THE END
OF THE
BEATLES?

ROCK&ROLL REFERENCE SERIES

TOM SCHULTHEISS, Series Editor

ROCK & ROLL REMEMBRANCES SERIES

TOM SCHULTHEISS, Series Editor

THE
END
OF THE
BEATLES?

by harry castleman
& walter j. podrazik

Sequel to *The Beatles Again*
and *All Together Now*:
The First Complete Beatles Discography

pierian press
1985

ISBN 0-87650-162-5
LC 84-60639

Copyright ©1985

by Walter J. Podrazik
and
Harry Castleman

THE PIERIAN PRESS
5000 Washtenaw Ave.
Ann Arbor, MI. 48104

contents

illustrations

introduction

The End Of The Beatles? is about music.

Like *All Together Now* and *The Beatles Again*, our previous two volumes, this book offers a wealth of background information on the preparation, packaging, and presentation of the record releases from John Lennon, Paul McCartney, George Harrison, and Ringo Starr. This includes not only the discs they issued as the Beatles, but also all of their solo efforts and work with other performers.

The End Of The Beatles is divided into five sections.

"The Magical Mystery Tour Rolls On" continues the year-by-year chronological discography begun in *All Together Now* and *The Beatles Again*, picking up the story from 1977's **Love Songs** album and carrying it through to December 31, 1983, adding nearly two hundred items along the way. This includes every new record release with which the Beatles have been associated as producers, writers, or performers.

"Pandemonium Shadow Ballet" provides background on records connected to the Beatles in other ways: spoken word packages ("Beatle Talk") and releases by such performers as Yoko Ono, Harry Nilsson, and the original cast of *Beatlemania* ("Family And Friends And Assorted Hangers-On").

"All Sales Final" examines bootleg records, including a detailed analysis of material done by the Beatles at their 1962 audition sessions and on the radio for the BBC in England.

"You Can't Say We Never Told You" offers eight in-depth essays on such topics as studio outtakes, audiophile discs, and publications devoted to the group.

Finally, the "Indexes And Instructions" section serves as a guide to using this book most effectively and efficiently.

All of these sections have been designed to make *The End Of The Beatles* a self-contained guide to the group, but without duplicating the information from *All Together Now* and *The Beatles Again*. Therefore, even when dealing with familiar territory (such as reissued tracks), we have gone out of our way in this volume to take a fresh approach, offering updated information and a new analysis of the material.

As a result, *The End Of The Beatles* can function quite well both as an individual volume and as part of the on-going chronology begun in *All Together Now* and continued in *The Beatles Again*. Of course, all three books do share a common theme: an appreciation of the music made by John, Paul, George, and Ringo.

****

Acknowledgments

We would like to thank the many people who responded so warmly and positively to both *All Together Now* and *The Beatles Again*, and who urged us to do a follow-up.

Special thanks to those that spoke to us in person or wrote to us about particular points, offering suggestions, corrections, and critical comments. We sincerely appreciate your input. In fact, several times this alerted us to items that might have otherwise slipped by unnoticed. So, stay in touch! (See page 447 for our mailing address.)

There are also many specific individuals, businesses, and institutions that have helped us hammer this book into final form. Our sincere thanks to all, and in particular —

Individuals

For beyond-the-call-of-duty observations and correspondence in Britain, thanks to Mark Lewisohn.

For beyond-the-call-of-duty observations and correspondence in the U.S., thanks to Don Wilkie.

For detailed comments on the developing manuscript, thanks to: Brad Elliott; Bill King; Elaine Macaluso; Michael Macaluso; Michael Tiefenbacher; Barbara Paulson

For special background perspectives, thanks to: Steve Holly, Laurence Juber, Michael McCartney, Harry Nilsson, Laura Gross, Dennis Elsas, Roger Scott, Nicholas Schaffner, and Terri Hemmert.

For special feedback, thanks to: Barbara Entman, Barbara Brown, Bernadette (Deco) Freeman, Danette Piekarczyk, Eileen

Berman, Peter Gibbon, and Micky Gibbon.

For items of information along the way, thanks to: Arno Guzek, Arthur Barry, Charles Reinhart, Cliff Yamasaka, Felice Lipsky, Joe Pope, Skip Groff, Joe Rufer, Joel Glazier, Koo Ogawara, Chip Largman, Norman Maslov, David Bacon, Renato Facconi, Rainer Moers, Peter Sills, Artillio Bergholtz, Estelle Fried, Les Share, Staffan Olander, Kevin O'Hare, Eddy Smit, Franco Settimo, Mark Carter, Allen Novak, and Fokke Zwaan.

For tea and sympathy, thanks to John O'Leary, Melanie Frey, Howard Leib, Beverly Weintraub, and Charlie Howell.

For New York numbering, thanks to PJ Haduch.

For network feeds and international shopping, thanks to Ed Mann and Holly Mann.

For a computer connection and sneak preview, thanks to Mark Guncheon and Kathy Willhoite.

For convention hospitality Merseyside, thanks to Jim Hughes and Liz Hughes.

For convention hospitality Stateside, thanks to Mark Lapidos and Carol Lapidos.

The Industry And Institutions

Allegiance/Takoma Records (special thanks to Howard Zelener)
Audiofidelity Enterprises (special thanks to Phil Goldschmiedt)
Beatlefest/Caromar Records (special thanks to Mark & Carol
    Lapidos)
Breaking Records (special thanks to Laurence & Hope Juber)
Carrere Records (special thanks to Freddy Cannon)
Charly/See For Miles Records (special thanks to Jean Luc Young)
Conn Records (special thanks to Ray Conn)
EMI, Ltd. (EMI, Parlophone, Capitol, Music For Pleasure, Apple
    Records) (special thanks to Martin Haxby and Charles Webster)
EMKA Productions Ltd. (special thanks to Steve O'Rourke)
EuroAtlantic Ltd. (special thanks to Denis O'Brien)
First American Records (special thanks to David Town)
Geffen Records
MGM/UA Home Entertainment (special thanks to Roy Eyre)
Mobile Fidelity Sound Lab (special thanks to Leslie Rosen)
MPL Productions, Ltd. (special thanks to Stephen Shrimpton)
Phonogram Ltd. (special thanks to Hugh Birley)
Polydor Ltd. (special thanks to Clive Fisher)
Raven Records (special thanks to Glenn A. Baker)
Rhino Records (special thanks to Harold Bronson)
Warner Bros. Records

The Library Of Congress—Motion Picture Broadcasting and Recorded
  Sound Division (special thanks to Gerald Gibson)
The New York Public Library—Rodgers and Hammerstein Archives
  Of Recorded Sound (special thanks to Gary Gisondi)
The Chicago Public Library—Music Division (special thanks to
  Richard Schwegel)
The Northwestern University Library—Special Collections Division
  (special thanks to Russell Maylone)

And, above all, special thanks to Tom Schultheiss for his exceptional
patience. Unfortunately, despite our best efforts over the past seven
years, he is still waiting for his copy of the Russian pressing of **Band
On The Run**.

Wally Podrazik
Harry Castleman
July 1, 1984

THE
MAGICAL
MYSTERY
TOUR
ROLLS ON

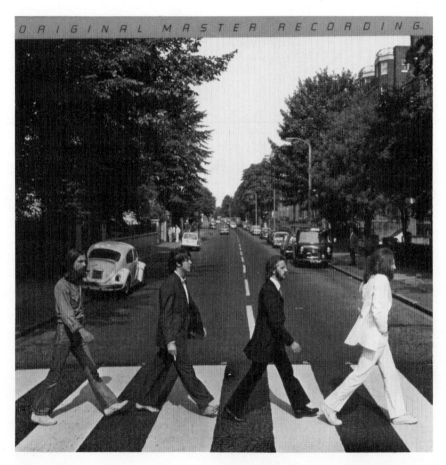

Abbey Road   **Mobile Fidelity Sound Lab MFSL 1-023 (LP)**

The End
Of The Beatles?

When was the end of the Beatles?

That's a deceptively simple rock trivia question.

The beginning was clear enough. The group first achieved world-wide fame in the "ninety days that shook the recording industry" (January to March 1964). Back then, John Lennon, Paul McCartney, George Harrison, and Ringo Starr came to America, appeared on *The Ed Sullivan Show*, headlined dozens of newspapers and magazines, and even held the top five positions on the U.S. singles chart simultaneously.

Ten years later, they were apart and pursuing their own careers, never to perform together again. Surely the end came some time in between. However (much to the regret of trivia aficionados) there was not really a public ending moment equivalent to the 1964 invasion. After all, the initial solo releases that came out in 1968, 1969, and 1970 were accompanied by new Beatles product. The four constantly turned up on each other's solo discs. They even had a record contract in effect until 1976.

By the time that expired, though, there was no doubt that the group's days together were finished. But in contrast to far too many other performers, they went their separate ways without an announced "final tour," "final album," or "final public appearance." It just happened. In fact, for John, Paul, George, and Ringo, the end of the group actually came much earlier than the public realized. Even while Beatles records topped the charts in the mid-1960s, they were already beginning to pursue their own solo interests, both personally and musically.

Yet for some who watched from the outside, the opposite was true — the Beatles never really ended at all. For the first generation that grew up with them, the group remained forever frozen in time, with their music a nostalgic key to youthful memories of everything from a first love to graduation day. For those that came in later, the Beatles were totally outside time. As with other stars of the past

3

such as Groucho Marx or Humphrey Bogart, their performances were captured and preserved at the height of their popularity and introduced to new generations through films, records, and photos. As a result, twenty years after first arriving in America, the Beatles could still make the cover of *Life* magazine, though they had not played a note together as a group in fourteen years.

Perhaps the best answer rests in a combination of elements — the individual careers of Lennon, McCartney, Harrison, and Starr going on simultaneously with the continued success of the Beatles as a group (through constant repackagings). In that sense, there really was not an end to the Beatles, just a shift in focus, with five career stories in progress rather than one.

In fact, by 1977 the number of U.S. top ten solo singles and albums released by John, Paul, George, and Ringo had just about matched their top ten output as a group. Yet in that same year there were also three new Beatles packages, including two with previously unreleased live material. Obviously, even after sixteen years of record releases, these five stories were far from . . . the end.

Love Songs   Capitol SKBL 11711 (LP)

Mull Of Kintyre   **Parlophone R 6018 (45)**

May.   Material for the next Wings album is recorded in the Virgin Islands aboard the yacht *Fair Carol*. The group is fined $15 one day by the area's National Park Commission for breaking the rule: "No amplified music after 10 p.m."

May 26.   *Beatlemania* begins its run at the Winter Garden Theater in New York. It never has an official opening night for critics.

September 12.   James Louis McCartney born.

September 16.   Marc Bolan, subject of Ringo Starr's 1974 documentary film *Born To Boogie*, dies in a car crash at age 29.

November.   Paul, Linda, and Denny Laine play live in the streets of Campbelltown, Scotland, along with the Campbelltown Pipes Band.

December.   *Billboard* magazine reports that fourteen-year-old Julian Lennon has formed a four-piece rock band at school in North Wales. Yes, they do some Beatles songs.

December.   George Harrison stops by a small country pub near his estate and plays a few songs. It's his first live public performance in Britain since 1969.

1977

What's A Mull?

At a lowkey press conference held in Tokyo's Hotel Okura early in October, John Lennon and Yoko Ono chatted with the local press, thanking the Japanese people for respecting their privacy during their visit. When asked about future performing and recording plans, Lennon replied that such activities had been put aside in favor of spending time with their two-year-old child, Sean. So even though there had not been a new record release from either John Lennon or Yoko Ono since 1975, that situation was to remain unchanged for at least another year (or longer) as they put all their creative energy into family life.

Though Lennon was in temporary retirement from the music business, Paul McCartney, George Harrison, and Ringo Starr remained active participants. Harrison, in fact, was just ending a year-long break from song writing and was preparing to begin work on another album. Paul and Ringo, meanwhile, had new records out for Christmas.

Ringo's album was actually a special children's disc presenting the adventures of a small white mouse from Liverpool called Scouse. He played the title role, with Adam Faith and Barbara Dickson as his co-stars and Donald Pleasence (who had written the story) as narrator. The record included fifteen songs (eight sung by Ringo) and came in a brightly colored cover showing Scouse the mouse standing in the snow next to a ship. Though the record did not chart and was not even released in the U.S., **Scouse The Mouse** was warmly received. Ringo was in fine voice, the music was good, and the story entertaining. The package made a perfect Christmas gift for children in England.

Paul McCartney's new release also turned up in many Christmas stockings. In fact, over just six weeks, his *Mull Of Kintyre* was practically embraced as a national anthem in Britain, topping the sales charts, dominating the airwaves, and playing in shops and homes throughout the country. By the end of December there were more than 1,200,000 copies sold in Britain alone. Eventually the disc became the best-selling single ever released in Britain, easily beating the previous champion (from 1963), *She Loves You*. *Mull Of Kintyre* also went on to top the charts throughout the world, with one major exception: the United States.

In the U.S., *Girls' School*, rather than *Mull Of Kintyre*, was promoted as the A-side. Actually, the single had been designated by McCartney as a double-A from the start (both sides were listed as number one in Britain), so Capitol's decision to push the hard rocker over the ballad merely reflected its judgment about the U.S. record market at the time. After all, *Girls' School* had strong musical hooks and clever (somewhat suggestive) lyrics. McCartney himself labeled it the story of a "pornographic St. Trinians" — referring to a series of humorous films and magazine cartoons by Ronald Searle about a fictional British schools for girls. He had even taken a number of the song's phrases from American newspaper ads for "adult" films, with titles such as *Curly Haired, School Mistress*, and *The Woman Trainer*. It seemed a perfect combination for U.S. success.

Instead, *Girls' School* never caught on Stateside and the single became one of McCartney's lowest charting U.S. solo releases. When *Mull Of Kintyre* took off in the rest of the world, Capitol made a belated effort to push it in the U.S. as an international hit, but that also failed. As a result, most Americans never had to deal with the questions: "What's a mull?" and "Where's Kintyre?"[1]

Despite the lack of U.S. chart success, *Mull Of Kintyre* was still a recognized international favorite, with all the attendant publicity and promotional tie-ins. For example, EMI inserted a notice in the millionth copy of the record to be pressed and shipped, informing the customer that he or she was entitled to a special prize. The winner received a Christmas hamper, presented by Denny Laine.

On a more practical level, there were a pair of promotional films made for the song, featuring the Campbeltown Pipes Band, residents of that town, the nearby coast line, and, of course, Paul, Linda, and Denny Laine. (Wings was temporarily down to a trio following the departure earlier in the year of Jimmy McCulloch and Joe English.) The three also appeared on Britain's Mike Yarwood television program on Christmas day to chat, show the *Mull Of Kintyre* film, and perform in a sketch. The film also played in the U.S. on such television programs as *The Midnight Special*.

All this helped to underscore Paul McCartney's continued success

---

[1] The Mull of Kintyre is a promontory point at the southern tip of the peninsula of Kintyre, which forms the extreme southern portion of Argyll Shire (county) in Scotland. It should not be confused with the isle of Mull some 80 miles to the northwest.

as an active solo artist. Counting *Mull Of Kintyre*, he had accumulated eighteen top ten solo singles and albums in Britain, and twenty-one in the U.S. Of course, each of the other former Beatles also had a healthy number of top ten singles and albums, though not quite as many as Paul, who released more than they did. Through the end of 1977, their totals were: John Lennon with nine top ten discs in Britain and ten in the U.S.; Ringo Starr with six top ten discs in Britain and nine in the U.S.; and George Harrison with five top ten discs in Britain and eight in the U.S.

Still, for those that preferred the music from the old days, the end of 1977 also brought another new Beatles compilation from EMI, **Love Songs**. The two-record set featured twenty-five romantic tunes packaged in an attractive, dark brown textured cover . . . just in time for Christmas giving.

****

ENTRY 573. This was the fourth two-record Beatles compilation, following the 1973 pair of greatest hits double albums and the 1976 thematic **Rock'n'Roll Music** collection. The "love songs" theme was the obvious flip-side companion. Back in 1976, the **Rock'n'Roll Music** package had been widely criticized for "looking cheap" with a bad caricature of the Beatles on the cover and a garish custom label featuring a glass of cola. In response, the package for **Love Songs** was designed to "look expensive" with: a classy "gold" embossed group shot stamped onto a pseudo-leather texture cover and repeated in black and white as a full-blown 12 by 14-inch gatefold illustration; a lyric booklet (in the U.S. edition) with the words to each song printed in script; and a tasteful custom label that used the cover photo as a sihouette backdrop to the song listings. The cover picture itself had been taken back in the late 1960s by commercial art photographer Richard Avedon and presented the four Beatles side-by-side as a smooth single entity. There was one change in emphasis, though, for this 1977 version: Paul McCartney was moved to a much more prominent position in the center of the group shot while Ringo Starr was relegated to Paul's previous spot on the side. After all, Paul *was* still with Capitol/EMI and had just come off a best selling world-wide tour!

A U.S. single of *Girl/You're Going To Lose That Girl* (Capitol 4506) was scheduled for release in November, but was canceled at the last moment — perhaps to avoid competition and confusion with McCartney's new single, *Girls' School/Mull Of Kintyre* (Entry 578). Or perhaps Capitol had second thoughts following the less-than-spectacular performance of its second "new" Beatles single in 1976, *Ob-La-Di, Ob-La-Da* (which had barely cracked *Billboard*'s top fifty). In any case, **Love Songs** had to make it without a hit single or special promotional hook — unlike **Rock'n'Roll Music**, which had been boosted by a top-ten single and interest in Paul McCartney's 1976 American tour. Instead, **Love Songs** was sold and displayed as a special thematic package. Though the set was not a top ten smash upon release (reaching only the top twenty in Britain and the top thirty in the U.S.), EMI reported that it turned out to be a *consistent* seller, no doubt appealing to many mainstream record buyers who had a soft spot in their hearts for these romantic Beatles ballads . . . whoops! That's *another* repackaging! (Entry 651).

Note: About 500 promo-only black vinyl versions of the *Girl* single were pressed and packaged in a Love Songs picture sleeve using the same custom label design. *Girl* appeared on both sides, in mono and stereo. In 1978, authentic looking gold vinyl "commercial" copies also turned up, featuring *You're Going To Lose That Girl* on the flip and the Love Songs picture sleeve and custom label. These, however, were privately pressed fakes.

ENTRY 574 & 575. An EP spin-off of EMI's greatest hits album series (prefix: NUT) launched in 1976 and 1977 with such 20-track compilations as **Hits Of The Mersey Era** and "Best of" collections from Peter and Gordon and Billy J. Kramer. For the moment, the Fourmost, Cilla Black, and Scaffold (see page 295) ended up with special EP releases. Album collections of their tracks turned up in 1982 and 1983 (Entries 696, 719, 736).

573.   OCT 21, 1977 (US) Capitol SKBL 11711 (2 LPs)
NOV 11, 1977 (UK) Parlophone PCSP 721 (2 LPs)
by The Beatles
LOVE SONGS   Prod: George Martin; †George Martin
(January 1969) and Phil Spector (March 1970)
side one
YESTERDAY–2:04
I'LL FOLLOW THE SUN–1:46
*I NEED YOU–*Harrison*–2:28*
GIRL–2:26
IN MY LIFE–2:23
*WORDS OF LOVE–*Buddy Holly*–2:10*
HERE, THERE AND EVERYWHERE–2:29
side two
*SOMETHING–*Harrison*–2:59*
AND I LOVE HER–2:27
IF I FELL–2:16
I'LL BE BACK–2:22
TELL ME WHAT YOU SEE–2:35
YES IT IS–2:40
side three
MICHELLE–2:42
IT'S ONLY LOVE–1:53
YOU'RE GOING TO LOSE THAT GIRL–2:18
EVERY LITTLE THING–2:01
FOR NO ONE–2:03
SHE'S LEAVING HOME–3:24
side four
†THE LONG AND WINDING ROAD–3:40
THIS BOY–2:11
NORWEGIAN WOOD (THIS BIRD HAS FLOWN)–2:00
YOU'VE GOT TO HIDE YOUR LOVE AWAY–2:08
I WILL–1:46
P.S. I LOVE YOU–2:02

574.   OCT 21, 1977 (UK) EMI 2695 (EP)
by The Fourmost   Prod: George Martin
side one
*HELLO LITTLE GIRL–*L/McC*–1:50*
*I'M IN LOVE–*L/McC*–2:07*
side two
(a little lovin')
(baby i need your lovin')

11

ENTRY 577. This mail-order-only sampler album was offered in the U.K. for 70p ($1.40) and a coupon appearing in *Melody Maker* (October 8 issue). Like similar two-record loss-leader sets from Warner Bros. in the U.S., this contained tracks from the company's latest releases, including potential hits (such as Foreigner's *Feels Like The First Time*) as well as more obscure material by artists such as Splinter (taken from their just-released album **Two Man Band**).

ENTRY 578. *Girls' School* was mostly recorded in London during March 1977 with the Wings lineup of Paul, Denny Laine, Jimmy McCulloch, Joe English, and Linda McCartney. The finishing touches on the track were completed in August.

Mull Of Kintyre was recorded in August at the "Spirit of Ranachan" house located in the Western Highlands of Scotland, on the peninsula of Kintyre. McCartney had some seven tons of RAK Mobile recording equipment brought to this beautiful, but remote, locale. The area's Campbeltown Pipe Band provided the distinctive Scottish music backing for the track. Jimmy McCulloch who officially left Wings late that summer, did not take part in the *Mull Of Kintyre* sessions.

In Britain, the single was stamped a "double A" and both sides were listed on the charts at No. 1, even though *Mull Of Kintyre* was obviously the main draw. In America, only *Girls' School* made the charts, reflecting Capitol's selection of that track as the side to promote. Both countries packaged the single in the same attractive picture sleeve, with art by Graham Hughes. (The *Mull* side featured a picture of the Mull of Kintyre promontory.) Both countries also issued the single on the Capitol label, continuing McCartney's occasional practice (begun with **Venus And Mars**) of using that 1950s style Capitol logo as his own "custom" label, even in Britain. Actually, though, the U.K. catalog number still followed the Parlophone sequence.

Soon after the release of the single, McCartney discovered the existence of a wartime repair ship named the *H.M.S. Mull of Kintyre*, which had been built in Canada for the Royal Navy and launched in1945. Naturally, an original cap bearing the name of the ship or (preferably) the ship itself is required for any truly *complete* collection.

Note: According to the U.S. Copyright Office, from 1973 through 1976 the author credit "McCartney" was the official pseudonym used by Paul and Linda McCartney to identify joint compositions (ending with *Soily*). From 1977 on (beginning with this single and the **London Town** album), "McCartney" meant just Paul McCartney alone.

575.   OCT 21, 1977 (UK) EMI 2998 (EP)
      by Cilla Black   Prod: George Martin
      side one
      (you're my world)
      IT'S FOR YOU–L/McC–*2:20*
      side two
      (alfie)
      (just a broken heart)

576.   OCT 21, 1977 (UK) Arcade ADEP 32 (2 LPs)
      by The Rolling Stones   Prod: Andrew Loog Oldham
      GET STONED
      side two
      cut one: *I WANNA BE YOUR MAN*–L/McC–*1:44*
      side three
      cut five: *WE LOVE YOU*–Mick Jagger/Keith Richards–
      4:39
        John and Paul: Backing Vocals

577.   OCTOBER 1977 (UK MAIL ORDER) WEA International
      MM 100 (LP)
      by Various Artists
      HOT PLATTER CORDON BLEU
      side one
      cut three: *LITTLE GIRL*–Robert J. Purvis/William
      Elliott–*3:14*
      by Splinter   Executive Producers: George Harrison and
      Dennis Morgan;   Prod: Norbert Putnam

578.   NOV 4, 1977 (US) Capitol 4504
      NOV 11, 1977 (UK) Parlophone (Capitol) R 6018
      by Wings   Prod: Paul McCartney
      A: Mull Of Kintyre–McCartney/Denny Laine–*4:42*
      A: Girls' School–McCartney–*4:34*

579.   NOV 7, 1977 (US) Arista AS 0292
      by The Alpha Band   Prod: Steven Soles
      A: YOU ANGEL YOU–Bob Dylan–*2:44*
        Ringo: Drums
      B: (not everything has a price)

GIRL

YOU'RE GOING TO LOSE THAT GIRL

From the album

LOVE SONGS

THE BEATLES

Girl   Capitol 4506 (45)

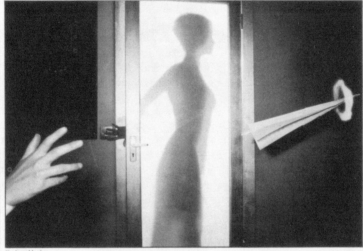

WINGS

Graham Hughes

GIRLS SCHOOL

Girls' School   Parlophone R 6018 (45)

ENTRY 581. The **Scouse The Mouse** album hit the stores just in time for Christmas, sporting colorful front and back cover art by Gerry Potterton (illustrator for the book) and receiving generally positive reviews. By the summer of 1978, though, it was almost impossible to find a copy anywhere in Britain. By the end of the year the record was officially out of print. As a result, **Scouse The Mouse** became an instant collector's item on both sides of the Atlantic, with the eight songs featuring Ringo's lead vocals eventually turning up on various bootleg packages. Unfortunately, this ignored nearly half the album and left the rather charming tale in shambles. The following program notes/listener's guide may help rectify that situation:

Scouse The Mouse: Written and Narrated by Donald Pleasence

Cast Of Characters

Scouse the Mouse—Ringo Starr	Polly Jolly—Polly Pleasence
Bonce the Mouse—Adam Faith	Little Boy—Henry Wolfe
Molly Jolly—Barbara Dickson	Ship's Captain—Michael Golden
Holly Jolly—Miranda Pleasence	Geoffrey the Cat—Henry Wolfe
(Sung by Lucy Pleasence)	Louey the Gull—Rick Jones
Mr. Jolly—Michael Golden	American Lady—Ruby Wax
Olly Jolly—Ben Chatterley	Pet Shop Voices—Gary Taylor

Side One: A small white mouse in the British seaport town of Liverpool bemoans his deadend life *Living In A Pet Shop*. It's noisy and crowded and there's no room for advancement. Other pet shop residents join in the chorus, singing in their own "animal" language. A young boy enters the shop, buys the white mouse, takes him home, and locks him in a cage. While feeding him that night, he names his new pet Scouse, after a type of stew served in Liverpool. Scouse soon discovers a surprise treat in his new home: television. From his vantage point in the cage, he spends hours watching everything on the "telly" and, in the process, learns how to speak English. He also decides that he wants to be a singing star, just like his favorite performers, the Jolly family. Over television he hears them doing their big hits, such as *Sing A Song For The Tragopan*, and — late at night — he begins singing and writing his own songs as well (*Scouse's Dream*).

On Christmas morning, Scouse gets his big break. The little boy gives him a rope ladder as a gift and Scouse immediately uses it to swing through the open cage door and down to the floor. He hides in a mouse hole till midnight, watching the Jollys singing on TV (*Snow Up Your Nose For Christmas*) and chatting with the hole's permanent resident, a brown Cockney mouse named Bonce. When the family is asleep, they sneak out to the dinner table for some supper. Scouse finds a mouse-sized British Airways bag among the toys, packs it with supplies, and heads out to the world (*Running Free*). He soon comes upon a nearby ship, the *Queen Elizabeth II*, bound for New York. With the voice of Bonce in his head bidding him farewell (*America (A Mouse's Dream)*), he hops aboard. On the ship, Scouse scoots into an open cabin door to avoid being crushed underfoot. He meets a young girl sitting and playing in bed. She is not at all surprised that Scouse can speak English because all the animals in *(continued)*

16

580.   DEC 2, 1977 (UK) EMI NUT 6 (LP)
        by Various Artists
        20 GOLDEN NUMBER ONES
        side one
            cut three: *BAD TO ME*–L/McC–*2:18*
                by Billy J. Kramer with The Dakotas   Prod: George
                Martin
        side two
            cut seven: *A WORLD WITHOUT LOVE*–L/McC–*2:38*
                by Peter and Gordon

581.   DEC 16, 1977 (UK) Polydor Super 2480 429 (LP)
            by Various Artists with Narration by Donald Pleasence
                Ringo: Vocals and Dialogue (%% Instrumental Cut and
                Additional Vocal Tracks by †Ben Chatterley;
                %Barbara Dickson; $Adam Faith; +Rick Jones;
                ††Lucy Pleasence)
        SCOUSE THE MOUSE   Prod: Hugh Murphy
        side one
            Living In A Pet Shop–Roger Brown–*2:33*
            Narration/Dialogue–*1:30*
            Ringo and Gary Taylor
            %(Sing A Song For The Tragopan–Roger Brown/Donald
                Pleasence–*2:48)*
            (Narration–*0:28*)
            Scouse's Dream–Roger Brown–*1:50*
            Narration/Dialogue–*1:48*
            Ringo and Adam Faith
            †(Snow Up Your Nose For Christmas)–Meira Pleasence/
                Donald Pleasence–*2:12)*
                    above track includes: Dialogue–*0:15*
                        Ringo and Adam Faith
            Narration/Dialogue–*1:35*
            Ringo and Adam Faith
            Running Free–Roger Brown–*2:25*
            Narration/Dialogue–*0:56*
            Ringo
            $(America (A Mouse's Dream)–Roger Brown–*2:55)*
            Narration/Dialogue–*0:45*
            Ringo and Miranda Pleasence
            ††(Scousey–Roger Brown–*2:30)*
            Narration/Dialogue–*0:55*
            Ringo and Miranda Pleasence

her dreams can talk. Of course, she assumes Scouse, too, is a dream, but admits it would be wonderful if he were real (*Scousey*). Scouse convinces her that he *is* real, so she offers him a selection of clothes from her doll collection. He chooses a yellow blazer and a pair of pants and, while dressing, sings a few lines from a song by the Jollys. The little girl recognizes it — for good reason. She is Holly Jolly. When the rest of the family enters, Holly introduces Scouse to them and urges him to sing!

Side Two: Hesitating only a moment, Scouse begins to sing for the Jollys (*Boat Ride*). Mr. Jolly chuckles in amazement, but then picks up his flute and accompanies Scouse, with the rest of the family joining in as well on the chorus. The next day, the Jollys take their new friend for a walk on deck, showing him off to the passersby. Upon learning Scouse can sing as well as talk, the ship's captain invites him to perform at a concert scheduled for that evening. Scouse accepts the offer and then makes a special point of inviting the captain's cat, Geoffrey, to the show. That night, the audience cheers the Jollys and Scouse singing *Scouse The Mouse*, a Molly Jolly solo on *The Passenger Pigeon*, and Polly Jolly and Scouse with *I Know A Place*. Scouse even directs a verse (in animal language) to Geoffrey the cat, urging him to be friendly . . . and not eat him! As the Jollys begin *Snow Up Your Nose For Christmas*, Scouse visits Geoffrey's table, where he is invited to a private "disco" cat party (three flights down) at midnight. When Scouse arrives carrying presents for the cats in his flight bag, he discovers that Geoffrey and the others really want to punish him for pretending to be human. After a ritual chant (*Caterwaul*) they lift Scouse with their paws and toss him out an open porthole into the water. Using his flight bag as a life preserver, Scouse sings for help (*S.O.S.*). Louey, a seagull with a Brooklyn accent, flies to his aid, grabs the straps of the flight bag, and carries Scouse to safety (*Ask Louey*).

At dawn, as the ship pulls into New York harbor, Louey drops Scouse onto the main deck. Holly Jolly greets him excitedly. Scouse, too, is excited. Looking at the New York City skyline — "It's dirty and big and beautiful!" — he realizes that his dream of fame is about to come true. Confidently, he sings the finale, *A Mouse Like Me*, as the ship's horn signals their arrival.

Note: When first released, the **Scouse The Mouse** album contained a 12 by 12-inch painting and drawing contest form for children (ages 5 to 10) living in the U.K. They had to color six pictures of Scouse and then fill a blank space with a Scouse sketch of their own. Two hundred winners were each to receive a copy of the *Scouse The Mouse* book, published by N.E.L. The contest deadline was February 28, 1978.

side two

Dialogue—*0:06*
  Ringo and Miranda Pleasence
Boat Ride—Roger Brown—*1:54*
Narration/Dialogue—*0:56*
  Ringo and Miranda Pleasence, Michael Golden, Henry
    Wolfe
Scouse The Mouse—Roger Brown—*2:42*
(Narration—*0:08*)
%(Passenger Pigeon—Roger Brown/Donald Pleasence—*1:20)*
(Narration—*0:05*)
I Know A Place—Roger Brown/Ruan O'Lochlainn/Donald
    Pleasence—*1:38*
Narration/Dialogue—*2:47*
  Ringo and Henry Wolfe
%%(Caterwaul—Jim Parker—*1:17)*
Narration/Dialogue—*0:47*
  Ringo and Henry Wolfe
S.O.S.—Roger Brown—*2:02*
Narration/Dialogue—*0:40*
  Ringo and Rick Jones
+(Ask Louey—Roger Brown/Donald Pleasence—*3:25)*
Narration/Dialogue—*0:32*
  Ringo and Miranda Pleasence
A Mouse Like Me—Ruan O'Lochlainn—*4:22*

February 17 & 18. An unauthorized advance airing of the **London Town** album over four radio stations in the U.S. and three in Canada. After official protests, the songs are taken off the air until the record's release the following month.

March 22. A promotional press conference with more silly Beatles reunion rumors. This time some (or all) might perform at a Memorial Day benefit for whales and dolphins. Or they might not. They don't.

March 22. *All You Need Is Cash* airs in the United States. Five days later it plays in Great Britain.

April 26. The *Ringo* television special airs in the U.S. It will not reach Britain for another five years (January 2, 1983).

May. An animated film short by Ian Emes, set to Linda McCartney's *Oriental Nightfish*, plays at the Cannes film festival.

July 18. The world premiere of the *Sgt. Pepper's Lonely Hearts Club Band* film at the Cinerama Dome in Los Angeles.

September. Wings recording sessions at Lympne Castle.

October 3. The Rockestra sessions at Abbey Road.

1978

London Town   Capitol SW 11777 (LP)

1978

All You Need Is Cash

In March 1978, the truth came out at last in both Britain and America, as the Rutles invaded the television airwaves. Ninety minutes later, they were gone, leaving behind bittersweet memories of youthful exuberance and personal lawsuits. They also left behind millions of fans who found in the Rutles one of the best presentations ever of the Beatles story.

The trouble with other documentaries about the Beatles – no matter how well done – was they they took themselves and the subject matter far too seriously. In the process, they lost a key element of the story: the humor. Monty Python's Eric Idle wrote a deliberate parody of the Beatles legend, substituting a new cast of characters and events for the originals. The result was *All You Need Is Cash*, a mock documentary about the Prefab Four which managed to convey an uncanny sense of such Fab Four events as the blossoming of Beatlemania, the rise and fall of Apple, and the bitter legal actions that helped send the Beatles on their separate ways.

One of the biggest boosters of the whole Rutles concept was George Harrison. He not only pointed to *All You Need Is Cash* as the best way to understand the madness of being a Beatle, he even appeared in the program, playing the part of a British reporter investigating the shaky state of Rutle Corps (Apple). As he chatted with Eric Manchester (Michael Palin in a send-up of Derek Taylor), office equipment and other valuables from the Rutles headquarters were wheeled out behind them, ending with the theft of the microphone they were using for the interview.[1]

Little more than a month after *All You Need Is Cash* aired on NBC in the U.S., Harrison appeared in another television special on NBC, *Ringo* – a one-hour musical comedy built around Ringo Starr. George opened the program with a mock press conference (complete with an allusion to the Rutles) that set up the premise,

---

[1] See page 337 for further details on the *All You Need Is Cash* special and the living lunchtime legend of the Rutles.

and then continued as narrator for the story.

Written by humorist Neil Israel, *Ringo* was loosely based on Mark Twain's *The Prince And The Pauper*, the story of a prince who switched places with one of his subjects, who was his exact twin. The special presented this tale as a fictionalized day in the life of Ringo Starr who, in order to get a few moments peace before a television concert, switched places with his twin, a Hollywood map salesman named Ognir Rrats (Ringo Starr spelled backwards). Ringo played both characters, with a little help from the special effects department and an occasional stand-in. Rounding out the cast and story were John Ritter as Ringo's manager, Art Carney as Ognir's cruel father, Carrie Fisher as Ognir's girlfriend, Vincent Price as Ringo's psychiatrist, and TV talk show host Mike Douglas as himself. At the conclusion Ringo switched back in time for the concert and then hired Ognir as his personal aide.

Though neither *All You Need Is Cash* or *Ringo* were big ratings successes in the U.S.,[1] both were well-received critically. However, Ringo's tie-in **Bad Boy** album did not fare as well and it became his last new record release until 1981.

There was one other Beatles take-off released in 1978, a feature length film starring Peter Frampton and the Bee Gees, *Sgt. Pepper's Lonely Hearts Club Band*. Unlike the Rutles or Ringo projects, this movie received scathing negative reviews. It also did quite poorly at the box office. Nonetheless, all the hoopla surrounding the production helped boost the Beatles own **Sgt. Pepper** album back onto the charts, along with a few other old packages.

The *Sgt. Pepper* film was the only flop associated with the Bee Gees that year. Otherwise, they were at the front of a red-hot boom in the sales of disco and dance music, led by the phenomonally successful **Saturday Night Fever** soundtrack album (eventually one of the best-selling packages of all time). The record even nosed out Paul McCartney, whose new **London Town** album was stuck behind it in the U.S. charts, unable to get to number one.

London Town was the result of more than a year's worth of work with Wings, including the month-long shipboard sessions in the Virgin Islands in 1977. However, by the time the album came out, both Jimmy McCulloch and Joe English had left the group. As a result, the front and back covers featured only Paul, Linda, and Denny Laine. Still, the trio pressed on, welcoming the British press for a special album kickoff party held aboard a launch on the Thames River (providing the opportunity for photos similar to the

---

[1] Due in part to NBC's generally weak lineup of series and specials at the time. For instance, Ringo's show was adjacent to a public affairs program featuring former U.S. President Gerald R. Ford.

London Town cover) and appearing with about fifty fans in a promotional film for the first single, *With A Little Luck*.

That soft-shuffle dance single shot to the top of the American charts and hit number five in Britain, helping the album to reach number two in the U.S. and number four in the U.K. No doubt the album would have done even better in Britain had *Mull Of Kintyre* been included, but McCartney was saving that chart-topping single for his end-of-the-year compilation disc. Besides, the presence of *Mull Of Kintyre* would not have helped all that much in the U.S. market, where it hadn't been a hit. However, neither did the two follow-up singles from the album (*I've Had Enough* and *London Town*), both of which failed to crack the top twenty.

The *With A Little Luck* film also included shots of a guest drummer, Steve Holly, a friend of Denny Laine's. By the time the promotional film for *I've Had Enough* was made some weeks later, Holly was aboard as a full-fledged member of Wings, along with another new addition, guitarist Laurence Juber.

With the Wings lineup once again complete, McCartney began work in June on the next album project, with sessions continuing into the following year at a variety of locations — including a medieval castle. The star-studded highlight took place in October, when Paul gathered nearly two dozen[1] top performers at the Abbey Road studios to form a superstar rock orchestra (dubbed "Rockestra") for two tracks: *So Glad To See You Here* and the instrumental *Rockestra Theme*.

To wrap up the year (and his current record contract), McCartney assembled a twelve-cut greatest hits album (**Wings Greatest**). And once again there was also a special package for those that preferred the music from the old days. This time, Capitol and EMI offered a fourteen-disc set (all the original British albums plus a bonus record) in a special blue box. The price? Only about $125.00. Of course, just in time for Christmas.

---

[1] See the Musician Credits index, page 481, for a complete list of the personnel.

ENTRY 582. From 1956 to 1962, Lonnie Donegan had two dozen top twenty hits in Britain, beginning with *Rock Island Line* and continuing with such chart toppers as *Puttin' On The Style* and the international smash *Does Your Chewing Gum Lose Its Flavor On The Bedpost Overnight?* What made him especially important to the aspiring teen musicians of Britain, though, was that he succeeded with a style of music (skiffle) that was perfectly suited to their limited range of available instruments (guitar, banjo, backyard washtub), while incorporating American jazz, folk, and blues influences. Many future British rock stars of the 1960s and 1970s cut their teeth on Donegan's music, so they happily came by to back him on a new album of folk and blues numbers, including fresh recordings of some previous Donegan hits. Ringo was the only former Beatle to turn up on this comeback album, though Paul McCartney spoke enthusiastically in support of the project in interviews at the time.

ENTRY 583. This Splinter single and Keni Burke's release that same day of *Keep On Singing/Day* (Dark Horse DRC 8522) were the final U.S. Dark Horse records to feature artists other than George Harrison. Thereafter, the company functioned merely as Harrison's own personal custom label.

ENTRY 584. Chrysalis pulled back the *Rock Island Line/Ham 'n' Eggs* single less than a month after release, deciding to go with the title cut instead. Neither Ringo track appeared on the flip side of the subsequent *Puttin' On The Style* single.

ENTRY 585. The first appearance of a previously released Beatles track on a British various artists compilation album. This package was a tie-in release to Tony Palmer's history of rock TV series called *All You Need Is Love*, so EMI licensed use of the original single to kick-off the record. Palmer's thirteen-part history first ran on British television in 1977, with the Beatles featured prominently in the episode first transmitted on May 14, which included the 1967 "Our World" performance of *All You Need Is Love*. The series ran in America on a syndicated basis, though in some cases U.S. stations only bothered to purchase the one hour focusing on the Beatles.

ENTRY 586. The final non-Harrison Dark Horse release in Britain.

ENTRY 587. The custom label for this single (and subsequent singles) from the **London Town** album consisted of the London skyline with sunny bright blue coloring on one side and a grey rainy tint on the other. The B-side's breezy instrumental *Cuff Link* riff was originally called *Off-The-Cuff Link*, but was changed just before release. On the album, the song served just that purpose.

582. JAN 9, 1978 (US) United Artists UA-LA 827-H (LP)
      JAN 27, 1978 (UK) Chrysalis CHR 1158 (LP)
          by Lonnie Donegan
          Ringo: Drums
      PUTTIN' ON THE STYLE   Prod: Adam Faith
      side one
          cut two: *Have A Drink On Me (Take A Whiff On Me)*–
          Lonnie Donegan/Huddie Ledbetter/Alan Lomax/
          John Lomax/Peter Buchanan–*3:00*
          cut three: *Ham 'n' Eggs*–Traditional/Arr. and Adapt. by
          Lonnie Donegan–*3:10*

583. JAN 23, 1978 (US) Dark Horse DRC 8523
          by Splinter   Executive Producers: George Harrison and
          Dennis Morgan;   Prod: Norbert Putnam
      A: MOTIONS OF LOVE–Parker McGee–*3:26*
      B: I NEED YOUR LOVE–Robert J. Purvis–*2:58*

584. FEB 3, 1978 (UK) Chrysalis CHS 2205
          by Lonnie Donegan   Prod: Adam Faith
      B: HAM 'N' EGGS–Traditional/Arr. and Adapt. by Lonnie
          Donegan–*3:10*
          Ringo: Drums
      A: (rock island line)

585. FEB 10, 1978 (UK) Theatre Projects 9199 995 (LP)
          by Various Artists
      ALL YOU NEED IS LOVE
      side one
          cut one: *ALL YOU NEED IS LOVE–3:57*
          by The Beatles   Prod: George Martin

586. MAR 3, 1978 (UK) Dark Horse K 17116
          by Splinter   Executive Producers: George Harrison and
          Dennis Morgan;   Prod: Norbert Putnam
      A: NEW YORK CITY (WHO AM I)–Robert J. Purvis–*3:49*
      B: BABY LOVE–Robert J. Purvis–*3:34*

587. MAR 23, 1978 (UK) Parlophone R 6019
      MAR 24, 1978 (US) Capitol 4559
          by Wings   Prod: Paul McCartney
      A: With A Little Luck–McCartney–*5:45*
      B: medley–3:10
          Backwards Traveller–McCartney–*1:07*
          Cuff Link–McCartney–*2:03*

25

ENTRY 588. The **London Town** album was recorded over a period of one year, beginning in February 1977. Sessions at Abbey Road took place February 7–March 31, October 25–December 1, and January 4–January 23, 1978. There were also sessions at Air London Studios December 3–December 14. And, for the entire month of May, Wings recorded aboard the yacht *Fair Carol* in the Virgin Islands.

A 36 by 24-inch poster packaged with the album featured a selection of shots from the island sessions, including a picture of a letter reminding the band members that several chartered boats had been recently visited by U.S. Customs officials in search of illegal drugs. On the other side of the poster there was a group shot of Paul, Linda McCartney, and Denny Laine – underscoring the fact that Jimmy McCulloch and Joe English were no longer part of the group even though their vocal and instrumental work was still included and fully credited on the album. That same group photo (by Graham Hughes) had previously been used as part of the *Mull Of Kintyre* picture sleeve.

Five songs on **London Town** were co-compositions by Denny Laine and Paul McCartney – including three songs with Paul on lead vocal – making this their most extensive collaboration ever. No doubt this helped account for the soft and gentle (almost fairy tale-like) atmosphere of the package, best shown on *London Town, Children Children*, and *Don't Let It Bring You Down*. Two songs were done with other performers in mind: *Name And Address* (in the style of Elvis Presley's 1950s Sun recordings) and *Girlfriend* (tailored for Michael Jackson's voice). Though Michael Jackson later recorded an excellent version of *Girlfriend* himself and included it on his 1979 **Off The Wall**, he and McCartney did not actually work together until they did the songs *Say Say Say, The Man*, and *The Girl Is Mine*. See Entries 720 and 748. In the summer of 1980, Jackson also released *Girlfriend* as a single in Britain (Epic EPC 8782).

Strong rockers capped both sides of the album, with the *Morse Moose And The Grey Goose* finale featuring particularly strong guitar work from Jimmy McCulloch. The basic instrumental guitar jam for that track took place at one of the shipboard sessions and kept on going even though the recording equipment also picked up some random radio noise (left in the final mix).

ENTRY 589. Recorded at the Band's farewell concert on November 24, 1976, at San Francisco's Winterland Arena. Though some other guests had extended solo shots, Ringo was content to sit in on the final song and an extended closing jam (which went on nearly thirty minutes).

ENTRY 590. This single was initially pegged as the first release from **Bad Boy** in Britain as well. The disc was assigned a catalog number (Polydor 2001 782) and release date (May 26, 1978), but copies were never pressed. Perhaps Polydor decided to cancel it after the same record flopped in the U.S. As a result, the album came out in Britain that June without a lead single. One month after that, *Old Time Relovin'* was given *Tonight* as its A-side and released as the only British single from **Bad Boy** (Entry 597).

588. MAR 31, 1978 (UK) Parlophone PAS 10012 (LP)
MAR 31, 1978 (US) Capitol SW 11777 (LP)
  by Wings
LONDON TOWN   Prod: Paul McCartney
side one
  London Town—McCartney/Denny Laine—*4:10*
  Cafe On The Left Bank—McCartney—*3:25*
  I'm Carrying—McCartney—*2:44*
  medley—*3:10*
    Backwards Traveller—McCartney—*1:07*
    Cuff Link—McCartney—*2:03*
  Children Children—McCartney/Denny Laine—*2:20*
  Girlfriend—McCartney—*4:31*
  I've Had Enough—McCartney—*3:02*
side two
  With A Little Luck—McCartney—*5:45*
  Famous Groupies—McCartney—*3:34*
  Deliver Your Children—McCartney/Denny Laine—*4:17*
  Name And Address—McCartney—*3:07*
  Don't Let It Bring You Down—McCartney/Denny Laine—*4:34*
  Morse Moose And The Grey Goose—McCartney/Denny Laine—*6:27*

589. APR 10, 1978 (US) Warner Brothers 3WS 3146 (3 LPs)
APR 14, 1978 (UK) Warner Brothers K 66076 (3 LPs)
  by The Band and Friends
  Ringo: Drums
THE LAST WALTZ   Prod: Robbie Robertson;   Co-Production: Rob Fraboni and John Simon
side five
  cut six: *I Shall Be Released*—Bob Dylan—*3:53*
  cut seven: *Ending Jam*—*1:29*

590. APR 17, 1978 (US) Portrait 6-70015
  by Ringo Starr   Prod: Vini Poncia;   Associate Producer: Ringo Starr
  A: *Lipstick Traces (On A Cigarette)*—Naomi Neville—*3:00*
  B: *Old Time Relovin'*—Starkey/Vini Poncia—*3:29*

ENTRY 591. The **Bad Boy** album was recorded in late 1977 at the Can-Base Studios (Nimbus 9 Productions) in Canada and at the Elite Recording Studios in the Bahamas. Unlike previous superstar Ringo productions, this album relied on generally anonymous session musicians under the banners Ringo's Roadside Attraction and Vini Poncia's Peaking Duck Orchestra and Chorus. Poncia and Ringo also served as producers for the set, partially in an effort to get it out in time to coincide with Ringo's April 26 TV special in the U.S. (though only three songs from the album were performed on the show: *Hard Times, Heart On My Sleeve*, and *A Man Like Me*).

Only two of the ten songs were Ringo/Vini Poncia compositions, down from seven at the **Ringo The 4th** sessions. The remaining tracks were cover versions, previously recorded and released as follows:

Bad Boy by the Jive Bombers in 1957 on Savoy 1508
   Originally *Brown Gal* by Lil Amstrong in 1936 on Decca 1092
      then *Lil Brown Gal* by Lil Armstrong in 1947 on Gotham 256
Hard Times by Peter Skellern in 1975 on (UK) Island ILPS 9352 **Hard Times (LP)**
Heart On My Sleeve by Bernard Gallagher and Graham Lyle in 1976 on A&M SP-4566 **Breakaway (LP)**
Lipstick Traces (On A Cigarette) by Benny Spellman in 1962 on Minit 644
Monkey See--Monkey Do by Michael Franks in 1976 on Reprise MS 2230 **Art Of Tea (LP)**
Tonight by Small Faces in 1977 on Atlantic SD 19113 **Playmates** (LP)
Where Did Our Love Go by the Supremes in 1964 on Motown 1060
A Man Like Me was merely a reworking of *A Mouse Like Me* from **Scouse The Mouse**

Lipstick Traces, Heart On My Sleeve, and *Hard Times* featured Ringo at his best interpreting a favorite oldie, a catchy love ballad, and an obscure album track (which George Harrison fans were already familiar with because Harrison appeared on another cut from that Peter Skellern record). Ringo's recording of *Hard Times*, in fact, was an excellent example of his skill at taking someone else's material and making it his own: he changed the pacing and emphasis of the original, giving the song a harder edge and stronger rhythm. This might have even made a much better choice as title cut to the entire album, and certainly should have been one of the singles.

The British package came out two months after the American release and featured a special custom label incorporating the Bad Boy logo from the cover.

ENTRY 592. See Entry 607 and page 316.

ENTRY 594. The British single was issued in a spooky Graham Hughes black-and-grey picture sleeve. Ads for this release and the promotional video included new Wings members Laurence Juber and Steve Holly, though neither played on the record.

591.   APR 17, 1978 (US) Portrait JR 35378 (LP)
JUN 16, 1978 (UK) Polydor 2310 599 (LP)
by Ringo Starr
BAD BOY   Prod: Vini Poncia;   Associate Producer: Ringo
Starr
side one
Who Needs A Heart—Starkey/Vini Poncia—*3:48*
Bad Boy—Lil Armstrong/Avon Long—*3:14*
Lipstick Traces (On A Cigarette)—Naomi Neville—*3:00*
Heart On My Sleeve—Bernard Gallagher/Graham Lyle—
3:20
Where Did Our Love Go—Eddie Holland/Lamont Dozier/
Brian Holland—*3:15*
side two
Hard Times—Peter Skellern—*3:31*
Tonight—Ian McLagan/John Pidgeon—*2:56*
Monkey See-Monkey Do—Michael Franks—*3:36*
Old Time Relovin'—Starkey/Vini Poncia—*4:16*
A Man Like Me—Ruan O'Lochlainn—*3:00*

592.   MAY 8, 1978 (US) RCA AFL-12798 (LP)
by Harry Nilsson   Prod: Richard Perry except †Harry
Nilsson   Ringo: Drums and †George: Cowbell
GREATEST HITS
side two
cut three: *SPACEMAN*—Harry Nilsson—*3:33*
†cut six: *DAYBREAK*—Harry Nilsson—*2:43*

593.   MAY 12, 1978 (UK) United Artists UP 36397
by The Bonzo Dog Band   Prod: Paul McCartney
side one
I'M THE URBAN SPACEMAN—Neil Innes—*2:23*
side two
(the intro and the outro)
(the strain)

594.   JUN 5, 1978 (US) Capitol 4594
JUN 16, 1978 (UK) Parlophone R 6020
by Wings   Prod: Paul McCartney
A: I'VE HAD ENOUGH—McCartney—*3:02*
B: DELIVER YOUR CHILDREN—McCartney/Denny Laine—
4:34

I've Had Enough   Parlophone R 6020 (45)

Sgt. Pepper's Lonely   Parlophone R 6022 (45)
Hearts Club Band

Sgt. Pepper's Lonely Hearts Club Band   Capitol 4612 (45)

ENTRY 595. As one of her first record releases, Kate Robbins (Paul's cousin) put out this song from the musical *Annie* (published by MPL). The record did not hit and became an overnight collectors item when Anchor went out of business in March 1979 as part of the worldwide reshuffling at ABC Records (its parent company). Even we don't have a copy. There is hope, though, because by 1981 Robbins had become a successful British television and singing star, so perhaps the track will appear on some future compilation album.

ENTRY 596. Ringo's third and final release (two singles and an album) for Portrait Records in America, though he would not formally depart the label until 1981. *Heart On My Sleeve* also appeared on side two, cut two of a 1978 various artists picture disc sampler album from CBS. This custom pressing was issued at the time as a promo-only giveaway for U.S. radio stations interested in a tie-in to the picture disc fad.

ENTRY 597. Ringo's final release for Polydor in Britain, concluding an association that began with **Rotogravure** in 1976.

ENTRY 599. Back in 1967 there had not been any singles taken from **Sgt. Pepper** in either the U.S. or the U.K. In the wake of the tremendous publicity surrounding the theatrical film release of *Sgt. Pepper's Lonely Hearts Club Band* in the summer of 1978, both countries rectified the situation, selecting the opening and closing tracks from the original album as a tie-in single. However, the new release flopped in both markets, peaking at 71 on the *Billboard* charts and at 63 on the *Music Week* charts. Nonetheless, in the U.S. two other aspects of Capitol's overall repromotion of **Sgt. Pepper** did work: a $15.98 picture disc version (released August 21) sold very well (see page 425) and, by late September, the eleven-year-old regular album was back in the American top twenty.

There were different picture sleeve designs on the American and British releases of the single.

ENTRY 600. The *London Town* single stalled at 60 on the *Music Week* charts in Britain and just broke the top forty in America (peaking at 39 in *Billboard*). This was Paul McCartney's final single for Capitol, though there was one more album released later that year, his greatest hits package (Entry 608).

ENTRY 601. Though George Harrison was merely listed in the general album credits and not identified with any particular song on **Along The Red Ledge**, further inquiries placed him on only one cut, *The Last Time*, playing acoustic guitar. Some copies of the album were pressed on red vinyl.

595. JUN 30, 1978 (UK) Anchor ANC 1054
by Kate Robbins Prod: Paul McCartney
*A: *Tomorrow*—Charles Strouse/Martin Charnin
B: *(crowds of you)*

596. JUL 3, 1978 (US) Portrait 6-70018
by Ringo Starr Prod: Vini Poncia; Associate Producer:
Ringo Starr
A: *HEART ON MY SLEEVE*—Bernard Gallagher/Graham
Lyle—*3:07*
B: *WHO NEEDS A HEART*—Starkey/Vini Poncia—*3:48*

597. JUL 21, 1978 (UK) Polydor 2001 795
by Ringo Starr Prod: Vini Poncia; Associate Producer:
Ringo Starr
A: *TONIGHT*—Ian McLagan/John Pidgeon—*2:56*
B: *OLD TIME RELOVIN'*—Starkey/Vini Poncia—*3:29*

598. AUG 4, 1978 (UK) EMI NUT 14 (LP)
by Cliff Bennett and The Rebel Rousers Prod: Paul
McCartney and David Paramor
BEST OF CLIFF BENNETT AND THE REBEL ROUSERS
side one
cut one: *GOT TO GET YOU INTO MY LIFE*— L/McC—*2:29*

599. AUG 7, 1978 (US) Capitol 4612
SEP 22, 1978 (UK) Parlophone R 6022
by The Beatles Prod: George Martin
A: *MEDLEY*—*4:45*
SGT. PEPPER'S LONELY HEARTS CLUB BAND—*1:59*
WITH A LITTLE HELP FROM MY FRIENDS—*2:46*
B: *A DAY IN THE LIFE*—*5:03*

600. AUG 11, 1978 (UK) Parlophone R 6021
AUG 14, 1978 (US) Capitol 4625
by Wings Prod: Paul McCartney
A: *LONDON TOWN*—McCartney/Denny Laine—*4:10*
B: *I'M CARRYING*—McCartney—*2:44*

601. AUG 21, 1978 (US) RCA AFL 1-2804 (LP)
SEP 29, 1978 (UK) RCA PL 1-2804 (LP)
by Daryl Hall and John Oates
ALONG THE RED LEDGE Prod: David Foster
side one
cut three: *The Last Time*—Daryl Hall—*2:47*
George: Guitar

ENTRY 602. Recorded during David Bowie's 1978 world tour, his final live tour of the 1970s. The package was delayed a bit from its originally scheduled release to September as Bowie and RCA worked out whether this would be his final album for the company or merely the latest release in an extended contract. He stayed until 1983.

In December, RCA in Britain released about 20,000 copies of the set pressed on yellow vinyl — a perfect accompaniment to EMI's white, red, and blue vinyl Beatles releases from that October (see page 426).

ENTRY 604. One of twelve new "double A" single repackagings of old Elton John material, released as a boxed set: **Elton John--Double A** (DJM EJ 12). The discs were also available separately, following his British hits from *Lady Samantha* (10901) through *Pinball Wizard* (10912). As usual, record company interest in an artist's back catalog happened to coincide with the release of new material by a different company (*Part Time Love* from the **Single Man** album, distributed by Phonogram).

ENTRY 605. For years, new Beatles fans had been coming into record stores to "catch up" on the group by buying all the available records. In 1976, EMI successfully tapped this audience with a special rerelease program of the group's British singles. The company took the twenty-two original British singles, put them in new picture sleeves, added a new disc (*Yesterday*, which had not been previously issued as a single in the U.K.), and then watched them all land on the British charts. Obviously, many old fans, new fans, and collectors purchased the entire set at once. Thousands of copies were also exported to the U.S.

Afterward, some buyers even wrote to EMI asking for a storage box for their purchase, similar to the one given to record stores for display. Such requests were politely turned down because those boxes had been specifically designed and manufactured in limited quantity for retail and promotional purposes.

The 1978 **Beatles Collection** was designed to function in a similar way for a dozen British albums, gathering all of them in their original sleeves, along with a new album containing previously issued material that did not appear on the other discs. Unlike the singles, though, this collection came packaged as a boxed set, with copies issued in both the U.K. and the U.S. — meaning that, technically, all these British albums received their first official American release. The chief difference between the two sets was that the bonus Beatles **Rarities** disc in Britain included the German-language recordings of *I Want To Hold Your Hand* and *She Loves You*, while the American version went with the standard English-language tracks. Also, the 3,000 copies issued in America were numbered on the front cover of the box, underscoring the more limited nature of the Stateside release. In either country, though, **The Beatles Collection** was touted as the perfect Christmas gift.

Nonetheless, this seemingly straightforward project drew criticism *(continued)*

602. SEP 25, 1978 (UK) RCA PL 02913 (2 LPs)
     SEP 25, 1978 (US) RCA CPL 2-2913 (2 LPs)
        by David Bowie
     STAGE   Prod: David Bowie and Tony Visconti
     side two
        cut two: *Fame (live)*—Lennon/David Bowie/Carlos
           Alomar—*4:06*

603. SEP 29, 1978 (UK) RCA PB 9324
        by Daryl Hall and John Oates   Prod: David Foster
     A: THE LAST TIME—Daryl Hall—*2:47*
        George: Guitar
     B: (serious music)

604. OCT 13, 1978 (UK) DJM DJS 10911
        by Elton John   Prod: Gus Dudgeon
     A: LUCY IN THE SKY WITH DIAMONDS—L/McC—*5:59*
        John: Guitars and Backing Vocal
     A: (philadelphia freedom)

605. NOV 10, 1978 (UK) Parlophone BC 13 (14 LPs)
     DEC 1, 1978 (US) Capitol BC 13 (14 LPs)
        by The Beatles
     THE BEATLES COLLECTION
        A Boxed Set of 12 Original British Album Packages Plus
        One New Bonus Disc
        PLEASE PLEASE ME Parlophone PCS 3042
        WITH THE BEATLES Parlophone PCS 3045
        A HARD DAY'S NIGHT Parlophone PCS 3058
        BEATLES FOR SALE Parlophone PCS 3062
        HELP! Parlophone PCS 3071
        RUBBER SOUL Parlophone PCS 3075
        REVOLVER Parlophone PCS 7009
        SGT. PEPPER'S LONELY HEARTS CLUB BAND
           Parlophone PCS 7027
        THE BEATLES Apple PCS 7067/8 (2 LPs)
        YELLOW SUBMARINE Apple PCS 7070
        ABBEY ROAD Apple PCS 7088
        LET IT BE Apple PCS 7096
        RARITIES (see **605a** and **605b**)

The Beatles Collection   **Parlophone BC 13 (LPs)**

Rarities   Parlophone PCM 1001 (LP)

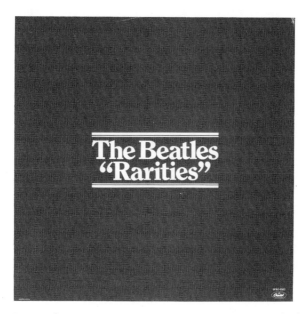

Rarities (inner sleeve)   Capitol SPRO 8969 (LP)

(Entry 605 continued)
(especially in America) in two areas: overall song selection and the bonus album. American fans in particular could not understand why readily available songs such as *She's A Woman* were considered "rarities," nor why some of the group's biggest hits such as *Hey Jude* were missing. They did *not* see the set for what EMI intended it to be: a collection of British albums. Rather, they expected it to serve as "the Beatles complete." In a way, though, this was just the latest reflection of the long-standing difference between the way Britain and America packaged the Beatles.

The chief difference between Beatles releases in Britain and America was that in Britain singles and albums were treated as separate entities. Throughout their active career as a group, the Beatles released far fewer singles in Britain than in America and usually did not include B-sides (sometimes even A-sides) on the companion albums. Capitol, on the other hand, used such material to generate extra albums for the American market, both for increased profit *and* because U.S. record buyers wanted such songs as *I Want To Hold Your Hand* and *She Loves You* on a new album released along with the singles. Consequently, throughout the 1960s there were very few tracks that never turned up on a regular album in America. At the same time in Britain, there were more than two dozen songs that never appeared on any British album and eight more than turned up just on a 1966 greatest hits package.

In preparing the 1978 boxed set, EMI decided to continue the policy of treating albums and singles separately. The company also decided to keep the album collection "pure" by including only the albums of new material that had been released in Britain from 1963 to 1970. Of course, this eliminated a great deal of duplication inherent with such double albums as the two 1973 greatest hits sets, the 1976 **Rock'n'Roll Music** set, and the 1977 **Love Songs** set. However, this also eliminated songs contained on **A Collection Of Beatles Oldies** from 1966, the **Magical Mystery Tour** album (released in England in 1976, but originally issued there in 1967 as a double EP set), and the American **Hey Jude** package (not released in England until 1979). Not including these meant that, for all practical purposes, many of the Beatles biggest hit singles were left out of the boxed set, along with a number of other cuts (all listed below):

Across The Universe (version one)	*Hello Goodbye*
Baby, You're A Rich Man	*Hey Jude*
Bad Boy	*I Am The Walrus*
The Ballad Of John And Yoko	*I Call Your Name*
Blue Jay Way	*I Feel Fine*
Day Tripper	*I Want To Hold Your Hand*
Don't Let Me Down	*I'll Get You*
Flying	*I'm Down*
The Fool On The Hill	*The Inner Light*
From Me To You	*Komm, Gib Mir Deine Hand*
(continued)	

605a **RARITIES** Prod: George Martin
British Edition Parlophone PSLP 261
Issue Separately Oct 19, 1979 as Parlophone PCM 1001
side one
ACROSS THE UNIVERSE (version one)—3:41
YES IT IS—2:40
THIS BOY—2:11
THE INNER LIGHT—Harrison—*2:36*
I'LL GET YOU—2:04
THANK YOU GIRL—2:01
KOMM, GIB MIR DEINE HAND—L/McC/Nicolas/
Hellmer—*2:23*
YOU KNOW MY NAME (LOOK UP THE NUMBER)—4:20
SIE LIEBT DICH—L/McC/Nicolas/Montague—*2:16*
side two
RAIN—2:59
SHE'S A WOMAN—2:57
MATCHBOX—Carl Perkins—*1:37*
I CALL YOUR NAME—2:02
BAD BOY—Larry Williams—*2:17*
SLOW DOWN—Larry Williams—*2:54*
I'M DOWN—2:30
LONG TALL SALLY—Enotris Johnson/Richard Penniman/
Robert Blackwell—*1:58*

605b **RARITIES** Prod: George Martin
American Edition Capitol SPRO 8969
side one
ACROSS THE UNIVERSE (version one)—3:41
YES IT IS—2:40
THIS BOY—2:11
THE INNER LIGHT—Harrison—*2:36*
I'LL GET YOU—2:04
THANK YOU GIRL—2:01
I WANT TO HOLD YOUR HAND—2:24
YOU KNOW MY NAME (LOOK UP THE NUMBER)—4:20
SHE LOVES YOU—2:18

(Entry 605 continued)

Lady Madonna
Long Tall Sally
Magical Mystery Tour
Matchbox
Old Brown Shoe
Paperback Writer
Penny Lane
Rain
Revolution
She Loves You
She's A Woman

Sie Liebt Dich
Slow Down
Strawberry Fields Forever
Thank You Girl
This Boy
We Can Work It Out
Yes It Is
You Know My Name (Look Up The Number)
Your Mother Should Know

Purists might argue the addition to the list of the original single versions of *Get Back, Let It Be, Love Me Do*, and *Please Please Me*. For the purposes of this discussion, we have decided to place them at the end of each list (like this one).

The British version of the Beatles **Rarities** bonus disc cut that list just about in half by gathering songs that had never appeared on any album in Britain, along with a few that had turned up only on the various 1970s double record compilation sets.

The British Release Information for the **Rarities** tracks:

Across The Universe — First issued in 1969 on **No One's Gonna Change Our World.**

Yes It Is — First issued in 1965 as the B-side to *Ticket To Ride.*

This Boy — First issued in 1963 as the B-side to *I Want To Hold Your Hand.* Also included on **Love Songs.**

The Inner Light — First issued in 1968 as the B-side to *Lady Madonna.*

I'll Get You — First issued in 1963 as the B-side to *She Loves You.*

Thank You Girl — First issued in 1963 as the B-side to *From Me To You.*

Komm, Gib Mir Deine Hand — Never previously released in Britain. First issued in 1964 as a single in Germany.

You Know My Name (Look Up The Number) — First issued in 1970 as the B-side to *Let It Be.*

Sie Liebt Dich — Never previously released in Britain. First issued in 1964 as a single in Germany.

Rain — First issued in 1966 as the B-side to *Paperback Writer.*

She's A Woman — First issued in 1964 as the flip to *I Feel Fine.*

Matchbox — First issued in 1964 on **Long Tall Sally** (EP). Also included on **Rock'n'Roll Music.**

I Call Your Name — First issued in 1964 on **Long Tall Sally** (EP). Also included on **Rock'n'Roll Music.**

Bad Boy — First issued in the U.K. in 1966 on **A Collection Of Beatles Oldies.** Originally issued in 1965 in the U.S. on **Beatles VI.** Also

(continued)

RAIN—2:59
SHE'S A WOMAN—2:57
*MATCHBOX—*Carl Perkins—*1:37*
I CALL YOUR NAME—2:02
*BAD BOY—*Larry Williams—*2:17*
*SLOW DOWN—*Larry Williams—*2:54*
I'M DOWN—2:30
*LONG TALL SALLY—*Enotris Johnson/Richard Penniman/ Robert Blackwell—*1:58*

In both countries, **THE BEATLES COLLECTION** contains the twelve British releases in their original sleeves with their contents unchanged:

PLEASE PLEASE ME   Prod: George Martin
First issued March 22, 1963
side one
I Saw Her Standing There—2:50
Misery—1:43
*Anna (Go To Him)—*Arthur Alexander—*2:56*
*Chains—*Gerry Goffin/Carole King—*2:21*
*Boys—*Luther Dixon/Wes Farrell—*2:24*
Ask Me Why—2:24
Please Please Me—2:00
side two
Love Me Do—2:19
P.S. I Love You—2:02
*Baby, It's You—*Hal David/Burt Bacharach/Barney Williams—*2:36*
Do You Want To Know A Secret—1:55
*A Taste Of Honey—*Ric Marlow/Bobby Scott—*2:02*
There's A Place—1:44
*Twist And Shout—*Bert Russell/Phil Medley—*2:32*

WITH THE BEATLES   Prod: George Martin
First issued November 22, 1963
side one
It Won't Be Long—2:11
All I've Got To Do—2:05
All My Loving—2:04
*Don't Bother Me—*Harrison—*2:28*
Little Child—1:46
*Till There Was You—*Meredith Willson—*2:12*
*Please Mr. Postman—*Brian Holland/Robert Bateman/Berry Gordy—*2:34*
side two
*Roll Over Beethoven—*Chuck Berry—*2:44*
Hold Me Tight—2:30
*You Really Got A Hold On Me—*William Robinson—*2:58*
I Wanna Be Your Man—1:59
*Devil In Her Heart—*Richard B. Drapkin—*2:23*
Not A Second Time—2:03
*Money (That's What I Want)—*Berry Gordy/Janie Bradford—*2:47*

(Entry 605 continued)
included on **Rock'n'Roll Music**.
Slow Down — First issued in 1964 on **Long Tall Sally** (EP). Also included
on **Rock'n'Roll Music**.
I'm Down — First issued in 1965 as the B-side to *Help!* Also included on
Rock'n'Roll Music.
Long Tall Sally — First issued in 1964 on **Long Tall Sally** (EP). Also in-
cluded on **Rock'n'Roll Music**.

The selection filled a number of holes for British fans. Previously, the two
German-language recordings had never appeared at all in England; six B-side
songs had never appeared on any British album; another was from an out-of-
print various artists album; and the remaining eight were scattered over **Rock
'n'Roll Music** and **Love Songs**. This would have been a helpful album for
British collectors released any time since 1970. The boxed set merely provided a first class showcase.

Unfortunately, the same could not be said for the package in America,
where the same basic lineup (minus the two German language tracks) was
much less impressive. There was only one true rarity (*Across The Universe*) and
only two B-sides that had never previously appeared on an American album.
Otherwise, the disc consisted of songs that were already on million-selling
albums that were still in print and easily accessible.

The American Release Information for the **Rarities** tracks:

Across The Universe — Never previously released in the U.S. First issued
in 1969 in the U.K. on **No One's Gonna Change Our World**.
Yes It Is — First issued in 1965 as the B-side to *Ticket To Ride*. Also in-
cluded on **Beatles VI** and **Love Songs**.
This Boy — First issued in 1964 on **Meet The Beatles**. Also included on
Love Songs.
The Inner Light — First issued in 1968 as the B-side to *Lady Madonna.*
I'll Get You — First issued in 1963 as the B-side to *She Loves You*. Also
included on **The Beatles Second Album** and as the B-side to *Sie Liebt
Dich.*
Thank You Girl — First issued in 1963 as the B-side to *From Me To You.*
Also included on **The Beatles Second Album** and as the B-side to
Do You Want To Know A Secret (twice reissued).
I Want To Hold Your Hand (replaced *Komm, Gib Mir Deine Hand* from
U.K.). First issued in 1963 as a single. Also included on **Meet The
Beatles** and **The Beatles 1962--1966**.
You Know My Name (Look Up The Number) — First issued in 1970 as
the B-side to *Let It Be.*
She Loves You (replaced *Sie Liebt Dich* from U.K.). First issued in 1963
as a single. Also included on **The Beatles Second Album** and **The
Beatles 1962--1966**.
(continued)

42

A HARD DAY'S NIGHT   Prod: George Martin
First issued July 10, 1964
side one
A Hard Day's Night–2:28
I Should Have Known Better–2:42
If I Fell–2:16
I'm Happy Just To Dance With You–1:59
And I Love Her–2:27
Tell Me Why–2:04
Can't Buy Me Love–2:15
side two
Anytime At All–2:10
I'll Cry Instead–1:44
Things We Said Today–2:35
When I Get Home–2:14
You Can't Do That–2:33
I'll Be Back–2:22
BEATLES FOR SALE   Prod: George Martin
First issued December 4, 1964
side one
No Reply–2:15
I'm A Loser–2:31
Baby's In Black–2:02
*Rock And Roll Music–*Chuck Berry*–2:02*
I'll Follow The Sun–1:46
*Mr. Moonlight–*Roy Lee Johnson*–2:35*
medley–2:30
      *Kansas City–*Jerry Leiber/Mike Stoller*–1:12*
      *Hey-Hey-Hey-Hey–*Richard Penniman*–1:18*
side two
Eight Days A Week–2:43
*Words Of Love–*Buddy Holly*–2:10*
*Honey Don't–*Carl Perkins*–2:56*
Every Little Thing–2:01
I Don't Want To Spoil The Party–2:33
What You're Doing–2:30
*Everybody's Trying To Be My Baby–*Carl Perkins*–2:24*
HELP!   Prod: George Martin
First issued August 6, 1965
side one
Help!–2:16
The Night Before–2:33
You've Got To Hide Your Love Away–2:08
*I Need You–*Harrison*–2:28*
Another Girl–2:02
You're Going To Lose That Girl–2:18
Ticket To Ride–3:03

(Entry 605 continued)

Rain — First issued in 1966 as the B-side to *Paperback Writer*. Also included on **Hey Jude**.

She's A Woman — First issued in 1964 as the flip to *I Feel Fine*. Also included on **Beatles '65**.

Matchbox — First issued in 1964 on **Something New**. Also issued as a single and included on **Rock'n'Roll Music**.

I Call Your Name — First issued in 1964 on **The Beatles Second Album**. Also included on **Rock'n'Roll Music**.

Bad Boy — First issued in 1965 on **Beatles VI**. Also included on **Rock'n' Roll Music**.

Slow Down — First issued in 1964 on **Something New**. Also issued as a single and included on **Rock'n'Roll Music**.

I'm Down — First issued in 1965 as the B-side to *Help!* Also included on **Rock'n'Roll Music**.

Long Tall Sally — First issued in 1964 on **The Beatles Second Album**. Also included on **Rock'n'Roll Music**.

Still, despite the flaws in the mish-mash contents of **Rarities**, the album might have been acceptable to American audiences as part of a complete Beatles collection. But, of course, **The Beatles Collection** was not complete. Even with the bonus album there were twenty-three titles unaccounted for.

Ten would have been taken care of by including the **Magical Mystery Tour** album in the set. The remaining thirteen titles could have served as the basis for another bonus disc, consisting of *The Ballad Of John And Yoko, Day Tripper, Don't Let Me Down, From Me To You, Hey Jude, I Feel Fine, I Want To Hold Your Hand (Komm, Gib Mir Deine Hand* in the U.S.), *Lady Madonna, Old Brown Shoe, Paperback Writer, Revolution, She Loves You (Sie Liebt Dich* in the U.S.), *We Can Work It Out* plus (perhaps) the original *Get Back, Let It Be, Love Me Do,* and *Please Please Me* singles. Combined with the already assembled **Rarities** album, this might have made an excellent thirty to thirty-four cut double bonus album. Instead, these tracks never turned up, so recipients of the boxed set were left to puzzle the absence of such "unimportant" songs as *Hey Jude* in a \$125.00 set.

Oddly, a boxed collection of American Beatles albums would not have left so many holes, though such a set would have been much larger, consisting of eighteen original album packages (not thirteen) plus a bonus disc of eight (not seventeen) songs: *Across The Universe, From Me To You, I'm Down, The Inner Light, Misery, Sie Liebt Dich, There's A Place, You Know My Name (Look Up The Number)* plus (perhaps) the original single releases of *Get Back, Let It Be, Love Me Do,* and *Please Please Me* to round out the set.
(continued)

Act Naturally—Johnny Russell/Vonie Morrison—*2:27*
It's Only Love—*1:53*
You Like Me Too Much—Harrison—*2:34*
Tell Me What You See—*2:35*
I've Just Seen A Face—*2:04*
Yesterday—*2:04*
Dizzy Miss Lizzy—Larry Williams—*2:51*

RUBBER SOUL   Prod: George Martin
First issued December 3, 1965

side one

Drive My Car—*2:25*
Norwegian Wood (This Bird Has Flown)—*2:00*
You Won't See Me—*3:19*
Nowhere Man—*2:40*
Think For Yourself—Harrison—*2:16*
The Word—*2:42*
Michelle—*2:42*

side two

What Goes On?—Lennon/McCartney/Starkey—*2:44*
Girl—*2:26*
I'm Looking Through You—*2:20*
In My Life—*2:23*
Wait—*2:13*
If I Needed Someone—Harrison—*2:19*
Run For Your Life—*2:21*

REVOLVER   Prod: George Martin
First issued August 5, 1966

side one

Taxman—Harrison—*2:36*
Eleanor Rigby—*2:11*
I'm Only Sleeping—*2:58*
Love You Too—Harrison—*3:00*
Here, There And Everywhere—*2:29*
Yellow Submarine—*2:40*
She Said She Said—*2:39*

side two

Good Day Sunshine—*2:08*
And Your Bird Can Sing—*2:02*
For No One—*2:03*
Dr. Robert—*2:14*
I Want To Tell You—Harrison—*2:30*
Got To Get You Into My Life—*2:31*
Tomorrow Never Knows—*3:00*

(Entry 605 continued)

Meet The Beatles	Yesterday And Today
The Beatles Second Album	Revolver
A Hard Day's Night	Sgt. Pepper
Something New	Magical Mystery Tour
Beatles '65	The Beatles
The Early Beatles	Yellow Submarine
Beatles VI	Abbey Road
Help!	Hey Jude
Rubber Soul	Let It Be

No doubt there were several reasons Capitol did not choose this release strategy: a deluxe set of British albums seemed more prestigious; presumably most American fans already had at least a few of the U.S. albums and would be less willing to duplicate those with a boxed set; eighteen albums would have been more costly than thirteen (even as imports); and, most importantly, at the time Capitol did not have the rights to two discs: **A Hard Day's Night** and **Let It Be** (both licensed to United Artists in the U.S.). In fact, **The Beatles Collection** marked the first time that those two titles were available through Capitol.

Yet despite all the shortcomings of **The Beatles Collection** as it was released, the set sold well. Ironically, the U.S. version (without the German language recordings on **Rarities**) even became the more valuable collector's item because there were only the initial 3,000 pressed and packaged. However, larger runs in England and the rest of Europe provided more than enough copies for export to interested buyers in the U.S. for years to come. After all, the boxed set did form a solid *base* for a complete Beatles collection, rounded out by **Magical Mystery Tour** (for *Baby You're A Rich Man, Blue Jay Way, Flying, The Fool On The Hill, Hello Goodbye, I Am The Walrus, Magical Mystery Tour, Penny Lane, Strawberry Fields Forever,* and *Your Mother Should Know*), **Hey Jude** (for *The Ballad Of John And Yoko, Don't Let Me Down, Hey Jude, Lady Madonna, Old Brown Shoe,* and *Revolution,* and **A Collection Of Beatles Oldies** (for *Day Tripper, From Me To You, I Feel Fine, I Want To Hold Your Hand, Paperback Writer, She Loves You,* and *We Can Work It Out*).

Meanwhile, even as **The Beatles Collection** continued to sell, the **Rarities** album took on a life of its own as interested fans bided their time, convinced that EMI would eventually issue the disc as a separate album. The waiting paid off. In September 1979, Capitol announced plans to release **Rarities** on its midline "budget" series (as Capitol SN-12009) in late October or November. At the same time, copies of an Australian version of the album began turning up in American import bins. This version featured the same blue cover design and simple list of songs that had been used in **The Beatles Collection** package. A British release in mid October improved the graphics slightly, darkening the blue and adding extensive liner notes by Hugh Fielder on the
(continued)

SGT. PEPPER'S LONELY HEARTS CLUB BAND   Prod: George
Martin
First issued June 1, 1967
side one
 Sgt. Pepper's Lonely Hearts Club Band—1:59
 With A Little Help From My Friends—2:46
 Lucy In The Sky With Diamonds—3:25
 Getting Better—2:47
 Fixing A Hole—2:33
 She's Leaving Home—3:24
 Being For The Benefit of Mr. Kite—2:36
side two
 Within You Without You—Harrison—*5:03*
 When I'm Sixty-Four—2:38
 Lovely Rita—2:43
 Good Morning Good Morning—2:35
 Sgt. Pepper's Lonely Hearts Club Band (Reprise)—1:20
 A Day In The Life—5:03
THE BEATLES   Prod: George Martin
First issued November 22, 1968
side one
 Back In The U.S.S.R.—2:45
 Dear Prudence—4:00
 Glass Onion—2:10
 Ob-La-Di, Ob-La-Da—3:10
 Wild Honey Pie—1:02
 The Continuing Story Of Bungalow Bill—3:05
 While My Guitar Gently Weeps—Harrison—*4:46*
 Happiness Is A Warm Gun—2:47
side two
 Martha My Dear—2:28
 I'm So Tired—2:01
 Blackbird—2:20
 Piggies—Harrison—*2:04*
 Rocky Raccoon—3:33
 Don't Pass Me By—Starkey—*3:52*
 Why Don't We Do It In The Road?—1:42
 I Will—1:46
 Julia—2:57
side three
 Birthday—2:40
 Yer Blues—4:01
 Mother Nature's Son—2:46
 *Everybody's Got Something To Hide Except Me And My Monkey—
  2:25*
 Sexy Sadie—3:15
 Helter Skelter—4:30
 Long, Long, Long—Harrison—*3:08*

(Entry 605 continued)

back cover.

Capitol, meanwhile, announced that it was canceling plans for its release of **Rarities** and was working instead on a revamped package for the American market. This came about chiefly due to the persistent efforts of twenty-seven-year-old Randall Davis, director of merchandising and advertising. When Davis heard about the plans to issue **Rarities** separately, he appealed to the powers-that-be to reconsider. He pointed out that while the British-oriented **Rarities** collection was acceptable as an element of **The Beatles Collection**, it made absolutely no sense as a separate American release. Even though a number of in-house sample copies had already been pressed, company executives decided Davis was right. They scrapped the scheduled **Rarities** package and put Davis in charge of assembling a new set. Thus, by the end of 1979, record buyers had the best of both worlds at work: a separate release of the British version of **Rarities** available and a special new American version in the works.

As part of his research for the new American **Rarities** package, Davis contacted a number of Beatles fans and experts, including ace collector and archivist Ron Furmanek and *All Together Now* co-author Wally Podrazik. Ten of the Podrazik suggestions (including the two-second "inner groove" to **Sgt. Pepper**) ended up on the revised album issued in 1980. Ron Furmanek's suggestions included an extended version of *And I Love Her* issued in Germany and the British mono mix of *Don't Pass Me By*. More importantly, though, he also brought Davis access to one of the most extensive collections of Beatles records and memorabilia in the world. Thus, when EMI could not find the original master tape to the first version of *Love Me Do*, Furmanek was able to supply a pristine copy of the original single for dubbing.

For full details on the final lineup and packaging for the American version of **Rarities** issued in 1980, see Entry 639. Before that disc came out, though, there was one more odd permutation released. Some dedicated fans decided to beat Capitol to the punch and issue their own package of rare tracks, using an official Capitol logo, elaborate cover artwork, and a similar lineup of songs. Their album was called **Collector's Items**.

This was a particularly audacious package. Not only did the label on the album exactly duplicate the color and logo then being used by Capitol, the back cover also touted all the "other" American Beatles albums on Capitol, with a picture of each one. To add a further air of legitimacy, **Collector's Items** was identified as being "For Promotional Use Only" — thus accounting for the absence of the disc on Capitol's list of new commercial releases. It was quite easy to mistake this for an official promotional album put together for radio station programmers. The front cover was a montage of Beatles collectibles, while the track selection was a straightforward collection of singles then unavailable on an American album (*indicated below), mixed with a few more esoteric oddities such as "true stereo" versions of songs (**indicated below).
(continued)

48

Revolution 1–4:13
Honey Pie–2:42
*Savoy Truffle–*Harrison*–2:55*
Cry Baby Cry–3:11
Revolution 9–8:15
Good Night–3:14

YELLOW SUBMARINE   Prod: George Martin
First issued in U.K. January 17, 1969
side one
Yellow Submarine–2:40
*Only A Northern Song–*Harrison*–3:23*
All Together Now–2:08
Hey Bulldog–3:09
*It's All Too Much–*Harrison*–6:27*
All You Need Is Love–3:46
side two   (Instrumentals by George Martin)
*(Pepperland–*George Martin*–2:18)*
*(Medley: Sea Of Time & Sea Of Holes–*George Martin*–5:16)*
*(Sea Of Monsters–*George Martin*–3:35)*
*(March Of The Meanies–*George Martin*–2:16)*
*(Pepperland Laid Waste–*George Martin*–2:09)*
*(Yellow Submarine In Pepperland–*L/McC*–*arr. George Martin*–2:10)*

ABBEY ROAD   Prod: George Martin
First issued September 26, 1969
side one
Come Together–4:16
*Something–*Harrison*–2:59*
Maxwell's Silver Hammer–3:24
Oh! Darling–3:28
*Octopus's Garden–*Starkey*–2:49*
I Want You (She's So Heavy)–7:49
side two
*Here Comes The Sun–*Harrison*–3:04*
Because–2:45
You Never Give Me Your Money–3:57
Sun King–2:31
Mean Mr. Mustard 1:06
Polythene Pam–1:13
She Came In Through The Bathroom Window–1:58
Golden Slumbers–1:31
Carry That Weight–1:37
The End–2:04
Her Majesty–0:23

(Entry 605 continued)

THE BEATLES COLLECTOR'S ITEMS   (US)   Capitol SPRO-9462
(bootleg)

side one	side two
Love Me Do (version one)	Penny Lane (DJ version)
From Me To You	**Baby, You're A Rich Man*
Thank You Girl	I Am The Walrus (with extra riffs)
All My Loving (with "hi-hat"	*The Inner Light*
cymbal)	Across The Universe (version one)
**This Boy*	*You Know My Name (Look Up The
Sie Liebt Dich	Number)
I Feel Fine	Sgt. Pepper Inner Groove
***She's A Woman*	
Help!	
***I'm Down*	

Nine of these cuts subsequently turned up on the 1980 version of the American **Rarities** package, leading some fans to speculate that Capitol's new track lineup was actually inspired by the **Collector's Items** album. This was not the case, though, because Randall Davis had developed the company's set independently. Besides, the duplication was generally limited to more obvious items such as singles not on an American album, the DJ version of *Penny Lane*, and the original versions of *Love Me Do* and *Across The Universe*.

Note: Though by 1982 fresh pressings of **Collector's Items** had made the disc fairly common on the bootleg market, initial distribution in late 1979 had been quite limited. One entertaining and probably accurate story has it that Capitol found out about the album when a legitimate record manufacturer doing it routinely called the company to check on some details regarding the label design. Upon learning of the unauthorized release, Capitol moved quickly to stop further pressings and distribution. When the disc resurfaced in 1981, the pressings were not as good, reflecting the use of lower quality facilities. Also, *I'm Down* was replaced by *Paperback Writer* in "true stereo" (actually just a bad amateur remix). Though this new record had a different catalog number (SPRO 9463), it usually turned up in the old jacket with the original number and track listing.

ENTRY 607.   The Harry Nilsson greatest hits albums released in the U.S. (Entry 592) and the U.K. had different track lineups. See page 316 for the complete contents of both editions.

An export version of the British album, called **Harry Nilsson's Greatest Hits** (RCA INTS 5233), was issued November 19, 1982.

LET IT BE Prod: George Martin (January 1969) and Phil Spector (March 1970)
First issued May 8, 1970
side one
Two Of Us–3:33
I Dig A Pony–3:55
Across The Universe–3:51
*I Me Mine–*Harrison*–2:25*
*Dig It–*Lennon/McCartney/Harrison/Starkey*–0:51*
Let It Be (version two)–4:01
*Maggie Mae–*P.D.–arr. Lennon/McCartney/Harrison/Starkey*–0:39*
side two
I've Got A Feeling–3:38
One After 909–2:52
The Long And Winding Road–3:40
*For You Blue–*Harrison*–2:33*
Get Back (version two)–3:09

606. FALL 1978 (US) Sire R-224095 (2 LPs)
   by Various Artists
   BRITISH GOLD
   side one
      cut three: *A WORLD WITHOUT LOVE–*L/McC*–2:38*
         by Peter and Gordon
   side three
      cut one: *AIN'T SHE SWEET–*Jack Yellen/Milton Ager*–2:12*
         by The Beatles Prod: Bert Kaempfert

607. NOV 17, 1978 (UK) RCA PL 42728 (LP)
   by Harry Nilsson Prod: Harry Nilsson
      Ringo: Drums
   HARRY NILSSON'S GREATEST MUSIC
   side one
      cut five: *SPACEMAN–*Harry Nilsson*–3:33*
      cut six: *KOJAK COLUMBO–*Harry Nilsson*–3:30*

ENTRY 608. Though labeled **Wings Greatest**, this album was really Paul McCartney's greatest hits, covering his solo career from the pre-Wings *Another Day* (1971) to his most recent number one, *With A Little Luck* (1978). The twelve-track lineup selected was quite impressive.

Five of the songs had hit number one on *Billboard*'s singles charts (*Uncle Albert/Admiral Halsey, My Love, Band On The Run, Silly Love Songs,* and *With A Little Luck*) and all but one had reached the top ten. The lone U.S. flop, *Mull Of Kintyre,* had been a tremendous hit elsewhere in the world, so it obviously belonged on the album. This careful balancing of successes in both the U.K. and the U.S. helped the package work effectively as an international release of hits. With the exception of *Mull Of Kintyre, Uncle Albert/Admiral Halsey* (not released as a single in England), and *Junior's Farm* (which only reached the top twenty in England), every track on the album had originally been a top ten hit on both sides of the Atlantic.

Even with that imposing lineup, though, the album still left out a few big songs including the number one *Listen To What The Man Said,* the top ten *Helen Wheels* and *Sally G,* and the popular studio version of *Maybe I'm Amazed* (from **McCartney**). Perhaps these songs did not fit into the overall flow of the package. Or perhaps McCartney wanted to keep a few of his early hits in reserve for a future volume two. For whatever reason, this led to the only mild criticism of the set among some fans: it was *too* selective. After all, since 1971 Paul McCartney had released twenty-one different singles in both Britain and America. There were more than a dozen tracks among these that had never appeared on an album. Why not do a two-record set similar to the 1973 Beatles greatest hits packages, combining big hits and more obscure tracks?

The most likely explanation is that Paul McCartney wanted to do a greatest hits package that really delivered nothing but hits. Unlike the other former Beatles, he had assembled enough solo successes to do just that. Why dilute the set? The more obscure items would have to wait for another album.

Still, McCartney did not ignore the opportunity to tie together a few loose ends. There were four tracks included on the album that had previously been available only as singles (*Another Day, Hi Hi Hi, Junior's Farm,* and *Mull Of Kintyre*) along with *Live And Let Die,* a single track that had turned up on the soundtrack album to the film. Of course, this still did not eliminate the need to purchase those five singles because the B-side to each one was also a non-album track.

Note: The art deco statue featured on the cover was photographed in Switzerland by Angus Forbes on October 15 and 16, 1978. Against the backdrop of mountains and snow, the statue appeared larger-than-life, but the poster included with the album cut it down to size. There, the statue was set on a piano top, behind a pair of parrots. It also turned up again on the cover of McCartney's next album, **Back To The Egg** (Entry 625), sitting on a fireplace mantelpiece.

608.   NOV 27, 1978 (US) Capitol S00--11905 (LP)
DEC 1, 1978 (UK) Parlophone PCTC 256 (LP)
by Paul McCartney/Wings
WINGS GREATEST   Prod: Paul McCartney except †George
Martin and Paul McCartney; %Paul and Linda McCartney
side one
ANOTHER DAY—Paul and Linda McCartney—*3:41*
SILLY LOVE SONGS—McCartney—*5:54*
†*LIVE AND LET DIE*—McCartney—*3:10*
JUNIOR'S FARM—McCartney—*4:20*
WITH A LITTLE LUCK—McCartney—*5:45*
BAND ON THE RUN—McCartney—*5:09*
side two
%*UNCLE ALBERT/ADMIRAL HALSEY*—Paul and Linda
McCartney—*4:50*
HI, HI, HI—Paul and Linda McCartney—*3:10*
LET 'EM IN—McCartney—*5:08*
MY LOVE—McCartney—*4:07*
JET—McCartney—*4:08*
MULL OF KINTYRE—McCartney/Denny Laine—*4:42*

WINGS GREATEST

ANOTHER DAY,
1971

UNCLE ALBERT/
ADMIRAL HALSEY
1971

SILLY
LOVE
SONGS,
1976

HI,HI,HI,
1972

LIVE AND
LET DIE
1973

LET 'EM IN
1976

JUNIOR'S
FARM,
1974

MY LOVE
1973

WITH A
LITTLE
LUCK
1978

JET
1973

BAND ON
THE RUN
1973

MULL OF
KINTYRE,
1977

PRODUCED BY PAUL McCARTNEY
EXCEPT LIVE AND LET DIE
CO-PRODUCED WITH GEORGE MARTIN

SLEEVE BY PAUL AND LINDA McCARTNEY
ASSISTED BY AUBREY POWELL & GEORGE HARDIE
PHOTOGRAPHY BY ANGUS FORBES
GROUP PHOTOGRAPH BY CLIVE ARROWSMITH

Wings Greatest (back cover)   **Capitol S00 11905 (LP)**

Wings Greatest (front cover) Capitol S00 11905 (LP)

"GOOD NIGHT TONIGHT"

Wings

Goodnight Tonight   Parlophone 12Y R 6023 (12-inch)

1979

March 16.   The ninety-minute *Wings Over The World* television special airs in the U.S. as a late night feature on CBS. On April 8 the program plays in England on BBC 2.

April 3.   The promotional film for *Goodnight Tonight* is shot at the Hammersmith Palais in London.

May 21.   Paul, George, and Ringo play at Eric and Patti's.

May 27.   "A Love Letter From John And Yoko."

June 8.   Ringo sits in on drums for Ron Wood's performance of *Buried Alive* on NBC's television concert program, *The Midnight Special*.

September 9.   Sid Bernstein's "Appeal to John, Paul, George and Ringo" runs in the New York *Times*.

September 27.   Former Wings guitarist Jimmy McCulloch is found dead.

October 24.   Paul McCartney is honored as "the most successful composer and recording artist of all time" (counting his Beatles and solo hits). He receives a disc made of rhodium.

December 26–29.   The concerts for the people of Kampuchea.

1979

How Long Can Disco On?

George Harrison's first album in more than two years seemed to come out of a time warp from the 1960s, completely ignoring the new wave, punk, and disco riffs of the 1970s. It was as if Harrison had gone back to the studio right after *Here Comes The Sun* and *Something* to record these tunes. As a result, the **George Harrison** album came across as fresh and upbeat, with the *Blow Away* single instantly familiar and accessible. To help support the release, Harrison did a few interviews and two promotional films, one set in a room with giant toys (for *Blow Away*) and the other set at a high speed raceway (for *Faster*). Both the single and the album cracked the U.S. top twenty and, in general, received very positive reviews and audience response.

Paul McCartney, meanwhile, entered the new year with a new contract and a new record label. Though staying with EMI for most of the world, Paul ended nearly fifteen years with Capitol Records in the U.S. and signed a multi-million dollar pact with Columbia Records. As part of the deal, he also brought along the rights to his previous solo releases (beginning with **McCartney**), which would shift to Columbia over the next few years.

McCartney's first disc on Columbia was a single, *Goodnight Tonight*, which the label pushed hard as a pop disco hit, complete with a special twelve-inch extended version. The song shot into the top five on both sides of the Atlantic, though some fans were outraged that McCartney had "sold out" and "gone disco."[1] They were in for quite a surprise, though, when the new album arrived several months later because there was not a note of disco on it. Even *Goodnight Tonight* had been omitted. Instead, **Back To The Egg** was a well-rounded back-to-the-basics pop rock album. There were strong new wave-ish tracks such as *Old Siam Sir*, effective pop ballads and love songs such as *Arrow Through Me*, and both of the cuts done the

---

[1] Actually, *Goodnight Tonight* did not even make *Billboard*'s disco charts. In reality, the song was very much a mainstream pop dance number.

previous year with the all-star Rockestra lineup. There were even promotional films for seven of the tracks. Nonetheless, **Back To The Egg** was not a chart topper and none of the singles pulled from it were big hits.

During the summer, McCartney took a break from Wings and did some experimental solo recording on his own. He also cut a solo Christmas single, *Wonderful Christmastime*, to be issued that November.

In September, Wings appeared as special surprise guest performers at the free Crickets concert that ended the fourth annual MPL-sponsored Buddy Holly Week celebration. For that, Denny Laine sang *Raining In My Heart*, Paul did *It's So Easy*, and everyone joined in for the grand finale, *Bo Diddley*. Two months later, Wings was back on the road as McCartney launched his first full-fledged concert tour of Britain since 1975. They began with a free show for Paul's old school:

The Wings Tour of Great Britain — 1979

November 23	Liverpool; Royal Court (Free concert for Liverpool Institute)
November 24,25,26	Liverpool; Royal Court
November 28,29	Manchester; Apollo
December 1	Southampton; Gaumont
December 2	Brighton; New Conference Centre
December 3	Lewisham; Odeon
December 5	London; Rainbow
December 7,8,9,10	London; Wembley Arena
December 12	Birmingham; Odeon
December 14	Newcastle; City Hall
December 15	Edinburgh; Odeon
December 16,17	Glasgow; Apollo

Songs performed at the shows included: *Got To Get You Into My Life; Getting Closer; Every Night; Again & Again & Again; I've Had Enough; No Words; Cook Of The House; Old Siam Sir; Maybe I'm Amazed; The Fool On The Hill; Let It Be; Hot As Sun; Spin It On; Twenty Flight Rock; Go Now; Arrow Through Me; Wonderful Christmastime; Coming Up; Goodnight Tonight; Yesterday; Mull Of Kintyre;* and *Band OnThe Run*.

Less than two weeks after the final show in Glasgow, Wings was back on stage as part of a series of charity concerts to benefit the United Nations emergency relief fund for the people of Kampuchea (Cambodia). The shows were set up in response to an appeal from United Nations' Secretary General Kurt Waldheim and spearheaded by Paul McCartney, who helped enlist the musicians and crews for four nights of music at London's Hammersmith Odeon. The performers were: December 26 — Queen; December 27 — Ian Dury,

Matumbi, The Clash; December 28 — The Pretenders, The Specials, The Who; December 29 — Rockpile, Elvis Costello, Wings, plus Surprise Guests.

Under normal conditions that would have been quite enough. However, it seemed that the press and public could not resist one last frenzy of Beatles reunion fever as the 1970s came to an end. Thus, the question that hung over the final night's show was: Will the Beatles reunite?

Actually, this talk had started back in September when promoter Sid Bernstein placed a full page ad in the New York *Times* suggesting that the former Beatles stage three benefit concerts to aid the "boat people" (refugees from Southeast Asia). When the U.N.'s Kurt Waldheim then began to query a number of musicians about some sort of benefit concert, tabloid papers such as the New York *Post* played up the possible scenario with banner headlines. The September 21st edition of the *Post* proclaimed: "The Beatles Are Back!" By the night of the final London show for Kampuchea, anything less than even a partial Beatles reunion was going to be judged a disappointment by Fleet Street.

Paul McCartney was the only former Beatle on stage. Rockestra, not John, George, and Ringo, were the surprise guests. An impressive assembly, to be sure, but not the Beatles.

Ironically, the former Beatles themselves had inadvertently helped fuel such wild speculation with two events earlier in the year. In May, at a private wedding reception for Eric Clapton and Patti Boyd, Paul, George, and Ringo had played together in an impromptu jam with fellow guests Ginger Baker, Jim Capaldi, Jack Bruce, Denny Laine, Mick Jagger, and Ray Cooper. Reportedly, their songs together included Lloyd Price's *Lawdy Miss Clawdy*, Jerry Lee Lewis's *High School Confidential*, and Eddie Cochran's *Something Else*.

Less than a week later, John Lennon and Yoko Ono emerged briefly from their self-imposed semi-retirement from public life by placing a full page ad in the New York *Times*, the Los Angeles *Times,* the London *Times*, and a Tokyo paper. Labeled "A Love Letter From John And Yoko To People Who Ask Us What, When, And Why," it essentially read: "Hi. We're doing fine. Family life is great. Thanks for caring. Keep on loving." However, the postscript to the letter attracted the most attention, referring to "three angels" looking over their shoulders as they wrote. Whether intended or not, to eager fans that clearly meant only one thing: Paul, George, and Ringo.

When that reunion did not take place, though, they were ready for something else: The return of John Lennon.

ENTRY 609 & 610. Less than two years after the legendary Hamburg Star Club tapes first hit the market as a two-record set, Pickwick brought them back to Stateside record buyers as two budget albums. In keeping with the spirit of the original Lingasong/Double H packaging, the new records clearly pointed out up front (on the front and back covers) that these were live recordings from 1962 in Germany, not polished studio tracks from England. Pickwick, in fact, did not even include a photo of the group anywhere on the jacket, going with a simple black-and-white design. Volume one used black lettering on a white background; volume two used white lettering on a black background.

For both volumes, the company did make a few changes from the original presentation of the music. First, the tracks appeared in a different order. More importantly, despite the fact that Lingasong had already spent some $100,000 "cleaning up" the recordings from their original state (done on a home tape recorder at 3¾ i.p.s. with one microphone), Pickwick brought in its own technicians to boost the vocals to a more prominent position in the new "final" mix. A commendable effort though, truth to be told, hard to notice and appreciate on these tracks. There was no getting around the fact that the sound quality of a seventeen-year-old homemade recording could not come close to the minimum standards expected by record buyers of the 1970s.

Pickwick also went back to the original tapes for a new song to include on this release. Unfortunately, *Hully Gully* (the last cut on volume one) did not feature the Beatles but another of the groups performing at the Star Club in 1962 (when Ted Taylor had arranged to have the recordings made of his own group, the Dominoes, and others working there at the time, including the Beatles). Perhaps the Beatles actually performed somewhere on this track (guitars or backing vocals), but the lead vocal and horn arrangements were definitely not from them.

So while the Pickwick albums did not really add any new Beatles material to this set of historic recordings, they did provide an inexpensive opportunity for American fans to acquire twenty-six of the thirty tracks released from the Star Club tapes. The four other songs, which had been issued on the original 1977 British and German packagings, remained unreleased in the U.S. The flip-side of that situation was that four songs issued on the original 1977 U.S. package remained unreleased in Britain:

On the original U.K. and German album		On the original 1977 U.S. album
I Saw Her Standing There	replaced by	*I'm Gonna Sit Right Down And Cry (Over You)*
Twist And Shout	replaced by	*Where Have You Been All My Life?*
Reminiscing	replaced by	*Till There Was You*
Ask Me Why	replaced by	*Sheila*

The reason for this trans-Atlantic discrepancy was simple. Back in 1977, when the live Star Club tapes first came out, the initial two-record set was issued first in Germany (on the Bellaphon label) and immediately exported. *(Continued)*

609. JAN 29, 1979 (US) Pickwick SPC-3661 (LP)
by The Beatles recorded live by Ted Taylor in 1962 except †
THE BEATLES FIRST LIVE RECORDINGS VOLUME ONE
side one
WHERE HAVE YOU BEEN ALL MY LIFE?—Barry Mann/
Cynthia Weil—*1:55*
A TASTE OF HONEY—Ric Marlow/Bobby Scott—*1:45*
YOUR FEET'S TOO BIG—Ada Benson/Fred Fisher—*2:18*
MR. MOONLIGHT—Roy Lee Johnson—*2:06*
BESAME MUCHO—Consuelo Velazquez/Selig Shaftel—
2:36
I'M GONNA SIT RIGHT DOWN AND CRY (OVER YOU)
—Joe Thomas/Howard Biggs—*2:43*
BE-BOP-A-LULA—Gene Vincent/Tex Davis—*2:29*
side two
HALLELUJAH, I LOVE HER SO—Ray Charles—*2:10*
'TILL THERE WAS YOU—Meredith Willson—*1:59*
SWEET LITTLE SIXTEEN—Chuck Berry—*2:45*
LITTLE QUEENIE—Chuck Berry—*3:51*
MEDLEY—*2:09*
KANSAS CITY—Jerry Leiber/Mike Stoller—*1:04*
HEY-HEY-HEY-HEY—Richard Penniman—*1:05*
(†hully gully—F. Smith/C. Goldsmith—*1:39)*

610. JAN 29, 1979 (US) Pickwick SPC 3662 (LP)
by The Beatles; recorded live by Ted Taylor in 1962
THE BEATLES FIRST LIVE RECORDINGS VOLUME TWO
side one
NOTHIN' SHAKIN' (BUT THE LEAVES ON THE TREES)
—Cirino Colacrai/Eddie Fontaine/Dianne Lampert/Jack
Cleveland—*1:15*
EVERYBODY'S TRYING TO BE MY BABY—Carl Perkins
—*2:25*
MATCHBOX—Carl Perkins—*2:35*
I'M TALKING ABOUT YOU—Chuck Berry—*1:48*
LONG TALL SALLY—Enotris Johnson/Richard Penni-
man/Robert Blackwell—*1:45*
ROLL OVER BEETHOVEN—Chuck Berry—*2:15*
HIPPY HIPPY SHAKE—Chan Romero—*1:42*

(Entry 609 & 610 continued)

The discs were not released in the U.S. for another two months, so something new had to be added to tout the American package and separate it from the imports. Thus, four new previously unreleased cuts were added, bumping four others from the original lineup. Of course, this meant that American fans who wished to acquire all thirty tracks had to buy both a domestic copy and an import. German and British fans had to do the same.

Later that year, Bellaphon solved that situation in Germany with a special one-disc companion package, repeating eight cuts but also including the four released in the U.S. (*indicated below):

LIVE IM THE STAR CLUB 1962 (West Germany) Bellaphon BI 15223

side one	side two
Twist And Shout	*I Saw Her Standing There*
Roll Over Beethoven	*A Taste Of Honey*
Sheila	*Mr. Moonlight*
Ask Me Why	*Where Have You Been All My Life?*
Till There Was You	*I'm Gonna Sit Right Down And Cry*
Long Tall Sally	*(Over You)*
	Sweet Little Sixteen

Copies of this record were also exported to England, where the four U.S. tracks remained unavailable on any British package until 1981 (Entry 681). That same year, the four European tracks also turned up in America (Entry 667).

Note: The Pickwick packages had been originally scheduled for release in October 1978 as BAN-90061 and BAN-90071 (numbers later used on a separate Canadian issuing), but were delayed. Upon release, these $3.98 budget discs ended up facing stiff competition from a familiar source: copies of the original two-record set from Linasong that turned up in the cut-out bins.

ENTRY 612 & 613. Though *Love Comes To Everyone* was initially targeted to be the first single from the new **George Harrison** album, at the last minute the very catchy *Blow Away* got the nod instead for both the U.S. and the U.K. That song was one of the first done by Harrison after a year-long layoff from songwriting in 1977 and, much to his surprise (and initial embarrassment), it turned out to be "one of *those* tunes" – very commercial.

Both countries packaged the single in an attractive picture sleeve using the back cover photo from the new album, though they selected two different island-inspired tracks for the respective B-sides. *Soft Touch* was written in the Virgin Islands, while the words to *Soft-Hearted Hana* were done when George saw the "non-touristy" side of the Haleakala volcano on the island of Maui in Hawaii. These songs also served as the American and British flip sides (trading places) when *Love Comes To Everyone* was issued as the follow-up single (Entries 619 & 621).

side two
FALLING IN LOVE AGAIN (CAN'T HELP IT)—Sammy
Lerner/Frederick Hollander—*1:57*
LEND ME YOUR COMB—Kay Twomey/Fred Wise/Ben
Weisman—*1:44*
SHEILA—Tommy Roe—*1:56*
RED SAILS IN THE SUNSET—Jimmy Kennedy/Will
Grosz—*2:00*
TO KNOW HER IS TO LOVE HER—Phil Spector—*3:02*
SHIMMY SHAKE—Joe South/Billy Land—*2:17*
I REMEMBER YOU—Johnny Mercer/Victor Schertzinger—
1:54

611. WINTER 1979 (US) Sire R-234021 (2 LPs)
by Various Artists
BRITISH ROCK CLASSICS
side one
cut one: *MY BONNIE*—Charles Pratt—*2:06*
by Tony Sheridan and The Beatles   Prod: Bert
Kaempfert

612. FEB 16, 1979 (UK) Dark Horse K 17327
by George Harrison   Prod: George Harrison and Russ
Titelman
A: Blow Away—Harrison—*3:59*
B: Soft Touch—Harrison—*4:00*

613. FEB 19, 1979 (US) Dark Horse DRC 8763
by George Harrison   Prod: George Harrison and Russ
Titelman
A: Blow Away—Harrison—*3:59*
B: Soft-Hearted Hana—Harrison—*4:03*

Blow Away   **Dark Horse DRC 8763 (45)**

George Harrison   **Dark Horse DHK 3255 (LP)**

ENTRY 614. The **George Harrison** album was recorded in 1978 from mid-April to October, with Russ Titelman sharing the producing chores. George began composing new material earlier in the year (actually starting with the music to *Love Comes To Everyone* in the fall of 1977), initially motivated by the desire to do some tunes that his friends on the Formula One race car circuit could enjoy. After all, through much of 1977 he had been entertained by their activities as professional racers, so it seemed only fair to return the favor. Appropriately, one of the new songs (*Faster*) was about Grand Prix racing, even taking its title from a book written by champion Jackie Stewart in 1973.

A visit to the Hawaiian islands in February 1978 provided a good deal of lyrical inspiration. While vacationing there, George wrote the words to *Love Comes To Everyone, If You Believe* (which he had begun on New Year's Day in England with Gary Wright), *Dark Sweet Lady* (for Olivia Trinidad), *Soft-Hearted Hana*, and *Here Comes The Moon*. On the last two, some "magic mushrooms" also supposedly added their influence — for the first time in years for George. (Well, it *was* a vacation.)

There were even connections to the Beatles days. *Here Comes The Moon* was an obvious companion to *Here Comes The Sun; Blow Away* sounded almost nostalgic, as if it had been done back in 1969 as well; and *Not Guilty* was a new recording of a song that had been left off the 1968 double album.

Harrison connected with Russ Titelman early on in the project when he came to Warner Bros. in Burbank looking for feedback not only on his newly recorded demo material but also on past work, bluntly asking three staff producers (Titelman, Ted Templeman, and Lenny Waronker) what songs of his they had liked — and disliked. Templeman, in response, cited *Deep Blue* as a personal favorite, so George put together a similar type of instrumental riff that became *Soft-Hearted Hana*. Titelman continued such positive encouragement during the production sessions. At his urging, for example, George developed some rough melodies into *Your Love Is Forever*, which he later described as one of his favorites on the album.

ENTRY 616 & 617. Recorded right after the 1978 Christmas holidays, both sides of this single were mixed and ready by February. Actually, the rough tracks for *Goodnight Tonight* had been done by McCartney himself more than a year earlier, following a visit to a dance club. He pulled out the tape in the midst of the **Back To The Egg** sessions when he decided it was time for a new Wings single. The group then built on the original recording. In contrast, *Daytime Nightime Suffering* was written over a weekend break and then immediately recorded at the Replica studios in the basement of MPL. The song even included baby James McCartney's unexpected "backing vocal" cry, which took place when Linda inadvertently stepped into mike range with him at the sessions.

The twelve-inch version was packaged in a colorful cardboard picture sleeve. In addition, the British package had a special inner sleeve with a sketch of some dancers. The U.S. disc had the line "disco single" on the label, while in Britain *Goodnight Tonight* was merely identified as the "full" or "long" version.

614. FEB 20, 1979 (US) Dark Horse DHK 3255 (LP)
FEB 23, 1979 (UK) Dark Horse K 56562 (LP)
by George Harrison
GEORGE HARRISON   Prod: George Harrison and Russ
Titelman
side one
Love Comes To Everyone—Harrison—*4:33*
Not Guilty—Harrison—*3:36*
Here Comes The Moon—Harrison—*4:46*
Soft-Hearted Hana—Harrison—*4:03*
Blow Away—Harrison—*3:59*
side two
Faster—Harrison—*4:40*
Dark Sweet Lady—Harrison—*3:20*
Your Love Is Forever—Harrison—*3:45*
Soft Touch—Harrison—*4:00*
If You Believe—Harrison/Gary Wright—*2:53*

615. FEB 26, 1979 (US) Capitol SM 11897 (LP)
by Billy J. Kramer with the Dakotas   Prod: George Martin
BEST OF BILLY J. KRAMER WITH THE DAKOTAS
side one
cut one: *I'LL KEEP YOU SATISFIED*—L/McC—*2:04*
cut two: *DO YOU WANT TO KNOW A SECRET*—L/McC—
1:59
cut four: *I CALL YOUR NAME*—L/McC—*2:00*
cut five: *FROM A WINDOW*—L/McC—*1:55*
side two
cut two: *BAD TO ME*—L/McC—*2:18*

616. MAR 16, 1979 (US) Columbia 3-10939
MAR 23, 1979 (UK) Parlophone R 6023
by Wings   Prod: Paul McCartney (A side); Paul McCartney
and Chris Thomas (B side)
*A: Goodnight Tonight—McCartney—*4:18*
*B: Daytime Nighttime Suffering—McCartney—*3:19*

617. MAR 26, 1979 (US) Columbia 23-10940 (12-inch)
APR 3, 1979 (UK) Parlophone 12Y R 6023 (12-inch)
by Wings   Prod: Paul McCartney (A side); Paul McCartney
and Chris Thomas (B side)
*A: Goodnight Tonight (long version)—McCartney—*7:25*
*B: Daytime Nighttime Suffering—McCartney—*3:19*

Goodnight Tonight   Parlophone 12Y R 6023 (12-inch)
(inner sleeve)

Daytime Nightime   Parlophone 12Y R 6023 (12-inch)
Suffering (inner sleeve)

The Songs Lennon And McCartney Gave Away   EMI NUT 18 (LP)

ENTRY 618. This twenty-track album brought together songs composed by John Lennon and Paul McCartney but then given to other artists and not recorded by the Beatles. Many of these recordings had been out of print for years. One ten-year-old cut (*Penina* from 1969) had never even been issued in Britain before. There were detailed liner notes by Tony Barrow providing background on each track.

Fourteen of the songs came from 1963 and 1964. During that time, most were not specifically written for the individual performers but, rather, were leftovers or old songs that John and Paul dusted off and gave away – usually to personal friends or other artists connected with NEMS. From 1965 on, they did this much less frequently, usually composing new material for a specific reason or artist.

Of course, many songs credited as Lennon-McCartney compositions were actually done individually, with only a minor amount of work together. Nonetheless, they were still credited to the writing *team* of John Lennon and Paul McCartney and, as such, formed a specific body of work. Strictly speaking, then, this album cheated a bit on the Lennon-McCartney hook in order to squeeze in a few songs composed and credited individually to Paul McCartney (*Catcall, Penina, Woman*) and John Lennon (*I'm The Greatest*).

At the same time, there were two songs left off this collection that did fit the premise of a Lennon-McCartney tune given to another performer: *Thingumybob* (given to the Black Dyke Mills Band in 1968) and *Goodbye* (given to Mary Hopkin in 1969). Most likely, these were not used due to the legal morass still surrounding non-Beatles product issued on Apple. One other track, *Give Peace A Chance*, was written and released by John in 1969 (as the Plastic Ono Band), but was still credited to Lennon-McCartney. That might have been a more appropriate track to include than Ringo's *I'm The Greatest* from 1973, especially because at the time *Give Peace A Chance* had not yet appeared in its entirety on any album. (In contrast, *I'm The Greatest* made its third album appearance.)

Overall, though, the collection covered the 1963--69 period very well. Of the material from the eleven artists included, the tracks (one each) by Carlos Mendes, the Strangers with Mike Shannon, Chris Barber, P.J. Proby, Tommy Quickly, and the Applejacks had been the most sought-after by fans.

Note: There were a few other songs no doubt left off because they broke from the strict definition of "songs they gave away." Nonetheless, these have been generally considered part of the canon of collectible cover versions. In two cases, the Lennon-McCartney song given to another artist was followed by a *later* release from the Beatles. *I Wanna Be Your Man* came out three weeks after a single version by the Rolling Stones, while *I Call Your Name* appeared nearly a year after a single by Billy J. Kramer. There were also a few instances in which a cover version came out after the original by the Beatles but was specifically "godfathered" by the group: *Do You Want To Know A Secret* by Billy J. Kramer, *Misery* by Kenny Lynch, and *I Saw Her Standing There* by Duffy Power (all in 1963), *You've Got To Hide Your Love Away* by the Silkie in 1965, and *Got To Get You Into My Life* by Cliff Bennett and the Rebel Rousers in 1966.

8. APR 13, 1979 (UK)   EMI NUT 18   (LP)
    by Various Artists (see individual cuts)
    THE SONGS LENNON AND MCCARTNEY GAVE AWAY
    side one
    I'M THE GREATEST—Lennon—*3:23*
    by Ringo Starr   Prod: Richard Perry
    ONE AND ONE IS TWO—L/McC—*2:10*
    by The Strangers with Mike Shannon
    FROM A WINDOW—L/McC—*1:55*
    by Billy J. Kramer   Prod: George Martin
    NOBODY I KNOW—L/McC—*2:27*
    by Peter & Gordon   Prod: Norman Newell
    LIKE DREAMERS DO—L/McC—*2:30*
    by The Applejacks   Prod: Mike Smith
    I'LL KEEP YOU SATISFIED—L/McC—*2:04*
    by Billy J. Kramer   Prod: George Martin
    LOVE OF THE LOVED—L/McC—*2:00*
    by Cilla Black   Prod: George Martin
    WOMAN—Paul McCartney—*2:21*
    by Peter & Gordon   Prod: John Burgess
    TIP OF MY TONGUE—L/McC—*2:02*
    by Tommy Quickly   Prod: Les Reed
    I'M IN LOVE—L/McC—*2:07*
    by The Fourmost   Prod: George Martin
    side two
    HELLO LITTLE GIRL—L/McC—*1:50*
    by The Fourmost   Prod: George Martin
    THAT MEANS A LOT—L/McC—*2:31*
    by P.J. Proby   Prod: Ron Richards
    IT'S FOR YOU—L/McC—*2:20*
    by Cilla Black   Prod: George Martin
    PENINA—Paul McCartney—*2:34*
    by Carlos Mendes
    STEP INSIDE LOVE—L/McC—*2:20*
    by Cilla Black   Prod: George Martin
    A WORLD WITHOUT LOVE—L/McC—*2:38*
    by Peter & Gordon   Prod: Norman Newell
    BAD TO ME—L/McC—*2:18*
    by Billy J. Kramer   Prod: George Martin
    I DON'T WANT TO SEE YOU AGAIN—L/McC—*1:59*
    by Peter & Gordon   Prod: Norman Newell
    I'LL BE ON MY WAY—L/McC—*1:38*
    by Billy J. Kramer   Prod: George Martin
    CATCALL—Paul McCartney—*3:03*
    by The Chris Barber Band   Prod: Chris Barber, Giorgio
        Gomelsky, Reggie King

ENTRY 620. Backed by an extensive ad campaign, this EMI greatest hits compilation featured twenty tracks from twenty British performers of the 1960s and 1970s, including nine number one hits. **A Monument To British Rock** also marked the first time songs by the Beatles both as a group and as solo artists were used on an EMI various artists package.

ENTRY 620a. More than nine years after this compilation album was released in the U.S., EMI issued the package in the U.K. The reason for the belated British release was simple: the **Hey Jude** album was very popular but, lacking a homegrown pressing, record dealers in England had to import copies. Oddly, EMI had actually issued a version of **Hey Jude** back in March 1970 (Apple CPCS 106), but that had been manufactured for export only. This new release, though, served both the British and export markets.

Still, the song selection on **Hey Jude** seemed a bit repetitious in 1979. Eight of the songs were readily available on at least one other U.K. greatest hits package and another, *I Should Have Known Better*, was on **A Hard Day's Night**. Only *Rain* was otherwise relatively hard to find on a U.K. album, having turned up only on **Rarities**, then unavailable as a separate release (but due to be issued as such in October).

Yet back in 1970, the opposite had been true. Though *Can't Buy Me Love* and *I Should Have Known Better* had been included on the United Artists soundtrack to **A Hard Day's Night**, neither had ever appeared on a Capitol album. More importantly, all the remaining tracks had only been on singles. In a way, then, **Hey Jude** had served the same purpose as the 1966 **Yesterday And Today**, gathering odd tracks onto a Capitol album for the first time. And until the greatest hits packages of 1973, this was the only way fans in either country could find these songs on an album.

Note: There were a total of eight Beatles discs issued in Britain between 1964 and 1970 for the export market:

(SEP 1964) *If I Fell* b/w *Tell Me Why* (Parlophone DP 562)
(APR 1965) **Something New** (Parlophone CPCS 101)
(AUG 1965) *Dizzy Miss Lizzy* b/w *Yesterday* (Parlophone DP 563)
(JAN 1966) *Michelle* b/w *Drive My Car* (Parlophone DP 564)
(MAR 1966) **Beatles VI** (Parlophone CPCS 104)
(APR 1966) **The Beatles' Second Album** (Parlophone CPCS 103)
(AUG 1968) *Hey Jude* b/w *Revolution* (Parlophone DP 570)
(MAR 1970) **Hey Jude** (Apple CPCS 106)

For further details on these export-only releases, consult issue six of *Beatles Now* magazine.

ENTRY 621. *Love Comes To Everyone* came in a picture sleeve featuring the front cover photo to the **George Harrison** album, but had an extremely short shelf life. Though the follow-up to a top twenty hit, this single failed even to make the "bubbling under" section of *Billboard*'s Hot 100 chart.

619. APR 27, 1979 (UK) Dark Horse K 17284
by George Harrison   Prod: George Harrison and Russ
Titelman
A: LOVE COMES TO EVERYONE—Harrison—*3:35*
B: SOFT-HEARTED HANA—Harrison—*4:03*

620. MAY 4, 1979 (UK) Harvest EMTV 17 (LP)
by Various Artists
A MONUMENT TO BRITISH ROCK
side one
cut two: *MY SWEET LORD*—Harrison—*4:39*
by George Harrison   Prod: George Harrison and Phil Spector
cut four: *GOT TO GET YOU INTO MY LIFE*—L/McC—*2:29*
by Cliff Bennett and The Rebel Rousers   Prod: Paul
McCartney and David Paramor
side two
cut one: *GET BACK*—*3:11*
by The Beatles with Billy Preston   Prod: George Martin
cut five: *IMAGINE*—Lennon—*2:59*
by John Lennon   Prod: John Lennon, Yoko Ono and
Phil Spector

620a. MAY 11, 1979 (UK) Parlophone PCS 7184 (LP)
by The Beatles
HEY JUDE   Prod: George Martin
side one
CAN'T BUY ME LOVE—*2:15*
I SHOULD HAVE KNOWN BETTER—*2:42*
PAPERBACK WRITER—*2:25*
RAIN—*2:59*
LADY MADONNA—*2:17*
REVOLUTION—*3:22*
side two
HEY JUDE—*7:11*
OLD BROWN SHOE—Harrison—*3:16*
DON'T LET ME DOWN—*3:34*
THE BALLAD OF JOHN AND YOKO—*2:58*

621. MAY 14, 1979 (US) Dark Horse DRC 8844
by George Harrison   Prod: George Harrison and Russ
Titelman
A: LOVE COMES TO EVERYONE—Harrison—*3:35*
B: SOFT TOUCH—Harrison—*4:00*

ENTRY 623 & 624. The initial singles from **Back To The Egg** in Britain and America showcased a pair of solid rockers, with the frenzied *Spin It On* acting as B-side to both. *Getting Closer* was actually an old song McCartney had written several years before, while *Old Siam, Sir* and *Spin It On* were freshly done in Scotland and reflected a more new wave-ish style. In fact, when Elvis Costello and two members of his band appeared as guests on Radio One's *Round Table* record review program in Britain, they were surprised to learn that McCartney was responsible for *Old Siam, Sir*, which they liked.

ENTRY 625. **Back To The Egg** was mostly recorded over a six-month period in 1978 (July to December), with a few final touches added the next year before the master tape was completed April 1. Sessions took place June 29–July 27 at the "Spirit of Ranachan" studio in Scotland, September 11–20 at Lympne Castle in Kent, October–November at EMI, and (for overdubs and fine-tuning) December at the portable Replica studio – an exact copy of Abbey Road's studio number two, located in the basement of MPL Productions in London. This schedule allowed McCartney to continue his habit of recording in unusual locations, but also to stick fairly close to home and family.

The sessions kicked off on June 29 with *To You*. Then McCartney and the band spent a few days laying down about a dozen vocal and instrumental demo tracks for the Rupert Bear cartoon project. Back to the album at hand for *Again And Again And Again* and *Arrow Through Me*, followed by *Winter Rose* and a rough guide version of *Love Awake*. *Spin It On* (virtually completed in one day, July 23) and *Old Siam, Sir* wrapped up work in Scotland.

Lympne (pronounced LIM) was **Back To The Egg**'s most exotic locale – a castle built in medieval times near the site of an old Roman fort. There, Wings recorded *We're Open Tonight* (in the well of an old stone spiral staircase), a new shorter version of *Love Awake, After The Ball, Million Miles*, and several straight literary readings by the castle's current owners, Harold and Dierdre Margary, whose voices were mixed in with two group instrumentals, *Reception* (along with random radio noise) and *The Broadcast*.

The superstar Rockestra session on October 3 provided the highlight of the recording back at Abbey Road, with the guest musicians laying down the basic backing tracks to *So Glad To See You Here* and *Rockestra Theme*. Appropriately, the cry of "Why haven't I had any dinner?" at the end of the *Rockestra Theme* was reminiscent of the big bands from another era (the 1930s and 1940s), which sometimes included a vocal chant from the boys in the band – as in Glenn Miller's *Pennsylvania 6–5000*. The following week, it was just Wings again for *Getting Closer* and *Baby's Request*.

Among the items added in subsequent overdubs: the vocals to *Winter Rose* and the synthesizer to *Getting Closer* (in March), the reggae reprise of *We're Open Tonight* at the end of *So Glad To See You Here*, and the Black Dyke Mills Band on *Love Awake* (April 1).

Note: **Back To The Egg** had a fried egg custom label: "sunny side up" on side one, "over easy" on side two. The only "egg" on the front cover, though, was a shot of the Earth taken from outer space.

622. MAY 1979 (US MAIL ORDER) Warner Brothers PRO A 796
(2 LPs)
by Various Artists
MONSTERS
side two
cut three: *NOT GUILTY*—Harrison—*3:36*
by George Harrison   Prod: George Harrison and Russ
Titelman

623. JUN 1, 1979 (UK) Parlophone R 6026
by Wings   Prod: Paul McCartney and Chris Thomas
A: Old Siam, Sir—McCartney—*4:11*
B: Spin It On—McCartney—*2:13*

624. JUN 4, 1979 (US) Columbia 3-11020
by Wings   Prod: Paul McCartney and Chris Thomas
A: Getting Closer—McCartney—*3:22*
B: Spin It On—McCartney—*2:13*

625. JUN 8, 1979 (UK) Parlophone PCTC 257 (LP)
JUN 11, 1979 (US) Columbia FC 36057 (LP)
by Wings and †Rockestra
BACK TO THE EGG   Prod: Paul McCartney and Chris
Thomas
side one
Reception—McCartney—*1:07*
Getting Closer—McCartney—*3:22*
We're Open Tonight—McCartney—*1:27*
Spin It On—McCartney—*2:13*
Again And Again And Again—Denny Laine—*3:33*
Old Siam, Sir—McCartney—*4:11*
Arrow Through Me—McCartney—*3:37*
side two
†Rockestra Theme—McCartney—*2:33*
To You—McCartney—*3:11*
medley—*3:57*
After The Ball—McCartney—*2:16*
Million Miles—McCartney—*1:41*
medley—*4:56*
Winter Rose—McCartney—*2:04*
Love Awake—McCartney—*2:52*
The Broadcast—McCartney—*1:28*
includes spoken excerpts from
The Sport Of Kings—Ian Hay—*0:18*
The Little Man—John Galsworthy—*0:43*
†So Glad To See You Here—McCartney—*3:19*
Baby's Request—McCartney—*2:48*

Back To The Egg   Columbia FC 36057 (LP)

Faster (frontside)   Dark Horse K 17423P
                                       (picture disc 45)

Faster (backside)   Dark Horse K 17423P
                                       (picture disc 45)

ENTRY 626. Despite the lead-off title track, this odd budget compilation drew primarily from Nilsson's 1971 **Aerial Pandemonium Ballet**.

ENTRY 627. This single was also issued as a picture disc (Dark Horse K17-423P) which, in fact, was far more common as an import to America than the black vinyl version. All royalties due Harrison from the sales of the record were donated to the Gunnar Nilsson cancer fund. (Nilsson was a racer who died of cancer in 1978.) This was an appropriate gesture because in interviews, on the sleeve to the single, and on the **George Harrison** album, Harrison acknowledged the inspiration provided by various Formula One drivers. He said *Faster* was: inspired by Jackie Stewart and Niki Lauda; in memory of Ronnie Peterson (a thirty-four-year-old Swedish Grand Prix driver killed in Milan in September 1978); done with special thanks to Jody Scheckter; and dedicated to the "Entire Formula One Circus." So as not to miss any of them, the *Faster* side of the picture disc featured photos of Stewart, Lauda, Scheckter, and Jochen Rindt, Jim Clark, Graham Hill, Emerson Fittipaldi, Stirling Moss and Juan Manuel Fangio.

Despite all the racing car dedications, though, one of the strongest aspects of *Faster* was that it did not only refer to racing. The song's descriptions of life in the fast lane easily applied to any situation that put a person in the public eye, such as being one of the Beatles.

Note: For atmosphere, *Faster* included the sounds of racing cars mixed in both at the beginning and at the second chorus. That was Mario Andretti and Ronnie Peterson driving their respective Lotuses at about 180 miles per hour.

ENTRY 627a. More than two years after its American release on Epic, the *Seaside Woman* single (Linda McCartney as Suzy and the Red Stripes) was issued in England. See page 293 and subsequent reissues for details.

ENTRY 628. Even though EMI touted this single as a double-A, the disc failed to rise any higher than number 60 on the British charts. Nonetheless, this was a surprisingly good performance by *Baby's Request*, considering that it had originally been intended as just a demo recording.

While on holiday in France, McCartney had met one of his favorite old singing groups, the Mills Brothers, backstage after one of their concerts. He was asked to write a song for them, thought it was a great idea, and turned out *Baby's Request* — doing a quick demo with Wings toward the end of the **Back To The Egg** sessions. The Mills Brothers never did do a recording, so McCartney decided to include his own demo version on the new album as the perfect final cut, following the thunderous *So Glad To See You Here* with Rockestra.

The *Baby's Request* side of the picture sleeve featured a tinted still from the promotional video, while the *Getting Closer* side showed a man walking a lobster. Why not a salamander as called for in the song? Because the picture was not set up especially for this sleeve — it was actually an old photo from Hipgnosis. See the 1978 book *Walk Away Rene—The Work Of Hipgnosis*, page 142 ("Unsold Ideas").

626. JUN 8, 1979 (UK) Camden CDS-1178 (LP)
by Harry Nilsson   Prod: John Lennon
SAVE THE LAST DANCE FOR ME
side one
cut one: *SAVE THE LAST DANCE FOR ME*—Doc Pomus/
Mort Shuman—*4:25*

627. JUL 13, 1979 (UK) Dark Horse K 17423
by George Harrison   Prod: George Harrison and Russ
Titelman
A: FASTER—Harrison—*4:40*
B: YOUR LOVE IS FOREVER—Harrison—*3:45*

627a AUG 10, 1979 (UK) A&M AMS 7461
by Suzy and The Red Stripes   Prod: Paul McCartney
A: SEASIDE WOMAN—McCartney—*3:36*
B: B-SIDE TO SEASIDE—McCartney—*2:36*

628. AUG 10, 1979 (UK) Parlophone R 6027
by Wings   Prod: Paul McCartney and Chris Thomas
A: GETTING CLOSER—McCartney—*3:22*
A: BABY'S REQUEST—McCartney—*2:48*

629. AUG 13, 1979 (US) Columbia 1-11070
by Wings   Prod: Paul McCartney and Chris Thomas
A: ARROW THROUGH ME—McCartney—*3:37*
B: OLD SIAM, SIR—McCartney—*4:11*

630. AUG 17, 1979 (UK) EMI NUT M 22 (LP)
by Various Artists
INSTRUMENTAL GEMS 1959--70
side two
cut one: *FLYING*—Lennon/McCartney/Harrison/
Starkey—*2:16*
by The Beatles   Prod: George Martin

631. OCT 8, 1979 (US) Warner Brothers BSK 3396 (LP)
NOV 9, 1979 (UK) Warner Brothers K 56751 (LP)
by Monty Python
MONTY PYTHON'S LIFE OF BRIAN (Original Soundtrack
Album)   Prod: Eric Idle and Graham Chapman
side two
closing song: *Always Look On The Bright Side Of Life*—
Eric Idle—*3:23*
Mixed by George Harrison and Phil MacDonald

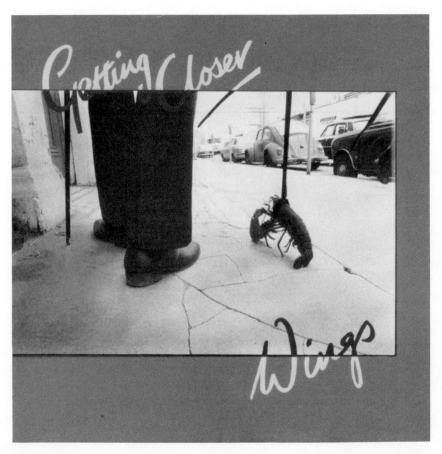

Getting Closer .   **Parlophone R 6027 (45)**

Baby's Request

Parlophone R 6027 (45)

ENTRY 631 & 632. George Harrison also spoke very briefly on a tie-in U.S. promotional album, **The Warner Bros. Music Show/Monty Python Examines The "Life Of Brian"** (Warner Bros. WBMS 110).

ENTRY 633. This Christmas single was recorded in the fall of 1979 and marked the first release credited solely to Paul McCartney since *Another Day* in 1971. It followed more than an album's worth of solo material done by McCartney during the summer, beginning soon after the release of **Back To The Egg**. However, those other tracks were not issued until the spring of 1980 (Entry 642).

The B-side was an instrumental adaptation of *Rudolph The Red-Nosed Reindeer*, a song originally done by Gene Autry in 1949 on Columbia 38610. McCartney's new recording featured a catchy violin riff performed by an anonymous delivery man (in his fifties or sixties) who had brought some rental sound equipment to the studio. When McCartney happened to mention that he was looking for a violin player to do a quick overdub for the *Rudolph* track, the man happily volunteered. Like a page from a Christmas storybook, it turned out that the delivery man was a musician who was picking up some extra money doing temporary work for the rental equipment company. He came back later with his own violin for the recording session with McCartney, but then took off before being paid and without leaving his name. MPL had to chase him down, but eventually found him and gave him his check for the session work. They could not have scripted a better "Christmas tale" for this record.

Wonderful Christmastime hit the top twenty in Britain but failed to make the American charts. Both countries issued the single in a picture sleeve featuring McCartney in a Santa Claus hat, but without the beard.

Note: Two McCartney and Wings tracks appeared on another Christmastime release, **Columbia's 21 Top 20** (A2S 700), a two-disc promotional item that included *Goodnight Tonight* (side two, cut two) and *Getting Closer* (side four, cut six).

ENTRY 634. Paul joined in the backing vocals on this tribute to pop radio by Lol Creme and Kevin Godley, former members of 10cc. The musician credits on the inner sleeve did not actually list McCartney's name (or anyone else's, for that matter) because they appeared in the form of pictures. Paul's photo was above a picture of several microphones.

ENTRY 635. Ringo was listed along with two other drummers (Jim Keltner and Zigaboo Modeliste) in the general credits to this first solo album from Ian McLagan, formerly a member of Small Faces. Most likely, Ringo did not play on every cut, though the liner notes did not provide a song-by-song breakdown.

There were two singles taken from the album: *Little Troublemaker* backed with *Hold On* was issued in the U.S. as Mercury 76046 on February 11, 1980. *La De La* backed with *Hold On* was issued in the U.K. as Mercury MER 1 on February 15, 1980. *La Da La* backed with *Headlines* was released as the follow-up single in the U.S. as Mercury 76058 on August 18, 1980.

632. OCT 19, 1979 (US) Warner Brothers WBS 49112
NOV 9, 1979 (UK) Warner Brothers K 17495
by Monty Python   Prod: Eric Idle and Graham Chapman;
Mixed by George Harrison and Phil MacDonald
A: *Always Look On The Bright Side Of Life*—Eric Idle—
3:23
B: *(brian)*

633. NOV 16, 1979 (UK) Parlophone R 6029
NOV 26, 1979 (US) Columbia 1-11162
by Paul McCartney   Prod: Paul McCartney
*A: *Wonderful Christmastime*—McCartney—*3:48*
*B: *Rudolph The Red-Nosed Reggae (Reindeer)*—John David
Marks—*1:46*

634. NOV 30, 1979 (UK) Polydor POLD 5029 (LP)
JAN 21, 1980 (US) Polydor PD 1 6257 (LP)
by Kevin Godley and Lol Creme
FREEZE FRAME   Prod: Kevin Godley and Lol Creme
side two
cut four: *Get Well Soon*—Kevin Godley/Lol Creme—*4:35*
Paul: Backing Vocal

635. DEC 10, 1979 (US) Mercury SRM 1 3786 (LP)
FEB 15, 1980 (UK) Mercury 9100 072 (LP)
by Ian McLagan
Ringo: Drums
TROUBLEMAKER   Prod: Geoff Workman
side one
La De La—Ian McLagan—*2:24*
Headlines—Ian McLagan—*2:57*
Truly—Carl Levy—*5:57*
Somebody—Ian McLagan—*2:57*
Movin' Out—Ian McLagan—*3:51*
side two
Little Troublemaker—Johnny Lee Schell—*2:27*
If It's Alright—Ian McLagan—*1:59*
Sign—Ian McLagan/Johnny Lee Schell—*3:23*
Hold On—Ian McLagan—*3:42*
Mystifies Me—Ron Wood—*5:23*

FREEZE FRAME · GODLEY CREME

Freeze Frame   **Polydor PD 1 6257 (LP)**

Wonderful Christmastime   **Columbia 1-11162 (45)**

February 18. Ringo and Barbara Bach begin filming *Caveman*.

February 27. The *Rockestra Theme* wins a Grammy Award.

May. At Cannes, the five-minute Oscar Grillo animated film of Linda McCartney's *Seaside Woman* wins the Palme d'Or (first prize) in the short film competition. On July 10, it goes into general release in Britain with the Peter Sellers movie *Being There*.

May 19. Ringo and Barbara Bach survive a car crash together.

June 22. Bert Kaempfert, producer of the Beatles first recording sessions in Germany, dies at the age of fifty-six.

November 26. Paul McCartney's *Rockshow* film has its world premiere at the Ziegfeld Theater in New York City.

December 8. (11:07 p.m.) John Lennon is pronounced dead on arrival at St. Luke's-Roosevelt Hospital in New York City. Shortly after midnight, Dr. Stephen Lynn makes the official announcement.

December 14. At the request of Yoko Ono, millions around the world pay tribute to the memory of John Lennon by observing ten minutes of silence, beginning at 2:00 p.m. New York time.

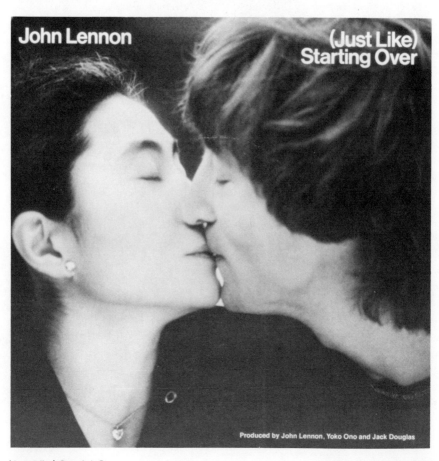

(Just Like) Starting Over   **Geffen GEF 49604 (45)**

1980

Coming Up
And Starting Over

On January 16, Paul McCartney and Wings landed in Japan, ready to begin a series of eleven sold out concert dates:

January 21,22,23,24,31 and February 1,2	Budokan, Tokyo
January 25,26	Aichi-ken Taiiku-kan, Nagoya
January 28	Osaka Festival Hall, Osaka
January 29	Osaka Furitsu Taiiku-kan, Osaka

More than 100,000 tickets has been sold for these shows, which looked as if they might be the first leg of a major world tour similar to McCartney's 1976 extravaganza. However, all plans had to be changed upon arrival that day when Japanese customs officials at the airport discovered in McCartney's luggage 219 grams (7.72 ounces) of marijuana with a "street value" in Tokyo of about $2,000.

Paul McCartney was arrested and taken to jail. He was held there (as prisoner number 22) without bail for ten days, facing a possible (though unlikely) maximum sentence of seven years imprisonment and a fine of $2,000. After protracted negotiations, McCartney was released at last on January 25 and immediately deported back to England. The entire Japanese tour was scrapped, with a reported $1.2 million of compensation given to various promoters.

Worldwide reaction to the arrest was a mixture of sympathetic support and mild bewilderment. ("Why didn't he have some underlings carry the stash?") Perversely, both airplay and record sales of McCartney product increased during the incident, though both were banned in Japan for a while.

This sobering experience left McCartney much more appreciative of his home and family . . .and quite uninterested in any new touring plans. Instead, after resting a bit, Paul dug out the tracks he had recorded by himself the previous summer and prepared them for release as his first pure solo album since 1970's **McCartney**. The obvious title: **McCartney II**.

To support the new release, Paul granted a number of print, radio, and television interviews, played ten different characters

87

simultaneously in a promotional film for the *Coming Up* lead single, and appeared in his nightclothes (with Linda) on the street outside the MPL offices as part of a live comedy sketch for NBC's *Saturday Night Live*. Paul and Linda hit the American airwaves with program correspondent Father Guido Sarducci (Don Novello) at about 12:30 a.m. New York time (5:30 a.m. London time).

Though the song *Coming Up* soon topped the U.S. charts and reached number two in Britain, there were actually two different versions involved. The U.K. hit was the A side of the single as taken from the **McCartney II** album, while U.S. programmers favored the flipside live version of *Coming Up* done by Wings at Glasgow the previous year. Columbia Records therefore wanted the live version on the new album. McCartney, who had previously turned down suggestions to include *Mull Of Kintyre* on **London Town** and *Goodnight Tonight* on **Back To The Egg**, definitely did not want a group recording on an otherwise solo album. As a compromise, he agreed to have a bonus one-sided single with the live version included with the initial shipments of the U.S. package. This allowed Columbia to tout **McCartney II** as "containing *Coming Up (Live At Glasgow)*."

The live cut was tremendously popular in the U.S., but many Stateside reviewers and programmers felt just the opposite about **McCartney II**, which was an odd-sounding deliberately experimental collection. They wondered why Paul didn't sound like Paul was supposed to sound! Partially as a result, the follow-up ballad *Waterfalls* was essentially ignored in the U.S., even though it was the most accessible track on the album. The song did hit the top ten in Britain and was followed by a third track from the album, the raucous *Temporary Secretary*.

With four consecutive solo singles (beginning with *Wonderful Christmastime* in November 1979), it appeared as if Paul might be abandoning Wings. This image was reinforced by news of solo projects by Denny Laine, Laurence Juber, and Steve Holly. Following the cancellation of the Japanese tour, Denny Laine had flown to Cannes to promote his wife Jo Jo at a recording industry convention. He also recorded and released a song inspired by the Japanese bust (*Japanese Tears*), staged a mini-tour of England (with Jo Jo and Steve Holly and a few other musicians), and put the finishing touches on a new solo album. Laurence Juber played on that, on some McCartney produced sessions for Ringo Starr in July, and on his own collection of instrumental tracks.

In the fall, though, Wings was back together in the studio, first for some overdubs on McCartney's often postponed Cold Cuts tracks (tentatively scheduled for release the following year) and then to rehearse material for a new album project. For that, Paul asked George Martin to act as producer. The two warmed up for their first new album in more than ten years by working on music for yet another long-standing McCartney project, the Rupert Bear cartoon, recording *All Stand Together* with the King's Sisters and the St. Paul's Boys Choir as backing singers. They then made plans to shift to Martin's studios on the island of Montserrat early the following year.

Meanwhile, for the first time in years, all of the other former Beatles were also involved in new album projects. George Harrison was wrapping up his **Somewhere In England** package. Ringo Starr was working with a variety of producers (including Paul and George) on **Can't Fight Lightning** (later called **Stop And Smell The Roses**). And, after five years, John Lennon was back.

On August 4, John Lennon and Yoko Ono ended their self-imposed retirement from recording and began work on a new album at the Hit Factory in New York City. In short order they had the album finished (with material left over), a contract with David Geffen's brand new label, and promotional interviews with *Newsweek, Playboy*, and the Los Angeles *Times*. Their first new single, *(Just Like) Starting Over* b/w *Kiss Kiss Kiss* came out in October, with the album **Double Fantasy** following a month later.

Much to their delight, the new songs were warmly received both by critics and fans, who even praised Yoko Ono's tracks. In fact, it seemed as if the five-year break was the best career move they could have made, because it turned their return into a major pop culture event – the latest verse in "The Ballad Of John And Yoko." And even those that did not like **Double Fantasy** at all usually tempered that judgment with the admission that the long-awaited return was most welcome anyway.

(Just Like) Starting Over headed straight into the U.S. top ten in only three weeks, with **Double Fantasy** close behind on the album charts. Yet already John and Yoko were at work on a follow-up publicity blitz that included a nude cover shot for *Rolling Stone*, a promotional film for the upcoming second single (*Woman*), a radio interview for the RKO network (slated for airing on Valentine's day), and a lengthy radio interview for the BBC.

They were most excited about *Walking On Thin Ice*, an upbeat Yoko Ono dance number that had not been included on **Double Fantasy**. Instead, John promised Yoko that it would be her first ever solo hit single. He was working on the final mix for the song on the night he died.

ENTRY 636. Proceeds and royalties from this album were donated to the Year of the Child campaign, launched by the United Nations in 1979.

ENTRY 637. See page 273.

ENTRY 639. A completely revamped version of the 1978 **Rarities** album (Entry 605b) specifically tailored for the American market. Besides offering a revised lineup of songs, the album also came in an elaborate new gatefold package. The front cover featured an embossed photo of the group centered on a tasteful off-white background, while the inside included a full color 12 by 12-inch panel devoted to the infamous "butcher" shot that had been used originally as the cover to **Yesterday And Today**. The back included detailed liner notes describing each cut and explaining the concept behind the package.

Actually, that had changed a bit since 1978, splitting the selections into two distinct categories: hard-to-find "rarities" and unusual recording "oddities." Among the rarities were three songs that had also appeared on the previous American **Rarities** album: *Across The Universe, The Inner Light*, and *You Know My Name (Look Up The Number)*. Another, *Sie Liebt Dich*, had been on the 1978 British package but not on the American version. Two more songs (*Misery* and *There's A Place*) filled a peculiar gap in the American market. Though both were easily obtainable in the U.K. (on the **Please Please Me** album), they had been unavailable on a U.S. album since 1964, when Vee Jay's **Introducing The Beatles** was deleted. One last track, the original British single version of *Love Me Do* (with Ringo on drums), had never been issued in the U.S.

These seven cuts functioned much like the original **Rarities** lineup in Britain, bringing together specific tracks that could not be found on a current album. The rest of the lineup on the new **Rarities** set, though, consisted primarily of oddities — that is, minor variations on particular recordings of familiar Beatles songs.

Three had small, but obvious, changes: *And I Love Her* (originally issued in Germany) repeated the guitar riff at the end of the song six times rather than four. *Penny Lane* (originally issued as a promotional single to U.S. radio stations) included an extra horn riff at the end. A newly-edited *I Am The Walrus* combined onto one version oddities that appeared on two different releases: a few extra beats in the middle of the song (from the Capitol single) and the intro riff repeated six times rather than four (from the British stereo disc).

The remaining cuts simply focused on the differences between stereo and monophonic releases. The mono versions of *Don't Pass Me By* and *Helter Skelter* were from the White Album, which had been issued only in stereo in the U.S. *Help!* was the mono recording from the U.S. single. And *I'm Only Sleeping* was from the British stereo version of **Revolver**.

A bit of gibberish that had appeared in the inner groove (leading to the label) on the U.K. version of **Sgt. Pepper** had been dropped from the U.S. release. **Rarities** ended with that two seconds of sound intact.

636. JAN 11, 1980 (UK) K-tel NE 1067 (LP)
by Various Artists
THE SUMMIT
side one
cut two: *JET*—McCartney—*4:08*
by Paul McCartney and Wings   Prod: Paul McCartney

637. JAN 18, 1980 (US) Vee Jay PRO-202 (LP)
JAN 23, 1981 (UK) Charly Records CRV 202 (LP)
by The Beatles; Interviews Conducted by Jim Steck and
Dave Hull; Editing and Background Music Produced
by Lou Adler
HEAR THE BEATLES TELL ALL
side one
Jim Steck Interviews John Lennon—13:14
side two
Dave Hull Interviews The Beatles—13:13

638. FEB 22, 1980 (UK) Music For Pleasure MFP 50469 (LP)
by Various Artists
ROCK ON THROUGH THE 60S
side two
cut six: *GOT TO GET YOU INTO MY LIFE*—L/McC—*2:29*
by Cliff Bennett and The Rebel Rousers   Prod: Paul
McCartney and David Paramor

639. MAR 24, 1980 (US) Capitol SHAL 12060 (LP)
by The Beatles
RARITIES   Prod: George Martin
side one
LOVE ME DO (version one)—2:22
MISERY—1:43
THERE'S A PLACE—1:44
SIE LIEBT DICH—L/McC/Nicolas/Montague—*2:16*
AND I LOVE HER—2:36
HELP!—2:16
I'M ONLY SLEEPING—2:58
I AM THE WALRUS—4:35
side two
PENNY LANE—3:00
HELTER SKELTER—3:38
DON'T PASS ME BY—Starkey—*3:45*
THE INNER LIGHT—Harrison—*2:36*
ACROSS THE UNIVERSE (version one)—3:41
YOU KNOW MY NAME (LOOK UP THE NUMBER)—4:20
SGT. PEPPER INNER GROOVE—0:02

THE BEATLES RARITIES

Rarities   **Capitol SHAL 12060 (LP)**

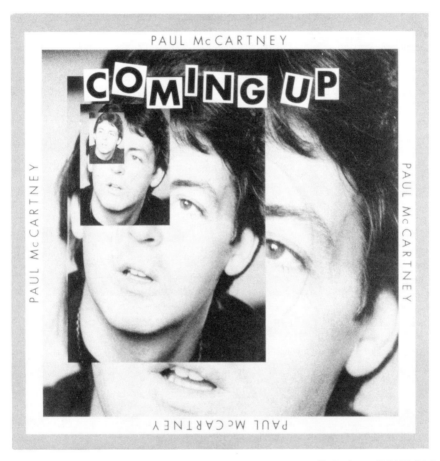

Coming Up   **Parlophone R 6035 (45)**

ENTRY 640. This lead single from the **McCartney II** album reached the top ten in both Britain and America, even topping *Billboard*'s charts for three weeks during the summer. However, the recording of *Coming Up* considered the *hit* version was different in the two countries.

Programmers in the U.K. generally went with the designated A-side studio version, which was typical of the techniques used by McCartney on his new solo album. Besides playing all the instruments, he also experimented with both the vocal and instrumental tracks, varying the speed to produce a sparse, somewhat tinny sound. The result was a catchy tune that sounded quite different from any other McCartney single. In the U.S., though, programmers did not care at all for a Paul McCartney record that did not sound like Paul McCartney. Yet they did like the song and so, very quickly, they flipped the disc over and went with the alternate version.

The live recording of *Coming Up* was taken from the last stop of the 1979 Wings tour of Britain — two nights (December 16 and 17) at the Apollo Theater in Glasgow. McCartney had included the song in the shows throughout the three-week tour as something brand new to spring on the audience, so this wrap-up performance was polished and confident as well as energetic. With a normal speed McCartney vocal and more time devoted to guitar and horn solos, this live recording ended up short one verse included in the studio version.

The other recording on side two was also by Wings, but from five years earlier with the lineup that included Jimmy McCulloch and Geoff Britton. This instrumental was one of the first tracks done at the **Venus And Mars** sessions and it brought the running time of the single to more than eleven minutes.

Both Britain and America issued the single in a black-and-white picture sleeve. There was also a promotional twelve-inch version (Columbia AS 775) in the U.S. In addition, Columbia included the live recording of *Coming Up* on side two, cut five of its year-end **Hitline '80** (Columbia A2S 890), a promo-only two record set for radio station programmers.

Note: The promotional video for *Coming Up* had its American premiere on the May 17, 1980, edition of NBC's *Saturday Night Live*. It was introduced live by Paul and Linda McCartney, in a trans-Atlantic hookup between London and New York, following a tongue-in-cheek interview with program correspondent Father Guido Sarducci. The video used the studio version of the song.

ENTRY 641. Pickwick's second packaging of the 1962 Star Club recordings was a straightforward two-record set, with the track order for any given side exactly the same as on the two 1979 volumes (Entries 609 & 610). This new release did not merely recycle leftover discs from that previous issuing, though. These were brand new pressings, combining different sides. (In 1979, side one had been coupled with side three, and side two with side four.)

The cover graphics were once again low key (without any pictures of the group) and clearly identified the contents as old, live recordings.

640. APR 11, 1980 (UK) Parlophone R 6035
APR 14, 1980 (US) Columbia 1-11263
by Paul McCartney (side one); Paul McCartney and Wings
(side two)   Prod: Paul McCartney
side one
Coming Up—McCartney—*3:49*
side two
*Coming Up (Live At Glasgow)—McCartney—*3:51*
*Lunch Box/Odd Sox—McCartney—*3:54*

641. MAY 5, 1980 (US) Pickwick PTP 2098 (2 LPs)
by The Beatles; recorded live by Ted Taylor in 1962 except †
THE HISTORIC FIRST LIVE RECORDINGS
side one
WHERE HAVE YOU BEEN ALL MY LIFE?—Barry Mann/
Cynthia Weil—*1:55*
A TASTE OF HONEY—Ric Marlow/Bobby Scott—*1:45*
YOUR FEET'S TOO BIG—Ada Benson/Fred Fisher—*2:18*
MR. MOONLIGHT—Roy Lee Johnson—*2:06*
BESAME MUCHO—Consuelo Velazquez/Selig Shaftel—*2:36*
I'M GONNA SIT RIGHT DOWN AND CRY (OVER YOU)
—Joe Thomas/Howard Biggs—*2:43*
BE-BOP-A-LULA—Gene Vincent/Tex Davis—*2:29*
side two
NOTHIN' SHAKIN' (BUT THE LEAVES ON THE TREES)
—Cirino Colacrai/Eddie Fontaine/Dianne Lampert/Jack
Cleveland—*1:15*
EVERYBODY'S TRYING TO BE MY BABY—Carl
Perkins—*2:25*
MATCHBOX—Carl Perkins—*2:35*
I'M TALKING ABOUT YOU—Chuck Berry—*1:48*
LONG TALL SALLY—Enotris Johnson/Richard Penni-
man/Robert Blackwell—*1:45*
ROLL OVER BEETHOVEN—Chuck Berry—*2:15*
HIPPY HIPPY SHAKE—Chan Romero—*1:42*
side three
HALLELUJAH, I LOVE HER SO—Ray Charles—*2:10*
'TILL THERE WAS YOU—Meredith Willson—*1:59*
SWEET LITTLE SIXTEEN—Chuck Berry—*2:45*
LITTLE QUEENIE—Chuck Berry—*3:51*
MEDLEY—*2:09*
KANSAS CITY—Jerry Leiber/Mike Stoller—*1:04*
HEY-HEY-HEY-HEY—Richard Penniman—*1:05*
(†hully gully—F. Smith/C. Goldsmith—*1:39)*

ENTRY 642. McCartney II was recorded "at home" over six weeks in the summer of 1979, beginning at McCartney's farm in Sussex and continuing in Scotland. As with his first solo album ten years before, McCartney composed, performed, produced, and engineered the entire project himself, with Linda popping in for occasional backing vocals.

McCartney originally conceived these home sessions as no more than an entertaining break from formal recording with Wings, not as the basis for a new album. He bypassed a recording console and plugged his microphones directly into the back of a sixteen-track tape machine. When particular songs did not work, he simply erased them and tried something else. He also reversed the usual approach to composing a song. Instead of starting with some words or a melody, McCartney began with drum and rhythm and bass tracks and then had to come up with a song to fit. For example, he turned the basic drum and bass tracks for *On The Way* into a blues-style number after seeing an episode of Alexis Korner's British TV series about blues music. *Nobody Knows* was also inspired by the same series.

The first thing done at these home sessions was *Front Parlour*, an instrumental recorded, appropriately, in the empty front parlor of McCartney's farm house, using the adjacent kitchen as an echo chamber for the snare drum. *Frozen Jap*, the other instrumental on the album, was *not* inspired by McCartney's jailing in Tokyo (that was six months later) but rather by the image of a snow-capped Mount Fuji. Still, to avoid any possible offense, the song title in Japan was changed to *Frozen Japanese*, dropping the shorthand slang.

Throughout the sessions, McCartney experimented with his vocals, using a variable speed recorder to raise and lower his tones. This was most noticeable on *Coming Up, Bogey Music* (inspired by the subterranean fantasy *Fungus The Bogeyman* by Raymond Briggs), the raucous *Temporary Secretary*, and the high-pitched wordplay of *Darkroom*. At the same time, he also included straightforward soft ballads: *One Of These Days*, written after a visit from a gentle Hare Krishna follower; *Summer's Day Song*, a classical music style piece; and *Waterfalls*, the only song on the album written before the home sessions began, and recorded as a change of pace after about eight improvised songs had been done.

By the time he finished, McCartney had enough material to fill two records. When he decided to release it, though, this was trimmed to a single disc — with two leftovers turning up as B-sides to singles (Entries 643 & 648).

Note: The seven-inch bonus single in the U.S. merely presented the live version of *Coming Up* (at 33 1/3), without anything on the flip side. In Japan, the package contained a far more valuable bonus: a coupon good for a chance at one of the 60,000 tour programs left from the aborted Japanese tour.

ENTRY 643. This obvious follow-up single to *Coming Up* hit the top ten in the U.K. but failed to crack *Billboard*'s Hot 100 (stalling at 106). The flip side (also from the **McCartney II** sessions) consisted of a simple repeated riff, with McCartney doing just what the title suggested: testing his equipment. In the process, he picked up the voice of Mel Blanc from a cartoon running on a nearby TV.

Note: The picture sleeve featured a painting by Christian Broutin.

side four
FALLING IN LOVE AGAIN (CAN'T HELP IT)—Sammy
Lerner/Frederick Hollander—*1:57*
LEND ME YOUR COMB—Kay Twomey/Fred Wise/Ben
Weisman—*1:44*
SHEILA—Tommy Roe—*1:56*
RED SAILS IN THE SUNSET—Jimmy Kennedy/Will
Grosz—*2:00*
TO KNOW HER IS TO LOVE HER—Phil Spector—*3:02*
SHIMMY SHAKE—Joe South/Billy Land—*2:17*
I REMEMBER YOU—Johnny Mercer/Victor Schertzinger—
1:54

642.   MAY 16, 1980 (UK) Parlophone PCTC 258 (LP)
MAY 26, 1980 (US) Columbia FC 36511 (LP)†
by Paul McCartney
McCARTNEY II   Prod: Paul McCartney
side one
Coming Up—McCartney—*3:49*
Temporary Secretary—McCartney—*3:13*
On The Way—McCartney—*3:36*
Waterfalls—McCartney—*4:40*
Nobody Knows—McCartney—*2:50*
side two
Front Parlour—McCartney—*3:30*
Summer's Day Song—McCartney—*3:24*
Frozen Jap—McCartney—*3:37*
Bogey Music—McCartney—*3:25*
Darkroom—McCartney—*2:18*
One Of These Days—McCartney—*3:35*
†Bonus Single (US only) Columbia AE7 1204
side one
   *Coming Up (Live At Glasgow)—McCartney—*3:51*
   by Paul McCartney and Wings   Prod: Paul McCartney

643.   JUN 13 1980 (UK) Parlophone R 6037
JUL 21, 1980 (US) Columbia 1-11335
   by Paul McCartney   Prod: Paul McCartney
A: WATERFALLS—McCartney—*4:40*
*B: Check My Machine—McCartney—*5:50*

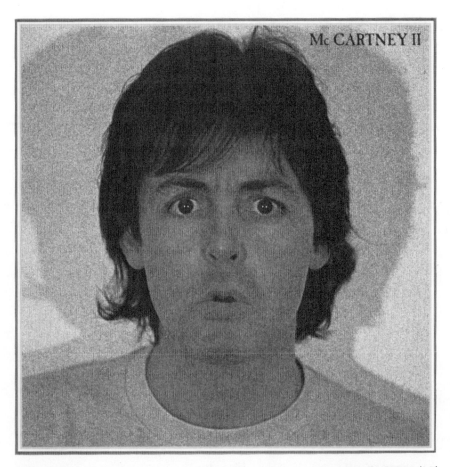

McCartney II   **Columbia FC 36511 (LP)**

Waterfalls

Columbia 1-11335 (45)

ENTRY 646. One of twelve new "double-A" single repackagings of old Rolling Stones material, following the group's career from *Come On* (STONE 1) to *Sympathy For The Devil* (STONE 12). The discs were available separately or in a special package to record dealers as **The Rolling Stones Singles Collection** (Decca BROWS 1). Each one came in a picture sleeve.

Consumers were also offered a special storage case – for purchase by mail for only £3.85 plus 90p postage (about $9). Unfortunately for Decca, it was possible to interpret the wording of the ads that ran in such publications as *Melody Maker* (September 6, 1980) as a generous offer to send the complete **Rolling Stones Singles Collection** (with discs) for that fee. The next week, the company ran a follow-up ad explaining that the singles and the case for the singles were *separate* purchases. £3.85 plus postage only brought the case!

If record buyers did not like that deal, they had only to wait a month. Then Decca offered another opportunity to purchase old Rolling Stones material (once again including *I Wanna Be Your Man*) on a new compilation album, **Solid Rock** (Entry 650).

ENTRY 647. Though Ringo Starr was merely listed in the general album credits and not identified as a musician for any particular songs on Harry Nilsson's **Flash Harry**, further inquiries placed him on *I've Got It!, How Long Can Disco On*, and (probably) *Old Dirt Road* (for old time's sake).

Old Dirt Road had its own unique hook, though. The song was one of two compositions written and recorded by John Lennon and Harry Nilsson back in 1974. (*Mucho Mungo/Mt. Elga*, for Nilsson's **Pussy Cats** album, was the other.) The Lennon version of *Old Dirt Road* had turned up immediately on his **Walls And Bridges** album, but this marked the first appearance of the song on a Harry Nilsson record. John Lennon was not involved in this new 1980 recording.

Ringo Starr, on the other hand, was around for his new composition with Nilsson, *How Long Can Disco On* (one of the best titles ever from the pair). Another old friend, Derek Taylor, did the liner notes for the package, warning that Nilsson had once said he'd stop making albums after number twenty-one – and that this was number nineteen.

Note: **Flash Harry** was the first album of new material from Harry Nilsson that did not come out in the U.S., following the end of his association with RCA. See page 317 for complete track details.

644. JUL 4, 1980 (UK) Music For Pleasure MFP 55024 (2 LPs)
by Various Artists with cuts by
†Cliff Bennett and The Rebel Rousers   Prod: Paul McCartney and David Paramor
%Cilla Black   Prod: George Martin
$The Fourmost   Prod: George Martin
+Billy J. Kramer with The Dakotas   Prod: George Martin
HITS FROM THE SWINGING SIXTIES
side one
+cut two: *DO YOU WANT TO KNOW A SECRET*–L/McC
–1:59
%cut four: *LOVE OF THE LOVED*–L/McC–*2:00*
side two
%cut three: *IT'S FOR YOU*–L/McC–*2:20*
$cut four: *HELLO LITTLE GIRL*–L/McC–*1:50*
side three
+cut five: *I'LL KEEP YOU SATISFIED*–L/McC–*2:04*
side four
†cut six: *GOT TO GET YOU INTO MY LIFE*–L/McC–
2:29

645. JUL 28, 1980 (US) K-tel TU 2640 (LP)
by Elton John   Prod: Gus Dudgeon
MILESTONES
side two
cut six: *LUCY IN THE SKY WITH DIAMONDS*–L/McC–*5:59*
John: Guitars and Backing Vocal

646. SEP 5, 1980 (UK) Decca STONE 1
by The Rolling Stones   Prod: Andrew Loog Oldham
A: I WANNA BE YOUR MAN–L/McC–*1:44*
A: (come on)

647. SEP 5, 1980 (UK) Mercury 6302 022 (LP)
by Harry Nilsson
Ringo: Drums
FLASH HARRY   Prod: Steve Cropper with Bruce Robb
side one
cut four: *Old Dirt Road*–Lennon/Harry Nilsson–*4:26*
side two
cut two: *I've Got It!*–Harry Nilsson/Perry Botkin, Jr.–
3:42
cut four: *How Long Can Disco On*–Starkey/Harry Nilsson
–2:54

Secret Friend   B SIDE   Paul McCartney

12 R6039

Secret Friend   **Parlophone 12 R 6039 (12-inch)**

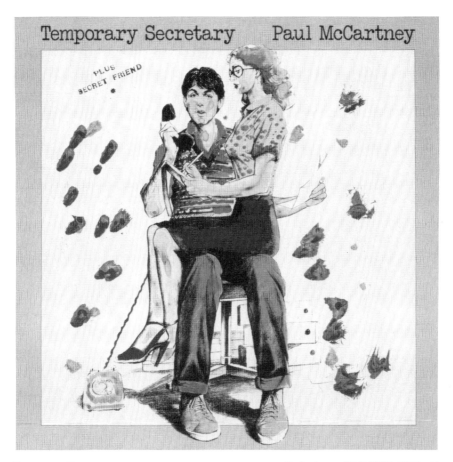

Temporary Secretary

Parlophone 12 R 6039 (12-inch)

ENTRY 648. A limited edition single (15,000 copies) issued only in Britain. The twelve-inch disc came in a full-color picture sleeve with a front cover cartoon drawing by Jeff Cummins showing Paul McCartney with a secretary on his lap. Both tracks on the record were from the **McCartney II** sessions.

Like *Coming Up, Temporary Secretary* featured several off-speed voices from McCartney, along with a constant electronic beat (produced by a sequencer machine) and a middle break based on Ian Dury's style of singing. Though it might have caught on as a novelty hit, *Temporary Secretary* was limited to the lower half of the British charts simply because there were only a small number of twelve-inch copies pressed, and no seven-inch equivalents. This was much more a one-time special release than the latest Paul McCartney single.

Secret Friend on the B-side was the real draw of the package. The song ran more than ten minutes and, in the process, provided a taste of what some of the cuts on **McCartney II** were probably like before editing. (*Darkroom*, for instance, had been shortened considerably in order to squeeze on the record.) As part of a special release, *Secret Friend* worked in its ten-minute version, even though the song could have been cut in half with no difficulty. However, had it been part of a two-record set with other lengthy tracks (the original plan for the **McCartney II** album), the result might have been too much even for ardent fans. With the B-side issuings of *Secret Friend* and *Check My Machine* (Entry 643), McCartney managed the perfect compromise, putting out just an album and a half.

Note: The Alfred Marks Bureau, dealers in "temporary secretaries," approached McCartney about using his song in its advertising. Though the company had obviously been part of the inspiration for *Temporary Secretary*, he turned them down.

ENTRY 651. This album offered nearly an hour of Beatles music on one disc (twenty cuts), including some of the group's most popular love songs. Ten of the selections, in fact, had previously appeared as part of the **Love Songs** compilation (Entry 573). But that had been back in 1977, and Christmas 1980 was rapidly approaching.

The overall track lineup held no real surprises, though it did include the once-rare first version of *Across The Universe* (recently reissued on both the U.K. and the U.S. editions of **Rarities**) and the single version of *Let It Be*.

Note: The front cover of **The Beatles Ballads** featured a fantasy painting of the Beatles (by John Patrick Byrne) below the album title, setting the four of them in a garden surrounded by domesticated animals. In Holland, that layout was changed a bit, with the picture enlarged to fill the entire front cover (on Parlophone 1A 062-07356).

648. SEP 15, 1980 (UK) Parlophone 12 R 6039 (12 inch)
by Paul McCartney   Prod: Paul McCartney
A: TEMPORARY SECRETARY—McCartney—*3:13*
*B: Secret Friend—McCartney—*10:30*

649. SEP 26, 1980 (UK) Mercury 6463 061 (LP)
by Rod Stewart   Prod: Rod Stewart
HOT RODS
side two
cut four: *MINE FOR ME*—McCartney—*4:02*

650. OCT 10, 1980 (UK) Decca TAB 1 (LP)
by The Rolling Stones   Prod: Andrew Loog Oldham
SOLID ROCK
side one
cut four: *I WANNA BE YOUR MAN*—L/McC—*1:44*

651. OCT 13, 1980 (UK) Parlophone PCS 7214 (LP)
by The Beatles
THE BEATLES BALLADS   Prod: George Martin except †
George Martin (January 1969) and Phil Spector (March
1970)
side one
YESTERDAY—*2:04*
NORWEGIAN WOOD (THIS BIRD HAS FLOWN)—*2:00*
DO YOU WANT TO KNOW A SECRET—*1:55*
FOR NO ONE—*2:03*
MICHELLE—*2:42*
NOWHERE MAN—*2:40*
YOU'VE GOT TO HIDE YOUR LOVE AWAY—*2:08*
ACROSS THE UNIVERSE (version one)—*3:41*
ALL MY LOVING—*2:04*
HEY JUDE—*7:11*
side two
SOMETHING—Harrison—*2:59*
THE FOOL ON THE HILL—*3:00*
TILL THERE WAS YOU—Meredith Willson—*2:12*
†*THE LONG AND WINDING ROAD*—*3:40*
HERE COMES THE SUN—Harrison—*3:04*
BLACKBIRD—*2:20*
AND I LOVE HER—*2:27*
SHE'S LEAVING HOME—*3:24*
HERE, THERE AND EVERYWHERE—*2:29*
LET IT BE—*3:50*

The Beatles Ballads   Parlophone PCS 7214 (LP)

The Beatles Ballads   Parlophone 1A 062-07356 (LP)

Rock 'N' Roll Music   Music For Pleasure MFP 50506 (LP)
— Volume One

Rock 'N' Roll Music   Capitol SN 16021 (LP)
— Volume Two

ENTRY 652. The first new material from John Lennon since the 1975 single of *Stand By Me* and *Move Over Ms. L. (Just Like) Starting Over* was the obvious teaser selection from the forthcoming **Double Fantasy** album (Entry 656), announcing the return with a 1950s style pop rocker. Lennon dubbed the track his "Elvis Orbison." This was one of the last songs he wrote while out in Bermuda (in preparation for the new album) and it reflected his invigorated, upbeat mood. The soft chimes of Yoko Ono's wishing bells provided an appropriate beginning to the track. Originally it was to be called merely *Starting Over*, but Lennon added the "Just Like" tag to avoid confusion with other similarly titled releases at the time, including a country hit.

While in Bermuda, Lennon had been overjoyed to discover that recordings by such new wave performers as the B-52s sounded quite a bit like Yoko Ono's records from the 1970s. At last the rest of the music world had caught on! *Kiss Kiss Kiss* showed that one of the "original punks" had not lost her touch. The song was a new wave style dance tune, complete with orgasmic screams and groans at the end. At the recording session for the song, Yoko had the lights in the studio dimmed and had screens put around her microphone area to avoid stares while she did her energetic and sexually suggestive vocals.

Note: The twelve-inch promotional version of the *(Just Like) Starting Over* single (Geffen PRO A-919) ran 4:17, longer than either the commercial single or the album track. However, the extra twenty-two seconds came at the end and merely extended the final fadeout. Both the regular single and the promotional disc came in a picture sleeve using the cover to **Double Fantasy.**

ENTRY 653 & 654. For this new release, the 1976 **Rock'n'Roll Music** double album was split into two separate packages, with the track order for any given side exactly the same as on the original (Entry 515). However, Capitol/EMI did not merely recycle leftover discs from the previous issuing. These were brand new pressings combining different sides. In 1976, side one of volume one had been coupled with side two of volume two, and side two of volume one with side one of volume two.

The packages were issued as budget albums in both the U.S. and the U.K. (list price: $5.98). With fourteen cuts each, they were an excellent bargain sampler of Beatles music. The newly coupled discs also worked much better than the original 1976 set. Volume one concentrated on cover versions of past rock classics (ten of the fourteen songs), while volume two presented chiefly group compositions (with only two cover versions).

In contrast to the frequently criticized artwork on the 1976 version of **Rock'n'Roll Music**, the cover picture used for the new packages was a tasteful group shot (circa 1965). This was set against a plain light background on the British edition and a small crowd of people on the American edition (giving the covers a somewhat darker tone).

Note: There were three other Beatles records shifted to the budget series at the same time as **Rock'n'Roll Music**. All three were solo efforts: Ringo Starr's **Ringo**, John Lennon's **Mind Games**, and George Harrison's **Dark Horse**. The track couplings were unchanged. See pages 437--439.

652. OCT 17, 1980 (US) Geffen GEF 49604
OCT 24, 1980 (UK) Geffen K 79186
by John Lennon and Yoko Ono   Prod: John Lennon,
Yoko Ono, and Jack Douglas
A: (Just Like) Starting Over—Lennon—*3:55*
B: Kiss Kiss Kiss—Yoko Ono—*2:41*

653. OCT 24, 1980 (UK) Music For Pleasure MFP 50506 (LP)
OCT 27, 1980 (US) Capitol SN 16020 (LP)
by The Beatles
ROCK 'N' ROLL MUSIC—VOLUME ONE   Prod: George
Martin
side one
TWIST AND SHOUT—Bert Russell/Phil Medley—*2:32*
I SAW HER STANDING THERE—*2:50*
YOU CAN'T DO THAT—*2:33*
I WANNA BE YOUR MAN—*1:59*
I CALL YOUR NAME—*2:02*
BOYS—Luther Dixon/Wes Farrell—*2:24*
LONG TALL SALLY—Enotris Johnson/Richard Penni-
man/Robert Blackwell—*1:58*
side two
ROCK AND ROLL MUSIC—Chuck Berry—*2:02*
SLOW DOWN—Larry Williams—*2:54*
MEDLEY—*2:30*
   KANSAS CITY—Jerry Leiber/Mike Stoller—*1:12*
   HEY-HEY-HEY-HEY—Richard Penniman—*1:18*
MONEY (THAT'S WHAT I WANT)—Berry Gordy/Janie
Bradford—*2:47*
BAD BOY—Larry Williams—*2:17*
MATCHBOX—Carl Perkins—*1:37*
ROLL OVER BEETHOVEN—Chuck Berry—*2:44*

ENTRY 655. This mail order package was sold by EMI's British-based record club, World Records, but also turned up as an import at selected record stores in America the following year. Unlike the 1978 **Beatles Collection**, which merely put existing Parlophone albums into a blue box, this set assembled 126 Beatles tracks from singles and albums and programmed them in essentially chronological order over eight new discs. There were also new cardboard sleeves for each record, with pictures from each era on the front cover and liner notes by Hugh Marshall on the back. All of this came in a large album box designed to resemble a wooden shipping crate, stamped "From Liverpool." Cost of the set: £29.75 (about $60).

Though **The Beatles Box** was not a complete collection of all 212 songs the group recorded and released for EMI between 1962 and 1970, it was a carefully selected condensation. For a mainstream record buyer interested in something in between the two-volume greatest hits albums and the fourteen-disc boxed set, this provided a perfect compromise and an excellent value (about half the cost of **The Beatles Collection**).

Compiler Simon Sinclair selected from the Beatles material quite well. The set included the A-sides to all twenty-two original British singles and all but six of the B-sides (leaving out *Ask Me Why, I'll Get You, Yes It Is, The Inner Light, Old Brown Shoe,* and *You Know My Name (Look Up The Number)*). Each album was represented by, on the average, between one-half and two-thirds of the original contents, though there were some exceptions: Only ten of the thirty tracks from the White Album turned up (with record two completely ignored) and only one of the four new songs on **Yellow Submarine** was used. In the other direction, all but one of the fourteen cuts on **Help** were used.

Only eight tracks from the British **Rarities** were included, leaving out more esoteric items such as *Sie Liebt Dich* and *Komm, Gib Mir Deine Hand.* Oddly, though, **The Beatles Box** did contain a handful of collector-oriented cuts (including some that had appeared on the 1980 American edition of **Rarities**), substituting them for the more familiar versions of the same songs. These included: *All My Loving* with the "hi-hat" cymbal opening used in Germany, *And I Love Her* with the extra two guitar riffs, *Penny Lane* with the extra horn riff, *I Am The Walrus* with the extra opening and middle riffs, *I Feel Fine* with a few seconds of whispering at the beginning, *Don't Pass Me By* in mono, the album version of *Please Please Me* with the mistake in the final verse, and the original single versions of *Love Me Do* and *Help.* In contrast to **Rarities, The Beatles Box** used the much more commercial version of *Across The Universe* from **Let It Be** rather than the one on the **No One's Gonna Change Our World** charity album. The **Let It Be** versions of *Get Back* and *Let It Be* were also chosen, over the single releases.

Still, these details were of little interest to buyers lured by such ad copy as "Hailed as the greatest songwriting talent since Irving Berlin, Rodgers & Hart, and other giants of music!" and "They didn't just make music . . . . They didn't just make news . . . . They Made History!" For them, the opportunity *(continued)*

654. OCT 24, 1980 (UK) Music For Pleasure MFP 50507 (LP)
OCT 27, 1980 (US) Capitol SN 16021 (LP)
by The Beatles
ROCK 'N' ROLL MUSIC—VOLUME TWO   Prod: George
Martin except † George Martin (January 1969) and Phil
Spector (March 1970)
side one
DIZZY MISS LIZZY—Larry Williams—*2:51*
ANYTIME AT ALL—*2:10*
DRIVE MY CAR—*2:25*
EVERYBODY'S TRYING TO BE MY BABY—Carl
Perkins—*2:24*
THE NIGHT BEFORE—*2:33*
I'M DOWN—*2:30*
REVOLUTION—*3:22*
side two
BACK IN THE U.S.S.R.—*2:45*
HELTER SKELTER—*4:30*
TAXMAN—Harrison—*2:36*
GOT TO GET YOU INTO MY LIFE—*2:31*
HEY BULLDOG—*3:09*
BIRTHDAY—*2:40*
†GET BACK (version two)—*3:09*

655. NOV 3, 1980 (UK MAIL ORDER) Parlophone SM 701-708
(8 LPs)
by The Beatles
THE BEATLES BOX   Prod: George Martin except † George
Martin (January 1969) and Phil Spector (March 1970)
record one: Parlophone SM 701
side one
LOVE ME DO (version one)—*2:22*
P.S. I LOVE YOU—*2:02*
I SAW HER STANDING THERE—*2:50*
PLEASE PLEASE ME—*2:00*
MISERY—*1:43*
DO YOU WANT TO KNOW A SECRET—*1:55*
A TASTE OF HONEY—Ric Marlow/Bobby Scott—*2:02*
TWIST AND SHOUT—Bert Russell/Phil Medley—*2:32*

111

(Entry 655 continued)
to have "all the good stuff" from the Beatles in one package was the chief draw.

In that light, one fascinating aspect of **The Beatles Box** is what songs from the EMI catalog were considered essential and what songs were expendable. (For example, none of George Harrison's Indian-influenced tracks were used.) All the songs omitted from the set have been marked with an asterisk (*) on the following list, which includes all the titles recorded and released by the Beatles from 1962 to 1970.

This list does not treat as separate entries different recordings of the same song, such as the album and single versions of *Get Back* and *Love Me Do*. *Revolution*, *Revolution 1*, and *Revolution 9* are listed separately, though, because they were treated as different songs. The German language versions of *She Loves You* and *I Want To Hold Your Hand (Sie Liebt Dich* and *Komm, Gib Mir Deine Hand)* are also listed as separate songs. The medley of *Kansas City* and *Hey Hey Hey Hey* is listed as one song.

Across The Universe	*Cry Baby Cry
Act Naturally	A Day In The Life
*All I've Got To Do	Day Tripper
All My Loving	*Dear Prudence
All Together Now	*Devil In Her Heart
All You Need Is Love	*Dig It
And I Love Her	*Dizzy Miss Lizzy
And Your Bird Can Sing	Do You Want To Know A Secret
*Anna (Go To Him)	Dr. Robert
Another Girl	*Don't Bother Me
*Anytime At All	Don't Let Me Down
*Ask Me Why	Don't Pass Me By
*Baby, It's You	Drive My Car
Baby, You're A Rich Man	Eight Days A Week
*Baby's In Black	Eleanor Rigby
Back In The U.S.S.R.	The End
*Bad Boy	Every Little Thing
The Ballad Of John And Yoko	*Everybody's Got Something To Hide
Because	Except Me And My Monkey
Being For The Benefit Of Mr. Kite	*Everybody's Trying To Be My Baby
*Birthday	Fixing A Hole
*Blackbird	*Flying
*Blue Jay Way	The Fool On The Hill
*Boys	For No One
Can't Buy Me Love	For You Blue
Carry That Weight	From Me To You
*Chains	Get Back
Come Together	*Getting Better
The Continuing Story Of	Girl
Bungalow Bill	*Glass Onion

(continued)

112

side two
FROM ME TO YOU–*1:49*
THANK YOU GIRL–*2:01*
SHE LOVES YOU–*2:18*
IT WON'T BE LONG–*2:11*
PLEASE MR. POSTMAN–Brian Holland/Robert Bateman/ Berry Gordy–*2:34*
ALL MY LOVING–*2:06*
ROLL OVER BEETHOVEN–Chuck Berry–*2:44*
MONEY (THAT'S WHAT I WANT)–Berry Gordy/Janie Bradford–*2:47*
record two: Parlophone SM 702
side one
I WANT TO HOLD YOUR HAND–*2:24*
THIS BOY–*2:11*
CAN'T BUY ME LOVE–*2:15*
YOU CAN'T DO THAT–*2:33*
A HARD DAY'S NIGHT–*2:28*
I SHOULD HAVE KNOWN BETTER–*2:42*
IF I FELL–*2:16*
AND I LOVE HER–*2:36*
side two
THINGS WE SAID TODAY–*2:35*
I'LL BE BACK–*2:22*
LONG TALL SALLY–Enotris Johnson/Richard Penniman/Robert Blackwell–*1:58*
I CALL YOUR NAME–*2:02*
MATCHBOX–Carl Perkins–*1:37*
SLOW DOWN–Larry Williams–*2:54*
SHE'S A WOMAN–*2:57*
I FEEL FINE–*2:20*
record three: Parlophone SM 703
side one
EIGHT DAYS A WEEK–*2:43*
NO REPLY–*2:15*
I'M A LOSER–*2:31*
I'LL FOLLOW THE SUN–*1:46*
MR. MOONLIGHT–Roy Lee Johnson–*2:35*
EVERY LITTLE THING–*2:01*
I DON'T WANT TO SPOIL THE PARTY–*2:33*
MEDLEY–*2:30*
    KANSAS CITY–Jerry Leiber/Mike Stoller–*1:12*
    HEY-HEY-HEY-HEY–Richard Penniman–*1:18*

Golden Slumbers
Good Day Sunshine
*Good Morning, Good Morning
*Good Night
Got To Get You Into My Life
Happiness Is A Warm Gun
A Hard Day's Night
Hello Goodbye
Help!
*Helter Skelter
Her Majesty
Here Comes The Sun
Here, There And Everywhere
*Hey Bulldog
Hey Jude
*Hold Me Tight
*Honey Don't
*Honey Pie
I Am The Walrus
I Call Your Name
*I Dig A Pony
I Don't Want To Spoil The Party
I Feel Fine
*I Me Mine
I Need You
I Saw Her Standing There
I Should Have Known Better
*I Wanna Be Your Man
I Want To Hold Your Hand
*I Want To Tell You
*I Want You (She's So Heavy)
*I Will
If I Fell
*If I Needed Someone
I'll Be Back
*I'll Cry Instead
I'll Follow The Sun
*I'll Get You
I'm A Loser
I'm Down
*I'm Happy Just To Dance With You
I'm Looking Through You
I'm Only Sleeping

I'm So Tired
In My Life
*The Inner Light
It Won't Be Long
*It's All Too Much
It's Only Love
*I've Got A Feeling
I've Just Seen A Face
Julia
Kansas City/Hey Hey Hey Hey
*Komm, Gib Mir Deine Hand
Lady Madonna
Let It Be
*Little Child
The Long And Winding Road
*Long, Long, Long
Long Tall Sally
Love Me Do
*Love You Too
Lovely Rita
Lucy In The Sky With Diamonds
*Maggie Mae
Magical Mystery Tour
Martha My Dear
Matchbox
Maxwell's Silver Hammer
*Mean Mr. Mustard
Michelle
Misery
Mr. Moonlight
Money (That's What I Want)
*Mother Nature's Son
The Night Before
No Reply
Norwegian Wood (This Bird Has
    Flown)
*Not A Second Time
Nowhere Man
Ob-La-Di, Ob-La-Da
Octopus's Garden
*Oh! Darling
*Old Brown Shoe
*One After 909

(continued)

(Entry 655 continued)
*Only A Northern Song
P.S. I Love You
Paperback Writer
Penny Lane
Piggies
Please Mr. Postman
Please Please Me
*Polythene Pam
Rain
Revolution
*Revolution 1
*Revolution 9
*Rock And Roll Music
*Rocky Raccoon
Roll Over Beethoven
*Run For Your Life
*Savoy Truffle
Sgt. Pepper's Lonely Hearts
    Club Band
*Sexy Sadie
*She Came In Through the
    Bathroom Window
She Loves You
*She Said She Said
She's A Woman
She's Leaving Home
*Sie Liebt Dich
Slow Down
Something
Strawberry Fields Forever
*Sun King
A Taste Of Honey
Taxman
Tell Me What You See
*Tell Me Why
Thank You Girl
*There's A Place

Things We Said Today
*Think For Yourself
This Boy
Ticket To Ride
*Till There Was You
*Tomorrow Never Knows
Twist And Shout
Two Of Us
*Wait
We Can Work It Out
*What Goes On
*What You're Doing
*When I Get Home
When I'm Sixty-Four
While My Guitar Gently Weeps
*Why Don't We Do It In The Road?
*Wild Honey Pie
With A Little Help From My Friends
*Within You Without You
*The Word
*Words Of Love
Yellow Submarine
*Yer Blues
*Yes It Is
Yesterday
You Can't Do That
*You Know My Name (Look Up The
    Number)
You Like Me Too Much
*You Never Give Me Your Money
*You Really Got A Hold On Me
You Won't See Me
Your Mother Should Know
You're Going To Lose That Girl
You've Got To Hide Your Love
    Away

Note: **The Beatles Box** was issued in Japan in 1981 as EMI/Odeon
EAS 77011-77018.

record six: Parlophone SM 706
side one
   SGT. PEPPER'S LONELY HEARTS CLUB BAND—1:59
   WITH A LITTLE HELP FROM MY FRIENDS—2:46
   LUCY IN THE SKY WITH DIAMONDS—3:25
   FIXING A HOLE—2:33
   SHE'S LEAVING HOME—3:24
   BEING FOR THE BENEFIT OF MR. KITE—2:36
   A DAY IN THE LIFE—5:03
side two
   WHEN I'M SIXTY-FOUR—2:38
   LOVELY RITA—2:43
   ALL YOU NEED IS LOVE—3:57
   BABY, YOU'RE A RICH MAN—3:07
   MAGICAL MYSTERY TOUR—2:48
   YOUR MOTHER SHOULD KNOW—2:33
   THE FOOL ON THE HILL—3:00
   I AM THE WALRUS—4:35
record seven: Parlophone SM 707
side one
   HELLO GOODBYE—3:24
   LADY MADONNA—2:17
   HEY JUDE—7:11
   REVOLUTION—3:22
   BACK IN THE U.S.S.R.—2:45
   OB-LA-DI, OB-LA-DA—3:10
   *WHILE MY GUITAR GENTLY WEEPS—*Harrison*—4:46*
side two
   THE CONTINUING STORY OF BUNGALOW BILL—3:05
   HAPPINESS IS A WARM GUN—2:47
   MARTHA MY DEAR—2:28
   I'M SO TIRED—2:01
   *PIGGIES—*Harrison*—2:04*
   *DON'T PASS ME BY—*Starkey*—3:52*
   JULIA—2:57
   ALL TOGETHER NOW—2:08
record eight: Parlophone SM 708
side one
   †*GET BACK (version two)—3:09*
   DON'T LET ME DOWN—3:34
   THE BALLAD OF JOHN AND YOKO—2:58
   †*ACROSS THE UNIVERSE—3:51*
   †*FOR YOU BLUE—*Harrison*—2:33*
   †*TWO OF US—3:33*
   †*THE LONG AND WINDING ROAD—3:40*
   †*LET IT BE (version two)—4:01*

The Beatles Box   Parlophone SM 701-708 (LPs)

The Beatles Box: Parlophone SM 701 (LP)
Record One

The Beatles Box: Parlophone SM 702 (LP)
Record Two

The Beatles Box: Parlophone SM 703 (LP)
Record Three

The Beatles Box: Parlophone SM 704 (LP)
Record Four

The Beatles Box: Parlophone SM 705 (LP)
Record Five

The Beatles Box: Parlophone SM 706 (LP)
Record Six

The Beatles Box: Parlophone SM 707 (LP)
Record Seven

The Beatles Box: Parlophone SM 708 (LP)
Record Eight

Double Fantasy

Geffen GHS 2001 (LP)

ENTRY 656. Double Fantasy was mostly recorded in August 1980 at the Hit Factory studios in New York City. Most of the songs had been written earlier in the year when John had been on holiday in Bermuda with Sean, and Yoko was working in New York. They played bits of music to each other during late night long distance calls.

Subtitled "A Heart Play," the album was sequenced as a back-and-forth dialogue between John and Yoko, with lead vocals on the fourteen songs evenly split between them. The approach was particularly effective on side one, which quickly moved from the opening chimes of *(Just Like) Starting Over* through the tensions of *Give Me Something, I'm Losing You,* and *I'm Moving On* to the peaceful bedtime story imagery of *Beautiful Boy (Darling Boy).* Even the use of Yoko's delicate wishing bells to open the album (and the single) was a deliberate contrast to the funeral death bell that had begun Lennon's first solo album in 1970. The two were obviously "starting over," only in a far more upbeat mood.

Two of the songs specifically dealt with explaining what, when, and why. *Cleanup Time,* written by Lennon in Bermuda, sprang out of the observation that people seemed to be getting their personal houses in order, as part of a general "cleanup time." *Watching The Wheels* was more direct, answering the question: What's John Lennon been doing the past five years?

John's *I'm Losing You* and Yoko's *I'm Moving On* formed the strongest couplet on the album. John's was written in a fit of frustration and anger down in Bermuda, when he was unable to reach Yoko by telephone. Yoko's described an angry break up. Originally, the songs also included licks from Cheap Trick's Rich Nielsen, Bun E. Carlos, and Robin Zander, but these were dropped from the final mix because they made the tracks a bit *too* heavy.

Side two offered some lighter moments, including Yoko's 1930s-style *I'm Your Angel,* John's bouncy *Dear Yoko,* and two deeply sincere love songs: Yoko's *Beautiful Boys* (written in response to Lennon's song for Sean, but directed to both of her "boys") and John's *Woman* (with a quotation from Chairman Mao spoken in the opening riff, describing all women as forming "the other half of the sky").

Double Fantasy ended with two Yoko Ono songs: the reassuring *Every Man Has A Woman Who Loves Him* and a "Japanese gospel number," *Hard Times Are Over,* featuring the Benny Cummings Singers and Kings Temple Choir as background singers. A bit from a spontaneous prayer by the group in the studio opened the final cut.

There were about twenty-two songs recorded at the **Double Fantasy** sessions, with the leftovers earmarked for either the follow-up album (page 413) or a special new single devoted to Yoko (Entry 666).

Note: Initial pressings of **Double Fantasy** listed the songs in the wrong order on the back cover, misplacing *Kiss Kiss Kiss, Woman, Dear Yoko,* and *Every Man Has A Woman Who Loves Him.* This was not corrected until early 1981, beginning with copies that hit the stores that spring.

ENTRY 657. See page 267.

side two

COME TOGETHER–4:16
SOMETHING–Harrison–2:59
MAXWELL'S SILVER HAMMER–3:24
OCTOPUS'S GARDEN–Starkey–2:49
HERE COMES THE SUN–Harrison–3:04
BECAUSE–2:45
GOLDEN SLUMBERS–1:31
CARRY THAT WEIGHT–1:37
THE END–2:04
HER MAJESTY–0:23

656. NOV 15, 1980 (US) Geffen GHS 2001 (LP)
NOV 17, 1980 (UK) Geffen K 99131 (LP)
by John Lennon and Yoko Ono
DOUBLE FANTASY   Prod: John Lennon, Yoko Ono and
Jack Douglas
side one

(Just Like) Starting Over–Lennon–3:55
Kiss Kiss Kiss–Yoko Ono–2:41
Cleanup Time–Lennon–2:57
Give Me Something–Yoko Ono–1:34
I'm Losing You–Lennon–3:58
I'm Moving On–Yoko Ono–2:19
Beautiful Boy (Darling Boy)–Lennon–4:01

side two

Watching The Wheels–Lennon–3:59
(Yes) I'm Your Angel–Yoko Ono–3:08
Woman–Lennon–3:32
Beautiful Boys–Yoko Ono–2:54
Dear Yoko–Lennon–2:33
Every Man Has A Woman Who Loves Him–Yoko Ono–
4:02
Hard Times Are Over–Yoko Ono–3:20

657. DEC 1, 1980 (US) Columbia PC 36987 (LP)
FEB 23, 1981 (UK) Parlophone CHAT 1 (LP)
by Paul McCartney; Interview Conducted by Vic Garbarini
THE McCARTNEY INTERVIEW
side one

An Interview With Paul McCartney For Musician: Player
& Listener Magazine–29:42
side two

An Interview With Paul McCartney For Musician: Player
& Listener Magazine–24:35

ENTRY 658--661. As part of McCartney's deal with Columbia Records, he brought his back catalog of solo material to his new label. This took place in stages, with the first five albums (**McCartney** through **Band On The Run**) coming out on Columbia about the same time as **McCartney II. Venus And Mars** followed later in the year. In each case, Columbia merely reissued the old album with a new label and number.

The same thing did not happen with McCartney's old singles. Despite the fact that many of them contained otherwise unavailable B-sides, Columbia did not reissue them. Instead, the company selected eight tracks for coupling as new "double-A" singles in the Hall Of Fame series. Only one song, *Goodnight Tonight* (Entry 658), was not also available on an album at the time. Two other titles, *My Love* and *Helen Wheels* (Entry 659 & 661) had originally been backed by the non-album B-sides of *The Mess* and *Country Dreamer*. However, *My Love* did have an unusual new flip side: the studio version of *Maybe I'm Amazed* from the 1970 **McCartney** album. This had never before been issued as a single in the U.S., though a live concert version by Wings had been a top ten hit in 1977. However, Columbia did not yet have the right to rerelease that single, so it had to go with the original version.

The following summer, Columbia added one more old Wings single to its catalog, the 1976 hit *Silly Love Songs* (Columbia 18-02171). This time, the record was not released as part of the Hall Of Fame series and it retained its original B-side, *Cook Of The House* (also available on the **Wings At The Speed Of Sound** album). However, *Silly Love Songs* was cut down to 3:26 from its original length of 5:54. This shorter time was not indicated on the label.

ENTRY 662. Denny Laine's first solo album since **Holly Days** in 1977 looked for all the world like a bootleg package, even though it was distributed in the U.K. by RCA. The cover was plain black with a minimum of artwork and lettering (though there were detailed liner notes on the back). In a way this was quite appropriate because the set contained a mixed bag of old and new tracks, including three previously unreleased Wings recordings.

Send Me The Heart was a country ballad written by McCartney and Laine and recorded in Nashville back in 1974. (The liner notes mistakenly placed it in 1973.) *I Would Only Smile* was a light pop tune from 1973 featuring the original Wings lineup including Henry McCullough on guitar and Denny Seiwell on drums. *Weep For Love* was the most recent of the three, recorded in 1979 at Lympne Castle during the **Back To The Egg** sessions. Had Paul McCartney released his often promised "Cold Cuts" album of finished outtake tracks in 1975 or 1976, the first two songs would probably have been on it.

Denny Laine did the lead vocals on each song and also served as overall producer for the album. However, if these had been released on a regular Wings album, Paul McCartney would no doubt have been listed as (at least) co-producer.

The U.S. release in 1983 touted the album as "Denny Laine and Friends" and even listed some of the guest musicians (including Paul and Linda) on the front cover. For the remaining cuts on the album, see page 307.

658. DEC 2, 1980 (US) Columbia Hall Of Fame 13-33405
by Wings   Prod: Paul McCartney except + Paul McCartney
and Chris Thomas
*A: *GOODNIGHT TONIGHT*—McCartney—*4:18*
+A: *GETTING CLOSER*—McCartney—*3:22*

659. DEC 2, 1980 (US) Columbia Hall Of Fame 13-33407
by Paul McCartney except + with Wings   Prod: Paul
McCartney
A: *MAYBE I'M AMAZED*—McCartney—*3:42*
+A: *MY LOVE*—McCartney—*4:07*

660. DEC 2, 1980 (US) Columbia Hall Of Fame 13-33408
by Paul McCartney and Wings   Prod: Paul McCartney (A
side); Paul and Linda McCartney   Prod: Paul and Linda
McCartney (+A side)
A: *JET*—McCartney—*4:08*
+A: *UNCLE ALBERT/ADMIRAL HALSEY*—Paul and Linda
McCartney—*4:50*

661. DEC 2, 1980 (US) Columbia Hall Of Fame 13-33409
by Paul McCartney and Wings   Prod: Paul McCartney
A: *BAND ON THE RUN*—McCartney—*5:09*
A: *HELEN WHEELS*—McCartney—*3:45*

662. DEC 5, 1980 (UK) Scratch SCR L 5001 (LP)
AUG 8, 1983 (US) Takoma TAK 7103 (LP)
by Denny Laine † with Paul McCartney and Wings
JAPANESE TEARS   Prod: Denny Laine
side one
cut four: *Send Me The Heart*—McCartney/Denny Laine—
3:38
side two
† cut six: *I Would Only Smile*—Denny Laine—*3:20*
† cut seven: *Weep For Love*—Denny Laine—*4:31*

663. DEC 5, 1980 (UK) K-tel NE 1111 (LP)
by David Bowie   Prod: David Bowie and Harry Maslin
THE BEST OF BOWIE
side two
cut three: *FAME*—Lennon/David Bowie/Carlos Alomar—
4:12

ENTRY 664. *My Sweet Lord* was the first solo release by any of the former Beatles to top the British charts during the 1970s. In fact, until 1976 it was also the *only* one to hit number one. Then Paul McCartney followed with *Let 'Em In* (1976) and *Mull Of Kintyre* (1977), the most successful single ever released in Britain. However, none of McCartney's tracks were available for this non-EMI compilation.

664.   DEC 5, 1980 (UK) CBS 10020 (2 LPs)
by Various Artists
THE GUINNESS ALBUM: HITS OF THE 70'S
side one
cut nine: *MY SWEET LORD*—Harrison—*4:39*
by George Harrison   Prod: George Harrison and Phil
Spector

SEASON OF GLASS
YOKO ONO

Season Of Glass   **Geffen GHS 2004 (LP)**

1981

January 18. Yoko Ono's "In Gratitude" ad appears worldwide.
April 10. The U.S. premiere of Ringo's film *Caveman*, a prehistoric comedy with a dialogue vocabulary of fifteen words.
April 27. The wedding of Ringo Starr and Barbara Bach.
April 27. Denny Laine officially ends his ten-year musical association with Paul McCartney. With the departure of Steve Holly and Laurence Juber earlier in the yaer, this marks the end of Wings as a functioning group.
June 15. Yoko Ono is sued for copyright infringement (on her song *I'm Your Angel*) by the composers of *Makin' Whoopee!*
October 4. A judge orders John "Duff" Lowe to surrender to Paul McCartney a 1958 demo disc of *That'll Be The Day* b/w *In Spite Of All Danger*, featuring Lowe, John, Paul, and George.
December 12. To wrap up an appearance on Britain's *Parkinson* TV talk show, Ringo, Tim Rice, Jimmy Tarbuck, and Michael Parkinson do an impromptu version of *Singing The Blues*.

1981

Seasons Of Glass

Sales of Beatles and John Lennon discs skyrocketed following Lennon's death. In the U.S., where **Double Fantasy** and *(Just Like) Starting Over* were already heading up the charts, both shot to the top. In Britain, where the two discs had already peaked and were actually on the way down, both reversed direction and went back up. They became the first John Lennon solo records to top the British single and album charts simultaneously.

In January, a rerelease of *Imagine* also reached number one in Britain, followed in February by *Woman*, the second single from **Double Fantasy**. A cover version of Lennon's *Jealous Guy* by Roxy Music hit number one there in March. Stateside, there were seven albums by the Beatles, six by John Lennon, and one by Paul McCartney (a newly-released interview disc) on the charts at the same time — more than at the peak of Beatlemania in the 1960s. *Woman* was also a big hit, spending twelve weeks in the top ten.

On January 18, Yoko Ono publicly thanked everyone for their concern, love, and generosity through an ad ("In Gratitude") run in newspapers throughout the world. The following month, she released *Walking On Thin Ice* (subtitled "For John"), the track Lennon had been working on the night he died. A third single from **Double Fantasy**, *Watching The Wheels*, followed in March. No doubt every Lennon track on **Double Fantasy** could have been issued successfully as a single, but Yoko Ono and Geffen stopped at three, the usual limit for a superstar album.

There were still some unreleased Lennon tracks left over from the **Double Fantasy** sessions that might have been rushed out, but Yoko held them back until she was better prepared to deal with their release. Instead, she focused her energies on recording a brand new solo album, **Season Of Glass**, which dealt with her pain, anger, and frustrations.

For many fans, **Season Of Glass** provided a unique opportunity to share similar feelings. At the same time, there were also many other tributes, memorials, and dedications of every sort. For example,

129

in January 1981 the government of Israel announced plans for a John Lennon Peace Forest to be planted in the Galilee region, near Safad, which was described as the ancient home of "intellectuals, mystics, and scholars." Closer to home, New York mayor Ed Koch signed a city ordinance on April 16 designating a three-block section of Central Park as "Strawberry Fields." And, of course, there were records, books, posters, and other such items — some pure exploitation, others sincere expressions of deeply felt emotions.

Despite all this activity, in February and March gossip writers and tabloid reporters became obsessed with the possibility of something more, the "ultimate" tribute to John Lennon: a reunion of the three remaining Beatles. This slant allowed Fleet Street to dust off all the old Beatles reunion stories and give them a new twist: Paul, George, and Ringo should get together in the recording studio to do a memorial record for John Lennon.

In February, when Paul McCartney went to George Martin's studio on the island of Montserrat to begin work on his new album, and Ringo Starr and other rock superstars showed up to play on some tracks, the rumor mongers went crazy over the scenario: two former Beatles on a remote desert island, with their original producer and other big name rock stars! What else could this be but a memorial reunion?

In fact it was nothing of the sort. The previous year George Martin and Paul McCartney had planned to spend about a month recording at Martin's AIR studios on the island. They had also decided that the new disc would feature guest musicians, so Ringo Starr, Stevie Wonder, Carl Perkins, and Stanley Clarke (among others) were invited to come over and play. That was it. Ironically, at the same time there *was* a memorial disc in the works by a former Beatle, only that was being done in another part of the world — by George Harrison.

Harrison's **Somewhere In England** album had been scheduled for release back in November 1980, but that had been delayed for two reasons: to avoid competing with **Double Fantasy** and because Warner Bros. wanted him to replace four tracks with more upbeat material. One of those new songs turned into George Harrison's tribute to John Lennon, *All Those Years Ago*.

Actually, that song had strated out as a track for Ringo Starr's next solo album. Following the death of Lennon, though, Harrison decided to use the tune himself. He took the basic instrumental (with Ringo on drums) and put new words to it. Then he contacted McCartney and arranged for a backing vocal overdub by Paul, Linda, and Denny Laine. The result was a "reunion" on tape of the three former Beatles in memory of John Lennon. Upon release in early May, the single became a worldwide hit. However, the album stalled short of the top ten and the follow-up single of *Teardrops* could not crack the U.S. top 100.

Yet at the same time, the radio airwaves were saturated with Beatles music. In fact, while *All Those Years Ago* just missed reaching number one in the U.S. a medley of old Beatles tunes performed by "Stars On 45" had topped the charts. Clearly there was plenty of room for the Beatles as nostalgia, but the death of John Lennon seemed to have reminded people of just how long ago Beatlemania had been. New individual efforts (especially by George and Ringo) now needed a tremendous boost merely to get noticed, no matter how good they were.

Ringo ran into such difficulties with his new album. First, he had to go label shopping after splitting with Portrait Records. Along the way, he revamped the album package a bit, dropping the *Can't Fight Lightning* title cut and substituting a new moniker, **Stop And Smell The Roses**. He landed eventually at Neil Bogart's new label, Boardwalk. Yet even though Ringo's album was one of only a handful of new releases from the company, it was still essentially lost in the rush of Christmas product. Obviously, the tremendous surge of interest in old Beatles product all year did not automatically transfer to a new Ringo Starr record.

Still, with all the talk of somber memorial albums and formal tributes, it was somehow appropriate that when Paul, George, and Ringo really did have a reunion it was not in the recording studio. Instead, on April 27, they were all at the Marylebone Register Office in London. There, Ringo Starr and Barbara Bach were married — in the same place that Paul and Linda had exchanged vows twelve years before.

Afterward, at the reception, there was the inevitable musical jam. Paul played piano, George played guitar, and Ringo pounded an overturned champagne bucket with a pair of spoons. There was no stereo simulcast satellite hookup.

131

ENTRY 665. *Woman* was the obvious second single from **Double Fantasy**, described by Lennon as "the Beatle track" and "an Eighties version of *Girl*." The record was issued in a picture sleeve in both the U.S. and the U.K.

ENTRY 666. Convinced that the time was right at last for a Yoko Ono pop hit, John and Yoko had held back *Walking On Thin Ice* (from the **Double Fantasy** sessions) for separate release as a single. At first Lennon suggested that they issue it with one of his songs on the B-side, but Yoko quite correctly pointed out that people would then simply make the B-side the A-side. If this was to work, it would have to be by Yoko only. They planned to work the release especially hard at rock dance clubs, which had been receptive to the new wave-ish sounds of *Kiss Kiss Kiss*. For a while, this plan included the possibility of a special dance club pressing of the single, with a bonus track such as the once-banned *Open Your Box* from 1971.

For the B-side they retrieved another song from the early 1970s, a Yoko Ono ballad called *It Happened*. Unlike *Open Your Box* (which had slipped into the U.S. anyway on **Fly** as *Hirake*), this one had not turned up on any American release. John and Yoko (and Jack Douglas) edited and remixed the original 1973 recording adding a brief humorous exchange at the beginning.

Lennon had been working on the final mix for *Walking On Thin Ice* the day he died. Yoko decided that she had to see the project through to its conclusion, so she and Jack Douglas finished the mix and got the record out in less than two months. Instead of calling it something like "Yoko Only" it became "*Walking On Thin Ice* — For John." The backside of the picture sleeve (showing an ice-covered sidewalk) gave the background to the release, while the inner sleeve insert printed the words to both songs and the musician credits. There was also a twelve-inch promo version issued in the same style sleeve (Geffen PRO A 934), though the extra third track, *Hard Times Are Over*, was simply taken from **Double Fantasy**.

Walking On Thin Ice became the first Yoko Ono single ever to make *Billboard*'s Hot 100, peaking at 33. As predicted, the song also did well at the dance clubs, making it to number 13 on *Billboard*'s Disco charts.

Neither track from the *Walking On Thin Ice* single appeared on Yoko Ono's follow-up **Season Of Glass** album (page 290). However, in Britain Geffen was able to tout that record as "including the single *Walking On Thin Ice*." This was accomplished by putting copies of the single into the album package.

Note: The song *It Happened* had been issued once before, but only in Japan. Back in the fall of 1974, a version produced by Yoko Ono and David Spinozza served as the B-side to *Yume O Motou (Let's Have A Dream)*, performed by Yoko Ono and the Plastic Ono Super Band. See page 292 for further details.

ENTRY 667. This two-disc TV mail order package actually received its widest distribution in 1982 when it turned up in cut-out bins throughout the U.S. As with most such albums, the jacket did not fold out, so both records were stuck
(continued)

665. JAN 5, 1981 (US) Geffen GEF 49644
JAN 16, 1981 (UK) Geffen K 79195
    by John Lennon and Yoko Ono   Prod: John Lennon,
    Yoko Ono and Jack Douglas
A: WOMAN—Lennon—*3:32*
B: BEAUTIFUL BOYS—Yoko Ono—*2:54*

666. FEB 1, 1981 (US) Geffen GEF 49683
FEB 20, 1981 (UK) Geffen K 79202
    by Yoko Ono   Prod: John Lennon, Yoko Ono and Jack
    Douglas (A side);   John Lennon and Yoko Ono in
    1973 with Editing and Remixing by John Lennon, Yoko
    Ono and Jack Douglas in 1980 (B side)
*A: Walking On Thin Ice—Yoko Ono—*5:58*
*B: It Happened—Yoko Ono—*5:06*

667. FEBRUARY 1981 (US MAIL ORDER) Hall Of Music HMI-
2200 (2 LPs)
    by The Beatles; recorded live by Ted Taylor in 1962
**THE BEATLES LIVE AT THE STAR CLUB 1962,
HAMBURG, GERMANY**
side one
    INTRODUCTION OF THE BAND—*0:21*
    ROLL OVER BEETHOVEN—Chuck Berry—*2:15*
    HIPPY HIPPY SHAKE—Chan Romero—*1:42*
    SWEET LITTLE SIXTEEN—Chuck Berry—*2:45*
    A TASTE OF HONEY—Ric Marlow/Bobby Scott—*1:45*
    TILL THERE WAS YOU—Meredith Willson—*1:59*
side two
    I SAW HER STANDING THERE—*2:22*
    ASK ME WHY—*2:26*
    REMINISCING—King Curtis—*1:41*
    TWIST AND SHOUT—Bert Russell/Phil Medley—*2:03*

John Lennon
Woman

Photo: Jack Mitchell

Woman   **Geffen GEF 49644 (45)**

Walking On Thin Ice   Geffen GEF 49683 (45)

into the same pocket. The cover graphics were essentially the same as the 1977 Lingasong release, with the back cover photo from the original moved up to the front and the inside picture placed on the back.

For American fans, the most important aspect of this album was that it provided the first U.S. release of the four tracks not previously issued in the States. They all turned up on side two. Otherwise, the set clocked in a bit short, with only eighteen songs on the two records.

ENTRY 668. This single (recorded at 33 1/3) came in a dark black picture sleeve and contained John Lennon's final concert hall appearance, which took place on November 28, 1974, during an Elton John show at New York's Madison Square Garden. At the time, it was Lennon's first live performance in about two years and it came about as the result of an informal wager.

Earlier in 1974, Lennon had made a guest appearance on Elton John's recording of *Lucy In The Sky With Diamonds*, and Elton John had done the same on John's *Whatever Gets You Thru The Night*. Elton innocently asked Lennon if he would perform *Whatever Gets You Thru The Night* live in concert with him if it hit number one. Lennon agreed, never expecting that to happen. Much to his surprise, the song caught on and spent one week (November 16, 1974) at the top of *Billboard*'s Hot 100. Less than three weeks later, he was on stage with the Elton John Band. They played three songs together: the two single tracks and, for the wrap-up, *I Saw Her Standing There*, described by Lennon as being "a number of an old estranged fiance of mine called Paul."

Even though Elton John put out a live album from that concert tour in 1976 (**Here And There**), none of the Lennon tracks were included. Only their *I Saw Her Standing There* finale turned up, issued as the B-side to Elton John's 1975 hit, *Philadelphia Freedom* (Entry 436), though all three songs appeared on a bootleg (page 390). Following the issue of the 1981 single, the three cuts were added to a revamped version of the live album in Japan, **Elton John And John Lennon Live — 28 November 1974** (DJM K28P-200). In England, DJM included the songs on a special cassette and also licensed them to other labels (see page 431 and Entry 747).

Note: Though John Lennon's performance at the Elton John show was his final concert hall appearance, it was not his final public performance. That took place the following year as part of the television special "Salute To Sir Lew Grade," which aired June 13, 1975. On that program, Lennon played *Slippin' And Slidin'* from **Rock'n'Roll** (then his latest album) and *Imagine*.

ENTRY 669. *Watching The Wheels*, trimmed by about half a minute, became the third consecutive top ten single from **Double Fantasy**. A few months later a sticker on new copies of the album identified *I'm Losing You* as yet another single release, but that was never issued.

Note: The picture sleeve featured a candid photo of John and Yoko taken outside the Dakota by Paul Goresh, the person who had also snapped a picture of Lennon giving his autograph to Mark Chapman.

side three
MEDLEY—*2:09*
KANSAS CITY—Jerry Leiber/Mike Stoller—*1:04*
HEY-HEY-HEY-HEY—Richard Penniman—*1:05*
MR. MOONLIGHT—Roy Lee Johnson—*2:06*
LONG TALL SALLY—Enotris Johnson/Richard
Penniman/Robert Blackwell—*1:45*
LITTLE QUEENIE—Chuck Berry—*3:51*
BE-BOP-A-LULA—Gene Vincent/Tex Davis—*2:29*
side four
RED SAILS IN THE SUNSET—Jimmy Kennedy/Will
Grosz—*2:00*
EVERYBODY'S TRYING TO BE MY BABY—Carl
Perkins—*2:25*
MATCHBOX—Carl Perkins—*2:35*
I'M TALKING ABOUT YOU—Chuck Berry—*1:48*

668.   MAR 13, 1981 (UK) DJM DJS 10965
by The Elton John Band featuring John Lennon and the
Muscle Shoals Horns   recorded live   Prod: Gus
Dudgeon
side one
I SAW HER STANDING THERE—L/McC—*3:35*
side two
Introduction/Entrance Of John Lennon—*1:08*
Whatever Gets You Thru The Night—Lennon—*3:12*
Lucy In The Sky With Diamonds—L/McC—*6:05*

669.   MAR 16, 1981 (US) Geffen GEF 49695
MAR 27, 1981 (UK) Geffen K 79207
by John Lennon and Yoko Ono   Prod: John Lennon,
Yoko Ono and Jack Douglas
A: WATCHING THE WHEELS—Lennon—*3:30*
B: (YES) I'M YOUR ANGEL—Yoko Ono—*2:50*

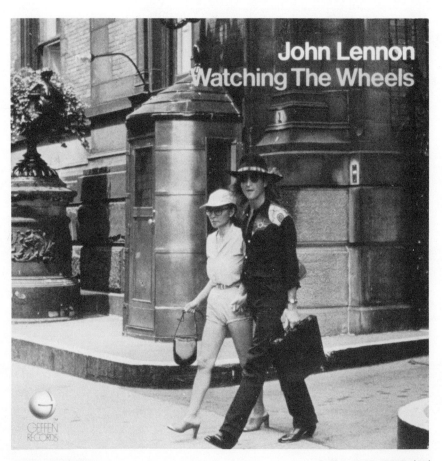

Watching The Wheels

Geffen GEF 49695 (45)

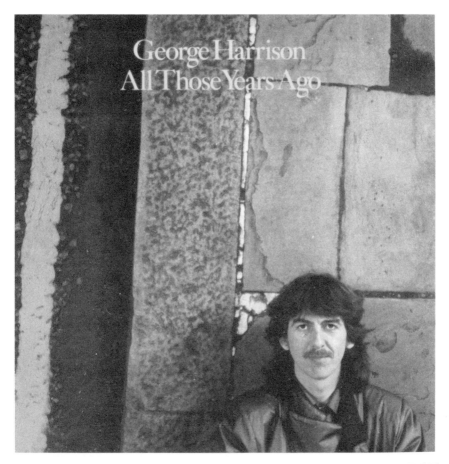

All Those Years Ago   Dark Horse DRC 49725 (45)

ENTRY 670. This live package contained highlights from the 1979 series of benefit concerts held at London's Hammersmith Odeon Theatre (December 26--29) to aid the United Nations relief efforts in Kampuchea (formerly known as Cambodia). The songs featuring McCartney with Wings and the all-star Rockestra were recorded on the final night and included a second live version of *Coming Up* (different from Entry 639) and the first commercially available recording of Paul singing Little Richard's 1957 hit, *Lucille*. That song and *Every Night* also appeared on a U.S. promotional sampler disc for the package (Atlantic PR 388).

Unfortunately for the fund raising effort, the album did not come out until more than a year after the event and could not even crack the U.S. top thirty.

ENTRY 671. The words to George Harrison's tribute to John Lennon appeared on the back of the picture sleeve. There was also a promo-only twelve-inch disc issued in the U.S. (Dark Horse PRO A 949).

ENTRY 672. Somewhere In England had originally been scheduled for release in November 1980, along with **Double Fantasy**, but was delayed and then completely revamped. The 1981 version had the same catalog number but a new cover, new track order, and four brand-new cuts: *All Those Years Ago, Blood From A Clone, Teardrops*, and *That Which I Have Lost*. (See page 393 for details on the 1980 set.)

Supposedly the 1980 lineup for the album had been rejected by Warner Bros. as too low-key and noncommercial. If that was the case, Harrison's new recordings answered those objections perfectly with a catchy superstar single (*All Those Years Ago*), an upbeat love song with strong keyboard work (*Teardrops*), spiritual consciousness set to a toe-tapping country-picker's beat (*That Which I Have Lost*), and an aggressive putdown of record company executives (*Blood From A Clone*). These combined with the remaining six songs from the original 1980 recordings to produce a well balanced new album.

Two tracks were cover versions of Hoagy Carmichael tunes: *Baltimore Oriole* (from 1942) and *Hong Kong Blues* (from 1939), which were both performed by Carmichael in the 1945 film *To Have And Have Not*. Though Harrison's version of *Baltimore Oriole* was only adequate, *Hong Kong Blues* was superb. In fact, that had been the lead-off track on the 1980 version of the album and would have made a perfect single. Another strong candidate for single release was a dance tune, *Unconsciousness Rules*. With all these upbeat tracks, *Life Itself* and *Writing's On The Wall*, slow Harrison spiritual numbers, worked quite effectively in contrast, one per side. Only *Save The World* was a disappointment. Perhaps the kindred *Tears Of The World* (one of the four songs left off the revised lineup) would have made a better choice to close the album.

Note: In contrast to the 1980 version, the new album featured an amusing front/back cover joke, with Harrison cleverly placed in front of "Holland Park Avenue Study," a painting by Mark Boyle hanging in London's Tate Gallery.

670. MAR 27, 1981 (US) Atlantic SD 2 7005 (2 LPs)
APR 3, 1981 (UK) Atlantic K 60153 (2 LPs)
by Various Artists with cuts by
Paul McCartney and Wings; † Rockestra
CONCERTS FOR THE PEOPLE OF KAMPUCHEA
Sound Producer: Chris Thomas
side four
Got To Get You Into My Life—L/McC—*2:57*
Every Night—McCartney—*4:17*
Coming Up—McCartney—*4:08*
†Lucille—Richard Penniman/Albert Collins—*3:03*
†Let It Be—L/McC—*4:12*
†Rockestra Theme—McCartney—*2:30*

671. MAY 4, 1981 (US) Dark Horse DRC 49725
MAY 15, 1981 (UK) Dark Horse K 17807
by George Harrison   Prod: George Harrison and Ray
Cooper
A: All Those Years Ago—Harrison—*3:43*
B: Writing's On The Wall—Harrison—*3:54*

672. JUN 1, 1981 (US) Dark Horse DHK 3492 (LP)
JUN 5, 1981 (UK) Dark Horse K 56870 (LP)
by George Harrison
SOMEWHERE IN ENGLAND   Prod: George Harrison and
Ray Cooper
side one
Blood From A Clone—Harrison—*3:58*
Unconsciousness Rules—Harrison—*3:04*
Life Itself—Harrison—*4:24*
All Those Years Ago—Harrison—*3:43*
Baltimore Oriole—Paul Francis Webster/Hoagy Carmichael—
3:57
side two
Teardrops—Harrison—*4:04*
That Which I Have Lost—Harrison—*3:42*
Writing's On The Wall—Harrison—*3:54*
Hong Kong Blues—Hoagy Carmichael—*2:54*
Save The World—Harrison—*4:56*

Somewhere In England (front cover)　　　　　　　　　**Dark Horse DHK 3492 (LP)**

SIDE ONE | SIDE TWO | Engineer *Phil McDonald*

Blood from a Clone | *Teardrops* | Produced by *George Harrison & Ray Cooper*
Unconsciousness Rules | *That Which I Have Lost*
Life Itself | *Writing's on the Wall*
All Those Years Ago | *Hong Kong Blues*
Baltimore Oriole | *Save the World* | Photography *Caroline Irwin*

Somewhere In England (back cover)   **Dark Horse DHK 3492 (LP)**

ENTRY 673. A limited edition boxed set similar in concept to **The Beatles Collection**, gathering all of John Lennon's solo efforts into one package. The silver toned box featured a mid-1970s photo of Lennon by Bob Gruen centered on the cover, with a machine-stamped autograph below.

Unlike the 1978 Beatles package, there was no bonus disc. After all, there were only two EMI releases from Lennon that had never been on an album: the single version of *Give Peace A Chance* and *Move Over Ms. L.* However, there was a bonus magazine: *The Liverpool Echo's Tribute To John Lennon,* a twenty-three-page collection of press clippings and photos.

At first EMI had balked at doing such a package, which not only might be criticized for being a cash-in exploitation, but which also might not sell well following the tremendous rush of Lennon album purchases over the Christmas holidays in 1980. The company's branch in Italy was the first to give it a try, issuing a special boxed set of Lennon material earlier in 1981. For that Italian collection, only seven album packages were used (**Shaved Fish** was omitted), but three singles were also included: *Instant Karma!/Who Has Seen The Wind, Power To The People/Open Your Box,* and *Happy Xmas (War Is Over)/Listen, The Snow Is Falling.* Instead of a bonus magazine, there was a large poster of the Lennon photo used in the 1968 **Beatles** double album.

With the viability of the set established, editions in other countries soon followed, including a British package. Copies quickly turned up in the import bins in America as well, sometimes carrying a price tag as low as $50 (less than $6 per album). This was quite a lure to those interested in building a complete John Lennon collection as quickly and inexpensively as possible.

Not surprisingly, **The John Lennon Boxed Set** omitted Lennon's experimental collaborations with Yoko Ono from 1968 and 1969. Those three albums, out of print since the mid-1970s, would have brought the set much closer to being a complete collection, with twelve discs. However, record buyers would no doubt have complained about three albums worth of offbeat sounds ranging from the random noise of **Two Virgins** to a baby's hearbeat on **Life With The Lions.** Only the 1969 **Wedding Album** contained anything familiar: a brief rendition of *Good Night* by Lennon to close side two. Nonetheless, a more complete picture of John Lennon's career would have included:

UNFINISHED MUSIC NO. 1 — TWO VIRGINS   Prod: John Lennon and
   Yoko Ono   First issued in the U.K. November 29, 1968, as Apple
   SAPCOR 2
side one
   Two Virgins—Lennon/Yoko Ono—*14:02*
      Two Virgins No. 1
      Together
      Two Virgins No. 2
      Two Virgins No. 3
      Two Virgins No. 4
      Two Virgins No. 5
      Two Virgins No. 6

(continued)

673. JUN 15, 1981 (UK) Parlophone JLB 8 (9 LPs)
by John Lennon
THE JOHN LENNON BOXED SET
A Boxed Set of 8 Original British Album Packages
**THE PLASTIC ONO BAND–LIVE PEACE IN TORONTO
1969**   Apple CORE 2001
JOHN LENNON/PLASTIC ONO BAND   Apple PCS 7124
IMAGINE   Apple PAS 10004
SOME TIME IN NEW YORK CITY   Apple PCSP 716
(2 LPs)
MIND GAMES   Apple PCS 7165
WALLS AND BRIDGES   Apple PCTC 253
ROCK 'N' ROLL   Apple PCS 7169
SHAVED FISH   Apple PCS 7173
This set contains the eight British releases in their original
sleeves with their contents unchanged:
THE PLASTIC ONO BAND–LIVE PEACE IN TORONTO 1969
Prod: John Lennon and Yoko Ono
First issued December 12, 1969
side one
Introduction Of The Band–1:44
*Blue Suede Shoes–*Carl Perkins–*2:09*
*Money (That's What I Want)–*Berry Gordy/Janie Bradford–*3:20*
*Dizzy Miss Lizzy–*Larry Williams–*3:25*
*Yer Blues–*L/McC–*3:50*
*Cold Turkey–*Lennon–*3:43*
*Give Peace A Chance–*L/McC–*3:30*
side two
*Don't Worry Kyoko (Mummy's Only Looking For Her Hand In The
Snow)–*Yoko Ono–*4:44*
*John, John (Let's Hope For Peace)–*Yoko Ono–*12:54*
JOHN LENNON/PLASTIC ONO BAND   Prod: John Lennon, Yoko
Ono and Phil Spector
First issued December 11, 1970
side one
*Mother–*Lennon–*5:29*
*Hold On (John)–*Lennon–*1:49*
*I Found Out–*Lennon–*3:33*
*Working Class Hero–*Lennon–*3:44*
*Isolation–*Lennon–*2:48*
side two
*Remember–*Lennon–*4:29*
*Love–*Lennon–*3:17*
*Well Well Well–*Lennon–*5:52*
*Look At Me–*Lennon–*2:49*
*God–*Lennon–*4:04*
*My Mummy's Dead–*Lennon–*0:48*

(Entry 673 continued)
side two
     Two Virgins—Lennon/Yoko Ono—*15:00*
     Hushabye Hushabye
     Two Virgins No. 7
     Two Virgins No. 8
     Two Virgins No. 9
     Two Virgins No. 10

UNFINISHED MUSIC NO. 2 – LIFE WITH THE LIONS   Prod: John Lennon and Yoko Ono.   First issued in the U.K. May 9, 1969, as Zapple 01
side one
     Cambridge 1969—Lennon/Yoko Ono—*26:30*
side two
     No Bed For Beatle John—Lennon/Yoko Ono—*4:45*
     Baby's Heartbeat—Lennon/Yoko Ono—*5:10*
     Two Minutes Silence—Lennon/Yoko Ono—*2:00*
     Radio Play—Lennon/Yoko Ono—*12:35*

WEDDING ALBUM   Prod: John Lennon and Yoko Ono.   First issued in the U.K. November 7, 1969 as Apple SAPCOR 11
side one
     John And Yoko—Lennon/Yoko Ono—*22:23*
side two
     Amsterdam—Lennon/Yoko Ono—*24:52*
        "John, John (Let's Hope For Peace)"—*5:18*
        "Amsterdam Interview"—*7:25*
        "Day In Bed"—*6:15*
        "Talking To The Press"—*3:15*
        "Bed Peace/Good Night"—L/McC—*2:05*
        "Hair Peace/Bed Peace"—*0:35*

These three albums were very much "John and Yoko at play," rather than collections of their songs. That came later, beginning with the **Live Peace In Toronto** album, which packaged individual songs by John Lennon and Yoko Ono on separate sides (John on side one, Yoko on side two). However, starting with the **John Lennon/Plastic Ono Band** album in 1970, the two usually split their efforts into separate releases, though they generally co-produced their respective sessions. As a result, for about three years individual albums from both of them usually hit the market at about the same time:
(continued)

146

IMAGINE   Prod: John Lennon, Yoko Ono and Phil Spector
First issued in U.K. October 8, 1971
side one
  Imagine–Lennon–*2:59*
  Crippled Inside–Lennon–*3:43*
  Jealous Guy–Lennon–*4:10*
  It's So Hard–Lennon–*2:22*
  I Don't Want To Be A Soldier, Mama, I Don't Want To Die–
    Lennon–*6:01*
side two
  Give Me Some Truth–Lennon–*3:11*
  Oh My Love–Lennon/Yoko Ono–*2:40*
  How Do You Sleep?–Lennon–*5:29*
  How?–Lennon–*3:37*
  Oh Yoko!–Lennon–*4:18*
SOME TIME IN NEW YORK CITY   Prod: John Lennon, Yoko Ono
and Phil Spector
First issued in U.K. September 15, 1972
side one
  Woman Is The Nigger Of The World–Lennon/Yoko Ono–*5:15*
  Sisters, O Sisters–Yoko Ono–*3:46*
  Attica State–Lennon/Yoko Ono–*2:52*
  Born In A Prison–Yoko Ono–*4:04*
  New York City–Lennon–*4:32*
side two
  Sunday Bloody Sunday–Lennon/Yoko Ono–*5:00*
  The Luck Of The Irish–Lennon/Yoko Ono–*2:54*
  John Sinclair–Lennon–*3:28*
  Angela–Lennon/Yoko Ono–*4:08*
  We're All Water–Yoko Ono–*7:15*
side three
  Cold Turkey–Lennon–*7:34*
  Don't Worry Kyoko–Yoko Ono–*17:12*
side four
  Well . . . (Baby Please Don't Go)–Walter Ward–*4:50*
  Jamrag–Lennon/Yoko Ono–*1:50*
  Scumbag–Lennon/Yoko Ono/Frank Zappa–*12:53*
  Au–Lennon/Yoko Ono–*3:25*
MIND GAMES   Prod: John Lennon
First issued in U.K. November 16, 1973
side one
  Mind Games–Lennon–*4:10*
  Tight A$–Lennon–*3:35*
  Aisumasen (I'm Sorry)–Lennon–*4:41*
  One Day (At A Time)–Lennon–*3:27*
  Bring On The Lucie (Freda Peeple)–Lennon–*4:11*
  Nutopian International Anthem–Lennon–*0:03*

147

(Entry 673 continued)
YOKO ONO/PLASTIC ONO BAND (Apple SAPCOR 17) was first issued
in the U.K. December 11, 1970, and accompanied the release of **John
Lennon/Plastic Ono Band.**

side one	side two
Why	*AOS*
Why Not	*Touch Me*
Greenfield Morning I Pushed	*Paper Shoes*
An Empty Baby Carriage	
All Over The City	

FLY (Apple SAPTU 101/2 – 2LPs) was first issued in the U.K. December 3, 1971, and accompanied the release of **Imagine.**

side one	side two
Midsummer New York	*Mind Holes*
Mind Train	*Don't Worry Kyoko*
side three	*Mrs. Lennon*
Airmale (Tone Deaf Jam)	*Hirake (Open Your Box)*
Don't Count The Waves	*Toilet Piece/Unknown*
You	*O'Wind (Body Is The Scar Of Your Mind)*
	side four
	Fly
	Telephone Piece

FEELING THE SPACE (Apple SAPCOR 26) was first issued in the U.K.
November 23, 1973, and accompanied the release of **Mind Games.**

side one	side two
Growing Pain	*A Thousand Times Yes*
Yellow Girl (Stand By For Life)	*Straight Talk*
Coffin Car	*Angry Young Woman*
Woman Of Salem	*She Hits Back*
Run, Run, Run	*Woman Power*
If Only	*Men, Men, Men*

In addition, **APPROXIMATELY INFINITE UNIVERSE** (Apple SAPDO
1001) came out in Britain in 1973 (February 16) without any accompanying
John Lennon release:

side one	side two
Yang Yang	*Approximately Infinite Universe*
Death Of Samantha	*Peter The Dealer*
I Want My Love To Rest Tonight	*Song For John*
What Did I Do!	*Catman (The Rosies Are Coming)*
Have You Seen A Horizon	*What A Bastard The World Is*
Lately	*Waiting For The Sunrise*

(continued)

148

side two

Intuition–Lennon–*3:05*
Out The Blue–Lennon–*3:19*
Only People–Lennon–*3:21*
I Know (I Know)–Lennon–*3:56*
You Are Here–Lennon–*4:06*
Meat City–Lennon–*2:52*

WALLS AND BRIDGES   Prod: John Lennon
First issued in U.K. October 4, 1974

side one

Going Down On Love–Lennon–*3:53*
Whatever Gets You Thru The Night–Lennon–*3:24*
Old Dirt Road–Lennon/Harry Nilsson–*4:10*
What You Got–Lennon–*3:06*
Bless You–Lennon–*4:39*
Scared–Lennon–*4:37*

side two

No. 9 Dream–Lennon–*4:44*
Surprise, Surprise (Sweet Bird Of Paradox)–Lennon–*2:33*
Steel And Glass–Lennon–*4:35*
Beef Jerky–Lennon–*3:24*
Nobody Loves You (When You're Down And Out)–Lennon–*5:07*
Ya Ya–Morgan Robinson/Clarence Lewis/Lee Dorsey–*1:06*

ROCK 'N' ROLL   Prod: John Lennon except † Phil Spector
First issued in U.K. February 21, 1975

side one

Be-Bop-A-Lula–Gene Vincent/Tex Davis–*2:36*
Stand By Me–Ben E. King/Jerry Leiber/Mike Stoller–*3:29*
Medley–*1:39*
    Rip It Up–Robert Blackwell/John Marascalco–*1:06*
    Ready Teddy–Robert Blackwell/John Marascalco–*0:33*
†*You Can't Catch Me*–Chuck Berry–*4:51*
Ain't That A Shame–Antoine Domino/Dave Bartholomew–*2:31*
Do You Want To Dance–Bobby Freeman–*2:53*
†*Sweet Little Sixteen*–Chuck Berry–*3:00*

side two

Slippin' And Slidin'–Richard Penniman/Edwin J. Bocage/Albert
    Collins/James Smith–*2:16*
Peggy Sue–Jerry Allison/Norman Petty/Buddy Holly–*2:02*
Medley–*3:40*
    Bring It On Home To Me–Sam Cooke–*2:03*
    Send Me Some Lovin'–Lloyd Price/John Marascalco–*1:37*
†*Bony Moronie*–Larry Williams–*3:50*
Ya Ya–Morgan Robinson/Clarence Lewis/Lee Dorsey–*2:17*
†*Just Because*–Lloyd Price–*4:25*

(Entry 673 continued)

side three
  *I Felt Like Smashing My Face
  In A Clear Glass Window
  Winter Song
  Kite Song
  What A Mess
  Shirankatta (I Didn't Know)
  Air Talk*

side four
  *I Have A Woman Inside My Soul
  Move On Fast
  Now Or Never
  Is Winter Here To Stay?
  Looking Over From My Hotel
  Window*

Only three Lennon albums were not accompanied by releases from Yoko Ono: **Walls And Bridges, Rock'n'Roll,** and the **Shaved Fish** "best of" collection. The first two were truly separate solo efforts because both were recorded during the couple's eighteen-month separation. In the other direction, three packages were put out combining songs by John Lennon and Yoko Ono: the 1971 *Happy Xmas* single, the 1972 **Some Time In New York City** album, and the 1980 **Double Fantasy** album.

Note: About the same time that **The John Lennon Boxed Set** hit the shops in Britain, Yoko Ono's **Season Of Glass** also came out. Though this album did not have any direct involvement by Lennon (it was recorded in 1981), it was treated by many fans and critics as an essential companion piece to any John Lennon collection. See page 290 for full track details.

ENTRY 674. Following several years of multi-platinum sales as a group, the members of Fleetwood Mac took some time off for solo projects. Drummer Mick Fleetwood did his solo recording at the Ghana Film Industries studio in Accra, Ghana, West Africa in January and February 1981. Some sessions were also filmed for an accompanying video release. The song with George Harrison, *Walk A Thin Line*, was the only track on the album that had previously been recorded by Fleetwood Mac as well, appearing on the group's 1979 **Tusk** album.

ENTRY 675. To tie-in with a British tour that summer, Bob Dylan released this lead single from his forthcoming **Shot Of Love** album (Entry 680).

ENTRY 676. Issued as part of the Warner Bros. "double A" oldie singles series, which used a separate sequence of numbers from the company's regular releases. Later in the year there were two more such singles, one from Harrison and another from Lennon (Entries 691 & 692).

SHAVED FISH Prod: John Lennon, Yoko Ono and Phil Spector
except † John Lennon; % John And Yoko; $ Phil Spector
First issued October 24, 1975
side one
%Give Peace A Chance–L/McC–*0:59*
%Cold Turkey–Lennon–*4:59*
$Instant Karma! (We All Shine On)–Lennon–*3:12*
Power To The People–Lennon–*3:04*
Mother–Lennon–*5:03*
Woman Is The Nigger Of The World–Lennon/Yoko Ono–*4:37*
side two
Imagine–Lennon–*2:59*
†Whatever Gets You Thru The Night–Lennon–*3:04*
†Mind Games–Lennon–*4:10*
†No. 9 Dream–Lennon–*4:44*
Medley–*4:15*
  Happy Xmas (War Is Over)–Lennon/Yoko Ono–*3:25*
  †Give Peace A Chance–L/McC–*0:50*

674. JUN 30, 1981 (UK) RCA LP 5044 (LP)
JUN 30, 1981 (US) RCA AFL 1 4080 (LP)
by Mick Fleetwood
THE VISITOR Prod: Richard Dashut and Mick Fleetwood
side two
  cut one: *Walk A Thin Line*–Lindsey Buckingham–*3:19*
  George: Twelve String Guitar, Slide Guitar, Backing Vocal

675. JUL 3, 1981 (UK) CBS A1406
by Bob Dylan Prod: Chuck Plotkin and Bob Dylan
A: Heart Of Mine–Bob Dylan–*3:32*
  Ringo: Drums
B: (let it be me)

676. JUL 6, 1981 (US) Geffen 0408
by John Lennon Prod: John Lennon, Yoko Ono and Jack
Douglas
A: (JUST LIKE) STARTING OVER–Lennon–*3:55*
A: WOMAN–Lennon–*3:32*

ENTRY 677 & 678. Audio Fidelity Records took over the British packaging of the Star Club tapes in 1981 and came up with a simple, sensible release strategy: three individual budget discs with ten tracks each (on the company's Phoenix label) and one deluxe two-record set with all thirty tracks. For quick reference, the thirty tracks (with lead vocalists) are listed below:

Ask Me Why (Lead Vocal: John)
Be-Bop-A-Lula (Lead Vocal: Horst Obber)
Besame Mucho (Lead Vocal: Paul)
Everybody's Trying To Be My Baby (Lead Vocal: George)
Falling In Love Again (Can't Help It) (Lead Vocal: Paul)
Hallelujah, I Love Her So (Lead Vocal: Horst Obber)
Hippy Hippy Shake (Lead Vocal: Paul)
I Remember You (Lead Vocal: Paul)
I Saw Her Standing There (Lead Vocal: Paul)
I'm Gonna Sit Right Down And Cry (Over You) (Lead Vocal: John)
I'm Talking About You (Lead Vocal: John)
Kansas City/Hey Hey Hey Hey (Lead Vocal: Paul)
Lend Me Your Comb (Lead Vocal: John and Paul)
Little Queenie (Lead Vocal: Paul)
Long Tall Sally (Lead Vocal: Paul)
Matchbox (Lead Vocal: Ringo)
Mr. Moonlight (Lead Vocal: John)
Nothin' Shakin' (But The Leaves On The Trees) (Lead Vocal: George)
Red Sails In The Sunset (Lead Vocal: Paul)
Reminiscing (Lead Vocal: Paul)
Roll Over Beethoven (Lead Vocal: George)
Sheila (Lead Vocal: George)
Shimmy Shake (Lead Vocal: Paul and John)
Sweet Little Sixteen (Lead Vocal: John)
A Taste Of Honey (Lead Vocal: Paul)
Till There Was You (Lead Vocal: Paul)
To Know Her Is To Love Her (Lead Vocal: George with John and Paul)
Twist And Shout (Lead Vocal: John)
Where Have You Been All My Life? (Lead Vocal: John)
Your Feet's Too Big (Lead Vocal: Paul)

Two of the budget sets came first. In contrast to all previous packagings of the Star Club tapes, these albums not only featured photos of the group on the front, the shots were from 1963, not the Hamburg days. The back cover liner notes, though, correctly identified the music as raw, live recordings from the Beatles' concert days in Germany. The third budget disc came out in early 1983. (Entry 694).

Note: One song previously reported to be on the Star Club tapes never turned up: *My Girl Is Red Hot* (Lead Vocal: John). Presumably it could not be salvaged.

ENTRY 679. The British release came in a picture sleeve.

677. JUL 17, 1981 (UK) Phoenix PHX 1004 (LP)
by The Beatles; recorded live by Ted Taylor in 1962
EARLY YEARS (1)
side one
I SAW HER STANDING THERE–*2:22*
ROLL OVER BEETHOVEN–Chuck Berry–*2:15*
HIPPY HIPPY SHAKE–Chan Romero–*1:42*
SWEET LITTLE SIXTEEN–Chuck Berry–*2:45*
LEND ME YOUR COMB–Kay Twomey/Fred Wise/Ben
Weisman–*1:44*
side two
TWIST AND SHOUT–Bert Russell/Phil Medley–*2:03*
MR. MOONLIGHT–Roy Lee Johnson–*2:06*
A TASTE OF HONEY–Ric Marlow/Bobby Scott–*1:45*
BESAME MUCHO–Consuelo Velazquez/Selig Shaftel–
2:36
REMINISCING–King Curtis–*1:41*

678. JUL 17, 1981 (UK) Phoenix PHX 1005 (LP)
by The Beatles; recorded live by Ted Taylor in 1962
EARLY YEARS (2)
side one
NOTHIN' SHAKIN' (BUT THE LEAVES ON THE TREES)
–Cirino Colacrai/Eddie Fontaine/Dianne Lampert/Jack
Cleveland–*1:15*
TO KNOW HER IS TO LOVE HER–Phil Spector–*3:02*
LITTLE QUEENIE–Chuck Berry–*3:51*
FALLING IN LOVE AGAIN (CAN'T HELP IT)–Sammy
Lerner/Frederick Hollander–*1:57*
ASK ME WHY–*2:26*
side two
RED SAILS IN THE SUNSET–Jimmy Kennedy/Will
Grosz–*2:00*
EVERYBODY'S TRYING TO BE MY BABY–Carl
Perkins–*2:25*
MATCHBOX–Carl Perkins–*2:35*
I'M TALKING ABOUT YOU–Chuck Berry–*1:48*
SHIMMY SHAKE–Joe South/Billy Land–*2:17*

679. JUL 20, 1981 (US) Dark Horse DRC 49785
JUL 31, 1981 (UK) Dark Horse K 17837
by George Harrison   Prod: George Harrison and Ray
Cooper
A: TEARDROPS–Harrison–*3:20*
B: SAVE THE WORLD–Harrison–*4:56*

Early Years (1)   Phoenix PHX 1004 (LP)

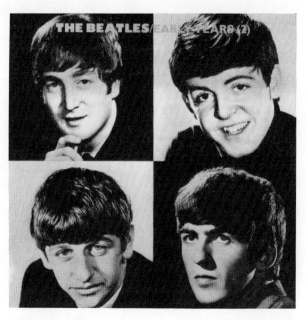

Early Years (2)   Phoenix PHX 1005 (LP)

Teardrops

Dark Horse K 17837 (45)

ENTRY 680. The album version of *Heart Of Mine* ran one minute longer than the track on both the British and American singles (Entries 675 & 683).

ENTRY 681. With this two-record set, all thirty of the Star Club tracks were gathered onto one package for the first time. This also marked the first U.K. appearance of the four tracks not previously issued in Britain.

In contrast to the two albums from Audio Fidelity issued the previous month, (Entries 677 & 678), the front cover to this set was plain white with only a few nondescript markings: the album title, five names (John Lennon, Paul McCartney, George Harrison, Ringo Starr, and Stuart Sutcliffe), and the word "Beatles" embossed in five-inch-high white-on-white lettering. The back cover featured a list of song titles, the Chris White liner notes (continued inside) that first appeared on the original 1977 package, and a late 1963 Dezo Hoffmann collarless jackets group shot (used on the back cover to the American **Meet The Beatles** album).

There were also a few errors. One song identification was completely wrong: *Can't Help It/Blue Angel* was really *Reminiscing*. (The Beatles' cover version of a song from the film *The Blue Angel* appeared on side three: *Falling In Love Again (Can't Help It)*.) Two titles were slightly mangled: *Nothin' Shakin' (But The Leaves On The Trees)* and *I'm Talking About You*. And, as with *every* previous Star Club packaging, Chuck Berry's *I'm Talking About You* was mistakenly identified as a similarly-titled Ray Charles song. As usual, all song title and author credit errors have been corrected for our listings.

A more serious error was the placement of Stuart Sutcliffe's name on the front cover. Though nowhere on the package did it say he played on the tracks, the implication was certainly there. In fact, though, Sutcliffe had left the Beatles in 1961 to live in Germany and had died in April 1962, right before the group's first appearance at the Star Club.

Then there was the matter of the recording date. According to the liner notes, the performance recorded took place at the club in April 1962, when Pete Best was still the official drummer for the group but Ringo Starr happened to be "sitting in" as a replacement. Though that did happen occasionally back then, it was not the case for these recordings. Ringo was on drums as a full-fledged member of the group because, in fact, the tapes were recorded in late 1962 — probably in December, during the group's last concert series at the Star Club. For a complete explanation of the confusion surrounding the recording date, see our article in the November 1977 issue of *Stereo Review*, "The Case of the Belittled Beatles Tapes" (reprinted in *The Beatles Again*).

Despite these minor mistakes, **Historic Sessions** emerged as probably the best packaging yet of the Star Club tapes, providing interested fans the opportunity to acquire all thirty songs with one purchase.

Note: The following summer, all the Star Club tracks were issued once again — this time as a series of special collector's singles by Collectable Records, an established U.S. label specializing in oldies. There were fifteen discs (all thirty songs), each with a different picture cover. They were also sold together in a plastic bag with a bonus poster featuring photos of all the picture sleeves.

(continued)

680.   AUG 10, 1981 (US) Columbia TC 37496 (LP)
AUG 21, 1981 (UK) CBS 85178 (LP)
by Bob Dylan   Prod: Chuck Plotkin and Bob Dylan
SHOT OF LOVE
side one
cut two: *Heart Of Mine*—Bob Dylan—*4:32*
Ringo: Drums

681.   AUG 14, 1981 (UK) Audiofidelity Enterprises AFE LD
1018 (2 LPs)
by The Beatles; recorded live by Ted Taylor in 1962
HISTORIC SESSIONS
side one
INTRODUCTION OF THE BAND—*0:21*
I'M GONNA SIT RIGHT DOWN AND CRY (OVER YOU)
—Joe Thomas/Howard Biggs—*2:43*
I SAW HER STANDING THERE—*2:22*
ROLL OVER BEETHOVEN—Chuck Berry—*2:15*
HIPPY HIPPY SHAKE—Chan Romero—*1:42*
SWEET LITTLE SIXTEEN—Chuck Berry—*2:45*
LEND ME YOUR COMB—Kay Twomey/Fred Wise/Ben
Weisman—*1:44*
YOUR FEET'S TOO BIG—Ada Benson/Fred Fisher—*2:18*
side two
TWIST AND SHOUT—Bert Russell/Phil Medley—*2:03*
MR. MOONLIGHT—Roy Lee Johnson—*2:06*
A TASTE OF HONEY—Ric Marlow/Bobby Scott—*1:45*
BESAME MUCHO—Consuelo Velazquez/Selig Shaftel—*2:36*
REMINISCING—King Curtis—*1:41*
MEDLEY—*2:09*
KANSAS CITY—Jerry Leiber/Mike Stoller—*1:04*
HEY-HEY-HEY-HEY—Richard Penniman—*1:05*
WHERE HAVE YOU BEEN ALL MY LIFE?—Barry Mann/
Cynthia Weil—*1:55*
side three
'TILL THERE WAS YOU—Meredith Willson—*1:59*
*NOTHIN' SHAKIN' (BUT THE LEAVES ON THE
TREES)*—Cirino Colacrai/Eddie Fontaine/Dianne
Lampert/Jack Cleveland—*1:15*
TO KNOW HER IS TO LOVE HER—Phil Spector—*3:02*
LITTLE QUEENIE—Chuck Berry—*3:51*
FALLING IN LOVE AGAIN (CAN'T HELP IT)—Sammy
Lerner/Frederick Hollander—*1:57*
ASK ME WHY—*2:26*
BE-BOP-A-LULA—Gene Vincent/Tex Davis—*2:29*
HALLELUJAH, I LOVE HER SO—Ray Charles—*2:10*

(Entry 681 continued)
For easy reference, all fifteen singles are listed below. The title and author credits generally followed the information from **Historic Sessions**, including such mistakes as identifying *Reminiscing* as *Can't Help It/Blue Angel*. See Entries 707a--707o (pages 192--193) for the specific track details on each disc.

COL 1501.   *A:* *I'm Gonna Sit Right Down And Cry (Over You)*
                B: *Roll Over Beethoven*

COL 1502.   *A:* *Hippy Hippy Shake*
                B: *Sweet Little Sixteen*

COL 1503.   *A:* *Lend Me Your Comb*
                B: *Your Feet's Too Big*

COL 1504.   *A:* *Where Have You Been All My Life?*
                B: *Mr. Moonlight*

COL 1505.   *A:* *A Taste Of Honey*
                B: *Besame Mucho*

COL 1506.   *A:* *Till There Was You*
                B: *Everybody's Trying To Be My Baby*

COL 1507.   *A:* *Nothin' Shakin' (But The Leaves On The Trees)*
                B: *Kansas City/Hey Hey Hey Hey*

COL 1508.   *A:* *To Know Her Is To Love Her*
                B: *Little Queenie*

COL 1509.   *A:* *Falling In Love Again (Can't Help It)*
                B: *Sheila*

COL 1510.   *A:* *Be-Bop-A-Lula*
                B: *Hallelujah, I Love Her So*

COL 1511.   *A:* *Red Sails In The Sunset*
                B: *Matchbox*

COL 1512.   *A:* *I'm Talking About You*
                B: *Shimmy Shake*

COL 1513.   *A:* *Long Tall Sally*
                B: *I Remember You*

COL 1514.   *A:* *Ask Me Why*
                B: *Twist And Shout*

COL 1515.   *A:* *I Saw Her Standing There*
                B: *Reminiscing*

These singles allowed the flexibility of acquiring any number of specific songs without buying an entire album. This packaging also made it possible to completely avoid the two tracks that did not feature lead vocals by one of the Beatles because both songs (*Be-Bop-A-Lula* and *Hallelujah, I Love Her So*) were coupled onto the same disc (1510).

ENTRY 683. Ths single came in a picture sleeve.

SHEILA—Tommy Roe—*1:56*

RED SAILS IN THE SUNSET—Jimmy Kennedy/Will Grosz—*2:00*

EVERYBODY'S TRYING TO BE MY BABY—Carl Perkins—*2:25*

MATCHBOX—Carl Perkins—*2:35*

I'M TALKING ABOUT YOU—Chuck Berry—*1:48*

SHIMMY SHAKE—Joe South/Billy Land—*2:17*

LONG TALL SALLY—Enotris Johnson/Richard Penniman/Robert Blackwell—*1:45*

I REMEMBER YOU—Johnny Mercer/Victor Schertzinger—*1:54*

682. AUG 21, 1981 (UK) Pickwick SHM 3088 (LP)
      by Elton John   Prod: Gus Dudgeon
      THE ALBUM
      side two
      cut one: *LUCY IN THE SKY WITH DIAMONDS*—L/McC—*5:59*
      John: Guitars and Backing Vocal

683. SEP 14, 1981 (US) Columbia 18-02510
      by Bob Dylan   Prod: Chuck Plotkin and Bob Dylan
      A: HEART OF MINE—Bob Dylan—*3:30*
      Ringo: Drums
      B: (the groom's still waiting at the altar)

684. SEP 22, 1981 (US) Columbia Special Products CSP P-16196 (LP)
      by Elton John   Prod: Gus Dudgeon
      BEST OF ELTON JOHN: VOLUME 1
      side one
      cut three: *LUCY IN THE SKY WITH DIAMONDS*—L/McC—*5:59*
      John: Guitars and Backing Vocal

685. SEP 28, 1981 (US) Warner Brothers BSK 3614 (LP)
      by Cheech and Chong   Prod: Lou Adler
      GREATEST HIT
      side one
      cut four: *BASKETBALL JONES FEATURING TYRONE SHOELACES*—Richard "Cheech" Marin/Thomas Chong—*4:04*
      George: Guitar

ENTRY 686. The lead single to **Stop And Smell The Roses** came in a picture sleeve that featured the album's front and back cover illustrations. Though *Wrack My Brain* stalled at 38, it still became Ringo's first American top forty hit since *A Dose Of Rock'n'Roll* five years before. Appropriately, the song was a lament on the difficulties of coming up with a popular tune.

ENTRY 687. At the urging of Barbara Bach, Ringo "got out of bed" to cut his first album in two years. For this new project, he put aside **Bad Boy**'s use of anonymous session musicians and returned to the highly successful formula of featuring other rock superstars as writers and backing musicians. This time, though, there was no overall producer for the album. Instead, the five different sessions had five different producers (each of the guest song writers).

Paul McCartney started things off in early July 1980 at the Superbear studios in Nice, France. With Linda McCartney, Laurence Juber, and Howie Casey along, he produced four tracks, including two new McCartney compositions, a cover version of a C&W favorite, and a song written by Ringo for Barbara Bach, *Can't Fight Lightning*. For that last number (essentially a one-line chant), Ringo switched instruments with Paul (he played guitar, McCartney played drums) while Barbara Bach and her twelve-year-old daughter Francesca joined in the background percussion. *Can't Fight Lightning* was even the working title of the album for a while in early 1981, but the track was dropped completely from the final lineup later in the year. Of the remaining McCartney numbers, *Sure To Fall (In Love With You)* was probably the best, serving as a lush and loving remake of the 1956 Carl Perkins hit single (Sun 235), though *Private Property* got the nod as the followup single.

George Harrison also turned in some excellent production work with his catchy *Wrack My Brain* original and a lively new recording of the eighteen-year-old *You Belong To Me*, which both Jo Stafford (Columbia 39811) and Patti Page (Mercury 5899) had landed in the top ten back in 1952. One other Harrison track for Ringo later became the basis for a top ten hit, but in a different form as *All Those Years Ago* (Entry 671).

Rounding out the package was a pair of recordings from Ron Wood and Stephen Stills, and three tracks produced by Harry Nilsson. *Drumming Is My Madness* was average, while *Stop And Take The Time To Smell The Roses*, the new title tune, was a light-hearted talking and singing collaboration complete with the sound of breaking glass, a car engine, and a plug for the album at the end. Wrapping up side two was a new version of *Back Off Boogaloo*, which worked in excerpts from and allusions to past numbers by Ringo and the Beatles, including *It Don't Come Easy, With A Little Help From My Friends, Help, Lady Madonna, Good Day Sunshine*, and *Baby, You're A Rich Man*. This "Starr's-on-45" cut even began with the opening riff to *It Don't Come Easy* before sliding into the main *Back Off Boogaloo* theme.

Note: John Lennon was also scheduled to participate in these sessions early in 1981, producing Ringo's recording of a new Lennon tune, *Life Begins At Forty*. Ringo dropped that from consideration for the album after John's death. Though he had the words and the music, a new recording must have seemed inappropriate.

160

686. OCT 26, 1981 (US) Boardwalk NB7-11-130
NOV 13, 1981 (UK) RCA 166
    by Ringo Starr   Prod: George Harrison (A side); Harry
    Nilsson (B side)
A: Wrack My Brain—Harrison—*2:20*
B: Drumming Is My Madness—Harry Nilsson—*3:30*

687. OCT 26, 1981 (US) Boardwalk NBI 33246 (LP)
NOV 20, 1981 (UK) RCA LP 6022 (LP)
    by Ringo Starr
STOP AND SMELL THE ROSES   Prod: Paul McCartney
    except † George Harrison; % Harry Nilsson; $ Ron Wood
    and Ringo Starr; + Stephen Stills
side one
    Private Property—McCartney—*2:44*
    †Wrack My Brain—Harrison—*2:20*
    %Drumming Is My Madness—Harry Nilsson—*3:30*
    Attention—McCartney—*3:18*
    %Stop And Take The Time To Smell The Roses—Starkey/
    Harry Nilsson—*3:13*
side two
    $Dead Giveaway—Starkey/Ron Wood—*3:24*
    †You Belong To Me—Pee Wee King/Redd Stewart/Chilton
    Price—*2:11*
    Sure To Fall (In Love With You)—Carl Perkins/Quinton
    Claunch/William Cantrell—*3:41*
    +You've Got A Nice Way—Stephen Stills/Michael Stergis—
    3:34
    %Back Off Boogaloo (version two)—Starkey—*3:16*

688. NOV 2, 1981 (UK) Music For Pleasure MFP 50541 (LP)
    by Various Artists
SAVILE'S TIME TRAVELS (20 GOLDEN HITS OF 1963)
side one
    cut one: *SHE LOVES YOU*—*2:18*
    by The Beatles   Prod: George Martin
    cut three: *DO YOU WANT TO KNOW A SECRET*—
    L/McC—*1:59*
    by Billy J. Kramer with The Dakotas   Prod: George
    Martin
    cut eight: *HELLO LITTLE GIRL*—L/McC—*1:50*
    by The Fourmost   Prod: George Martin

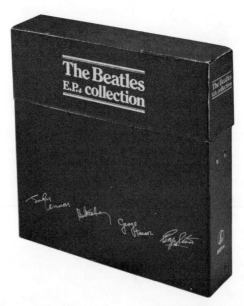

The Beatles EP Collection   Parlophone BEP 14 (EPs)

The Beatles (frontside)   Parlophone SGE 1 (EP)

SGE 1

THE BEATLES

A

THE INNER LIGHT____

Originally this was issued as the 'B' side of the single 'Lady Madonna' in 1968. However, this is the first time the track has been released in stereo.

BABY YOU'RE A RICH MAN___

Released in mono in 1967 as the 'B' side of 'All you need is Love', this stereo version has only appeared on the UK cassette of 'Magical Mystery Tour' and on the German issue of the 'Magical Mystery Tour' album.

B

SHE'S A WOMAN____

This stereo track was originally issued in mono as the 'B' side of 'I feel fine' in 1964. It is only available in stereo on an Australian album and was recently included in the box set compilation 'The Beatles Box' issued by World Records.

THIS BOY____

Never before issued in stereo in the UK although it has appeared on releases in both Canada and Australia. It was originally the 'B' side of 'I want to hold your hand' released in 1963.

The Beatles (backside)   **Parlophone SGE 1 (EP)**

ENTRY 689. For the debut album by British stage star Elaine Paige, co-producer Tim Rice added words to one of Paul McCartney's instrumentals from the 1970 **McCartney** album. Though not a true "collaboration" between the two writers in the strict sense of the word, this was still somewhat "in the family" because McCartney and Rice had been friends going back to the 1960s. (Rice even produced several Scaffold tracks.) More importantly, they continued to work together on various projects into the 1980s, though usually not on vinyl. For instance, in October 1981, Tim Rice's publishing company, Pavilion Books, put out the British version of the book *Paul McCartney, Composer And Artist*.

Appropriately, Elaine Paige had developed her London stage reputation in the title role of the Tim Rice and Andrew Lloyd Webber hit, *Evita*. She later went on to star in Webber's T.S. Eliot musical, *Cats*.

Note: Actually, another artist beat Elaine Paige with a record of *Hot As Sun*, using the published Tim Rice lyrics. Noosha Fox released the tune as a single July 25, 1981, on Earlobe Records ELB-S-105, backed with *The Cheapest Nights*. However, this recording did not have any direct connection with Tim Rice (Peter Wingfield produced the disc), so Elaine Paige still had the first "official" release.

ENTRY 690. Though the Wings B-side to this Denny Laine single was taken from the 1980 **Japanese Tears** album, the A-side was meant to be the preview track to a new album, **Anyone Can Fly**. In contrast to the previous album, all of the songs were freshly recorded following Laine's departure from Wings earlier in 1981, so there was no involvement by Paul McCartney on *Who Moved The World?* or any of the other new songs. However, the **Anyone Can Fly** album did not follow the single as scheduled. In 1982, Laine put the entire project on the shelf. (See page 306.)

Note: Though an obvious title for a post-Wings solo release, *Anyone Can Fly* was actually the name of a book Denny Laine had been reading back in 1979 at the **Back To The Egg** sessions at Lympne castle. He was learning how to be a pilot.

ENTRY 691 & 692. In contrast to the previous John Lennon release earlier in the year (Entry 676), these two new offerings in the Warner Bros. "double A" singles series did not have hits on both sides. The George Harrison disc coupled *All Those Years Ago* with the unsuccessful follow-up, which had not even hit *Billboard*'s Hot 100. Nonetheless, *Teardrops* did provide a more attractive flip side than the less commercial *Writing's On The Wall*. Apparently that same reasoning was used for the John Lennon single, replacing *I'm Your Angel*, the original Yoko Ono B-side to *Watching The Wheels*, with *Beautiful Boy (Darling Boy)*, a Lennon cut from **Double Fantasy** that had not even been issued as a single before this release.

164

689.   NOV 2, 1981 (UK) WEA K 58385 (LP)
       by Elaine Paige
       ELAINE PAIGE   Prod: Tim Rice and Andrew Powell
       side two
       cut three: *Hot As Sun*—McCartney/words by Tim Rice—
       3:15

690.   NOV 9, 1981 (UK) Rock City RC 7001
       by Denny Laine with Paul McCartney and Wings
       B: WEEP FOR LOVE—Denny Laine—*4:31*
       A: (who moved the world?)

691.   NOV 9, 1981 (US) Dark Horse 0410
       by George Harrison   Prod: George Harrison and Ray
           Cooper
       A: ALL THOSE YEARS AGO—Harrison—*3:43*
       A: TEARDROPS—Harrison—*3:20*

692.   NOV 9, 1981 (US) Geffen 0415
       by John Lennon   Prod: John Lennon, Yoko Ono and
           Jack Douglas
       A: WATCHING THE WHEELS—Lennon—*3:30*
       A: BEAUTIFUL BOY (DARLING BOY)—Lennon—*4:01*

693.   DEC 7, 1981 (UK) Parlophone BEP 14 (15 EPs)
       by The Beatles
       THE BEATLES EP COLLECTION
       A Boxed Set Of 13 Original British EP Packages Plus
           One New Bonus Disc
       TWIST AND SHOUT   Parlophone GEP 8882
       THE BEATLES' HITS   Parlophone GEP 8880
       THE BEATLES (NO. 1)   Parlophone GEP 8883
       ALL MY LOVING   Parlophone GEP 8891
       LONG TALL SALLY   Parlophone GEP 8913
       EXTRACTS FROM THE FILM A HARD DAY'S NIGHT
           Parlophone GEP 8920
       EXTRACTS FROM THE ALBUM A HARD DAY'S NIGHT
           Parlophone GEP 8924
       BEATLES FOR SALE   Parlophone GEP 8931
       BEATLES FOR SALE (NO. 2)   Parlophone GEP 8938
       THE BEATLES' MILLION SELLERS   Parlophone GEP 8946
       YESTERDAY   Parlophone GEP 8948
       NOWHERE MAN   Parlophone GEP 8952
       MAGICAL MYSTERY TOUR   Parlophone SMMT 1/2
           (2 EPs)
       THE BEATLES (see **693a**)

ENTRY 693. A companion package to the 1978 Beatles album collection, gathering all the British EP releases into a similar boxed set. In fact, the box for the EPs was exactly the same color and design as the box for the albums, only five inches smaller.

Like **The Beatles Collection, The Beatles EP Collection** even contained a bonus disc. Unlike **Rarities** in the album collection, though, **The Beatles** bonus EP was not issued separately. Fortunately for most record buyers, this was no great loss. By 1981, such rarities as *Sie Liebt Dich* and the first version of *Across The Universe* had already become quite accessible through the **Rarities** albums, so the new EP was left with such "desirable" items as "true" stereo recordings of *This Boy, She's A Woman*, and *Baby, You're A Rich Man*. This was in ironic contrast to the rest of the set because all the other EPs had been originally issued only in mono (with the exception of **Magical Mystery Tour**, which had been released in both mono and stereo).

Though at one time a few Beatles tracks had been available in the U.K. only on an EP (such as the four songs on **Long Tall Sally**), this was no longer true. The many compilation albums since the mid 1960s (especially **Rarities**) had eliminated any need for the EPs except as odd curiosities. As such, though, they still functioned quite well, serving as nicely packaged British equivalents to the American practice of squeezing extra singles from each Beatles album.

For each of the fifty-eight EP tracks listed below, the first British album that contained the song appears in parentheses. (* indicates a compilation album)

Act Naturally **(Help)**
All My Loving **(With The Beatles)**
And I Love Her **(A Hard Day's Night)**
Anna (Go To Him) **(Please Please Me)**
Anytime At All **(A Hard Day's Night)**
Ask Me Why **(With The Beatles)**
Baby, You're A Rich Man **(Magical Mystery Tour)**
Baby's In Black **(Beatles For Sale)**
Blue Jay Way **(Magical Mystery Tour)**
Can't Buy Me Love **(A Hard Day's Night)**
Chains **(Please Please Me)**
Do You Want To Know A Secret **(Please Please Me)**
Drive My Car **(Rubber Soul)**
Eight Days A Week **(Beatles For Sale)**
Flying **(Magical Mystery Tour)**
The Fool On The Hill **(Magical Mystery Tour)**
*From Me To You **(A Collection Of Beatles Oldies)**
I Am The Walrus **(Magical Mystery Tour)**
(continued)

693a **THE BEATLES** Prod: George Martin
Bonus Disc: Parlophone SGE 1
side one
THE INNER LIGHT—Harrison—*2:36*
BABY, YOU'RE A RICH MAN—*3:07*
side two
SHE'S A WOMAN—*2:57*
THIS BOY—*2:11*
Besides the bonus disc, **THE BEATLES EP COLLECTION**
contains the thirteen British EP releases in their original
sleeves with their contents unchanged:
TWIST AND SHOUT Prod: George Martin
First issued July 12, 1963
side one
Twist And Shout—Bert Russell/Phil Medley—*2:32*
A Taste Of Honey—Ric Marlow/Bobby Scott—*2:02*
side two
Do You Want To Know A Secret—*1:55*
There's A Place—*1:44*
THE BEATLES' HITS Prod: George Martin
First issued September 6, 1963
side one
From Me To You—*1:49*
Thank You Girl—*2:01*
side two
Please Please Me—*2:00*
Love Me Do—*2:19*
THE BEATLES (NO. 1) Prod: George Martin
First issued November 1, 1963
side one
I Saw Her Standing There—*2:50*
Misery—*1:43*
side two
Anna (Go To Him)—Arthur Alexander—*2:56*
Chains—Gerry Goffin/Carole King—*2:21*
ALL MY LOVING Prod: George Martin
First issued February 7, 1964
side one
All My Loving—*2:04*
Ask Me Why—*2:24*
side two
Money (That's What I Want)—Berry Gordy/Janie Bradford—*2:47*
P.S. I Love You—*2:02*

(Entry 693 continued)
    *I Call Your Name (Rock'n'Roll Music)
    I Don't Want To Spoil The Party (Beatles For Sale)
    *I Feel Fine (A Collection Of Beatles Oldies)
    I Saw Her Standing There (Please Please Me)
    I Should Have Known Better (A Hard Day's Night)
    *I Want To Hold Your Hand (A Collection of Beatles Oldies)
    If I Fell (A Hard Day's Night)
    I'll Cry Instead (A Hard Day's Night)
    I'll Follow The Sun (Beatles For Sale)
    I'm A Loser (Beatles For Sale)
    *The Inner Light (Rarities)
    It's Only Love (Help)
    *Long Tall Sally (Rock'n'Roll Music)
    Love Me Do (Please Please Me)
    Magical Mystery Tour (Magical Mystery Tour)
    *Matchbox (Rock'n'Roll Music)
    Michelle (Rubber Soul)
    Misery (Please Please Me)
    Money (That's What I Want) (With The Beatles)
    No Reply (Beatles For Sale)
    Nowhere Man (Rubber Soul)
    P.S. I Love You (Please Please Me)
    Please Please Me (Please Please Me)
    Rock And Roll Music (Beatles For Sale)
    *She Loves You (A Collection Of Beatles Oldies)
    *She's A Woman (Rarities)
    *Slow Down (Rock'n'Roll Music)
    A Taste Of Honey (Please Please Me)
    Tell Me Why (A Hard Day's Night)
    *Thank You Girl (Rarities)
    There's A Place (Please Please Me)
    Things We Said Today (A Hard Day's Night)
    *This Boy (Love Songs)
    Twist And Shout (Please Please Me)
    When I Get Home (A Hard Day's Night)
    Words Of Love (Beatles For Sale)
    Yesterday (Help)
    You Like Me Too Much (Help)
    You Won't See Me (Rubber Soul)
    Your Mother Should Know (Magical Mystery Tour)
(continued)

LONG TALL SALLY   Prod: George Martin
First issued June 19, 1964
side one
Long Tall Sally—Enotris Johnson/Richard Penniman/Robert
   Blackwell—*1:58*
I Call Your Name—*2:02*
side two
Slow Down—Larry Williams—*2:54*
Matchbox—Carl Perkins—*1:37*

EXTRACTS FROM THE FILM A HARD DAY'S NIGHT   Prod:
George Martin
First issued November 4, 1964
side one
I Should Have Known Better—*2:42*
If I Fell—*2:16*
side two
Tell Me Why—*2:04*
And I Love Her—*2:27*

EXTRACTS FROM THE ALBUM A HARD DAY'S NIGHT   Prod:
George Martin
First issued November 6, 1964
side one
Anytime At All—*2:10*
I'll Cry Instead—*1:44*
side two
Things We Said Today—*2:35*
When I Get Home—*2:14*

BEATLES FOR SALE   Prod: George Martin
First issued April 6, 1965
side one
No Reply—*2:15*
I'm A Loser—*2:31*
side two
Rock And Roll Music—Chuck Berry—*2:02*
Eight Days A Week—*2:43*

BEATLES FOR SALE (NO. 2)   Prod: George Martin
First issued June 4, 1965
side one
I'll Follow The Sun—*1:46*
Baby's In Black—*2:02*
side two
Words Of Love—Buddy Holly—*2:10*
I Don't Want To Spoil The Party—*2:33*

(Entry 693 continued)

The number of EP tracks taken from each British album breaks down as follows:

Please Please Me (11 of the 14 tracks)
With The Beatles (3 of the 14 tracks)
A Hard Day's Night (9 of the 13 tracks)
Beatles For Sale (8 of the 14 tracks)
Help (4 of the 14 tracks)
Rubber Soul (4 of the 14 tracks)
*A Collection Of Beatles Oldies (4 of the 16 tracks)
Magical Mystery Tour (7 of the 11 tracks)
*Rock'n'Roll Music (4 of the 28 tracks)
*Love Songs (1 of the 25 tracks)
*Rarities (3 of the 17 tracks)

All five tracks on **Rock'n'Roll Music** and **Love Songs** also appeared on **Rarities**. Of course, the twelve songs on the four compilation albums (*indicated above) actually appeared in Britain first as a single or EP track, then as an album cut.

Perhaps the most delightfully humorous aspect of the EPs was the hard sell used on the backcovers. After all, these were glorified singles touting the albums. The best liner notes of this type appeared on the 1963 **Beatles' Hits**, in which publicist Tony Barrow urged record buyers to take the EP and preserve it for ten years. Then, in 1973, " . . . exhume it from your collection . . . and write me a very nasty letter if the pop people of the 70's aren't talking with respect about at least two of these titles as 'early examples of modern beat standards taken from The Lennon & McCartney Songbook!' "

In that same write-up, Barrow categorically stated that " . . . Lennon & McCartney have written enough songs to keep them in singles and albums from now until 1973 . . . . " No wonder some fans had the impression that there were dozens of finished tracks locked away in the EMI vaults. Clearly, Barrow was exaggerating just a wee bit.

The later EPs did not have such touts. In fact, they did not have any liner notes at all. And from **Revolver** on, there was no longer any need for such EP rereleases of album material. The final EP package, **Magical Mystery Tour**, consisted entirely of brand new songs.

THE BEATLES' MILLION SELLERS Prod: George Martin
First issued December 6, 1965
side one
She Loves You—2:18
I Want To Hold Your Hand—2:24
side two
Can't Buy Me Love—2:15
I Feel Fine—2:20
YESTERDAY Prod: George Martin
First issued March 4, 1966
side one
Yesterday—2:04
Act Naturally—Johnny Russell/Vonie Morrison—2:27
side two
You Like Me Too Much—Harrison—2:34
It's Only Love—1:53
NOWHERE MAN Prod: George Martin
First issued July 8, 1966
side one
Nowhere Man—2:40
Drive My Car—2:25
side two
Michelle—2:42
You Won't See Me—3:19
MAGICAL MYSTERY TOUR Prod: George Martin
First issued December 8, 1967
side one
Magical Mystery Tour—2:48
Your Mother Should Know—2:33
side two
I Am The Walrus—4:35
side three
The Fool On The Hill—3:00
Flying—Lennon/McCartney/Harrison/Starkey—2:16
side four
Blue Jay Way—Harrison—3:50

January 30.   On the BBC's *Desert Island Discs*, Paul names the eight records he'd want on a desert island, including a song written by his dad, *Walking In The Park With Eloise* (which Paul recorded as the Country Hams) and John Lennon's *Beautiful Boy*.

February 24.   **Double Fantasy** wins the Grammy Award as album of the year. Yoko Ono and Sean appear to accept the award.

March 7.   The BBC marks the twentieth anniversary of the first British radio appearance of the Beatles with a two-hour special, "The Beatles At The Beeb," which airs in the U.S. in May.

April 20.   Formal dedication of the Strawberry Fields section of New York's Central Park.

July 15.   The *Take It Away* promotional film (directed by John McKenzie) premieres in Britain on *Top Of The Pops*.

October.   *The Compleat Beatles* video documentary is released, following last minute royalty arrangements with Apple.

October.   Mobile Fidelity Sound Lab issues an audiophile boxed set of thirteen British Beatles albums. List price: $325.

It Was Twenty Years Ago b/w From Me To You   Parlophone RP 5015 B (picture disc 45)

1982

Twenty Years On

In March 1982, Paul McCartney released his first new single since 1980, a simple ode to racial harmony called *Ebony And Ivory*. Paul had come up with the basic idea for the song a few years back, initially inspired by a TV talk show appearance by comic Spike Milligan (of *The Goon Show*), who made a simple keyboard analogy during the discussion: white keys produce certain notes, black keys produce other notes, and when combined they sound great together. So, too, with people . . . . McCartney liked the concept and began building a composition around it.

When the time came to consider recording the song, Paul decided that it would be particularly appropriate to carry over the "black and white together" theme by doing the track as a duet with a black performer. His first choice for the role was Stevie Wonder, who enthusiastically agreed to do it. They recorded the tune in February 1981 during McCartney's sessions in Montserrat at George Martin's AIR studios.

Upon release in 1982, the single became an immediate across-the-board hit. The song not only topped the pop singles charts in both Britain and America, it was also popular on both middle-of-the-road and black stations. *Ebony And Ivory* ended up the fourth biggest hit of the year in the U.S. and the ninth for the year in the U.K. The single also served as the perfect lead-in to McCartney's first new album project with George Martin since the Beatles days, **Tug Of War**.

Paul and George Martin had begun work on these sessions in late 1980. Early on, they decided that the album would not be a new Wings record, but rather a McCartney solo project. However, it would also be different from **McCartney II**. Instead of making it a totally solo effort (with Paul playing everything), they set up the sessions to showcase talented guest musicians, "casting" each song with whatever performers seemed best suited to the individual tunes.

Because McCartney had formed Wings so soon after splitting from the Beatles (primarily to have a functioning touring band), he

173

had never followed this almost inevitable route for a solo performer. In contrast, John, George, and Ringo had generally relied on guest musicians from the very beginning. For Paul, though, the idea was a fresh new personal treat with its own built-in excitement, such as having Stevie Wonder as his collaborator. It also meant the end of Wings as a functioning band. Though Denny Laine came along to Montserrat (as a guest musician), Steve Holly and Laurence Juber did not. For the foreseeable future, then, Paul McCartney's recordings would have to be regarded as true solo efforts.

Tug Of War was a critical, artistic, and sales success on both sides of the Atlantic. McCartney was particularly effective in promoting the album with key radio, television, and print interviews, and with excellent films for three tracks: *Ebony And Ivory, Take It Away*, and *Tug Of War*.

There was even material left over from the sessions. In fact, Martin and McCartney had initially wanted the package to be a two-record set, but they were discouraged from doing that because, at the time, overall record sales were in a slump throughout the music industry and the prospects for an expensive double album were quite uncertain. So they trimmed the set to one disc, saving the other tracks for possible inclusion on the next album.

At the same time work began on that follow-up disc, Paul was also involved in other projects. These included production of an animated film short featuring the character of Rupert Bear, an original full-length theatrical film (*Give My Regards To Broad Street*) written by, scored by, and starring Paul, and a guest vocal appearance with Michael Jackson on *The Girl Is Mine*, which was released in October as the lead single to Jackson's **Thriller**.

Ringo Starr had a role in *Give My Regards To Broad Street* and also appeared in two other McCartney films: the promotional footage for *Take It Away* (a track from **Tug Of War** that Ringo played on) and *The Cooler*, an eleven-minute short built around the three McCartney produced songs on Ringo's **Stop And Smell The Roses**. In May, *The Cooler* was entered in the short subject category at the Cannes film festival, but did not win. During that summer, it did have a brief theatrical run in Britain as it was quietly paired with *Grease 2*.

By then, Ringo was already working on his next solo album, with Joe Walsh as producer. The record (called **Old Wave**) was finished by August, but then Ringo once again ran into a release problem. Boardwalk was on the verge of fading, so the two parted ways and once again Ringo had to go shopping for a label. He did not find one in time for Christmas, so release of the new album was delayed into 1983.

George Harrison managed to get his latest package, **Gone Troppo**, issued in time for Christmas, but the album was quickly lost in the usual flood of new holiday product. Unfortunately, George chose not to do any tie-in interviews or personal appearances, and there were no promotional films. As a result, it was difficult to push the disc and the album became Harrison's least successful solo release on the U.S. charts since **Electronic Sound** in 1969. The lead single of *Wake Up My Love* could not crack the top fifty and the album did not even make it into the top 100.

In addition to those discs, there was also a bonanza of re-packaged material available for Christmas giving.

The John Lennon Collection offered six of the seven Lennon tracks from **Double Fantasy** in combination with songs from his EMI solo recordings. This was issued by EMI in Britain and by Geffen in the U.S., thus serving as the final package in that contract. Yoko Ono shifted to Polydor Records worldwide in October, taking along the rights to any future Lennon tracks, such as material done for **Milk And Honey**, the follow-up to **Double Fantasy**. Her first Poly-dor release, though, was a brand new solo album, **It's Alright**, which cracked the U.S. top 100. **The John Lennon Collection** hit the top forty in the U.S. and did even better in Britain, staying at number one throughout the Christmas holidays.

Part of this success was no doubt a reflection of renewed interest in the group resulting from EMI's promotion of the twentieth anni-versary of the release of *Love Me Do*. Stickers, posters, and ads appeared throughout Britain, reminding people that "It was twenty years ago" and asking "Did You know that John Lennon, Paul McCartney, George Harrison, and Ringo Starr used to be in a group called the Beatles?"

Love Me Do was officially rereleased (though it had never been out of print), packaged in a new picture sleeve and with a copy of its original red label. As the group's first single for EMI back in 1962, *Love Me Do* had reached only number seventeen on the charts. This time it scooted to number four. A new album compilation of Beatles tracks, **20 Greatest Hits**, hit the top ten as well. There was also a picture disc single of *Love Me Do*, a twelve-inch version, and even a boxed set of all twenty-six British single releases, in brand new picture sleeves. All of these sold well.

Twenty years on, the Beatles were obviously still a viable com-mercial act.

ENTRY 694. The ten-track companion to the previous two volumes in Audio Fidelity's British budget release of the Star Club tapes (Entries 677 & 678). This album completed the thirty-track lineup, including the four songs previously issued for the first time in Britain on **Historic Sessions** (Entry 681). Also taken from that album: a cut-down of the Chris White liner notes and the Dezo Hoffmann 1963 group shot (tinted for the front cover).

With the Star Club tracks out in England both as a series of three budget releases and as a regularly priced two-record set, there was no question about the availability of the material. However, there was another matter: Were the cuts *worth* having? For the average record buyer expecting the polish of studio releases from the Beatles or the "mixing board" quality of live recordings from the 1970s and 1980s, the answer was obvious: No.

For those willing to accept the low-grade sound, the tracks were of interest for a number of reasons. Eleven songs were live versions of familiar EMI studio tracks, offering the opportunity for direct comparison on: *Ask Me Why, Everybody's Trying To Be My Baby, I Saw Her Standing There, Kansas City/Hey Hey Hey Hey, Long Tall Sally, Matchbox, Mr. Moonlight, Roll Over Beethoven, A Taste Of Honey, Till There Was You,* and *Twist And Shout.* Two other songs (*Besame Mucho* and *To Know Her Is To Love Her*) were released on the 1982 Audio Fidelity packaging of the group's 1962 audition tapes (Entry 713), once again offering the chance to compare live and studio versions.

Fifteen songs from the Star Club recordings were unavailable on any other regular commercial record release. However, seven of these were also performed by the group for the BBC. Four of them (*Hippy Hippy Shake, Lend Me Your Comb, Nothin' Shakin',* and *Sweet Little Sixteen*) aired on "The Beatles at the Beeb" radio special (page 386), two (*I'm Gonna Sit Right Down And Cry* and *I'm Talking About You*) appeared on a low-quality bootleg record (page 385), and one (*Sheila*) has not yet surfaced.

Eight songs have not turned up through any other source: *Falling In Love Again, I Remember You, Little Queenie, Red Sails In The Sunset, Reminiscing, Shimmy Shake, Where Have You Been All My Life,* and *Your Feet's Too Big.* The two cuts that featured Star Club waiter Horst Obber on lead vocals (*Be-Bop-A-Lula* and *Hallelujah, I Love Her So*) can be safely ignored by almost everybody.

ENTRY 696. Colin Miles, supervisor of the EMI "NUT" compilation series back in the late 1970s, took the same idea to his own independent label, distributed by Charly Records. For the first batch of releases, he reissued a number of albums cut out by EMI, adding a new Fourmost collection. The biggest disappointment about the new Fourmost album was that it did not contain *Rosetta* and *Just Like Before,* both sides of a McCartney-produced single from 1969.

Note: See page 262 for a See For Miles checklist.

694.   JAN 22, 1982 (UK) Phoenix PHX 1011 (LP)
by The Beatles recorded live by Ted Taylor in 1962
RARE BEATLES
side one
BE-BOP-A-LULA–Gene Vincent/Tex Davis–*2:29*
LONG TALL SALLY–Enotris Johnson/Richard Penniman/Robert Blackwell*–1:45*
YOUR FEET'S TOO BIG–Ada Benson/Fred Fisher–*2:18*
I'M GONNA SIT RIGHT DOWN AND CRY (OVER YOU)
–Joe Thomas/Howard Biggs–*2:43*
WHERE HAVE YOU BEEN ALL MY LIFE?–Barry Mann/Cynthia Weil–*1:55*
side two
SHEILA–Tommy Roe–*1:56*
HALLELUJAH, I LOVE HER SO–Ray Charles–*2:10*
'TILL THERE WAS YOU–Meredith Willson–*1:59*
MEDLEY–*2:09*
    KANSAS CITY–Jerry Leiber/Mike Stoller–*1:04*
    HEY-HEY-HEY-HEY–Richard Penniman–*1:05*
I REMEMBER YOU–Johnny Mercer/Victor Schertzinger–*1:54*

695.   FEB 1, 1982 (US) Boardwalk NB7-11-134
by Ringo Starr   Prod: Paul McCartney (A side); Harry Nilsson (B side)
A: PRIVATE PROPERTY–McCartney–*2:44*
B: STOP AND TAKE THE TIME TO SMELL THE ROSES–Starkey/Harry Nilsson–*3:13*

696.   FEB 26, 1982 (UK) See For Miles/Charly CM 104 (LP)
by The Fourmost   Prod: George Martin
FIRST AND FOURMOST
side one
    cut one: *HELLO LITTLE GIRL*–L/McC–*1:50*
    cut two: *I'M IN LOVE*–L/McC–*2:07*

697.   MAR 1, 1982 (UK) Mercury 6359 098 (LP)
AUG 9, 1982 (US) Mercury SRM-1-4054 (LP)
by Gary Brooker
LEAD ME TO THE WATER   Prod: Gary Brooker
side one
    cut one: *Mineral Man*–Gary Brooker–*3:20*
    George: Guitar

Rare Beatles   Phoenix PHX 1011 (LP)

20 ORIGINAL TRACKS

JAMES BOND THEME   KINGSTON CALYPSO   UNDER THE MANGO TREE   FROM RUSSIA WITH LOVE   GOLDFINGER   007   THUNDERBALL   YOU ONLY LIVE TWICE
ON HER MAJESTY'S SECRET SERVICE   WE HAVE ALL THE TIME IN THE WORLD   DIAMONDS ARE FOREVER   LIVE AND LET DIE   JUST A CLOSER WALK WITH THEE
BOND MEETS SOLITAIRE   THE MAN WITH THE GOLDEN GUN   NOBODY DOES IT BETTER   BOND '77   MOONRAKER   FOR YOUR EYES ONLY

James Bond Greatest Hits   Liberty   EMTV 007   (LP)

ENTRY 698. This special twenty track collection from EMI's Liberty label gathered the title songs and some incidental music to a dozen James Bond films, including Paul McCartney's recording of *Live And Let Die*. As indicated by the catalog number prefix (EMTV), this package was targeted for a special tie-in advertising campaign on British television (budget: £200,000). See Entry 759 for the U.S. version of this package.

Note: The original 1973 single of *Live And Let Die* indicated only George Martin as producer. McCartney's 1978 greatest hits album (Entry 608) listed both Martin and McCartney as producers. The 1973 soundtrack album and this new compilation avoided the issue altogether and simply offered no production credit for that specific track. Of course, even with Martin's name as the only one listed, it is always safe to assume that, on his own records, Paul McCartney had significant input leading to the finished product.

ENTRY 699. *The Beatles' Movie Medley* was not so much a single as a glorified commercial trailer for the new **Reel Music** compilation. In a sense, though, it was the perfect solution to the problem of promoting an album that contained fourteen familiar songs, twelve of which had *already* appeared on singles in America (*You've Got To Hide Your Love Away* and *Magical Mystery Tour* were the lone exceptions). Instead of going with any particular track, which might have been treated as a familiar oldie rather than as a new release, Capitol used a medley that showcased half the contents of the album. The lure of this "new" Beatles recording apparently did the trick, because the medley hit number twelve on *Billboard*'s charts.

EMI did not issue the single in England until two months after its American release. Even though this followed a rush of imported copies from the U.S., the new British package also did well, cracking the top ten. Both countries offered the single in a picture sleeve (reproducing the cover to **Reel Music**) and with the custom label from the album (a film reel).

Note: The B-side to *The Beatles' Movie Medley* was originally scheduled to be another edited track, *Fab Four On Film*. This had been done by United Artists back in 1964 as an "open-ended" promotional interview for local DJs, giving them the chance to "ask" the Beatles about *A Hard Day's Night*. Capitol's Randall Davis edited the comments together into one long track running 6:30. The disc (Capitol B-5100) got as far as promotional copies to radio stations, in both seven-inch and twelve-inch (Capitol SPRO 9758) form. Then, at the last minute, the B-side was changed to another song from *A Hard Day's Night, I'm Happy Just To Dance With You* (previously the B-side to *If I Fell* and *not* on **Reel Music**). This was the coupling that went out to the general public.

ENTRY 700. **Reel Music** offered four songs from **A Hard Day's Night**, three each from **Help** and **Let It Be**, and two each from **Magical Mystery Tour** and **Yellow Submarine**. *The Beatles' Movie Medley* was not included, presumably because it would have been superfluous alongside the full length versions of the songs. There was also a twelve-page, full-color "souvenir program," displaying stills, promotional posters, and lobby cards from each film.

Note: Capitol pressed some gold vinyl copies for radio station giveaways.

698. MAR 8, 1982 (UK) Liberty EMTV 007 (LP)
by Various Artists
JAMES BOND GREATEST HITS
side two
cut two: *LIVE AND LET DIE*—McCartney—*3:10*
by Paul McCartney and Wings   Prod: George Martin and
Paul McCartney

699. MAR 15, 1982 (US) Capitol B 5107
MAY 24, 1982 (UK) Parlophone R 6055
by The Beatles   Prod: George Martin except † George
Martin (January 1969) and Phil Spector (March 1970)
**A: The Beatles' Movie Medley*—*3:56*
MAGICAL MYSTERY TOUR—*0:31*
ALL YOU NEED IS LOVE—*0:34*
YOU'VE GOT TO HIDE YOUR LOVE AWAY—*0:35*
I SHOULD HAVE KNOWN BETTER—*0:47*
A HARD DAY'S NIGHT—*0:22*
TICKET TO RIDE—*0:31*
†GET BACK (version two)—*0:36*
B: I'M HAPPY JUST TO DANCE WITH YOU—*1:59*

700. MAR 22, 1982 (US) Capitol SV 12199 (LP)
MAR 29, 1982 (UK) Parlophone PCS 7218 (LP)
by The Beatles
REEL MUSIC   Prod: George Martin except † George
Martin (January 1969) and Phil Spector (March 1970)
side one
A HARD DAY'S NIGHT—*2:28*
I SHOULD HAVE KNOWN BETTER—*2:42*
CAN'T BUY ME LOVE—*2:15*
AND I LOVE HER—*2:27*
HELP!—*2:16*
YOU'VE GOT TO HIDE YOUR LOVE AWAY—*2:08*
TICKET TO RIDE—*3:03*
MAGICAL MYSTERY TOUR—*2:48*
side two
I AM THE WALRUS—*4:35*
YELLOW SUBMARINE—*2:40*
ALL YOU NEED IS LOVE—*3:46*
†LET IT BE (version two)—*4:01*
†GET BACK (version two)—*3:09*
†THE LONG AND WINDING ROAD—*3:40*

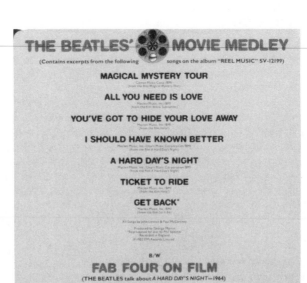

Fab Four On Film   Capitol B-5100 (45)
b/w The Beatles' Movie Medley

I'm Happy Just To Dance With You   Capitol B 5107 (45)
b/w The Beatles' Movie Medley

Reel Music   **Capitol SV 12199 (LP)**

ENTRY 701 & 703. Paul McCartney and Stevie Wonder recorded *Ebony And Ivory* together at George Martin's Air Studios on the island of Montserrat on February 27, 1981, as part of the **Tug Of War** sessions.

Upon release, *Ebony And Ivory* served as the perfect lead single for the **Tug Of War** album, not only topping the pop charts but also giving McCartney his first placement on *Billboard*'s Soul charts (where *Ebony And Ivory* cracked the top ten). Black-oriented stations simply treated the disc as a new Stevie Wonder release that happened to be with Paul McCartney.

Stevie Wonder was not on the B-side, which contained a folk-ish acoustic number by Paul and Denny Laine. In addition, the twelve-inch pressing of the single included a solo McCartney recording of *Ebony And Ivory* without Stevie Wonder. Neither track was on the **Tug Of War** album (Entry 704).

Note: To tout the forthcoming **Tug Of War** album, Columbia sent radio stations a promotional twelve-inch disc: **McCartney — A Sample From "Tug Of War" April, 1982** (Columbia AS 1444). This contained *Ebony And Ivory* on one side and *Ballroom Dancing* and *The Pound Is Sinking* on the other. See page 427 for further details. Later, at Christmastime, *Ebony And Ivory* and the follow-up *Take It Away* single also turned up on Columbia's year-end promotional two-record set, **Columbia's 24 For 82** (Columbia A2S 1588). *Take It Away* was on side one (cut three) and *Ebony And Ivory* on side two (cut six).

ENTRY 702. This package on Audio Fidelity's Phoenix label contained four of the recordings done by the Beatles in Germany backing singer Tony Sheridan. It came out alongside **The Beatles — Circa 1960 — In The Beginning**, Polydor's album with all eight of the songs from those 1961 sessions, plus four filler tracks that the Beatles did not play on (*Let's Dance, What'd I Say, Ruby Baby,* and *Ya Ya*), credited to the Beat Brothers. However, the reissuing of that record in the fall of 1981 had eliminated the gatefold sleeve of the original while raising the list price to $8.98.

The **First Movement** disc listed for only $3.98, yet even as a budget release there were problems with the new package. The liner notes were misleading and inaccurate, not only garbling a few points in Beatles history but also incorrectly identifying the Beatles as the backing group on the four Beat Brothers songs. Some copies of the album also carried the sticker: "Attention Collectors — Unreleased Tracks." Considering the number of times these songs had been issued and reissued since the mid-1960s, that claim was hilarious. Actually, the stickers were left over from Audio Fidelity's release of the Star Club tracks in 1981, though strictly speaking the tout was not correct for those packages either. Perhaps the more accurate line proved too unwieldy: "Attention Collectors! Once Again Available! Previously released recordings that were out of print and hard to find for a while. Now you can buy them again!"

Note: Less than four months later, the same tracks used on **First Movement** appeared on another reissue package, **The Savage Young Beatles** (Entry 709). In August 1983, the list price of the Polydor package was lowered to $5.98. That is still the best one to buy. (See Entry 247.)

184

701. MAR 26, 1982 (UK) Parlophone R 6054
MAR 29, 1982 (US) Columbia 18-02860
  by Paul McCartney †with Stevie Wonder   Prod: George Martin
†*A: Ebony And Ivory*—McCartney—*3:41*
**B: Rainclouds*—McCartney/Denny Laine—*3:07*

702. MAR 29, 1982 (UK) Phoenix PHX 339 (LP)
  by Tony Sheridan and The Beatles, and † The Beatles
  Prod: Bert Kaempfert (Additional cuts by % Tony
  Sheridan and The Beat Brothers)
FIRST MOVEMENT
side one
  †*CRY FOR A SHADOW*—Lennon/Harrison—*2:22*
  %*(let's dance)*
  IF YOU LOVE ME, BABY—Charles Singleton/Waldenese
  Hall—*2:52*
  %*(what'd i say)*
side two
  SWEET GEORGIA BROWN—Ben Bernie/Maceo Pinkard/
  Kenneth Casey—*2:03*
  %*(ruby baby)*
  %*(ya ya)*
  WHY—Tony Sheridan/Bill Crompton—*2:55*

703. APR 2, 1982 (UK) Parlophone 12R 6054 (12 inch)
APR 12, 1982 (US) Columbia 44 02878 (12 inch)
  by Paul McCartney †with Stevie Wonder   Prod: George Martin
side one
  †*Ebony And Ivory*—McCartney—*3:41*
side two
  *Rainclouds—McCartney/Denny Laine—*3:07*
  **Ebony And Ivory (solo version)*—McCartney—*3:41*

Ebony And Ivory   **Parlophone 12 R 6054 (12-inch)**

Tug Of War   Columbia TC 37462 (LP)

ENTRY 704. After initial rehearsals at Pugin's Hall in the quiet Kent village of Tenterden in late 1980, recording for **Tug Of War** began in February 1981 at George Martin's Air Studios in the Caribbean, and continued in London through the rest of the year. The basic tracks for more than half the album were done that first month at Montserrat, with Dave Mattacks, Steve Gadd, Stanley Clarke, Ringo, Carl Perkins, and Stevie Wonder stopping by to play.

Ringo's appearance on *Take It Away* marked the first time that a fellow former Beatle turned up on a McCartney solo disc. Appropriately, the song had been initially conceived for Ringo before Paul decided that it better suited his own voice.

Stanley Clarke performed on two tunes, a quiet ballad (*Somebody Who Cares*) and a schizoid ode to love and financial affairs (*The Pound Is Sinking*), which actually sounded like a combination of two different song fragments, ala *Uncle Albert/Admiral Halsey*.

Carl Perkins had been a Beatles favorite from the early days, so his visit provided an opportunity to share memories and songs. Paul wrote *Get It* the night before Perkins arrived. He, in turn, wrote *My Old Friend* (not used on **Tug Of War**) as a thank-you to Paul. They also shared humorous stories. The laughter from Perkins at the end of *Get It* was his response to a quip — since edited out — from McCartney. (See page 461 for details.)

Stevie Wonder also came up with a song, after they had recorded *Ebony And Ivory*. *What's That You're Doing?* evolved out of a late night studio jam with him on synthesizer and McCartney on drums. The two worked out the riffs and then let go, with Wonder even tossing in a *She Loves You* tribute line at the end.

Back in London, Martin and McCartney polished the tracks and recorded other numbers. The sweeping title song featured military snares, full orchestration, and (to open) grunts and groans from the indoor tug-of-war national championships, recorded live at Huddersfield by engineer Eddie Klein. In the other direction, *Here Today*, McCartney's Lennon-inspired song, was a simple, sad vocal backed with a string quartet.

Rounding out the set were: a thirty-two-second experimental transition track (*Be What You See*); a ballad inspired by a peaceful night aboard the catamaran *Wanderlust* during the 1977 Virgin Island recording sessions for **London Town**; the Latin-style *Dress Me Up As A Robber*; and McCartney's one-cut **Quadrophenia**, *Ballroom Dancing*, a nostalgic return to the teen dances of his youth, plus *I'll Give You A Ring* (Entries 706 & 707).

There was even material left over from these sessions. Some of it was used on the follow-up **Pipes Of Peace** (Entry 754).

ENTRY 706 & 707. Both the seven-inch and twelve-inch singles featured a full color sleeve, a trimmed and tightened version of *Take It Away*, and a catchy new non-album B-side, *I'll Give You A Ring* (written back in the 1970s). *Dress Me Up As A Robber* was unchanged from **Tug Of War** on the twelve inch.

ENTRY 707a--707o (pages 192--193). See also pages 156--158.

704.   APR 26, 1982 (UK) Parlophone PCTC 259 (LP)
APR 26, 1982 (US) Columbia TC 37462
by Paul McCartney † with Stevie Wonder; % with Carl
Perkins
TUG OF WAR   Prod: George Martin
side one
Tug Of War—McCartney—*4:21*
Take It Away—McCartney—*4:13*
Somebody Who Cares—McCartney—*3:19*
†What's That You're Doing?—McCartney/Stevie Wonder—
6:21
Here Today—McCartney—*2:26*
side two
Ballroom Dancing—McCartney—*4:06*
The Pound Is Sinking—McCartney—*2:52*
Wanderlust—McCartney—*3:50*
%Get It—McCartney—*2:30*
Be What You See—McCartney—*0:32*
Dress Me Up As A Robber—McCartney—*2:40*
†Ebony And Ivory—McCartney—*3:41*

705.   JUN 7, 1982 (US) Capitol SVBB-12220 (2 LPs)
by The Beach Boys   Prod: The Beach Boys
SUNSHINE DREAM
side two
cut four: *VEGETABLES*—Brian Wilson/Van Dyke Parks—
2:05
Paul: Backing Vocal and Munching Sounds

706.   JUN 21, 1982 (UK) Parlophone R 6056
JUN 21, 1982 (US) Columbia 18-03018
by Paul McCartney   Prod: George Martin
A: TAKE IT AWAY—McCartney—*3:59*
*B: I'll Give You A Ring—McCartney—*3:05*

707.   JUL 5, 1982 (UK) Parlophone 12R 6056 (12 inch)
JUL 26, 1982 (US) Columbia 44-03019 (12 inch)
by Paul McCartney   Prod: George Martin
side one
TAKE IT AWAY—McCartney—*3:59*
side two
*I'll Give You A Ring—McCartney—*3:05*
DRESS ME UP AS A ROBBER—McCartney—*2:40*

Take It Away   **Parlophone 12R 6056 (12-inch)**

Tug Of War   Parlophone R 6057 (45)

707a. JUL 6, 1982 (US) Collectable Records COL 1501
by The Beatles; recorded live by Ted Taylor in 1962
A: *I'M GONNA SIT RIGHT DOWN AND CRY (OVER YOU)*—Joe Thomas/Howard Biggs—*2:43*
B: *ROLL OVER BEETHOVEN*—Chuck Berry—*2:15*

707b. JUL 6, 1982 (US) Collectable Records COL 1502
by The Beatles; recorded live by Ted Taylor in 1962
A: *HIPPY HIPPY SHAKE*—Chan Romero—*1:42*
B: *SWEET LITTLE SIXTEEN*—Chuck Berry—*2:45*

707c. JUL 6, 1982 (US) Collectable Records COL 1503
by The Beatles; recorded live by Ted Taylor in 1962
A: *LEND ME YOUR COMB*—Kay Twomey/Fred Wise/Ben Weisman—*1:44*
B: *YOUR FEET'S TOO BIG*—Ada Benson/Fred Fisher—*2:18*

707d. JUL 6, 1982 (US) Collectable Records COL 1504
by The Beatles; recorded live by Ted Taylor in 1962
A: *WHERE HAVE YOU BEEN ALL MY LIFE?*—Barry Mann/Cynthia Weil—*1:55*
B: *MR. MOONLIGHT*—Roy Lee Johnson—*2:06*

707e. JUL 6, 1982 (US) Collectable Records COL 1505
by The Beatles; recorded live by Ted Taylor in 1962
A: *A TASTE OF HONEY*—Ric Marlow/Bobby Scott—*1:45*
B: *BESAME MUCHO*—Consuelo Velazquez/Selig Shaftel—*2:36*

707f. JUL 6, 1982 (US) Collectable Records COL 1506
by The Beatles; recorded live by Ted Taylor in 1962
A: *TILL THERE WAS YOU*—Meredith Willson—*1:59*
B: *EVERYBODY'S TRYING TO BE MY BABY*—Carl Perkins—*2:25*

707g. JUL 6, 1982 (US) Collectable Records COL 1507
by The Beatles; recorded live by Ted Taylor in 1962
A: *NOTHIN' SHAKIN' (BUT THE LEAVES ON THE TREES)*—Cirino Colacrai/Eddie Fontaine/Dianne Lampert/Jack Cleveland—*1:15*
B: *MEDLEY*—*2:09*
KANSAS CITY—Jerry Leiber/Mike Stoller—*1:04*
HEY-HEY-HEY-HEY—Richard Penniman—*1:05*

707h. JUL 6, 1982 (US) Collectable Records COL 1508
by The Beatles; recorded live by Ted Taylor in 1962
A: TO KNOW HER IS TO LOVE HER—Phil Spector—*3:02*
B: LITTLE QUEENIE—Chuck Berry—*3:51*

707i. JUL 6, 1982 (US) Collectable Records COL 1509
by The Beatles; recorded live by Ted Taylor in 1962
A: FALLING IN LOVE AGAIN (CAN'T HELP IT)—Sammy
Lerner/Frederick Hollander—*1:57*
B: SHEILA—Tommy Roe—*1:56*

707j. JUL 6, 1982 (US) Collectable Records COL 1510
by The Beatles; recorded live by Ted Taylor in 1962
A: BE-BOP-A-LULA—Gene Vincent/Tex Davis—*2:29*
B: HALLELUJAH, I LOVE HER SO—Ray Charles—*2:10*

707k. JUL 6, 1982 (US) Collectable Records COL 1511
by The Beatles; recorded live by Ted Taylor in 1962
A: RED SAILS IN THE SUNSET—Jimmy Kennedy/Will
Grosz—*2:00*
B: MATCHBOX—Carl Perkins—*2:35*

707l. JUL 6, 1982 (US) Collectable Records COL 1512
by The Beatles; recorded live by Ted Taylor in 1962
A: I'M TALKING ABOUT YOU—Chuck Berry—*1:48*
B: SHIMMY SHAKE—Joe South/Billy Land—*2:17*

707m. JUL 6, 1982 (US) Collectable Records COL 1513
by The Beatles; recorded live by Ted Taylor in 1962
A: LONG TALL SALLY—Enotris Johnson/Richard
Penniman/Robert Blackwell—*1:45*
B: I REMEMBER YOU—Johnny Mercer/Victor Schertzinger
—*1:54*

707n. JUL 6, 1982 (US) Collectable Records COL 1514
by The Beatles; recorded live by Ted Taylor in 1962
A: ASK ME WHY—*2:26*
B: TWIST AND SHOUT—Bert Russell/Phil Medley—*2:03*

707o. JUL 6, 1982 (US) Collectable Records COL 1515
by The Beatles; recorded live by Ted Taylor in 1962
A: I SAW HER STANDING THERE—*2:22*
B: REMINISCING—King Curtis—*1:41*

ENTRY 708. Laurence Juber's collection of old standards (thus, the album's title) was mostly recorded in early 1980 during the long break in Wings activities following the aborted Japanese tour. However, *Maisie*, the only Juber original on the album and the only track to feature McCartney and other members of Wings, was done quite a bit earlier. The song had been recorded during the 1978 and 1979 **Back To The Egg** sessions, but did not make the album.

All the songs on **Standard Time** were published by MPL. For the complete track lineup, see page 310.

ENTRY 709. This ten-inch disc from Charly Records included four of the recordings done by the Beatles backing Tony Sheridan in 1961. Like the **First Movement** release earlier in the year (Entry 702), four songs that the Beatles did not play on rounded out the contents. Fortunately, **The Savage Young Beatles** did not mistakenly attribute these other songs to the Beatles. Nonetheless, the inclusion of the four filler tracks was disappointing because there had been only eight songs from the sessions ever issued at all.

The Beatles backing vocalist Tony Sheridan (*except the Beatles solo)
    Recorded May 1961 in Germany
Ain't She Sweet (John Lennon lead vocal)
Cry For A Shadow (Instrumental)
My Bonnie (Lies Over The Ocean) (see below)
Nobody's Child
Take Out Some Insurance On Me, Baby (also called: *If You Love Me, Baby*)
The Saints (When The Saints Go Marching In)
Sweet Georgia Brown (see below)
Why

The original issuing of the *My Bonnie* single in Germany (Polydor 24 673) included a thirty-five-second intro verse, sung in English on copies labeled "twist" and in German on copies labeled "rock." Subsequent reissues rarely included the English intro and never included the German intro. In addition, the original 1962 release of *Sweet Georgia Brown* on Polydor EP 21485 did not have the references to the Beatles' haircuts and popular following – those were added in a new Sheridan vocal used on all subsequent issuings of the track. Despite the many repackagings of the Tony Sheridan material with the Beatles, the only disc that contained all three of these rare versions was an authorized limited edition seven-inch EP issued by Polydor in Sweden in 1982 for a Beatles fan organization. See page 248.

Note: **The Savage Young Beatles** title was first used on an unauthorized collection in the mid-1960s.

ENTRY 713. This third single from **Tug Of War** trimmed the opening grunts and groans from the title track and coupled it with the Carl Perkins/Paul McCartney duet. The single failed to crack the top fifty in either the U.K. or the U.S. The British single came in a picture sleeve.

708. JUL 9, 1982 (US) Breaking Records BREAK 1 (LP)
by Laurence Juber
STANDARD TIME Prod: Laurence Juber and Richard Niles
side one
cut three: *Maisie*—Laurence Juber—*3:10*
Paul: Bass

709. JUL 30, 1982 (UK) Charly CFM 701 (10 inch)
by Tony Sheridan and The Beatles, and †The Beatles
Prod: Bert Kaempfert (Additional cuts by %Tony
Sheridan and The Beat Brothers)
THE SAVAGE YOUNG BEATLES
side one
WHY—Tony Sheridan/Bill Crompton—*2:55*
†*CRY FOR A SHADOW*—Lennon/Harrison—*2:22*
%*(let's dance)*
%*(ya ya)*
side two
%*(what'd i say)*
%*(ruby baby)*
TAKE OUT SOME INSURANCE ON ME, BABY—Charles
Singleton/Waldenese Hall—*2:52*
SWEET GEORGIA BROWN—Ben Bernie/Maceo Pinkard/
Kenneth Casey—*2:03*

710. AUG 6, 1982 (UK) RSO RSO 91
by Cream Prod: Felix Pappalardi
A: BADGE—Harrison/Eric Clapton—*2:45*
B: (tales of brave ulysses)

711. AUG 6, 1982 (UK) RSO RSOX 91 (12 inch)
by Cream Prod: Felix Pappalardi
side one
BADGE—Harrison/Eric Clapton—*2:45*
side two
(tales of brave ulysses)
(white room)

712. SEP 6, 1982 (UK) Parlophone R 6057
SEP 13, 1982 (US) Columbia 38-03235
by Paul McCartney † with Carl Perkins Prod: George
Martin
A: TUG OF WAR—McCartney—*4:00*
†*B: GET IT*—McCartney—*2:30*

ENTRY 713--715. Songs from the Beatles 1962 audition tapes had been available on various bootleg records since the late 1970s. For reasons outlined in the "All Sales Final" chapter, we have chosen to treat Audio Fidelity's release of this material as the first legimate commercial issuing. See pages 353--358. for a thorough discussion of the topic, including details of the packages put out by Backstage Records in 1982 and PAC Records in 1981, as well as some reasons *not* to treat the Audio Fidelity records as legitimate.

The three Audio Fidelity albums were an appropriate addition to the company's other Beatles packages: the Tony Sheridan recordings (Entry 702) and Star Club tapes (Entries 677, 678, 681, 694). These new records contained twelve cover versions of songs not written by the Beatles, including two tracks later recorded for the **With The Beatles** album, *Till There Was You* and *Money*. (See page 352 for detailed background information on the original recordings of all these songs.) The sets omitted three Lennon/McCartney originals that were not otherwise available from EMI: *Hello Little Girl, Like Dreamers Do,* and *Love Of The Loved.* These had been included on several bootleg packages.

All twelve songs appeared on the full price ($7.98 list) **Complete Silver Beatles** album (thus the title). There were also two seven-song budget albums ($3.98 list each) issued in America, with two tracks used on both volume one and volume two (*Three Cool Cats* and *Searchin'*). Even though the Beatles had long since dropped the "Silver" moniker at the time of these recordings, Audio Fidelity still used it in the titles, also adding a silvertone finish to all three album jackets.

In order to avoid sides that ran less than ten minutes each on the budget discs, Audio Fidelity extended the running time of seven songs. This was done by making copies of some sections of the recordings and editing these back into the same songs. As a result, a song such as *Searchin'* did not fade out after 2:54 — instead the main verse and chorus repeated once again, stretching the cut to 3:44. The following seven songs were altered that way:

> *Memphis, Tennessee* added 27 seconds
> *Money (That's What I Want)* added 38 seconds
> *Searchin'* added 50 seconds
> *September In The Rain* added 28 seconds
> *Sure To Fall (In Love With You)* added 52 seconds
> *Take Good Care Of My Baby* added 34 seconds
> *Three Cool Cats* added 22 seconds

Though collector-purists objected to such editing, the company justified it by pointing out that the budget sets were aimed at casual record buyers who would be far more upset by a six-minute side than by a Beatles song that had been "tampered with." Besides, on **The Complete Silver Beatles** the recordings ran unaltered.

Compared to the company's previous packages of the Star Club tapes and the Tony Sheridan recordings, there were remarkably few errors. The only major mistake was incorrectly printing John Lennon as the lead vocalist on two songs sung by Paul McCartney (*Searchin'* and *Sure To Fall*).

The liner notes for all three volumes were written by Wally Podrazik.

713.   SEP 10, 1982 (UK) Audiofidelity AFELP 1047 (LP)
       SEP 27, 1982 (US) Audio Rarities AR 2452 (LP)
       by The Beatles
       THE COMPLETE SILVER BEATLES   Prod: Mike Smith
       side one
       Three Cool Cats—Jerry Leiber/Mike Stoller—*2:16*
       Crying, Waiting, Hoping—Buddy Holly—*1:56*
       Besame Mucho—Consuelo Velazquez/Selig Shaftel—*2:32*
       Searchin'—Jerry Leiber/Mike Stoller—*2:54*
       The Sheik Of Araby—Harry B. Smith/Ted Snyder/Frances
         Wheeler—*1:35*
       Money (That's What I Want)—Berry Gordy/Janie Bradford
         —*2:18*
       side two
       To Know Her Is To Love Her—Phil Spector—*2:26*
       Take Good Care Of My Baby—Gerry Goffin/Carole King—
         2:16
       Memphis, Tennessee—Chuck Berry—*2:12*
       Sure To Fall (In Love With You)—Carl Perkins/William E.
         Cantrell/Quinton Claunch—*1:55*
       Till There Was You—Meredith Willson—*2:54*
       September In The Rain—Al Dubin/Harry Warren—*1:49*

714.   SEP 27, 1982 (US) Phoenix-10 PHX 352 (LP)
       by The Beatles
       THE SILVER BEATLES—VOL. 1   Prod: Mike Smith
       side one
       Three Cool Cats—Jerry Leiber/Mike Stoller—*2:38*
       Memphis, Tennessee—Chuck Berry—*2:39*
       Besame Mucho—Consuelo Velazquez/Selig Shaftel—*2:32*
       The Sheik Of Araby—Harry B. Smith/Ted Snyder/Frances
         Wheeler—*1:35*
       side two
       Till There Was You—Meredith Willson—*2:54*
       Searchin'—Jerry Leiber/Mike Stoller—*3:44*
       Sure To Fall (In Love With You)—Carl Perkins/William E.
         Cantrell/Quinton Claunch—*2:47*

The Silver Beatles — Vol. 1   Phoenix-10 PHX 352 (LP)

The Silver Beatles — Vol. 2   Phoenix-10 PHX 353 (LP)

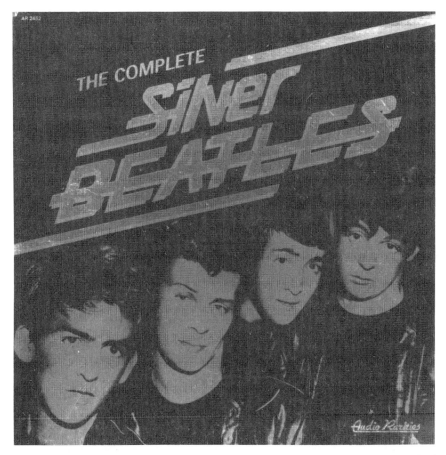

The Complete Silver Beatles   Audio Rarities AR 2452 (LP)

ENTRY 716 & 717. Initial plans for this greatest hits set in Britain called for a twenty-six track two-disc package. In that form, **The Beatles Greatest Hits** (Parlophone EMTVS 34) included the A-side to each of the twenty-two Beatles singles issued from 1962 to 1970, with both sides of four "double-A" releases. The lineup was as follows:

Side 1) *Love Me Do; Please Please Me; From Me To You; She Loves You; I Want To Hold Your Hand; Can't Buy Me Love; A Hard Day's Night.*

Side 2) *I Feel Fine; She's A Woman; Ticket To Ride; Help!; We Can Work It Out; Day Tripper; Paperback Writer.*

Side 3) *Yellow Submarine; Eleanor Rigby; Penny Lane; Strawberry Fields Forever; All You Need Is Love; Hello Goodbye; Lady Madonna.*

Side 4) *Hey Jude; Get Back; The Ballad Of John And Yoko; Something; Let It Be.*

At the last minute this idea was scrapped in favor of one record, **20 Greatest Hits**, containing only those songs that had hit number one in Britain (according to the charts compiled by *Record Retailer* magazine, later *Music Week*). This brought the British package in line with the twenty-track approach taken in other countries such as the United States. Besides, EMI was also releasing all the British singles in a new boxed set that fall (Entry 735), so the double album would have been too repetitious.

The exception to the "number one" rule in Britain was *Love Me Do*, which had reached only number seventeen in the U.K. back in 1962. That track was included to tie-in with the special rerelease of *Love Me Do* on October 4, twenty years after the original issue. However, both that single and the new album did not use the original version with Ringo on drums (see Entry 724).

Artwork for the **20 Greatest Hits** package was simple and did not even feature a group shot on the cover. There was a great deal of detailed information on the back, though, listing for each track the recording date, release date, and date the disc hit number one in Britain. Obviously EMI had done some house cleaning in the file room because, for the first time, the company offered specific recording dates for each song, even making a distinction between tracks done in one day and those done over a longer period but *begun* on a specific date (indicated by the line "recording commenced").

Love Me Do recorded September 11, 1962

From Me To You recorded March 4, 1963

She Loves You recording commenced July 1, 1963

I Want To Hold Your Hand recording commenced October 17, 1963

Can't Buy Me Love recording commenced February 25, 1964

A Hard Day's Night recording commenced April 16, 1964

I Feel Fine recording commenced October 18, 1964

Ticket To Ride recording commenced February 15, 1965

Help recording commenced April 13, 1965

Day Tripper recording commenced October 16, 1965

We Can Work It Out recording commenced October 20, 1965

(continued)

715.   SEP 27, 1982 (US) Phoenix-10 PHX 353 (LP)
        by The Beatles
        THE SILVER BEATLES–VOL. 2   Prod: Mike Smith
        side one
        Searchin'–Jerry Leiber/Mike Stoller–*3:44*
        Take Good Care Of My Baby–Gerry Goffin/Carole King–
        2:50
        Money (That's What I Want)–Berry Gordy/Janie Bradford
        –*2:56*
        side two
        To Know Her Is To Love Her–Phil Spector–*2:26*
        Three Cool Cats–Jerry Leiber/Mike Stoller–*2:38*
        September In The Rain–Al Dubin/Harry Warren–*2:17*
        Crying, Waiting, Hoping–Buddy Holly–*1:56*

716.   OCT 11, 1982 (UK) Parlophone PCTC 260 (LP)
        by The Beatles
        20 GREATEST HITS   Prod: George Martin
        side one
        LOVE ME DO–*2:19*
        FROM ME TO YOU–*1:49*
        SHE LOVES YOU–*2:18*
        I WANT TO HOLD YOUR HAND–*2:24*
        CAN'T BUY ME LOVE–*2:15*
        A HARD DAY'S NIGHT–*2:28*
        I FEEL FINE–*2:20*
        TICKET TO RIDE–*3:03*
        HELP!–*2:16*
        DAY TRIPPER–*2:37*
        WE CAN WORK IT OUT–*2:10*
        side two
        PAPERBACK WRITER–*2:25*
        YELLOW SUBMARINE–*2:40*
        ELEANOR RIGBY–*2:11*
        ALL YOU NEED IS LOVE–*3:57*
        HELLO GOODBYE–*3:24*
        LADY MADONNA–*2:17*
        HEY JUDE–*7:11*
        GET BACK–*3:11*
        THE BALLAD OF JOHN AND YOKO–*2:58*

(Entry 716 & 717 continued)

Paperback Writer recording commenced April 13, 1966
Yellow Submarine recording commenced May 26, 1966
Eleanor Rigby recording commenced April 20, 1966
All You Need Is Love recording commenced June 14, 1967
Hello Goodbye recording commenced October 2, 1967
Lady Madonna recording commenced February 3, 1968
Hey Jude recording commenced July 29, 1968
Get Back recording commenced January 23, 1969
The Ballad Of John And Yoko recorded on April 14, 1969

In America, the back cover notes did not make such distinctions and instead simply identified each recording session as taking place in one day.

The American version of **20 Greatest Hits** had the same basic packaging as the British album, but a slightly different lineup because it was based on *Billboard*'s charts for the U.S. This eliminated six British hits that had failed to top the U.S. charts (*From Me To You, Day Tripper, Yellow Submarine, Eleanor Rigby, Lady Madonna*, and *The Ballad Of John And Yoko*). In their place were six American hits that had not reached number one in Britain, with recording data listed as:

Eight Days A Week recorded October 6, 1964
Yesterday recorded February 16, 1965 (see Entry 735)
Penny Lane recorded December 29, 1966
Come Together recorded July 21, 1969
Let It Be recorded January 26, 1969; final mix March 1970 (see Entry 735)
The Long And Winding Road recorded January 26, 1969; final mix March 1970

Each of these should have read "recording commenced." In addition, the "final mix" date for *Let It Be* was incorrect because it referred to the **Let It Be** album track, not the single track included on the **20 Greatest Hits** album. And, in a garbled cross-Atlantic transcription, the recording date for *I Want To Hold Your Hand* was incorrectly listed as October 7, rather than October 17.

The differences between the lineups on the British and American collections wisely reflected the popularity of individual songs in particular markets. (The EMI branch in each major country had the option of tailoring the **20 Greatest Hits** album to serve its own needs.) Inexplicably, the most popular Beatles single ever in the U.S., *Hey Jude*, was shortened by two minutes on the American package, simply by fading out early. Of course, various U.S. radio stations had been doing that on their own for years, so this merely provided an "official" cut-down version.

ENTRY 719. Mike (McGear) McCartney did the liner notes for this compilation. One previously undisclosed Paul McCartney-Scaffold connection came to light in these: McCartney's lead guitar work on *Goose*, originally issued in the U.K. June 27, 1969, as the B-side to *Charity Bubbles* (Parlophone R 5784). The U.S. release was on Bell 821. According to Tim Rice (in the 1982 book *Abbey Road*), Paul also played on the A-side. See page 296 for a complete track listing for this album.

717.　OCT 11, 1982 (US) Capitol SV 12245 (LP)
by The Beatles
20 GREATEST HITS　Prod: George Martin except †George
Martin (January 1969) and Phil Spector (March 1970)
side one
SHE LOVES YOU–2:18
LOVE ME DO–2:19
I WANT TO HOLD YOUR HAND–2:24
CAN'T BUY ME LOVE–2:15
A HARD DAY'S NIGHT–2:28
I FEEL FINE–2:20
EIGHT DAYS A WEEK–2:43
TICKET TO RIDE–3:03
HELP!–2:16
YESTERDAY–2:04
WE CAN WORK IT OUT–2:10
PAPERBACK WRITER–2:25
side two
PENNY LANE–3:00
ALL YOU NEED IS LOVE–3:36
HELLO GOODBYE–3:24
HEY JUDE–5:05
GET BACK–3:11
COME TOGETHER–4:16
LET IT BE–3:50
†THE LONG AND WINDING ROAD–3:40

718.　OCT 18, 1982 (UK) See For Miles/Charly CM 111 (LP)
by Various Artists
20 ONE HIT WONDERS
side one
cut nine: *I'M THE URBAN SPACEMAN–*Neil Innes*–2:23*
by The Bonzo Dog Band　Prod: Paul McCartney

719.　OCT 18, 1982 (UK) See For Miles/Charly CM 114 (LP)
by Scaffold　Prod: Paul McCartney except †Norrie
Paramor and Tim Rice
THE SCAFFOLD SINGLES A'S AND B'S
side one
†cut seven: *CHARITY BUBBLES–*Mike McGear/Roger
McGough*–2:40*
cut eleven: *LIVERPOOL LOU–*Dominic Behan*–2:58*
side two
†cut six: *GOOSE–*Mike McGear/Roger McGough*–2:34*
cut nine: *TEN YEARS AFTER ON STRAWBERRY
JAM–*McCartney*–2:52*

20 Greatest Hits

Capitol SV 12245 (LP)

The Scaffold Singles A's And B's

See For Miles/Charly CM 114 (LP)

ENTRY 720 & 721. After working together on songs for McCartney's next album (see Entries 753 and 754), Michael Jackson and Paul teamed up on a track for Jackson's new **Thriller** album (Entry 734). Their duet on *The Girl Is Mine* reached the top ten in both the U.S. and U.K.

Both countries issued the disc in a picture sleeve. In addition, Epic in Britain put out a seven-inch picture disc (Epic EPC A11-2729) that November. Meanwhile, Epic in America issued the song on the label's series of bargain price one-sided singles, and also put out a special DJ-only edited version (running 3:32) that eliminated the rap between McCartney and Jackson at the end of the song. That DJ single had the same catalog number but a different mix number (ZSS 169202 versus ZSS 169138).

ENTRY 722. Though *Searchin'* was the obvious track to pull from **The Complete Silver Beatles** for single release, the disc failed to chart. The three-track single was issued in a picture sleeve with the cover photo used on the album.

ENTRY 723. There was a promotional twelve-inch version of this single released in the U.S. as Dark Horse PRO A-1075.

ENTRY 724. When EMI rereleased *Love Me Do* on October 4, the company did not use the original single track with Ringo on drums, but rather the version featuring Andy White on drums and Ringo on tambourine. That second recording was the one first included on the 1963 **Please Please Me** album and then on all subsequent releases of the song in both the U.K. and the U.S. Late in 1963, it even replaced the original version on new pressings of the British single. As a result, the first version of *Love Me Do* became a collector's item, eventually turning up on the 1980 **Rarities** package released in the U.S. Back then, however, Capitol had been forced to make a dub from a commercial single because the original EMI master tape could not be located.

Two years later the tape still had not been found. Nonetheless, following the initial press coverage of the *Love Me Do* rerelease, and subsequent interest in the original version, the company dug up a clean dub of its own (from Beatles fan Mark Cousins) and included the track on a special follow-up twelve-inch disc. Like the seven-inch rerelease the previous month, this new record came in a gold-tinted picture sleeve with a red Parlophone label similar to the one in use back in 1962.

Note: *Love Me Do* was also reissued in the same picture sleeve in the U.S., though there was no twelve-inch version. In addition, the song turned up on the promotional **Capitol In-Store Sampler** album (SPRO 9867/9868) issued at the time (side one, cut eight).

ENTRY 725. For its release as a tie-in single with the new **John Lennon Collection,** *Love* was remixed to boost the quiet piano passages at the beginning and end of the track. This recording just missed cracking the British top forty, stopping at 41. The B-side was not included on the new compilation album.

The single came in a picture sleeve.

720.   OCT 25, 1982 (US) Epic 34-03288
OCT 29, 1982 (UK) Epic EPC A2729
  by Michael Jackson with Paul McCartney   Prod: Quincy
    Jones
A: The Girl Is Mine—Michael Jackson—*3:41*
    Paul: Lead Vocal Duet with Michael Jackson
B: (can't get outta the rain)

721.   OCT 25, 1982 (US) Epic ENR-03372 (1 side)
  by Michael Jackson with Paul McCartney   Prod: Quincy
    Jones
side one
The Girl Is Mine—Michael Jackson—*3:41*
    Paul: Lead Vocal Duet with Michael Jackson
side two
    There is no B-side track.

722.   OCT 29, 1982 (UK) Audiofidelity AFS 1
  by The Beatles   Prod: Mike Smith
side one
SEARCHIN'—Jerry Leiber/Mike Stoller—*2:54*
side two
MONEY (THAT'S WHAT I WANT)—Berry Gordy/Janie
    Bradford—*2:18*
TILL THERE WAS YOU—Meredith Willson—*2:54*

723.   OCT 29, 1982 (UK) Dark Horse 929864-7
NOV 1, 1982 (US) Dark Horse 7-29864
  by George Harrison   Prod: George Harrison, Ray Cooper,
    and Phil McDonald
A: Wake Up My Love—Harrison—*3:33*
B: Greece—Harrison—*3:57*

724.   NOV 1, 1982 (UK) Parlophone 12R 4949 (12 inch)
  by The Beatles   Prod: George Martin
side one
LOVE ME DO—*2:19*
P.S. I LOVE YOU—*2:02*
side two
LOVE ME DO (version one)—*2:22*

725.   NOV 1, 1982 (UK) Parlophone R 6059
  by John Lennon   Prod: John Lennon, Yoko Ono, and
    Phil Spector
A: LOVE—Lennon—*3:17*
B: GIVE ME SOME TRUTH—Lennon—*3:11*

Searchin'   Audiofidelity AFS 1 (45)

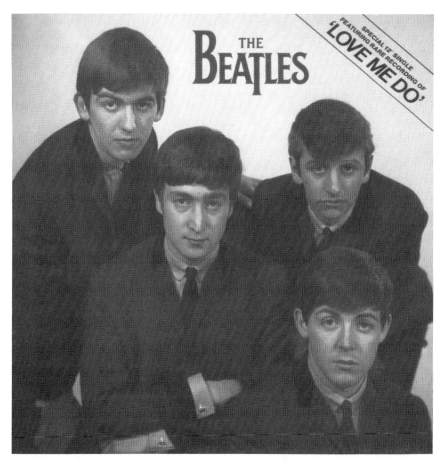

Love Me Do   Parlophone 12R 4949 (12-inch)

ENTRY 726. **The John Lennon Collection** was a seventeen-track compilation that gathered onto one tasteful package nearly all of Lennon's solo singles and a few select album cuts, including all but one of his **Double Fantasy** tracks. The package did very well in the British Christmas market, becoming the U.K.'s best selling album for the final quarter of 1982.

For EMI, the agreement with Geffen Records for use of the **Double Fantasy** material meant that all but one John Lennon release (*Cleanup Time*) was available on a Parlophone album. For Geffen in America, it meant additional mileage from the only Lennon songs the company had (see Entry 729). The result was a close to definitive John Lennon solo collection, going from the original *Give Peace A Chance* single (complete on an album for the first time) to **Double Fantasy**'s closing Lennon track, *Dear Yoko*.

Only three singles were missing from the collection, *Cold Turkey, Mother*, and *Woman Is The Nigger Of The World*. These were passed over in favor of the softer *Love* (newly released as a single) and *Jealous Guy* (which had been a hit as done by Roxy Music in early 1981 — see page 318.

Unlike the 1975 **Shaved Fish** collection, none of the songs were trimmed. As a result, **The John Lennon Collection** ran more than one hour. The front, back, and inner sleeve photos for the album were from the December 1980 Annie Leibovitz sessions. All the song lyrics were also included.

ENTRY 727. With the exception of *Dream Away* (done for the 1981 film *Time Bandits*), **Gone Troppo** was recorded in the spring and early summer of 1982 at George Harrison's elaborate home studios. The bright and gaudy cover and sleeve graphics — designed by former Bonzo Dog Band-er "Legs" Larry Smith — set the mood for the package as "troppo" (Australian slang for silly or "out to lunch" or gone mad).

The record itself opened with the upbeat single release, *Wake Up My Love* (featuring sharp synthesizer work reminiscent of *Teardrops*) and the sweet melody changes of *That's The Way It Goes*. Then the "troppo" mood took over with a Jimmy Buffett style ode to island living (*Gone Troppo*), a Mediterranean instrumental with a pun-filled vocal undertone at the end (*Greece*), and a novelty oldie (*I Really Love You*). For that last number, a remake of a 1961 hit single (Cub 9095) by the Stereos, Harrison even stepped into the role of backing singer, sharing the distinctive doo-wop vocals with Willie Greene, Bobby King, and Pico Pena.

Side two was strictly non-troppo, featuring four typically lush Harrison ballads and love songs, plus the album's ace-in-the-hole, *Dream Away* (running one verse longer than in the *Time Bandits* film). Had Harrison heeded the requests to release this closing credits tune when *Time Bandits* became an unexpected hit in 1981, he probably would have had an out-of-the-blue chart success to boost the new album. Instead, **Gone Troppo** failed to crack *Billboard*'s Hot 100, *Wake Up My Love* did not break the top fifty, and neither disc charted in Britain. Warner Bros. did not even release the follow-up American single (Entry 739) in Britain.

726. NOV 1, 1982 (UK) Parlophone EMTV 37 (LP)
by John Lennon
THE JOHN LENNON COLLECTION   Prod: John Lennon,
Yoko Ono and Jack Douglas except †John Lennon, Yoko
Ono and Phil Spector; %John Lennon; $Phil Spector;
+John Lennon and Yoko Ono
side one
+*GIVE PEACE A CHANCE*–L/McC–*4:49*
$*INSTANT KARMA! (WE ALL SHINE ON)*–Lennon–*3:18*
†*POWER TO THE PEOPLE*–Lennon–*3:15*
%*WHATEVER GETS YOU THRU THE NIGHT*–Lennon–
3:24
%*NO. 9 DREAM*–Lennon–*4:44*
%*MIND GAMES*–Lennon–*4:10*
†*LOVE*–Lennon–*3:17*
†*HAPPY XMAS (WAR IS OVER)*–Lennon/Yoko Ono–*3:25*
side two
†*IMAGINE*–Lennon–*2:59*
†*JEALOUS GUY*–Lennon–*4:10*
%*STAND BY ME*–Ben E. King/Jerry Leiber/Mike Stoller–
3:29
(JUST LIKE) STARTING OVER–Lennon–*3:55*
WOMAN–Lennon–*3:32*
I'M LOSING YOU–Lennon–*3:58*
BEAUTIFUL BOY (DARLING BOY)–Lennon–*4:01*
WATCHING THE WHEELS–Lennon–*3:30*
DEAR YOKO–Lennon–*2:33*

727. NOV 5, 1982 (UK) Dark Horse 923734-1 (LP)
NOV 8, 1982 (US) Dark Horse 1-23734 (LP)
by George Harrison
GONE TROPPO   Prod: George Harrison, Ray Cooper, and
Phil McDonald
side one
Wake Up My Love–Harrison–*3:33*
That's The Way It Goes–Harrison–*3:32*
I Really Love You–Leroy Swearingen–*2:53*
Greece–Harrison–*3:57*
Gone Troppo–Harrison–*4:27*
side two
Mystical One–Harrison–*3:43*
Unknown Delight–Harrison–*4:14*
Baby Don't Run Away–Harrison–*3:57*
Dream Away–Harrison–*4:27*
Circles–Harrison–*3:45*

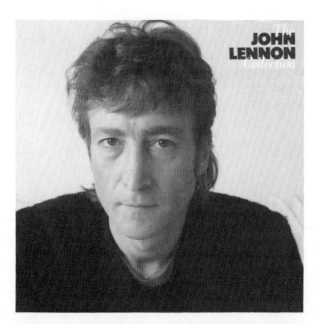

The John Lennon Collection   **Parlophone EMTV 37 (LP)**

Gone Troppo   **Dark Horse 1-23734 (LP)**

Love   Parlophone R 6059 (45)

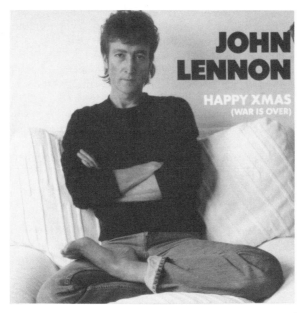

Happy Xmas (War Is Over)   Geffen 7-29855 (45)

ENTRY 729. As part of the deal with EMI for use of John Lennon's **Double Fantasy** tracks, Geffen Records got the American rights to **The John Lennon Collection**. This allowed the company to rerelease the only Lennon material it had, accompanied by songs that were still available in the U.S. on various Capitol albums.

Geffen made things a bit confusing for American record buyers, though. Instead of releasing the album with all seventeen tracks, the company dropped two: *Happy Xmas (War Is Over)* and *Stand By Me*. However, these songs were offered as a bonus on the cassette version of the album in order to encourage purchase of the cassette and to discourage home taping of the record. Perhaps this strategy swayed some record buyers. Others simply opted for an import copy of EMI's British package, completely ignoring either Geffen release.

The decision to issue *Happy Xmas* as a single (Entry 732) made things even more confusing. Though not on the new album, the song was packaged in a picture sleeve featuring the back cover photo to **The John Lennon Collection**. This set up a perfect promotional tie-in, then effectively undercut it. As a result, Capitol's **Shaved Fish** remained the only U.S. album with *Happy Xmas*.

In contrast to the chart-topping success of **The John Lennon Collection** in Britain, the American version did not even crack *Billboard*'s top thirty.

ENTRY 730. This best of collection was released by A&M Records following Billy Preston's shift to Motown. Though Preston's most famous single appearance was on another label and unavailable (backing the Beatles in 1969 on *Get Back*), his own solo recording of *Get Back* from the 1978 *Sgt. Pepper* film appeared instead. In addition, there was also a different recording of Preston's best known solo track for Apple, *That's The Way God Planned It*. Obviously, the legal complications surrounding Apple had still not been cleared up.

Note: The last time any non-Beatles Apple material turned up on a new compilation record was in late 1975 on the Sire **History Of British Rock, Vol. 3** (Entry 461), which included Badfinger's *Day After Day* and Mary Hopkin's *Those Were The Days*. After that, all the recordings by Apple's roster disappeared from the scene, with the original albums and singles hitting the cut-out bins in late 1976.

As a result, songs originally recorded for Apple had to be rerecorded for subsequent release on other labels. James Taylor did that with *Something In The Way She Moves* and *Carolina In My Mind* for his 1976 **James Taylor's Greatest Hits** (Warner Bros. 2979). Mary Hopkin rerecorded *Those Were The Days* and *Goodbye* for licensing and packaging by Key Seven Music in 1980 on **Those Were The Days** (Excelsior XMP-6014), **24 More Great Heartbreakers And Tear Jerkers** (Excelsior 2XMP-4406), and (*Goodbye* only) **Super Hits Of The 60's** (Exact Productions EX-202). An odd exception to this rerelease problem was John Tavener's **The Whale** which came out on Ring O' Records in 1978. Apparently it helped to have one of the original owners of Apple behind the effort.

214

728.　NOV 5, 1982　(UK)　Cambra CR 028　(2 LPs)
　　　by Various Artists with cuts by
　　　The Beatles;　recorded live by Ted Taylor in 1962
THE POP EXPLOSION
side two
　　cut five: *LONG TALL SALLY*—Enotris Johnson/Richard
　　Penniman/Robert Blackwell—*1:45*
side three
　　cut four: *TILL THERE WAS YOU*—Meredith Willson—*1:59*
side four
　　cut three: *MR. MOONLIGHT*—Roy Lee Johnson—*2:06*

729.　NOV 8, 1982　(US)　Geffen GHSP 2023　(LP)
　　　by John Lennon
THE JOHN LENNON COLLECTION　Prod: John Lennon,
Yoko Ono, and Jack Douglas except †John Lennon, Yoko
Ono, and Phil Spector; %John Lennon; $Phil Spector;
+John Lennon and Yoko Ono
side one
+GIVE PEACE A CHANCE—L/McC—*4:49*
$INSTANT KARMA! (WE ALL SHINE ON)—Lennon—*3:18*
†POWER TO THE PEOPLE—Lennon—*3:15*
%WHATEVER GETS YOU THRU THE NIGHT—Lennon—*3:24*
%NO. 9 DREAM—Lennon—*4:44*
%MIND GAMES—Lennon—*4:10*
†LOVE—Lennon—*3:17*
side two
†IMAGINE—Lennon—*2:59*
†JEALOUS GUY—Lennon—*4:10*
(JUST LIKE) STARTING OVER—Lennon—*3:55*
WOMAN—Lennon—*3:32*
I'M LOSING YOU—Lennon—*3:58*
BEAUTIFUL BOY (DARLING BOY)—Lennon—*4:01*
WATCHING THE WHEELS—Lennon—*3:30*
DEAR YOKO—Lennon—*2:33*

730.　NOV 15, 1982　(US)　A&M SP-3205　(LP)
　　　by Billy Preston　Prod: Billy Preston
　　　George: Lead Guitar
BEST OF BILLY PRESTON
side two
　　cut five: *I WROTE A SIMPLE SONG*—Billy Preston/Joe
　　Greene—*3:28*

ENTRY 732. Capitol's *Happy Xmas (War Is Over)* single (backed with Yoko Ono's *Listen, The Snow Is Falling*) was still in stock when the Geffen single came out, so the two were side-by-side in some stores. Geffen also sent out twelve-inch promo copies of its disc (Geffen PRO A 1079).

ENTRY 733. **It's Alright** was recorded and mixed at the Hit Factory in New York City in mid 1982. For the first time since 1973's **Feeling The Space**, Yoko Ono acted as sole producer. See page 291 for full track details.

On *Never Say Goodbye* she mixed in an old tape of John Lennon shouting "Yoko!" This was the only cut on the album to incorporate such a technique. The song was later released as the second single from the album (Entry 738).

The back cover to **It's Alright** showed Yoko and Sean (captioned "keepers of the wishing well") standing in New York's Central Park, with a photo of John superimposed to their right.

ENTRY 734. *The Girl Is Mine* provided a powerful worldwide launch for Michael Jackson's **Thriller**. He followed up with a pair of number one singles from the album (*Billie Jean* and *Beat It*), turning it into one of the biggest sellers of all time by the end of 1983. In the U.S. **Thriller** was quickly issued on the Half Speed Mastered series (Epic HE 48112), as a compact digital disc (Epic EK 38112), and as a picture disc (Epic 8E8-38867). In the U.K. there was also a picture disc (Epic EPC 11-85930) and a compact digital disc (Epic CDEPC 85930).

Note: Reflecting its international popularity, *The Girl Is Mine* became the first song since 1977 to be issued as a single in Israel, normally an album-only market. The record (CBS/Epic 2729) was pressed on pink vinyl and packaged in a picture sleeve. Appropriately, the previous single accorded such an honor was McCartney's own *Mull Of Kintyre*.

ENTRY 735. The companion package to the 1978 Beatles album collection and the 1981 EP collection. Like the previous two, this came in a special storage box. The label on each single was a faithful duplication of the one used on the original release. As with the **20 Greatest Hits** albums issued in October, the package also included recording date information for each track.

Though there was no new single created especially for the set, there was an even better bonus: each of the discs came in a special picture sleeve. Because British Beatles singles had rarely been packaged in this way originally, this meant that there were twenty-two newly designed sleeves in the set. (Only *Penny Lane, Let It Be, Sgt. Pepper*, and *The Beatles' Movie Medley* simply reprinted previous picture sleeve artwork.) Though at the time only *Love Me Do* was available outside the boxed set in its new sleeve, the success of that reissue set the stage for similar releases by EMI at the twentieth anniversary of each subsequent single. Thus, British fans were given the choice of acquiring the singles in their new sleeves all at once or "on the installment plan." (Actually, some stores broke open the boxes and sold the discs separately on the spot.)

(continued)

216

731.   NOV 22, 1982 (UK) K-tel NE 1201 (2 LPs)
       by The Rolling Stones   Prod: Andrew Loog Oldham
       STORY OF THE STONES
       side two
       cut three: *WE LOVE YOU*—Mick Jagger/Keith Richards—*4:39*
       John and Paul: Backing Vocals
       side three
       cut three: *I WANNA BE YOUR MAN*—L/McC—*1:44*

732.   NOV 29, 1982 (US) Geffen 7-29855
       by John Lennon   Prod: John Lennon, Yoko Ono, and
       Phil Spector (A side); John Lennon, Yoko Ono, and
       Jack Douglas (B side)
       A: HAPPY XMAS (WAR IS OVER)—Lennon/Yoko Ono—
       3:25
       B: BEAUTIFUL BOY (DARLING BOY)—Lennon—*4:01*

733.   NOV 29, 1982 (US) Polydor PD-1-6364 (LP)
       DEC 10, 1982 (UK) Polydor POLD 5073 (LP)
       by Yoko Ono
       IT'S ALRIGHT   Prod: Yoko Ono
       side one
       cut two: *Never Say Goodbye*—Yoko Ono—*4:25*
       John: Shout

734.   NOV 29, 1982 (US) Epic QE 38112 (LP)
       DEC 3, 1982 (UK) Epic EPC 85930 (LP)
       by Michael Jackson   Prod: Quincy Jones
       THRILLER
       side one
       cut three: *The Girl Is Mine*—Michael Jackson—*3:41*
       Paul: Lead Vocal Duet with Michael Jackson

735.   DEC 6, 1982 (UK) Parlophone BSC 1 (26 45s)
       by The Beatles   Prod: George Martin except +George
       Martin and Phil Spector
       THE BEATLES SINGLES COLLECTION
       A Boxed Set of 26 Original British Singles
       Packaged in new picture sleeves (except †) with the
       original contents unchanged:

(Entry 735 continued)

Perhaps the most fascinating aspect of the boxed set for American fans was that it presented the singles according to their British release scheme — usually only about three discs per year. This was in dramatic contrast to the schedule in America before 1967, when there would easily be twice as many issued. Thus, such points as the dominance of Lennon or McCartney during particular years or the absence of Harrison from either an A or B side until 1968 became much easier to follow. The following chart summarizes these points:

Tracks released as singles by the Beatles in Britain from 1962 to 1970:

(A or B Side) *Title* (Main Writer) (LEAD VOCAL) [Date recording commenced]

(A) *Love Me Do* (Paul) (JOHN & PAUL) [11 Sep 62]
(B) *P.S. I Love You* (Paul) (JOHN & PAUL) [11 Sep 62]

(A) *Please Please Me* (John) (JOHN & PAUL) [26 Nov 62]
(B) *Ask Me Why* (John) (JOHN) [26 Nov 62]

(A) *From Me To You* (John & Paul) (JOHN & PAUL) [4 Mar 63]
(B) *Thank You Girl* (John & Paul) (JOHN & PAUL) [4 Mar 63]

(A) *She Loves You* (John & Paul) (JOHN & PAUL) [1 Jul 63]
(B) *I'll Get You* (John & Paul) (JOHN & PAUL) [1 Jul 63]

(A) *I Want To Hold Your Hand* (John & Paul) (JOHN & PAUL) [17 Oct 63]
(B) *This Boy* (John) (JOHN & PAUL) [17 Oct 63]

(A) *Can't Buy Me Love* (Paul) (PAUL) [25 Feb 64]
(B) *You Can't Do That* (John) (JOHN) [6 Feb 64]

(A) *A Hard Day's Night* (John) (JOHN) [16 Apr 64]
(B) *Things We Said Today* (Paul) (PAUL) [2 Jun 64]

(A) *I Feel Fine* (John) (JOHN & PAUL) [18 Oct 64]
(A) *She's A Woman* (Paul) (PAUL) [2 Oct 64]

(A) *Ticket To Ride* (John) (JOHN) [15 Feb 65]
(B) *Yes It Is* (John) (JOHN) [16 Feb 65]

(A) *Help!* (John) (JOHN) [13 Apr 65]
(B) *I'm Down* (Paul) (PAUL) [14 Apr 65]

(continued)

218

Parlophone R 4949 *First issued October 5, 1962*
  A: Love Me Do—2:19
  B: P.S. I Love You—2:02
Parlophone R 4983 *First issued January 11, 1963*
  A: Please Please Me—2:00
  B: Ask Me Why—2:24
Parlophone R 5015 *First issued April 12, 1963*
  A: From Me To You—1:49
  B: Thank You Girl—2:01
Parlophone R 5055 *First issued August 23, 1963*
  A: She Loves You—2:18
  B: I'll Get You—2:04
Parlophone R 5084 *First issued November 29, 1963*
  A: I Want To Hold Your Hand—2:24
  B: This Boy—2:11
Parlophone R 5115 *First issued March 20, 1964*
  A: Can't Buy Me Love—2:15
  B: You Can't Do That—2:33
Parlophone R 5160 *First issued July 10, 1964*
  A: A Hard Day's Night—2:28
  B: Things We Said Today—2:35
Parlophone R 5200 *First issued November 27, 1964*
  A: I Feel Fine—2:20
  B: She's A Woman—2:57
Parlophone R 5265 *First issued April 9, 1965*
  A: Ticket To Ride—3:03
  B: Yes It Is—2:40
Parlophone R 5305 *First issued July 23, 1965*
  A: Help!—2:16
  B: I'm Down—2:30
Parlophone R 5389 *First issued December 3, 1965*
  A: We Can Work It Out—2:10
  B: Day Tripper—2:37
Parlophone R 5452 *First issued June 10, 1966*
  A: Paperback Writer—2:25
  B: Rain—2:59
Parlophone R 5493 *First issued August 5, 1966*
  A: Yellow Submarine—2:40
  A: Eleanor Rigby—2:11
†Parlophone R 5570 *First issued February 17, 1967*
  A: Penny Lane—3:00
  A: Strawberry Fields Forever—4:05
Parlophone R 5620 *First Issued July 7, 1967*
  A: All You Need Is Love—3:57
  B: Baby, You're A Rich Man—3:07
Parlophone R 5655 *First issued November 24, 1967*
  A: Hello Goodbye—3:24
  B: I Am The Walrus—4:35

(Entry 735 continued)

(A) *We Can Work It Out* (Paul & John) (PAUL & JOHN) [20 Oct 65]
(A) *Day Tripper* (John) (JOHN & PAUL) [16 Oct 65]

(A) *Paperback Writer* (Paul) (PAUL) [13 Apr 66]
(B) *Rain* (John) (JOHN) [13 Apr 66]

(A) *Yellow Submarine* (Paul) (RINGO) [26 May 66]
(A) *Eleanor Rigby* (John & Paul) (PAUL) [20 Apr 66]

(A) *Penny Lane* (Paul) (PAUL) [29 Dec 66]
(A) *Strawberry Fields Forever* (John) (JOHN) [24 Nov 66]

(A) *All You Need Is Love* (John) (JOHN) [14 Jun 67]
(B) *Baby, You're A Rich Man* (John & Paul) (JOHN & PAUL) [11 May 67]

(A) *Hello Goodbye* (Paul) (PAUL) [2 Oct 67]
(B) *I Am The Walrus* (John) (JOHN) [25 Sep 67]

(A) *Lady Madonna* (Paul) (PAUL) [3 Feb 68]
(B) *The Inner Light* (George) (GEORGE) [6 Feb 68]

(A) *Hey Jude* (Paul) (PAUL) [29 Jul 68]
(B) *Revolution* (John) (JOHN) [14 Aug 68]

(A) *Get Back* (Paul) (PAUL) [23 Jan 69]
(B) *Don't Let Me Down* (John) (JOHN) [22 Jan 69]

(A) *The Ballad Of John And Yoko* (John) (JOHN) [14 Apr 69]
(B) *Old Brown Shoe* (George) (GEORGE) [25 Feb 69]

(A) *Something* (George) (GEORGE) [25 Feb 69]
(A) *Come Together* (John) (JOHN) [21 Jul 69]

(A) *Let It Be* (Paul) (PAUL) [25 Jan 69]
(B) *You Know My Name (Look Up The Number)* (John) (JOHN) [8 Jun 67]

Tracks released as singles by the Beatles in Britain from 1976 to 1982:

(A) *Yesterday* (Paul) (PAUL) [14 Jun 65]
(B) *I Should Have Known Better* (John) (JOHN) [6 Feb 64]

(continued)

Parlophone R 5675 *First issued March 15, 1968*
  A: Lady Madonna—2:17
  B: The Inner Light—Harrison—*2:36*
Apple R 5722 *First issued August 30, 1968*
  A: Hey Jude—7:11
  B: Revolution—3:22
Apple R 5777 *First issued April 11, 1969*
  A: Get Back—3:11
  B: Don't Let Me Down—3:34
Apple R 5786 *First issued May 30, 1969*
  A: The Ballad Of John And Yoko—2:58
  B: Old Brown Shoe—Harrison—*3:16*
Apple R 5814 *First issued October 31, 1969*
  A: Something—Harrison—*2:59*
  A: Come Together—4:16
† Apple R 5833 *First issued March 6, 1970*
  A: Let It Be—3:50
  B: You Know My Name (Look Up The Number)—4:20
Parlophone R 6013 *First issued March 5, 1976*
  A: Yesterday—2:04
  B: I Should Have Known Better—2:42
Parlophone R 6016 *First issued June 25, 1976*
  A: Back In The U.S.S.R.—2:45
  B: Twist And Shout—Bert Russell/Phil Medley—*2:32*
† Parlophone R 6022 *First issued September 22, 1978*
  A: Medley: 4:45
    Sgt. Pepper's Lonely Hearts Club Band—1:59
    With A Little Help From My Friends—2:46
  B: A Day In The Life—5:03
† Parlophone R 6055 *First issued May 24, 1982*
  *A: The Beatles' Movie Medley—3:56
    Magical Mystery Tour—0:31
    All You Need Is Love—0:34
    You've Got To Hide Your Love Away—0:35
    I Should Have Known Better—0:47
    A Hard Day's Night—0:22
    Ticket To Ride—0:31
    +Get Back (version two)—0:36
  B: I'm Happy Just To Dance With You—1:59

(Entry 735 continued)

(A) *Back In The U.S.S.R.* (Paul) (PAUL) [22 Aug 68]
(B) *Twist And Shout* (cover) (JOHN) [11 Feb 63]

(A) *Sgt. Pepper's Lonely Hearts Club Band* (Paul) (PAUL) [2 Feb 67]
  With A Little Help From My Friends (Paul) (RINGO) [29 Mar 67]
(B) *A Day In The Life* (John & Paul) (JOHN & PAUL) [19 Jan 67]

(A) *The Beatles' Movie Medley* [editing commenced 18 Jan 82]
(B) *I'm Happy Just To Dance With You* (John) (GEORGE) [1 Mar 64]

    The four singles issued after 1970 were in the spirit of the many special U.S. couplings over the years. On *Back In The U.S.S.R.*, EMI even placed a song not written by the Beatles on the B-side (*Twist And Shout*) something the group never did on any other British single.

    Naturally, the new British singles set also turned up in American import bins. However, these copies carried a special export catalog number (Parlophone BSCP 1) and contained a special bonus, the *Love Me Do* picture disc. See page 426 for further information on the British picture disc singles.

    Note: An insert sheet included in the boxed set listed the release date and highest British chart position for each single, as well as the recording data offered on the American version of the **20 Greatest Hits** album (Entry 717). *Let It Be* was off by only one day, listed on the U.S. album as January 26, 1969, rather than January 25. However, the discrepancy on *Yesterday* was four months: February 16, 1965 in the U.S. versus June 14, 1965 in the U.K. The June date was the correct one.

The Beatles Singles Collection   Parlophone BSC 1 (45s)

Love Me Do   Parlophone R 4949 (45)

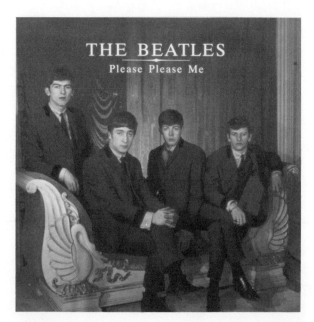

Please Please Me   **Parlophone R 4983 (45)**

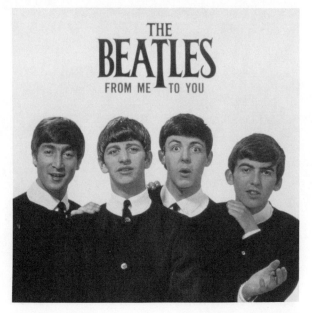

From Me To You   **Parlophone R 5015 (45)**

She Loves You   Parlophone R 5055 (45)

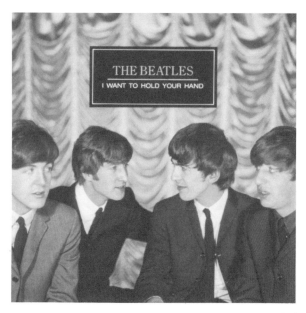

I Want To Hold Your Hand   Parlophone R 5084 (45)

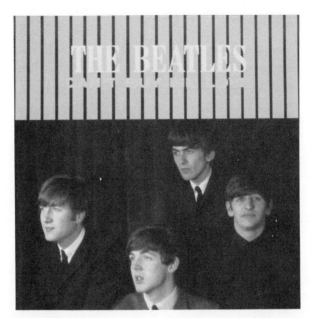

Can't Buy Me Love   Parlophone R 5115 (45)

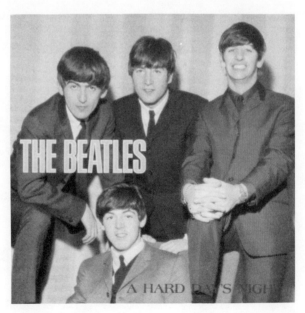

A Hard Day's Night   Parlophone R 5160 (45)

I Feel Fine   Parlophone R 5200 (45)

Ticket To Ride   Parlophone R 5265 (45)

Help   Parlophone R 5305 (45)

We Can Work It Out   Parlophone R 5389 (45)

Paperback Writer   Parlophone R 5452 (45)

Yellow Submarine   Parlophone R 5493 (45)

Penny Lane   Parlophone R 5570 (45)

All You Need Is Love   Parlophone R 5620 (45)

Hello Goodbye   Parlophone R 5655 (45)

Lady Madonna   Parlophone R 5675 (45)

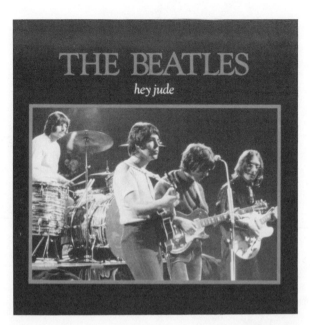

Hey Jude   **Apple R 5722 (45)**

Get Back   **Apple R 5777 (45)**

The Ballad Of John And Yoko   Apple R 5786 (45)

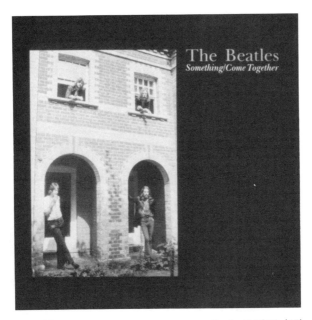

Something   Apple R 5814 (45)

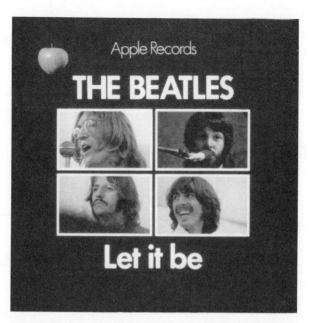

Let It Be   Apple R 5833 (45)

Yesterday   Parlophone R 6013 (45)

Back In The U.S.S.R.   Parlophone R 6016 (45)

The Beatles' Movie Medley   Parlophone R 6055 (45)

Say Say Say   Columbia 44-04169 (12-inch)

1983

May 9.   KYST in Houston adopts an all-Beatles format as K-BTL (Beatle Radio No. 9). This "All Beatles, All The Time" set-up does not last six months.

June 4.   *Ringo's Yellow Submarine: A Voyage Through Beatles Magic* begins airing weekly on U.S. radio stations. On the last episode (November 26), Ringo takes calls from listeners.

October 4.   Shooting begins in Los Alamos, California, for the *Say Say Say* promotional film, directed by Bob Giraldi.

October.   Julian Lennon signs with Charisma Records worldwide.

October 24.   Yoko Ono announces plans to donate millions of dollars to various philanthropies as a humanitarian response to the terrorist bombing of a U.S. Marines base in Beirut.

November 7.   Ringo Starr and Barbara Bach play a pair of bisexual dress designers on the NBC made-for-television film of the Judith Krantz novel *Princess Daisy*.

December 1.   Yoko Ono joins Paul, George, and Ringo for a business meeting at the Dorchester Hotel in London.

1983

From Under Wraps

Immediately after the death of John Lennon in 1980, publishers throughout the world filled the newsstands and bookstores with Beatles and Lennon-related material. Old books and magazines were reprinted, while others were put together virtually overnight to cash in on the surge of interest. Generally, these recycled the same old press release stories and photos over and over again. Nonetheless, they sold well enough to justify contracts for even more books about the group, especially those with a John Lennon connection. In 1983, these began to hit the market.

The chief characteristic of the new books was an apparent obsession to "tell all." This generally meant details of sexual escapades, drug use, and behind-the-scenes business intrigues. Such tales virtually guaranteed coverage by the supermarket tabloids and gossip columnists, and brought out from under wraps personal aspects of the Beatles story that had never really been shared with the general public before.

There were two main problems with the books: 1) as personal reminiscing, they reflected just one person's (sometimes bitter) perspective; 2) they almost inevitably ignored the music.

They were not, however, ignored by the press and the public. So once again, the Beatles were big sellers, this time in the bookshops. And despite their flaws, these books did offer fascinating reading, in the "bare-your-soul" spirit of John Lennon's own *Lennon Remembers* (his candid conversations with *Rolling Stone* in 1970) and in dramatic contrast to the wide-eyed innocence of such presentations as the 1964 documentary album, **The Beatles' Story**.

For those interested in less salacious experiences, there were two public exhibitions in 1983 which offered a peek at other items previously under wraps: "The Beatles At Abbey Road" and "Give Peace A Chance."

"Give Peace A Chance" was an exhibit staged at the Peace Museum in Chicago. Yoko Ono contributed for display personal mementos relating to her activities with John on behalf of the peace movement in the 1960s and 1970s. The setup included the Gibson guitar used at the 1969 *Give Peace A Chance* bed-in, a billboard-size "War Is Over! If You Want It!" poster from 1971, and even one of the acorn boxes they sent to world leaders back in 1969 as a symbol to be planted for peace. All of this was incorporated into a gallery layout showcasing the history of the peace movement and the role of musicians in it, from the 1940s to the present. Appropriately, the exhibition captured the best aspects of the John Lennon and Yoko Ono peace events of the late 1960s and early 1970s, giving those who weren't there a taste of the times. The "Give Peace A Chance" exhibit was on display in Chicago from September 11, 1983 to January 31, 1984. Just as it was opening, "The Beatles At Abbey Road" was ending its successful seven-week run in England.

The audio-visual presentation of "The Beatles At Abbey Road"[1] offered fans a once-in-a-lifetime opportunity to hear the Beatles on tape and to see the group on film while seated in EMI's studio number two — the place where much of the music had been recorded. Throughout the summer (July 18 to September 11), thousands of fans from all over the world stopped by for a taste of Beatles nostalgia.

Back Stateside, Ringo Starr offered his perspective on Beatles history every week (for twenty-six weeks) on his own prerecorded radio show carried throughout the U.S.: *Ringo's Yellow Submarine: A Voyage Through Beatles Magic*. The program began in June and featured Ringo as a guest DJ, telling a few anecdotes and playing Beatles music. For the final program, he took calls live from listeners throughout the country, discussing everything from "genuine" Beatles memorabilia ("made last week in Taiwan") to his latest album, **Old Wave**, which most listeners had never heard!

The fate of **Old Wave** was a stinging reminder that, despite the continuing nostalgic interest in the Beatles, new solo efforts by former members were not guaranteed automatic acceptance. In the case of **Old Wave**, Ringo found himself unable to arrange either a U.S. or U.K. record release deal for the completed album, which had been recorded in the summer of 1982. A year later, in the summer of 1983, he decided to have it released anyway in other markets, including Canada (on RCA) and West Germany (on Bellaphon). This allowed fans in Britain and the U.S. to pick up imported copies, with the possibility that a deal could still be struck for those markets. However, that never happened.

The problem with **Old Wave** had nothing to do with the quality of the material. Some of it was pretty good, with songs such as *She's About A Mover* and *I Keep Forgettin'* particularly strong. Instead, as

---

[1] See page 403 for a detailed description of "The Beatles At Abbey Road."

the title suggested, it was indeed "old wave" – the music did not sound like anything currently topping the charts. As a result, any major release in the U.K. or U.S. would have to have been accompanied by a major, innovative promotional push. Apparently, there were few companies interested in expending the effort. There were too many tempting new acts to go with instead.

Even Paul McCartney, certified the best-selling composer and performer in music history, ran into problems in 1983. Though his *Say Say Say* duet with Michael Jackson reached the top of the charts in the U.S., it did not pull the subsequent **Pipes Of Peace** album up with it. In fact, **Pipes Of Peace** became McCartney's first regular studio album to miss the U.S. top ten in his twenty-year chart career, covering releases with the Beatles, Wings and purely solo.

The record also received many negative reviews. Perhaps those were inevitable, though, because any follow-up to the critically acclaimed **Tug Of War** was bound to suffer in comparison. Even so, **Pipes Of Peace** was the source and inspiration for some superb promotional filmwork, including the con-men-on-the-run setting for *Say Say Say* and the World War I battlefield for the *Pipes Of Peace* title track. These revealed McCartney to be better than ever in the increasingly important visual format.

Appropriately, back home in Britain, **Pipes Of Peace** was much more successful for Paul. After *Say Say Say* just missed topping the charts, a *Pipes Of Peace* single caught on over the Christmas season and rolled straight on to number one.

So, on the verge of 1984 – with its inevitable nostalgic slant celebrating the twentieth anniversary of the Beatles landing in America – Paul McCartney still had his hit making prowess as a solo artist mostly intact. George Harrison and Ringo Starr had to fight a little harder to be heard on record, though they were also doing quite well with filmwork (producing and performing, respectively). And John Lennon was about to enter the picture one more time as Yoko Ono prepared to release the album they had planned as the follow-up to **Double Fantasy, Milk And Honey**.

ENTRY 736 & 740. In March 1982, EMI deleted the twenty-track **Songs Lennon And McCartney Gave Away** compilation (Entry 618), so record buyers once again had to search out each of those songs, either on new collections by the artists (such as **The Very Best Of Cilla Black**) or on new various artists compilations (such as **Remember . . . A Collection Of Pop Memories**).

Of course, a visit to a secondhand record shop might still turn up a copy of **The Songs Lennon And McCartney Gave Away**, or perhaps even previous releases of the individual tracks. Consult *All Together Now* and *The Beatles Again* for further details on these. There were also six reissues overlooked in both books:

1) *I'll Be On My Way* by Billy J. Kramer and The Dakotas as the B-side to *Trains And Boats And Planes* in the U.S. in 1964, replacing the initial flip side, *That's The Way I Feel*, but keeping the same catalog number (Imperial 66115).

2) *Bad To Me* by Billy J. Kramer and The Dakotas on side two, cut five of the 1964 U.S. various artists compilation **The Original Golden Greats** (Liberty LST 7500).

3) *Those Were The Days* by Mary Hopkin on side two, cut ten of the 1972 U.K. various artists compilation **20 Fantastic Hits Volume Two** (Arcade 2891 002).

4) *Step Inside Love* by Cilla Black on side two, cut five of the 1973 U.K. various artists compilation **Pure Gold On EMI** (EMI EMK 251).

5) *Bad To Me* by Billy J. Kramer and The Dakotas and *A World Without Love* by Peter and Gordon on the 1977 British various artists double album **Superstars Tribute To The Beatles** (Arcade ADE P21)--on side one, cut three and side three, cut five respectively.

6) *Tip Of My Tongue* by Tommy Quickly on side one, cut four of the 1977 British various artists double album **The 60's File** (Pye FILD 006).

Some dedicated Beatles fans provided another source for hard-to-find tracks: licensed and authorized limited edition records. Four such seven-inch discs were put out in Sweden by Buttercup Records and were available by mail from Steffan Olander and Lennart Malmbjer, Box 4, S-240 17 Sodra Sandby, Sweden. The first three were *One And One Is Two* by The Strangers with Mike Shannon (Buttercup BIC 101), *Tip Of My Tongue* by Tommy Quickly (Pye 7N 45629), and *Like Dreamers Do* by The Applejacks b/w *I'll Keep You Satisfied* by Billy J. Kramer (Decca FR 13793). There were picture sleeves for the first and third discs, while the second came in a special Pye sleeve. *I'll Keep You Satisfied* was not the original 1963 Parlophone recording with the Dakotas but a 1973 rerecording done by Kramer for Decca as a solo release (Decca F 13426).

The fourth single was a six-track EP (Polydor 2230 114) featuring material from the 1961 sessions with Tony Sheridan along with Ringo Starr's 1977 *Just A Dream* (his only non-album solo B-side for Polydor), Cream's 1969 *Badge* (featuring George Harrison), and Roger Daltrey's 1977 *Giddy* (written by Paul McCartney). See page 248 for details of the Tony Sheridan tracks on that disc.

736.   JAN 17, 1983 (UK) Parlophone EMTV 38 (LP)
       by Cilla Black   Prod: George Martin
       THE VERY BEST OF CILLA BLACK
       side one
          cut one: *LOVE OF THE LOVED*—L/McC—*2:00*
          cut four: *IT'S FOR YOU*—L/McC—*2:20*
       side two
          cut three: *STEP INSIDE LOVE*—L/McC—*2:20*

737.   JAN 24, 1983 (UK) Capitol CL 258
       by Steve Miller   Prod: Glyn Johns and Steve Miller
       side one
       (the joker)
       side two
       (living in the u.s.a.)
       MY DARK HOUR—Steve Miller—*3:05*
       Paul: Bass Guitar, Drums, and Backing Vocal

738.   JAN 25, 1983 (US) Polydor 810 556-7
       by Yoko Ono   Prod: Yoko Ono
       A: NEVER SAY GOODBYE—Yoko Ono—*3:24*
       John: Shout
       B: (loneliness)

739.   FEB 7, 1983 (US) Dark Horse 7-29744
       by George Harrison   Prod: George Harrison, Ray Cooper,
          and Phil McDonald
       A: I REALLY LOVE YOU—Leroy Swearingen—*2:53*
       B: CIRCLES—Harrison—*3:45*

740.   FEB 11, 1983 (UK) Cambra CR 070 (2 LPs)
       by Various Artists
       REMEMBER . . . A COLLECTION OF POP MEMORIES
       side one
          cut four: *TIP OF MY TONGUE*—L/McC—*2:02*
          by Tommy Quickly   Prod: Les Reed
       side three
          cut five: *LUCY IN THE SKY WITH DIAMONDS*—
          L/McC—*5:59*
          by Elton John   Prod: Gus Dudgeon
          John: Guitars and Backing Vocal

ENTRY 741. *Never Say Goodbye* from **It's Alright** (Entry 733) was trimmed and tightened for single release (Entry 738), then remixed into an extended length version for this subsequent twelve-inch package.

ENTRY 742. Fans of Eric Clapton, Jack Bruce, and Ginger Baker no doubt passed up this Cream compilation as yet another unnecessary addition to the seemingly endless series of repackagings for all three performers. The disc appeared briefly on *Billboard*'s "Bubbling Under" listings and did not even chart in Britain. Nonetheless, for George Harrison fans interested in obtaining *Badge*, this was actually a pretty good album, offering a well-rounded sampling of Cream tracks in addition to George's only guest shot with the group.

ENTRY 743. This twenty-track compilation gathered material by a dozen different Mersey-based performers, providing an excellent sampling of their music from the mid-1960s. The liner notes by Spencer Leigh (from BBC Radio Merseyside) included details on Ringo Starr's involvement with an odd 1964 release by Rory Storm and the Hurricanes, *America* — from *West Side Story*. The record was produced by Beatles' manager Brian Epstein (his one-and-only time in such a role), who arranged for the London sessions at EMI, brought the group down, and chose the songs. During the recording, Ringo dropped by and joined Rory Storm's brother-in-law Shane Fenton (later known as Alvin Stardust) on the backing vocals. The song was originally issued November 13, 1964 as Parlophone R 5197 b/w *Since You Broke My Heart*.

How I Won The War, the final cut on the record, was not really typical Merseyside fare. However, it was from a rare John Lennon-related disc, so that was excuse enough for inclusion on the collection. This montage of sound effects, voices, and music had been issued originally as a tie-in single with the 1967 *How I Won The War* film (there was no soundtrack album) and emphasized the John Lennon connection by listing his character (Musketeer Gripweed) as the main artist. In fact, Lennon's voice could barely be picked out in the cacophony of noise.

741. FEB 22, 1983 (US) Polydor 810 575-1 (12-inch)
by Yoko Ono   Prod: Yoko Ono
A: *NEVER SAY GOODBYE (long version)*—Yoko Ono—*4:27*
John: Shout
B: *(loneliness)*

742. MAR 4, 1983 (UK) RSO Deluxe RSD-5021 (LP)
APR 4, 1983 (US) RSO 811 639-1 Y-1 (LP)
by Cream   Prod: Felix Pappalardi
STRANGE BREW – THE VERY BEST OF CREAM
side one
cut one: *BADGE*—Harrison/Eric Clapton—*2:45*

743. APR 15, 1983 (UK) See For Miles/Charly CM 118 (LP)
by Various Artists
LIVERPOOL 1963--1968
side one
cut seven: *AMERICA*—Leonard Bernstein/Stephen
Sondheim—*2:29*
by Rory Storm and The Hurricanes   Prod: Brian Epstein
Ringo: Backing Vocal
side two
cut ten: *HOW I WON THE WAR*—Ken Thorne—*3:00*
by Musketeer Gripweed and the Third Troop
John: Voice

744. JUN 6, 1983 (UK) Music For Pleasure MFP 5620 (LP)
by Various Artists
SAVILE'S TIME TRAVELS (20 GOLDEN HITS OF 1964)
side one
cut one: *I WANT TO HOLD YOUR HAND*—*2:24*
by The Beatles   Prod: George Martin
cut eight: *A WORLD WITHOUT LOVE*—L/McC—*2:38*
by Peter and Gordon   Prod: Norman Newell

745. JUN 16, 1983 (GERMANY) Bellaphon 100.16.012
by Ringo Starr   Prod: Joe Walsh
A: *In My Car*—Starkey/Joe Walsh/Mo Foster/Kim Goody—
3:13
B: *As Far As We Can Go*—Russ Ballard—*3:52*

Liverpool 1963–1968   See For Miles/Charly CM 118 (LP)

Never Say Goodbye   Polydor 810 575-1 (12-inch)

ENTRY 745 & 746. In contrast to the round robin of producers and players on **Stop And Smell The Roses**, the **Old Wave** album was recorded in mid 1982 at Startling Studios with a core group of five musicians. Dubbed the "Rock & Rock Review," Mo Foster (bass), Chris Stainton and Gary Brooker (keyboards), producer Joe Walsh (guitars), and Ringo handled most of the tracks themselves. The two exceptions were *Everybody's In A Hurry But Me* (a free flowing jam with such guests as John Entwistle and Eric Clapton) and *She's About A Mover* (with a completely different lineup). In addition, Barbara Bach joined in on *I'm Going Down* (screaming) and *Be My Baby* (human handclaps). Ringo also wrote the song *Alibi* for her.

Joe Walsh and Ringo were the main writers on most of the songs. Of the cover versions, *I Keep Forgettin'* was a special favorite – an oldie by Chuck Jackson from 1962 (Wand 126) that Ringo had always wanted to record. Moving up three years, *She's About A Mover* had originally been done in 1965 by the Sir Douglas Quintet (Tribe 8308).

The album's title, a reverse of the term "New Wave," was inspired by Barbara's daughter Francesca who asked old pro Ringo if he was "Old Wave." "Yes," came the reply," and that's what we'll call the new album." Appropriately, the front cover photo of Ringo was from the old days, taken at a photobooth "somewhere in Northern England."

Note: Though not released in either the U.S. or the U.K., **Old Wave** was imported into both countries from Canada and West Germany. The single, however, rarely turned up.

ENTRY 747. Two of John Lennon's three songs performed live on stage with Elton John back in 1974 appeared on this mixed bag compilation. The third song, *I Saw Her Standing There*, had been on a British various artists compilation album back in mid 1977 – on side two, cut ten of **Superstars Tribute To The Beatles** (Arcade ADE P21), a two-record, forty-track set. Oddly, though all three songs appeared in England on singles (Entries 551 and 668) and on a special cassette (page 431) issued by DJM, the company never put them on any of its Elton John albums.

ENTRY 748. This twofer package offered Leon Russell's first two solo albums from the early 1970s. As with the original release of **Leon Russell** (Entry 244), there were no track-by-track musician credits, only a general listing which included both Ringo Starr and George Harrison. Further research indicated that Ringo played on *Shoot Out At The Plantation* and *Delta Lady*, and that neither appeared on *Song For You, Hummingbird*, and *Roll Away The Stone*. Harrison's tracks and any other Ringo contributions have not yet been identified among the remaining six titles: *Dixie Lullaby, I Put A Spell On You, Prince Of Peace, Give Peace A Chance, Hurtsome Body*, and *Pisces Apple Lady*.

746. JUN 16, 1983 (GERMANY) Bellaphon 260.16.029 (LP)
JUN 24, 1983 (CANADA) RCA DXL 1-3233 (LP)
by Ringo Starr
OLD WAVE   Prod: Joe Walsh
side one
In My Car—Starkey/Joe Walsh/Mo Foster/Kim Goody—*3:13*
Hopeless—Starkey/Joe Walsh—*3:17*
Alibi—Starkey/Joe Walsh—*4:00*
Be My Baby—Joe Walsh—*3:44*
She's About A Mover—Doug Sahm—*3:52*
side two
I Keep Forgettin'—Jerry Leiber/Mike Stoller—*4:18*
Picture Show Life—John Reid/John Slate—*4:21*
As Far As We Can Go—Russ Ballard—*3:52*
Everybody's In A Hurry But Me—Starkey/Joe Walsh/John
Entwhistle/Eric Clapton/Chris Stainton—*2:35*
I'm Going Down—Starkey/Joe Walsh—*3:34*

747. JUN 27, 1983 (UK) Everest Records CBR 1027 (LP)
by Elton John (see below)
THE NEW COLLECTION
side one
cut six: *WHATEVER GETS YOU THRU THE NIGHT*—
Lennon—*3:12*
cut seven: *LUCY IN THE SKY WITH DIAMONDS*—
L/McC—*6:05*
by The Elton John Band featuring John Lennon (guitar
and vocal) and the Muscle Shoals Horns recorded live
Prod: Gus Dudgeon

748. JUL 28, 1983 (US) MCA SRC 2-38013 (2 LPs)
by Leon Russell   Prod: Denny Cordell and Leon Russell
Ringo: Drums; George: Guitar (see notes)
**LEON RUSSELL/LEON RUSSELL AND THE SHELTER
PEOPLE**
record one: Leon Russell
side one
cut four: *SHOOT OUT ON THE PLANTATION*—Leon
Russell—*3:10*
side two
cut one: *DELTA LADY*—Leon Russell—*4:00*

ENTRY 749. This package of Cream and Jimi Hendrix cuts was part of a continuing British mail order series presenting selected tracks from rock's past. Surprisingly, *Badge* was the first Beatles-related recording to turn up on one of the albums.

Note: In the U.S., a mail order record series featuring Grammy Award tracks was advertisied late in 1983, with the first discs scheduled for release in January 1984. The 100 disc series was dubbed **The Official Grammy Awards Archive Collection**, with cuts by the Beatles, George Harrison, and Paul Mc-Cartney slated for inclusion.

ENTRY 750. **20 Greatest Hits** combined the contents of two previous Audio Fidelity releases from 1982, **First Movement** (Entry 702) and **The Complete Silver Beatles** (Entry 713). Unfortunately, this new package retained the four Tony Sheridan cuts from **First Movement** that had nothing to do with the Beatles.

Audio Fidelity also issued **First Movement** as a picture disc in Britain in October 1983 (Audiofidelity PXS 339P).

Note: The only recent repackaging of material by the Beatles and Tony Sheridan that broke from the usual rerelease of the same familiar tracks was a six-cut seven-inch EP issued in Sweden in late 1982. This was put together by Stefan Olander and Lennart Malmbjer as a special limited edition, authorized pressing (Polydor 2230 114) offered for sale by mail order. Side one featured three particularly rare items from the group's 1961 sessions for Polydor in Germany backing Tony Sheridan: the slow intro piece sung in German for *My Bonnie*, the same intro piece sung in English (both from Entry 1), and the original recording of *Sweet Georgia Brown* (from Entry 5a). The thirty-five second *My Bonnie* intros (in either language) had been left off virtually every release of the song since the original 1961 German single. Oddly, the new Swedish EP did not include the actual song *My Bonnie*, just the two intros. *Sweet Georgia Brown*, meanwhile, ran intact. Since 1963 that song had only ever appeared in rerecorded form in both the U.S. and the U.K. because Tony Sheridan had done a new lead vocal for the track prior to its rerelease from the vaults. See page 194 for further information on the group's 1961 recording work in Germany. Ringo Starr's *Just A Dream*, Cream's *Badge*, and Roger Daltrey's *Giddy* rounded out the EP, which was available from Buttercup Records. (See page 240 for the mailing address.)

There was one other fan sponsored limited edition reissue of *My Bonnie*, which included the German language spoken intro along with the complete song (in stereo) b/w *Cry For A Shadow*. This single (Polydor 2801 033) came in a picture sleeve and was issued as a special tie-in to the October 24, 1978, Beatles convention sponsored by the Beatles Information Center in Koln, West Germany. There were only 500 copies made (numbered on the individual sleeves) and most of these were given out free to those attending the convention.

749.   SEPTEMBER 1983 (UK MAIL ORDER) History Of Rock
       HRL 016 (2 LPs)
       by Jimi Hendrix and Cream (see below)
       THE HISTORY OF ROCK – VOLUME 16 (Jimi Hendrix
       and Cream)
       side four
           cut two: *BADGE*–Harrison/Eric Clapton–*2:45*
           by Cream   Prod: Felix Pappalardi

750.   SEP 10, 1983 (UK) Phoenix P20-623 (LP)
       by The Beatles   Prod: Mike Smith except
       †Tony Sheridan and The Beatles; and %The Beatles
       Prod: Bert Kaempfert (Additional cuts by $Tony
       Sheridan and The Beat Brothers)
       20 GREATEST HITS
       side one
           %CRY FOR A SHADOW–Lennon/Harrison–*2:22*
           $(let's dance)
           †IF YOU LOVE ME, BABY–Charles Singleton/Waldenese
           Hall–*2:52*
           $(what'd i say)
           †SWEET GEORGIA BROWN–Ben Bernie/Maceo Pinkard/
           Kenneth Casey–*2:03*
           $(ruby baby)
           $(ya ya)
           †WHY–Tony Sheridan/Bill Crompton–*2:55*
           TO KNOW HER IS TO LOVE HER–Phil Spector–*2:26*
       side two
           THREE COOL CATS– Jerry Leiber/Mike Stoller–*2:16*
           CRYING, WAITING, HOPING–Buddy Holly–*1:56*
           BESAME MUCHO–Consuelo Velazquez/Selig Shaftel–*2:32*
           SEARCHIN'–Jerry Leiber/Mike Stoller–*2:54*
           THE SHEIK OF ARABY–Harry B. Smith/Ted Snyder/
           Frances Wheeler–*1:35*
           MONEY (THAT'S WHAT I WANT)–Berry Gordy,/Janie
           Bradford–*2:18*
           TAKE GOOD CARE OF MY BABY–Gerry Goffin/Carole
           King–*2:16*
           MEMPHIS, TENNESSEE–Chuck Berry–*2:12*
           SURE TO FALL (IN LOVE WITH YOU)–Carl Perkins/
           William E. Cantrell/Quinton Claunch–*1:55*
           TILL THERE WAS YOU–Meredith Willson–*2:54*
           SEPTEMBER IN THE RAIN–Al Dubin/Harry Warren–*1:49*

ENTRY 752 & 753. Back in the Christmas season of 1980--1981, Michael Jackson contacted Paul McCartney and suggested they get together and write some hits. At the time, Jackson had a string of top ten songs taken from **Off The Wall**, while McCartney was working on his follow-up to the chart topping *Coming Up* and **McCartney II**. In the spring, they got together in England and wrote the basics of two songs (*Say Say Say* and *The Man*), with subsequent work done in Los Angeles and London. At first, both were candidates for **Tug Of War**, but when McCartney and George Martin decided to keep that album to only one disc, the Jackson/McCartney numbers were held back for the follow-up. Meanwhile, Michael Jackson was at work on his own album and, in the spring of 1982, Paul came by Los Angeles to share the vocals on *The Girl Is Mine*. Though the third song done by the pair, that was the first to be released, serving as the lead single to Jackson's **Thriller** in October 1982. *Say Say Say* and *The Man* followed at last in October 1983.

In the U.S., *Say Say Say* topped *Billboard*'s Hot 100 and reached number two on the black singles chart. The song hit number one in Britain on *Music Week*'s special twelve-inch chart, but peaked at number two on the regular singles listing.

The British chart movements of *Say Say Say* were, in fact, rather unusual. After quickly reaching number ten in its second week, the disc dropped back down the singles chart, then shot back up to number three. Apparently, the revival came as the result of the *Say Say Say* promotional film, which hit the British airwaves just in time to boost interest and sales. Oddly, the film had absolutely nothing to do with the actual words to the song except that it provided the perfect accompaniment to the energetic vocal performance by McCartney and Jackson. The two played con men in the American West (much like the characters in the film *Butch Cassidy And The Sundance Kid*), who performed in a traveling medicine/magic/dance hall show. Naturally, this provided Michael Jackson the opportunity for some flashy dancing, along with good natured clowning with Paul. Of course, they gave their "ill gotten gains" to a local orphanage.

Both the seven-inch and twelve-inch packages for *Say Say Say* came in a bright blue picture sleeve. The twelve-inch featured two extended length versions of the song (one an instrumental) remixed by John "Jellybean" Benitez, who was responsible for other successful remixes at the time such as *Tell Her About It* by Billy Joel, *Say It Isn't So* by Daryl Hall and John Oates, and *Everyday I Write The Book* by Elvis Costello and the Attractions.

Note: When asked by Father Guido Sarducci in 1980 to name the animal he would most want to be, Paul replied, "Koala bear." For the moment, the B-side *Ode To A Koala Bear* would have to do.

751. SEP 10, 1983 (UK) Phoenix P20 629 (LP)
by The Beatles; recorded live by Ted Taylor in 1962
20 GREAT HITS
side one
TWIST AND SHOUT–Bert Russell/Phil Medley–*2:03*
MR. MOONLIGHT–Roy Lee Johnson–*2:06*
A TASTE OF HONEY–Ric Marlow/Bobby Scott–*1:45*
MEDLEY–*2:09*
   KANSAS CITY–Jerry Leiber/Mike Stoller–*1:04*
   HEY-HEY-HEY-HEY–Richard Penniman–*1:05*
I SAW HER STANDING THERE–*2:22*
ROLL OVER BEETHOVEN–Chuck Berry–*2:15*
HIPPY HIPPY SHAKE–Chan Romero–*1:42*
SWEET LITTLE SIXTEEN–Chuck Berry–*2:45*
YOUR FEET'S TOO BIG–Ada Benson/Fred Fisher–*2:18*
NOTHIN' SHAKIN' (BUT THE LEAVES ON THE TREES)
   –Cirino Colacrai/Eddie Fontaine/Dianne Lampert/Jack
   Cleveland–*1:15*
side two
LITTLE QUEENIE–Chuck Berry–*3:51*
ASK ME WHY–*2:26*
BE-BOP-A-LULA–Gene Vincent/Tex Davis–*2:29*
HALLELUJAH, I LOVE HER SO–Ray Charles–*2:10*
RED SAILS IN THE SUNSET–Jimmy Kennedy/Will
   Grosz–*2:00*
EVERYBODY'S TRYING TO BE MY BABY–Carl
   Perkins–*2:25*
MATCHBOX–Carl Perkins–*2:35*
I'M TALKING ABOUT YOU–Chuck Berry–*1:48*
SHIMMY SHAKE–Joe South/Billy Land–*2:17*
LONG TALL SALLY–Enotris Johnson/Richard Penni-
   man/Robert Blackwell–*1:45*

752. OCT 3, 1983 (UK) Parlophone R 6062
OCT 3, 1983 (US) Columbia 38-04168
by Paul McCartney †with Michael Jackson   Prod: George
Martin
†A: *Say Say Say*–McCartney/Michael Jackson–*3:55*
*B: *Ode To A Koala Bear*–McCartney–*3:45*

ENTRY 754. Though George Martin and Paul McCartney had been building toward two records of material for **Tug Of War** before cutting it to a single disc, **Pipes Of Peace** was not just record two released eighteen months later. Instead, the album contained a mixture of completely new songs, and tracks that had been close to finished at the previous sessions. Along the way, other tunes and some alternate recordings were discarded.

The older material used included the *Hey Hey* instrumental (which grew out of a jam in Montserrat by Stanley Clarke, McCartney, and Steve Gadd), *Average Person* (at one time planned as the second cut on **Tug Of War** instead of *Take It Away*) and *Keep Under Cover* (both brought pretty much intact), and *Say Say Say* and *The Man* (finished and polished for the new album). *Sweetest Little Show*, which had been kicking around throughout the sessions and at one time was part of a three-song medley, at last fell into place on its own, building to a McCartney acoustic solo at the end, complete with applause.

The soft uplifting tone of the *Pipes Of Peace* title track reflected the strong love orientation on the rest of the newer material: *So Bad* (a delicate "Philadelphia Soul" style love ballad), *The Other Me* (Paul close-miked and completely alone at the guitar, synthesizer, and piano), and *Through Our Love* — the sweeping finale not only to **Pipes Of Peace** but also to the entire three-year "War & Peace" recording venture. *Tug Of Peace* served as a final tie-in to the previous album, weaving in and out of both title tunes accompanied by the thumping of some thirty garden canes on the studio floor — with Martin and McCartney swinging about fifteen each.

In contrast to the detailed track-by-track musician credits on **Tug Of War**, **Pipes Of Peace** offered only general thanks to about a dozen musicians and centerspread photos of Paul and seven others: Linda McCartney, Ringo Starr, Michael Jackson, Andy Mackay, Eric Stewart, Stanley Clarke, and Steve Gadd. Yet even these seven were not on every cut.

Also unlike **Tug Of War, Pipes Of Peace** did not top the album charts, peaking at number four in the U.K. and at number fifteen in the U.S.

Note: The overall packaging of **Pipes Of Peace** reinforced the upbeat imagery. Clive Barker's chrome sculpture "Van Gogh's Chair" appeared on the ivory-colored cover (surrounded by various pipes), the inner sleeve, and the custom record label for side two, while Van Gogh's prototype painting "Chair And Pipe" appeared on the other side of the inner sleeve. There was a different custom label on side one: a delightful reproduction of the 1940s Parlophone label design. (In the U.S. the same was done with the Columbia label.) Finally, the jacket also carried a quotation from Indian poet Rabindranath Tagore: "In love all of life's contradictions dissolve and disappear."

753. OCT 3, 1983 (UK) Parlophone 12R 6062 (12-inch)
OCT 10, 1983 (US) Columbia 44-04169 (12-inch)
by Paul McCartney †with Michael Jackson   Prod: George
Martin †and remixed by John "Jellybean" Benitez
side one
†Say Say Say (long version)–McCartney/Michael Jackson–
5:40
side two
*† *Say Say Say (instrumental)*–McCartney/Michael
Jackson–*7:00*
**Ode To A Koala Bear*–McCartney–*3:45*

754. OCT 31, 1983 (UK) Parlophone PCTC 1652301 (LP)
OCT 31, 1983 (US) Columbia QC 39149 (LP)
by Paul McCartney †with Michael Jackson
PIPES OF PEACE   Prod: George Martin
side one
Pipes Of Peace–McCartney–*3:51*
†Say Say Say–McCartney/Michael Jackson–*3:55*
The Other Me–McCartney–*3:55*
Keep Under Cover–McCartney–*3:03*
So Bad–McCartney–*3:18*
side two
†The Man–McCartney/Michael Jackson–*3:52*
Sweetest Little Show–McCartney–*2:58*
Average Person–McCartney–*4:23*
Hey Hey–McCartney/Stanley Clarke–*2:56*
Tug Of Peace–McCartney–*2:45*
Through Our Love–McCartney–*3:26*

Pipes Of Peace (back cover)   **Columbia QC 39149 (LP)**

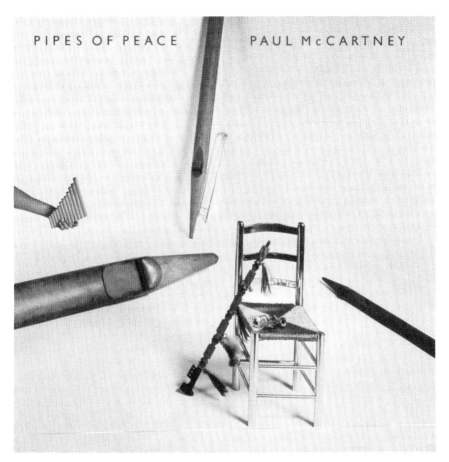

PIPES OF PEACE   PAUL McCARTNEY

Pipes Of Peace (front cover)   **Columbia QC 39149 (LP)**

ENTRY 755. Bill Harry, founder and editor of the legendary *Mersey Beat* music newspaper in the early 1960s, compiled and annotated this two-record sampler of work by Mersey-based performers from 1963 to 1966. The thirty-seven cut package included tracks by the era's biggest stars such as the Beatles, Cilla Black, and Billy J. Kramer, as well as more obscure performers such as the Chants, Dennisons, and Mojos. This gave the set an advantage over the See For Miles **Liverpool 1963–1968** collection released a few months earlier because that one had only non-hit tracks, even by popular performers such as Cilla Black and Billy J. Kramer. For the curious, **Mersey Beat** even included a post-Beatles track by Pete Best, *I'm Gonna Knock On Your Door*.

Note: Though we've never had any particular interest in Pete Best's solo work, some fans have added his records to their collections as odd novelty items, right on through to **The Beatle That Time Forgot** (Phoenix PHX 340) released in 1982. For those so inclined we suggest consulting issue 77 of the collector's magazine *Goldmine* for a detailed article/discography on Best. Be wary, though. One collector wrote to tell us of a Pete Best single issued on Capitol (*Carousel Of Love* b/w *Want You*) that, he said, was not by former Beatle Pete Best but by Australian singer-songwriter Peter Best. Imagine how tired *he* must be of explaining why he was kicked out of the Beatles.

ENTRY 757--757b. All three Beatles-related discs added to the Old Gold nostalgia singles series had track couplings that had not been issued in Britain previously. However, two of them did have Stateside equivalents put out back in the 1960s: Billy J. Kramer's *Bad To Me* b/w *Little Children* (Entry 54) and Peter and Gordon's *A World Without Love* b/w *Nobody I Know* (Entry 139).

755. OCT 31, 1983 (UK) Parlophone PCSP 1783293 (2 LPs)
by Various Artists
MERSEY BEAT
side one
cut one: *SHE LOVES YOU–2:18*
by The Beatles   Prod: George Martin
side two
cut one: *LOVE OF THE LOVED–*L/McC*–2:00*
by Cilla Black   Prod: George Martin
side three
cut one: *I WANT TO HOLD YOUR HAND–2:24*
by The Beatles   Prod: George Martin
cut five: *BAD TO ME–*L/McC*–2:18*
by Billy J. Kramer with The Dakotas   Prod: George
Martin
side four
cut four: *AMERICA–*Leonard Bernstein/Stephen
Sondheim*–2:29*
by Rory Storm and The Hurricanes   Prod: Brian Epstein
Ringo: Backing Vocal

756. NOV 4, 1983 (UK) Cambra CR 103 (2 LPs)
by Various Artists
THE POP EXPLOSION VOLUME 2
side one
cut five: *CRY FOR A SHADOW–*Lennon/Harrison*–2:22*
by The Beatles   Prod: Bert Kaempfert
side two
cut three: *WHY–*Tony Sheridan/Bill Crompton*–2:55*
by Tony Sheridan and The Beatles   Prod: Bert
Kaempfert

757. NOV 25, 1983 (UK) Old Gold OG 9367
by Billy J. Kramer with The Dakotas   Prod: George Martin
A: *DO YOU WANT TO KNOW A SECRET–*L/McC*–1:59*
B: *(trains and boats and planes)*

757a. NOV 25, 1983 (UK) Old Gold OG 9372
by Billy J. Kramer with The Dakotas   Prod: George Martin
A: *BAD TO ME–*L/McC*–2:18*
B: *(little children)*

757b. NOV 25, 1983 (UK) Old Gold OG 9381
by Peter and Gordon   Prod: Norman Newell
A: *A WORLD WITHOUT LOVE–*L/McC*–2:38*
B: *NOBODY I KNOW–*L/McC*–2:27*

ENTRY 758. Following the tremendous success of each release from Michael Jackson's **Thriller** album, Epic in Britain put together a special limited edition singles package (instead of a greatest hits album), drawing from both **Thriller** and Jackson's 1979 **Off The Wall** album. The new records (including *The Girl Is Mine*) were pressed on red vinyl. The nine-disc package even hit the British album charts, peaking at number 66.

ENTRY 759. There was no mention of Wings on this American version of EMI's successful British collection of James Bond movie music (Entry 698). Instead, the artist identification under *Live And Let Die* was simply a vocal credit to Paul McCartney.

ENTRY 760. This album included a printed 5 by 8-inch insert note from Yoko Ono, commenting on the various segments of the interview. See page 273 for further details.

ENTRY 761. The follow-up single to *Say Say Say* consisted of two tracks from **Pipes Of Peace**. *So Bad* was promoted as the A-side in the U.S. while *Pipes Of Peace* was the A-side in the U.K. In both cases, the other song served as the B-side flip. Both singles also came in picture sleeves.

   Pipes Of Peace seemed particularly appropriate for the Christmas season. Besides the obvious message in the lyrics, the recording featured a children's choir in the background. As a further seasonal tie-in, the promotional film for the song was set on a World War I battlefield in France on Christmas Day 1914, recreating a spontaneous one-day truce that was declared by the British and German trench soldiers facing each other. For the film, McCartney played a dual role and appeared on both sides of the battleline.

   So Bad was a simple love ballad featuring McCartney's upper-range vocals. Paul had sung the song at home while working toward the final version, and when his young son seemed a bit left out by lines always directed toward "the girls," Paul added the answer couplet of a girl singing to a boy.

   In Britain, the single was a tremendous success, reaching number one on the charts. This marked the first time that a McCartney solo single hit number one in Britain – two previous U.K. chart toppers had been with Wings (*Mull Of Kintyre*) and Stevie Wonder (*Ebony And Ivory*). The chart performance of *Pipes Of Peace* also brought George Martin a special honor, moving him into a tie for the top spot in the *Guinness Book Of Records* category of producers with the most number one singles in the U.K. In addition, the **Pipes Of Peace** album was also pulled back into the top ten.

   The disc did not fare as well Stateside. Despite the fact that *So Bad* was the follow-up release to a top-selling song (*Say Say Say* was number one in the U.S. the week *So Bad* came out), the new single stalled at number 23 and failed to pump new chart life into the **Pipes Of Peace** album.

758. NOV 25, 1983 (UK) Epic MJ 1 (9 45s)
by Michael Jackson
MICHAEL JACKSON 9 SINGLES PACK
record five: Epic MJ 5
A: THE GIRL IS MINE—Michael Jackson—*3:41*
Paul: Lead Vocal Duet with Michael Jackson
B: (can't get outta the rain)

759. NOV 28, 1983 (US) Liberty LO 51138 (LP)
by Various Artists
JAMES BOND 13 ORIGINAL THEMES
side two
cut one: *LIVE AND LET DIE*—McCartney—*3:10*
by Paul McCartney and Wings   Prod: George Martin
and Paul McCartney

760. DEC 5, 1983 (US) Polydor 817 238-1 Y-1 (LP)
DEC 16, 1983 (UK) Polydor 817 238-1 (LP)
by John Lennon and Yoko Ono; Interview Conducted by
David Sheff
HEART PLAY – **unfinished dialogue** –
side one
Section One—*6:27*
Section Two—*13:41*
Section Three—*0:53*
side two
Section Four—*4:37*
Section Five—*6:02*
Section Six—*4:05*
Section Seven—*6:00*
includes *WOMAN*—Lennon—*0:32*
Prod: John Lennon, Yoko Ono, and Jack Douglas

761. DEC 5, 1983 (UK) Parlophone R 6064
DEC 5, 1983 (US) Columbia 38-04296
†A side in UK; ††A side in US
by Paul McCartney   Prod: George Martin
†A: PIPES OF PEACE—McCartney—*3:25*
††A: SO BAD—McCartney—*3:18*

259

So Bad   **Columbia 38-04296 (45)**

Pipes Of Peace

Parlophone R 6064 (45)

ENTRY 762. Since the See For Miles series began in early 1982, nine of the packages have had some connection to the Beatles.

CM 101 **Off The Beatle Track** by George Martin
    A reissue of the 1964 album Parlophone PCS 3057
CM 104 **First And Fourmost** by The Fourmost (Entry 696)
CM 106 **World Without Love** by Peter & Gordon
    A reissue of the 1977 **Best Of** EMI NUT 8 (Entry 562)
CM 107 **Listen** by Billy J. Kramer
    A reissue of the 1977 **Best Of** EMI NUT 9 (Entry 563)
CM 108 **Got To Get You Into My Life** by Cliff Bennett
    A reissue of the 1978 **Best Of** EMI NUT 14 (Entry 598)
CM 111 **20 One Hit Wonders** by Various Artists (Entry 718)
CM 114 **The Scaffold Singles A's And B's** by Scaffold (Entry 719)
CM 118 **Liverpool 1963--1968** by Various Artists (Entry 743)
CM 119 **Sixties Lost And Found Volume 2** by Various Artists

Entry 763. Guitarist John Williams (from the Australian instrumental group Sky) performed Paul McCartney's signature theme for the film *The Honorary Consul*, scheduled for British theatrical release in early 1984 along with a soundtrack album. John McKenzie, who directed McCartney's *Take It Away* promotional film, was the director for *The Honorary Consul*. There was not any American record tie-in to the earlier 1983 U.S. showing of the movie, which had played under the title *Beyond The Limit* rather than *The Honorary Consul* (the name of the Graham Greene novel the film was based on). It bombed in the U.S.

The single came in a picture sleeve.

ENTRY 765--767. *Beatle Book* writer Mark Lewisohn penned the liner notes for all three of these albums, making them the first Star Club packages to have the song titles listed correctly.

On December 19, Breakaway Records also issued the twelve Beatles audition tracks as **The Audition Tapes** (Breakaway BWY 72). This record contained the same track lineup as the 1982 Audio Fidelity set **The Complete Silver Beatles** (Entry 713). See page 357 and the "New Numbers" section (page 436) for further details.

A week after the three Breakaway Star Club albums came out, Audio Fidelity released its own three-record boxed set, **The Beatles Historic Sessions** (PHX 31). This contained all thirty Star Club songs on two discs (as on Entry 681) along with the twelve audition cuts (as on Entry 713).

Note: In his 1975 book *The Man Who Gave The Beatles Away*, Allan Williams suggested that if the tapes of the Beatles performing live at the Star Club were ever released on record, they could be worth "about ten million quid." We can't help but wonder, though: Did he mean that one album would sell ten million copies or that there would be ten million different packages?

762. DEC 9, 1983 (UK) See For Miles/Charly CM 123 (UK)
by Various Artists
SIXTIES LOST AND FOUND VOLUME 2
side two
cut nine: *LIKE DREAMERS DO*–L/McC–*2:30*
by The Applejacks Prod: Mike Smith

763. DEC 19, 1983 (UK) Island IS 155
by John Williams Prod: Stanley Myers and Richard
Harvey
*A: Theme From "The Honorary Consul"–McCartney–*3:45*
B: (clara's theme)

764. DEC 19, 1983 (US) Atlantic 13243
by The Beatles (A side); Tony Sheridan and The Beatles
(B side) Prod: Bert Kaempfert
A: AIN'T SHE SWEET–Jack Yellen/Milton Ager–*2:12*
B: SWEET GEORGIA BROWN–Ben Bernie/Maceo Pinkard/
Kenneth Casey–*2:03*

765. DEC 30, 1983 (UK) Breakaway BWY 85 (LP)
by The Beatles; recorded live by Ted Taylor in 1962
THE HAMBURG TAPES VOLUME ONE
side one
INTRODUCTION OF THE BAND–*0:21*
I'M GONNA SIT RIGHT DOWN AND CRY (OVER YOU)
–Joe Thomas/Howard Biggs–*2:43*
I SAW HER STANDING THERE–*2:22*
ROLL OVER BEETHOVEN–Chuck Berry–*2:15*
HIPPY HIPPY SHAKE–Chan Romero–*1:42*
LEND ME YOUR COMB–Kay Twomey/Fred Wise/Ben
Weisman–*1:44*
side two
YOUR FEET'S TOO BIG–Ada Benson/Fred Fisher–*2:18*
MR. MOONLIGHT–Roy Lee Johnson–*2:06*
A TASTE OF HONEY–Ric Marlow/Bobby Scott–*1:45*
WHERE HAVE YOU BEEN ALL MY LIFE?–Barry Mann/
Cynthia Weil–*1:55*
I REMEMBER YOU–Johnny Mercer/Victor Schertzinger–
1:54

766. DEC 30, 1983 (UK) Breakaway BWY 86 (LP)
by The Beatles; recorded live by Ted Taylor in 1962
THE HAMBURG TAPES VOLUME TWO
side one
TWIST AND SHOUT—Bert Russell/Phil Medley—*2:03*
SWEET LITTLE SIXTEEN—Chuck Berry—*2:45*
BESAME MUCHO—Consuelo Velazquez/Selig Shaftel—
2:36
REMINISCING—King Curtis—*1:41*
MEDLEY—*2:09*
   KANSAS CITY—Jerry Leiber/Mike Stoller—*1:04*
   HEY-HEY-HEY-HEY—Richard Penniman—*1:05*
side two
'TILL THERE WAS YOU—Meredith Willson—*1:59*
LITTLE QUEENIE—Chuck Berry—*3:51*
FALLING IN LOVE AGAIN (CAN'T HELP IT)—Sammy
Lerner/Frederick Hollander—*1:57*
BE-BOP-A-LULA—Gene Vincent/Tex Davis—*2:29*
MATCHBOX—Carl Perkins—*2:35*

767. DEC 30, 1983 (UK) Breakaway BWY 87 (LP)
by The Beatles; recorded live by Ted Taylor in 1962
THE HAMBURG TAPES VOLUME THREE
side one
ASK ME WHY—*2:26*
*NOTHIN' SHAKIN' (BUT THE LEAVES ON THE
TREES)*—Cirino Colacrai/Eddie Fontaine/Dianne
Lampert/Jack Cleveland—*1:15*
TO KNOW HER IS TO LOVE HER—Phil Spector—*3:02*
HALLELUJAH, I LOVE HER SO—Ray Charles—*2:10*
SHEILA—Tommy Roe—*1:56*
side two
RED SAILS IN THE SUNSET—Jimmy Kennedy/Will
Grosz—*2:00*
EVERYBODY'S TRYING TO BE MY BABY—Carl
Perkins—*2:25*
I'M TALKING ABOUT YOU—Chuck Berry—*1:48*
SHIMMY SHAKE—Joe South/Billy Land—*2:17*
LONG TALL SALLY—Enotris Johnson/Richard
Penniman/Robert Blackwell—*1:45*

PANDEMONIUM SHADOW BALLET

Beatle Talk... the way they were '64 with Red Robinson

Beatle Talk   Great Northwest Music Co. GNW 4007 (LP)

Beatle Talk

Since 1964 there have been only a handful of interview and documentary packages officially issued to the public by the various companies that have handled the Beatles. Of these, **The Beatles' Story** on Capitol, **The McCartney Interview** on Columbia, and John and Yoko's **Heart Play** on Polydor received the widest distribution, with all three making the American album charts.

However, independent entrepreneurs have also put together their own assortment of spoken word, documentary, and interview discs as the next-best-thing to releasing a real Beatles record. Often these just contained public statements made at press conferences, on the radio, or in off-the-cuff interviews and conversations. They provided at best a "pin-up picture" style visit with John, Paul, George, and Ringo rather than any deeply revealing insights. Nonetheless, such Beatle talk does serve as an appropriate souvenir of a particular era.

Here are some suggested talk items to sample. Remember, though, that while most people can play the music of the Beatles over and over again without getting tired of it, very few feel the same about talk discs. In fact, for some, *one* spin is quite enough.

****

The McCartney Interview (LP) (Entry 657)
US: Columbia PC 36987 (December 1980)
UK: Parlophone CHAT 1 (February 1981)

Vic Garbarini's 1980 interview with Paul McCartney was originally meant to be strictly a print piece for *Musician: Player & Listener* magazine. However, the session went so well that McCartney decided to allow the tapes to be used as a special promotional package to U.S. radio stations to help push **McCartney II**. Columbia released the interviews as a two-record set (Columbia A2S-821/AS 822 and AS 823) with one disc (AS 822) containing the entire interview

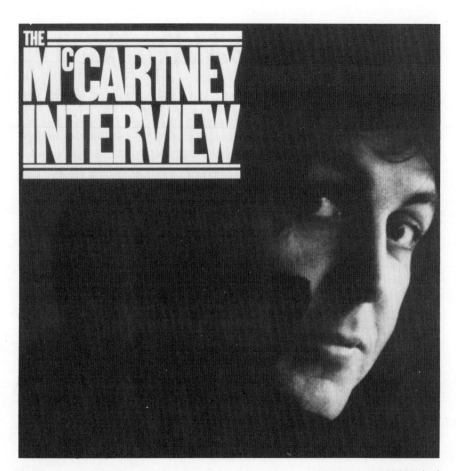

The McCartney Interview   Columbia PC 36987 (LP)

and the other (AS 823) banding the cuts and editing out the questions so that any local DJ could "interview" Paul — or, more likely, just mix the edited comments in with the music.

The two-record set became an instant collector's item, with interest in the package running so high that Columbia (and McCartney) decided to issue the interview as an authorized commercial release. For this, the banded disc was eliminated as superfluous and the complete interview was packaged with the same art as the original promotional copies. The commercial version came out in a limited quantity of 57,000 on Columbia's "Nice Price" $5.98 budget line, so there would be no mistaking the record as a regular "new" McCartney album.

The McCartney Interview hit American stores in early December 1980 and was soon swept up in the buying frenzy following John Lennon's death, even spending three weeks on *Billboard*'s album charts (peaking at 158). In Britain, the album was not released until early 1981 when EMI issued and deleted the record on the same day (February 23). This served to underscore the limited nature of the pressing, though it was also a clever publicity gimmick that helped to concentrate record store orders into a very short period, thereby boosting the album into the British charts (even cracking the top forty) for a few weeks. The instant deletion also meant that, as in the U.S., there was to be no mistaking this for a regular McCartnet album.

As on the original promotional package, the commercial copies of **The McCartney Interview** carried a "topic guide" to each side, though the individual segment timings were dropped. With the wide range of subjects covered — including McCartney's Beatles years — this album functioned quite well as a release to the general public. In 1982, it was nominated for a Grammy award in the category of "Best Spoken Word, Documentary, or Drama Recording," but lost out to an Orson Welles reading of the horror classic, "Donovan's Brain."

Topic Guide to **The McCartney Interview** Album
(time of McCartney comments on the banded promo album):

Side One:

1. *McCartney II (1:28)*
2. *Negative criticism of Beatles & Wings (0:50)*
3. *His influences (0:30)*
4. *Venus & Mars/Wild Life (2:22)*
5. *Band On The Run (1:28)*
6. *Musical Direction/Ringo/George/Hey Jude (1:04)*

7. *The White Album/Tension/Helter Skelter (1:11)*
8. *Abbey Road (0:21)*
9. *Musical Background/Trumpet, guitar, piano/learning bass in Hamburg (2:53)*
10. *Early Beatles mixes/Motown & Stax influences (0:31)*
11. *The Sgt. Pepper Story/The Beach Boys' Pet Sounds (2:04)*
12. *Rubber Soul/Revolver (0:50)*
13. *Fame & success/Paul's & John's reactions (1:55)*
14. *Stage fright during the Beatles and Wings (1:01)*
15. *How Wings started (1:18)*
16. *New Wave/Early Beatles (0:56)*
17. *Creating the Beatles' sound/Love Me Do & early songs (1:17)*

Side Two:

1. *The Beatles' conquest of America (3:10)*
2. *Beatles' haircuts & image (1:46)*
3. *Paying dues in Hamburg & Liverpool/early tours (3:00)*
4. *Weathering pressures/The break-up (2:20)*
5. *Video of Coming Up/Reliving the Beatle image (0:54)*
6. *Playing bass (0:50)*
7. *Lennon-McCartney songwriting/Dislike of formulas (0:41)*
8. *Beatles' imitators (0:58)*
9. *I Am The Walrus/The Black Carnation/Sgt. Pepper L.P. Cover (0:56)*
10. *New Wave/Bowie, Ferry, Elvis (1:01)*
11. *Pop Music & Radio (0:49)*
12. *Getting Married/Changing Perspective/Waterfalls (1:14)*
13. *Give Ireland Back To The Irish, Hi Hi Hi/Banned songs/Children's songs/ Mary Had A Little Lamb (1:20)*

****

John Lennon and Yoko Ono Interviews (1966 to 1980)

John Lennon's 1966 press conference remarks commenting on the "Beatles are more popular than Jesus Christ" controversy received worldwide attention. They even turned up on a mail order album, **I Apologize** (Sterling Products 8893 6481) for those that wanted to preserve the moment and judge for themselves Lennon's explanation and official "apology." Most people at the time seemed satisfied and Lennon's comments helped diffuse some of the tension surrounding what was to be the final Beatles tour of the United States.

A few years later, Lennon was back before the press, this time with Yoko Ono. The two were constantly in the public spotlight with their avant garde art events, bed-ins, and demonstrations for peace. Along the way they granted dozens of interviews, including several that turned up on disc. The most widely distributed record of these was their own **Wedding Album** (see Entry 227 and page 146).

There were also more obscure records.

In 1969, John and Yoko talked on San Francisco radio station KYA, which soon thereafter offered its listeners copies of a special promotional seven-inch disc containing the interview.

On October 8, 1971, John and Yoko held a press conference at the Everson Museum in Syracuse, New York, to help publicize the opening of Yoko Ono's one-woman museum show, "This Is Not Here." Lennon was there officially only as a guest artist at the exhibition but, as usual, the press took the opportunity to work in as many Beatles-related questions as possible, even bluntly asking about George, Ringo, or Paul's participation in the event. Different five-minute excerpts from these conversations (with some overlap) turned up on consecutive editions of **The History Of Syracuse Music** (side two, cut six of Volume VIII/IX and side two, cut seven of Volume X/XI) issued in the mid-1970s. Oddly, the cover to the first package had photos of John, Yoko, and . . . Paul McCartney and Wings! The latter was there, however, because an interview with Syracuse boy Joe English also appeared on the set.

When Lennon and Ono settled in New York City in 1972, they spent some time with such Greenwich Village types as Abbie Hoffman, Jerry Rubin, and "street" singer David Peel. John and Yoko even produced an Apple album by Peel, **The Pope Smokes Dope** (Entry 321), which included a brief snatch of conversation between them to open the track *The Ballad Of New York City – John Lennon/Yoko Ono*. Years later, Peel dug out a two-minute recording of Lennon talking and used it as one of the tracks on his 1977 **Bring Back The Beatles** album, issued on his own Orange Records (Orange 004). He also released that *John Lennon Interview* track as a seven-inch picture disc (Orange 70079PD). In 1980, Peel included two more interview clips on his **John Lennon For President** album (Orange 005), *The Yoko Ono Interview* (0:58) and *The John And Yoko Interview* (1:47).

By then, John and Yoko were on the verge of emerging from five years out of the public eye. Once again, they were ready and willing to talk . . . .

****

271

Heart Play —unfinished dialogue—   **Polydor 817 238-1 Y-1 (LP)**

Heart Play – unfinished dialogue – (LP) (Entry 760)
US: Polydor 817 238-1 Y-1 (December 1983)
UK: Polydor 817 238-1 (December 1983)

As part of the overall promotion for **Double Fantasy** in 1980, John Lennon and Yoko Ono granted a number of interviews from September through December. These included radio sessions with the BBC and the RKO network and, for print, discussions with writers from *Newsweek*, the Los Angeles *Times*, and *Playboy*. Of these, the *Playboy* interviews conducted in September by David Sheff probably provided the best detailed insights into "what, when, and why" – that is, what had John and Yoko been *doing* since 1975 and what were they planning now?

The full-fledged interview text ran in the January 1981 issue of *Playboy* (on sale in early December), with a follow-up article detailing Lennon's comments on his songs appearing in the April 1981 issue. For Christmas 1981, Playboy Press published the conversations in book form as *The Playboy Interviews With John Lennon And Yoko Ono*. This ran nearly 200 pages and included both magazine pieces, along with other material from the interview sessions that had been left out of the articles due to space limitations.

The 1983 **Heart Play** record included selected excerpts from the interview tapes. Because those talk sessions had not been recorded with a commercial record release in mind, the sound quality fluctuated from very good to just acceptable. Nonetheless, they still emerged as a very powerful and touching visit with John and Yoko, who were fresh, eager, and hopeful about their new work together.

The same week that Polydor shipped **Heart Play** in the U.S., NBC's radio network service called The Source presented another excellent Lennon interview program, "John Lennon: A Day On The Radio." This was taken from a February 1975 visit by Lennon to New York radio station WNEW to promote his **Rock'n'Roll** album. John was relaxed, in good humor, and an excellent "guest" disc jockey. The two-hour special was sent to stations either via satellite or on three transcription discs (NBC 83-49).

****

Hear The Beatles Tell All (LP) (Entry 637)
US: Vee Jay PRO 202 (January 1980)
UK: Charly Records CRV 202 (January 1981)

This interview disc was originally issued as a promotional album by Vee Jay Records back in the fall of 1964. That year, the company repackaged its only Beatles music album in three different guises, so this was actually a refreshing change for radio programmers. Nonetheless, Vee Jay's days as a Beatles label were numbered back then, and by the end of 1964 Capitol had won the legal rights to all the Beatles songs previously issued by the company. Vee Jay retained ownership of its specially-produced interview album and, some fifteen years later, the company issued **Hear The Beatles Tell All** as a budget commercial release for the general public. The album sold well enough as a legitimate piece of Beatles history and, in 1981, Charly Records put it out in Britain as well.

The interviews themselves held up surprisingly well. Jim Steck's one-on-one chat with John Lennon on side one was particularly good. Dave Hull's conversation with all the Beatles on side two was a bit more typical of the era, but still provided an excellent taste of the Beatles' public persona, circa 1964.

****

The American Tour With Ed Rudy (LP)
US: Radio Pulsebeat News News Documentary #2 (May 1964)

In the summer of 1964, radio reporter Ed Rudy hit the U.S. top twenty narrating an album package of Beatles interviews taken from their first American visit, including press conferences, phone calls, and in-flight chat. His **American Tour** album was the first successful Beatles interview/documentary package, selling without the aid of even one Beatles song.

That album was only one of several discs done by Ed Rudy while covering the Beatles. He had actually done a special DJ album dubbed **"Beatlemania" Tour Coverage** (News Documentary #1) prior to the commercial release of **The American Tour**, using essentially the same material (first gathered while covering the Beatles in February 1964). After his chart success with **The American Tour**, Rudy put out two more albums: **The New U.S. Tour** (News Documentary #3) and, in 1965, a live "tribute" album called **The Great American Tour 1965 Live "Beatlemania" Concert** (Lloyds LL 1007/1008). For the "Beatlemania" album, Rudy took the sounds of the screaming audience at a Beatles concert and overdubbed a soundalike group called the Liverpool Lads to cover the Beatles music.

There was no Ed Rudy album in 1966. However, the "Ring Around the Pops" organization stepped in with **Beatle-Views** (BV-1966), an album of interviews conducted during the group's final U.S. tour. Ken Douglas served as narrator for the package.

None of these albums followed **The American Tour** onto the charts and soon all of them were out of print. In October 1980, Ed Rudy reissued **The American Tour** as a $10 mail order item sporting a new cover featuring a picture of the Beatles. (Previously, there had only been the album title and a picture of Rudy himself.) He even autographed the new album at no extra charge.

****

The Beatles' Story (2 LPs) (Entry 106)
  US: Capitol STBO 2222 (November 1964)

Capitol followed Ed Rudy's successful album in the fall of 1964 with its own "official" documentary package, **The Beatles' Story**, a deluxe two-record set. This did even better than Rudy's, hitting the U.S. top ten with a slick, glossy history written and narrated by John Babcock, Al Wiman, and Roger Christian, and produced by Gary Usher and Roger Christian. They incorporated background narration, inerviews, crowd reactions, instrumental versions of Beatles songs, and bits of real Beatles music – including the opening riffs to *Twist And Shout* done live at the 1964 Hollywood Bowl concert and Capitol's first attempt at a *Beatles Medley (Things We Said Today/ I'm Happy Just To Dance With You/Little Child/Long Tall Sally/ She Loves You)*.

The Beatles' Story was never out of print from the 1960s through the 1980s. This preserved Capitol's presentation of the group as those "four lovable mop tops" long after they themselves had trashed that image.

Thus, for the 1980s, both **The Beatles' Story** and the Ed Rudy discs functioned best as historical curiosities, illustrating the type of coverage and image that followed the Beatles back in 1964. As such, they were of primary interest to ardent Beatles completists – or to those looking for a dose of wide-eyed innocence after a session with one of those "tell-all" Beatles books of the 1970s and 1980s.

****

Una Sensazionale Intervista Die Beatles (7-inch)
  + Tre Dischi Apple (plus 3 discs)
  Italy: Apple DPR 108 (November 1968)

In August 1968, Apple in Britain packaged its first four single releases into a limited edition presentation packet dubbed "Our First Four." These sets of *Hey Jude, Those Were The Days* (Mary Hopkin), *Sour Milk Sea* (Jackie Lomax), and *Thingumybob* (Black Dyke Mills Brass Band) were delivered to a select number of key locations both in and out of the record industry, including the Royal Palace.

275

A few months later, Apple in Italy put together its own four record package. This one was available for purchase commercially, however, and contained *Quelli Erano Giorni* (*Those Were The Days* in Italian by Mary Hopkin), *Sour Milk Sea* (Jackie Lomax), *Maybe Tomorrow* (Iveys), and, from the Beatles, a special interview disc, *Una Sensazionale Intervista con I Beatles.* That interview was conducted back in England by British DJ Kenny Everett, who talked with the Beatles during the recording sessions for the White Album. It appeared as the A and B sides of the single (running 3:25 and 3:47 respectively), providing a taste of Beatles nonsense from late in their career.

Though not many copies of the interview disc turned up in the U.S. and U.K., during the mid-1970s the material was pirated on various bootleg packages, including a blatant counterfeit of the original single.

****

The Beatles Talk Down Under (LP)
   UK: Goughsound Records GP 5001 (May 1982)
   US: Raven PVC 8911 (May 1982)

Even after the Beatles became worldwide stars, the focus of attention for their releases and career milestones usually fell on either Britain (their home) or the United States. As a result, the rest of the world often appeared to be little more than a footnote, no matter how large the crowds or how successful the events. In 1981, as a bit of national boosterism, Australian Glenn A. Baker put together *The Beatles Down Under*, a book about the record-breaking 1964 tour of Australia and New Zealand by the Beatles. (During their nineteen day swing the group played 32 concerts before more than 200,000 people.)

Baker and Warren Barnett also collected interviews done on the tour and packaged them as a companion record release, **The Beatles Talk Down Under**. The album came out in Australia, then in England and the United States. Running nearly an hour, the record offered conversations from every step of the "down under" tour, beginning with a taped message sent by the Beatles from England to DJ Barry Ferber and ending with their farewell airport interviews in Sydney on July 1, 1964. There was even a day-by-day itinerary presented on the back cover liner notes.

The Beatles Talk Down Under proved particularly good at conveying the sense of developing press coverage in an on-going tour, including the mini-drama of "When will Ringo rejoin the group?" He had missed a number of concerts beginning June 4 due to an attack of tonsillitis, so substitute drummer Jimmy Nicol replaced him for about ten days. By June 15, Ringo was back, just in time for the first of six concerts in Melbourne.

The front cover of the album contained a clear, upfront caption describing the contents: "This album does not contain any music performed by the Beatles and is not a Capitol or EMI Records product. It is comprised of interviews and press conferences only." The material ran in chronological order as follows:

Side One:

1. *Message From England* (March 1964) *0:55*
2. *Hong Kong* (June 10) *2:18*
3. *Darwin* (June 11) *1:12*
4. *Sydney* (June 11) *7:00*
5. *Adelaide* (June 12/13) *10:00*
6. *Sydney* (June 14) *3:30*
7. *Melbourne* (June 15/17) *5:52*
8. *Sydney* (June 18/21) *5:06*

Side Two:

1. *Wellington* (June 22/23) *5:30*
2. *Auckland/Dunedin* (June 24/25) *14:55*
3. *Brisbane* (June 29/30) *2:48*
4. *Sydney* (July 1) *9:52*

****

The Beatles Tapes From The David Wigg Interviews (2 LPs) (Entry 519)
    UK: Polydor 2683 068 (July 1976)
    US: PBR International 7005/6 (1978)

The 1976 British **Beatles Tapes** album was a collection of interviews by David Wigg, done separately with John, Paul, George, and Ringo between 1968 and 1973. The conversations were packaged in a deluxe two-record set with each of the four sides devoted to one of the Beatles. Instrumental versions of Beatles songs served as transition between segments. Despite the tasteful packaging and clear identification of the contents, the Beatles were upset with the album, in part because the interviews had not been granted with a record release in mind. Nonetheless, after some legal protests, the release of **The Beatles Tapes** was allowed to stand and, two years later, it was licensed for American release. The U.S. edition included more elaborate cover artwork and was even pressed on blue colored vinyl,

277

The Beatles Tapes From The
David Wigg Interviews

Polydor 2683 068 (LP)

The Beatles Talk Down Under

Raven PVC 8911 (LP)

but the new package did not sell well and was very quickly out of print. However, import copies of the original British edition continued to sell in the U.S. into the 1980s.

****

Beatle Talk (LP)
US: The Great Northwest Music Co. GNW 4007 (November 1978)

The Beatle Interviews (LP)
UK: Everest CBR 1008 (June 1982)

The Beatles Talk With Jerry G (picture disc LP)
US: Backstage BSR 1165 (October 1982)

The Beatles Talk With Jerry G — Volume 2 (picture disc LP)
US: Backstage BSR 1175 (August 1983)

In 1978 the Great Northwest Music Company revived the idea of packaging Beatles public press conferences with **Beatle Talk**, a twenty-minute album narrated by DJ Red Robinson. He was one of the reporters who recorded their comments at press conferences held in 1964 (Vancouver) and 1966 (Seattle). Four years later, Robinson and his press conference tapes turned up again, in Britain, on the 1982 **Beatle Interviews** album on Everest. This also contained John Lennon's famous "apology" in Chicago over the "Beatles are more popular than Jesus Christ" remark.

Meanwhile, Backstage Records put some Beatles press conference material and an extensive interview with Pete Best on its May 1982 packages of the group's audition tapes (see page 360), then topped that in October with **The Beatles Talk With Jerry G**, a picture disc album devoted entirely to Beatles conversations recorded back in 1964 and 1965 by DJ Jerry G. Bishop. Backstage put out the following year yet another picture disc interview album, **The Beatles Talk With Jerry G — Volume 2**.

****

Timeless (picture disc LP)
US: Silhouette Music SM 10004 (March 1981)

Timeless II (picture disc LP)
US: Silhouette Music SM 10010 (February 1983)

Timeless II½ (7-inch picture disc at 33 1/3)
US: Silhouette Music SM 1451 (April 1983)

279

Beatles press conferences made up the bulk of the material on these souvenir picture discs, issued in 1981 and 1983. **Timeless** also contained bland cover versions of Beatles music and tributes to John Lennon, along with various news reports about his death.

Strictly for those that prefer hanging their records on the wall.

****

The Beatles also talked on a number of promotional discs such as *The Beatles Introduce New Songs*. Consult "Not For You" in *The Beatles Again* and "Bootlegs" in *All Together Now* for further details on such releases.

Since then, a number of other promotional talk items have come to our attention. George Harrison spoke briefly on a 1979 U.S. promo interview record **(The Warner Bros. Music Show: Monty Python Examines The "Life Of Brian")** plugging the Monty Python *Life Of Brian* film (see page 82).

In Britain back in 1966, all four Beatles appeared on a special flexi-disc, *Sound Of The Stars* (Lyn 996), along with other British pop stars such as Cilla Black. This was available free to readers of the British music weekly *Disc & Music Echo* in exchange for two coupons clipped from the paper. Radio Caroline's Tom Lodge conducted the generally light and frivolous interview with the group.

Eight years later, in 1974, John Lennon joined in the celebration of the first anniversary of London's Capitol Radio (October 16, 1974) by adding his message of congratulations (lasting all of six seconds) to a special British promo-only single called *Happy First Birthday From Cuddley Capital — Starring K. Everett Esq And Everybody Who Is Anybody* (Warner Bros. SAM 20).

During that same era, Lennon's voice also appeared on two radio station promotion records issued under the banner: "What's It All About?" Paul McCartney and Ringo Starr also turned up on the series.

What's It All About?
John Lennon & Mind Games (1973)
John Lennon & Rock'n'Roll (1975)
Paul & Linda McCartney On Tour With Wings (1976)
The Beatles (1978)
John Lennon (1981)
Ringo Starr (1981)

These seven-inch discs were part of a regular series sent to U.S. stations for use as short public service-religious programs. Each one ran between four and five minutes, including music, interviews, and narration – all inevitably leading to the question: "What's it all about?" The ready answer: God (specifically, Jesus Christ).

All the interview comments appeared to be taken from public press conferences and were certainly not done specifically for this series. Nonetheless, the use of the Beatles – John Lennon in particular – for such a pop-religion project was an odd juxtaposition of image and values.

In the case of the first disc, there was obviously old territory to cover. With the song *Mind Games* serving as background music, the narrator expressed general admiration of Lennon, but then went on to criticize his pop philosophizing, even working in a replay of the 1966 press conference apology for saying the Beatles were bigger than Jesus Christ.

The second Lennon disc included excerpts from *Can't Buy Me Love, Michelle, Be-Bop-A-Lula, God*, and *Imagine* and was far more upbeat, focusing on Lennon as a positive force who could get people to think: "What's it all about?" The record ended with a verse from *Imagine*, strategically skipping the lines that suggested that *no* (organized) religion was one of the ideals of a perfect world.

The Paul and Linda McCartney program included excerpts from *Silly Love Songs, Band On The Run, Listen To What The Man Said*, and *Jet*, along with press conference comments by Jimmy McCulloch, Joe English, Linda, and Paul. Naturally, the program pointed out McCartney's dissatisfaction with LSD and Eastern meditation from the 1960s, though the main theme of the narration was that even a successful superstar like Paul McCartney still felt the need to search for an answer.

The 1978 Beatles program was standard stuff, using bits of *Twist And Shout, I Saw Her Standing There, Help, Strawberry Fields Forever, Yesterday, A Hard Day's Night, Get Back, Lady Madonna, Come Together, Let It Be*, and *The End* in the narration. Ringo's 1981 program included selections from *Yellow Submarine, I Wanna Be Your Man, You're Sixteen, With A Little Help From My Friends*, and *It Don't Come Easy*.

Finally, the 1981 John Lennon program was a career retrospective. Part one traced the Beatles days, with excerpts from *A Day In The Life, A Hard Day's Night, Help, I Am The Walrus, Strawberry Fields Forever, Lucy In The Sky With Diamonds, Revolution*, and *Come Together*. The second half of the show focused on Lennon's solo career. Once again, there was a carefully chosen excerpt from *Imagine*, as well as selections from *Give Peace A Chance, The Ballad Of John And Yoko, Instant Karma, Whatever Gets You Thru The Night, (Just Like) Starting Over*, and *God*. The narration presented John Lennon as a modern spiritual pop poet who believed in the divine potential of humanity.

281

****

In 1979, Mercury Records added to the talk category with its two-record promotional album **The Ultimate Radio Bootleg, Vol. III** (Mercury MK 2-121). This included a brief *Transcontinental Beatle Interview* (meaning it was over the phone) conducted by Chicago DJs Art Roberts and Ron Riley back in 1964 for WLS radio. In 1982 Capitol Records even came close to issuing an official interview track on the flipside of *The Beatles' Movie Medley* (Entry 699), but pulled back at the last minute.

The following checklist serves as a guide to these promotional discs, as well as to the other talk records discussed either here in *The End Of The Beatles?* (*), in *The Beatles Again* (%), or in *All Together Now* (†). All are U.S. releases unless otherwise indicated.

*†**The American Tour With Ed Rudy** (News Documentary #2)
%**Band On The Run Open-End Interview** (Apple)
***The Beatle Interviews** (Everest CBR 1008) (UK only)
***Beatle Talk** (Great Northwest Music Co. GNW 4007)
***Beatle-Views** (BV-1966)
*"**Beatlemania" Tour Coverage** (News Documentary #1)
†*The Beatles And Murray The K – As It Happened* (Fairway OV-526-1)
*%†**The Beatles Christmas Album** (Apple SBC 100 in US) and (Apple LYN 2153 in UK)
%*The Beatles Introduce New Songs* (Capitol PRO 2720)
%*The Beatles Open-End Interview* (Capitol Compact 33 PRO 2548/2549)
%*The Beatles Second Open-End Interview* (Capitol Compact 33 PRO 2598/2599)
*†**The Beatles' Story** (Capitol STBO 2222)
***The Beatles Talk Down Under** (Raven PVC 8911 in US) and (Goughsound GP 5001 in UK)
***The Beatles Talk With Jerry G** (Backstage BRS 1165)
***The Beatles Talk With Jerry G—Volume 2** (Backstage BSR 1175)
*%**The Beatles Tapes From The David Wigg Interviews** (Polydor 2683 068 in UK) and (PBR International 7005/6 in US)
***Bring Back The Beatles** (Orange Records 004)
†%**Dark Horse Radio Special** (Dark Horse 1974)
%*Dialogue From The Motion Picture "Let It Be"* (Beatles Promo 1970)
%**Earth News Interviews**
*_Fab Four On Film_ (Capitol B 5100)
%†**Get Off: Anti-Drug Public Service Announcements**
***Great American Tour 1965—Live "Beatlemania" Concert** (Lloyds LL 1007/1008)
*_Happy First Birthday From Cuddley Capital—Starring K. Everett Esq And Everybody Who Is Anybody_ (Warner Bros. SAM 20) (UK only)

*%†**Hear The Beatles Tell All** (Vee Jay PRO 202 in US) and (Charly CRV 202 in UK)

***Heart Play—unfinished dialogue—** (Polydor 817 238-1 Y-1 in US) and (Polydor 817 238-1 in UK)

***History Of Syracuse Music Vols. VIII/IX**

***History Of Syracuse Music Vols. X/XI**

***I Apologize** (Sterling Products 8893 6481)

†*IBBW Interview* (Tom Clay—*Remember, We Don't Like Them, We Love Them*)

%**An Introduction To Roy Harper** (Chrysalis PRO 620)

***John Lennon: A Day On The Radio** (NBC 83-49)

***John Lennon For President** (Orange Records 005)

**The John Lennon Interview* (Orange Records 70079PD)

%*John Lennon On Ronnie Hawkins* (Cotillion PR 104/105)

%*KFWBeatles Talk* (RB 2637/2638)

*KYA Peace Talk

***The McCartney Interview** (Columbia PC 36987 in US) and (Parlophone CHAT 1 in UK)

***The New U.S. Tour With Ed Rudy** (News Documentary #3)

%**Personal Music Dialogue At 33 1/3** (Dark Horse PRO 649)

**Sound Of The Stars* (Lyn 996) (UK only)

***Timeless** (Silhouette Music SM 10004)

***Timeless II** (Silhouette Music SM 10010)

***Timeless II½** (Silhouette Music SM 1451)

***The Ultimate Radio Bootleg, Vol. III** (Mercury MK 2-121)

**Una Sensazionale Intervista con I Beatles* (Apple DPR 108) (Italy only)

***The Warner Bros. Music Show: Monty Python Examines The "Life Of Brian"** (Warner Bros. WBMS 110)

**What's It All About?* (various editions)

   John Lennon & Mind Games (1973)

   John Lennon & Rock'n'Roll (1975)

   Paul & Linda McCartney On Tour With Wings (1976)

   The Beatles (1978)

   John Lennon (1981)

   Ringo Starr (1981)

****

The Last Word

The best "talk" album by the Beatles was the 1970 **Beatles Christmas Album** (Entry 270), which collected the seven recorded messages they sent to their fan club members from 1963 to 1969. Early messages consisted of John, Paul, George, and Ringo delivering cheery greetings for the holiday season, while later ones evolved into elaborate sound and music skits. All were quite entertaining and served as delightful visits with the Fab Four.

The Beatles Christmas Album was available from the official Beatles fan club until the organization shut down in 1972. Since then, bootleggers have put out counterfeit copies of the original album package and, in 1982 and 1983, a few companies even tried to pass off their discs as legitimate releases under such titles as Christmas Reflections (Desert Vibrations Heritage Series HSRD-SP1) and Happy Michaelmas (Adirondack Group AG-8146). However, these were all unauthorized and illegal.

When a company called Richy Records announced plans for a similar release in late 1983 — citing the previous Happy Michaelmas as a precedent-setting "legitimate" package — Apple and EMI at last went to court. They won a preliminary injunction barring the album's issuance until a full trial on the matter could be held some time in 1984, effectively arguing that if anyone had the rights to release those tracks it was EMI.

Unfortunately, this meant that until such a legal release of The Beatles Christmas Album, some of the best Beatles talk ever recorded remained officially unavailable to millions of interested fans.

Family
And Friends
And Assorted Hangers-On

Even without direct musical involvement by Lennon, McCartney, Harrison, or Starr, releases from their "extended family" (and friends) have always held a special attraction — and have sometimes even turned into fan favorites themselves. This section covers recent ventures in this area, along with a selection of tributes, novelty-items, and parodies. Included is material from:

Yoko Ono
Linda McCartney
Scaffold
Mike McCartney (McGear)
Roger McGough
John Gorman
Denny Laine
Laurence Juber
Professor Longhair
Zoot Money
The Cimarons
Harry Nilsson
Roxy Music
Phil Collins
Elton John
Queen

Billy Joel
Pink Floyd
Mike Oldfield
Paul Simon
Royal Liverpool Philharmonic
    Orchestra
Royal Philharmonic Orchestra
Beatlemania
*Sgt. Pepper's Lonely Hearts
    Club Band*
Stars On 45
Beatlesongs (Selected Beatles
    Novelties)
Peter Sellers
The Rutles

It's Alright   **Polydor PD 1 6364 (LP)**

My Man   **Polydor PD 2224 (45)**

Yoko Ono. With the release of **Double Fantasy** in 1980, Yoko Ono at last won grudging acceptance among critics and the general public. As a result, when she continued her recording career following the death of John Lennon, people were at least willing to give her new records a chance.

One reason for this new attitude was that rock music itself had changed, with the styles of some new wave artists actually quite reminiscent of Yoko Ono ten years before. What had seemed so alien back in 1969 could turn up in the 1980s as a dance club smash or even a top forty hit.

Beyond that, however, was the fact that **Double Fantasy** had emphasized ballads and more accessible rock songs from Yoko. Even though she had been writing and singing such music since the early 1970s (*Mrs. Lennon* and *Midsummer New York* on **Fly**, for instance), her image as an abstract screamer kept most people from ever noticing other sides of her work. Thus, songs such as *Beautiful Boys, I'm Moving On*, and *Hard Times Are Over* came as a pleasant surprise. At the same time, her upbeat new wave-ish *Kiss Kiss Kiss* proved popular at New York dance clubs.

Sensing that the time was at last right for a Yoko Ono solo hit, John and Yoko selected for single release two tracks not included on **Double Fantasy**: a strong dance number (*Walking On Thin Ice*) and a soft ballad (*It Happened*). Lennon had been working on the final mix of the A-side the night he died.

After some soul-searching, Yoko released the single in early 1981 (Entry 666), explaining her decision to do so in the liner notes on the picture sleeve. These also gave a bit of the history behind the song *It Happened*, which had previously been released in Japan in 1974. Apparently Lennon had found the nearly seven-year-old recording among Yoko's old tapes, fell in love with it, and boldly proclaimed, "I'll make it a hit!" He, Yoko, and Jack Douglas then edited and remixed the song. For its fresh release, there was even a newly recorded conversation between John and Yoko as they walked through Central Park in New York City during a promotional film/photo session, with Lennon gently ribbing Yoko's business acumen. "Hey Yoko," he said, "Why don't you buy that building? Then you could have one room to keep your fur coats and one to keep cats in."

Walking On Thin Ice marked the first time that a Yoko Ono solo single ever hit the charts. Still, that was just completing a task she had begun with John. A truly solo effort followed, **Season Of Glass**, recorded at the same studio as **Double Fantasy** (New York's Hit Factory), with the same core of musicians.

At first Yoko had Phil Spector supervise the production, but when that arrangement failed to work out, she finished producing

No, No, No   **Geffen GEF 49802 (45)**

the album herself. She turned out fourteen tracks that dealt both directly and obliquely with her emotions. *No, No, No*, for instance, contained angry screams, gunshots, and sirens. *Goodbye Sadness*, on the other hand, was a simple sad ballad. Even five-year-old Sean joined in, telling *A Little Story* that John had taught him.

The cover of the album was particularly striking, with the New York City skyline as seen from a window in their apartment at the Dakota in the background and Lennon's blood-stained glasses beside a half-filled glass of water in the foreground. Despite the disturbing images in the music and on the package (or perhaps because of them), **Season Of Glass** received generally positive reviews. For many Beatles fans, in fact, the album served as a very special contact with Yoko Ono, sharing extremely sensitive feelings and emotions.

Season Of Glass reached 49 on *Billboard*'s charts. It would probably have done even better had the *Walking On Thin Ice* track been included. Instead, two new singles were taken from the album: *No, No, No* and *Goodbye Sadness.*

No, No, No came in a picture sleeve that featured a photo of Yoko in the streets of New York on the frontside and a drawing by Sean on the back. In addition, Sean's *A Little Story* was mixed into the *No, No, No* track over an instrumental bridge. The same packaging was used for the promotional 12-inch disc, which featured three additional songs from the album on the flip side. To help promote the follow-up *Goodbye Sadness* single, Yoko put together a special film for the fall 1981 premiere of NBC's *Saturday Night Live.*

Despite these efforts, neither single hit the charts. In 1982, Yoko Ono and Geffen Records split. To close their deal, Geffen released one more album, a Lennon greatest hits package (Entry 729).

Yoko, meanwhile, signed with Polydor Records worldwide. Her first release for the company was the **It's Alright** album, with the song *My Man* issued as a lead single. Subtitled "An Air Play," **It's Alright** contained ten generally upbeat tracks, with Yoko acting as sole producer right from the start. On one cut, *Never Say Goodbye*, she mixed in an old tape of John shouting her name. Otherwise the songs were remarkably straightforward ballads and dance tunes, once again recorded at the Hit Factory, though with a different set of musicians from **Double Fantasy** and **Season Of Glass.**

My Man was issued in an attractive rainbow picture sleeve and also released to radio stations as a promotional 12-inch (Polydor PRO 192). The follow-up, *Never Say Goodbye* backed with *Loneliness*, was issued as a commercial 12-inch single, with both songs remixed into new extended versions. Once again, though, neither single hit the charts. However, **It's Alright** did crack the *Billboard* top 100, coming in at 98.

In December 1983, Polydor issued a John and Yoko talk album (Entry 760 and page 273), with the remaining tracks from the **Double Fantasy** sessions scheduled for release in early 1984. (See page 413.)

JUN 8, 1981 (US) Geffen GHS-2004 (LP)
JUN 12, 1981 (UK) Geffen K 99164 (LP)
    by Yoko Ono and †Sean Ono Lennon
SEASON OF GLASS Prod: Yoko Ono and Phil Spector
side one
*Goodbye Sadness—*Yoko Ono*—3:48*
*Mindweaver—*Yoko Ono*—4:24*
*†A Little Story—*Sean Ono Lennon*—1:08*
*Even When You're Far Away—*Yoko Ono*—4:12*
*Nobody Sees Me Like You Do—*Yoko Ono*—3:31*
*Turn Of The Wheel—*Yoko Ono*—2:41*
*Dogtown—*Yoko Ono*—3:22*
*Silver Horse—*Yoko Ono*—3:03*
side two
*I Don't Know Why—*Yoko Ono*—4:18*
*Extension 33—*Yoko Ono*—2:45*
*No, No, No—*Yoko Ono*—2:43*
*Will You Touch Me—*Yoko Ono*—2:37*
*She Gets Down On Her Knees—*Yoko Ono*—4:13*
*Toyboat—*Yoko Ono*—3:31*
*Mother Of The Universe—*Yoko Ono*—4:26*

AUG 26, 1981 (US) Geffen GEF 49802
    by Yoko Ono Prod: Yoko Ono and Phil Spector
A: MEDLEY—3:37
        *NO, NO, NO—*Yoko Ono*—3:37*
        *A LITTLE STORY—*Sean Ono Lennon*—0:42*
*B: WILL YOU TOUCH ME—*Yoko Ono*—2:36*

Promotional 12-inch (US) Geffen PRO A-975 (AUG 1981)
    by Yoko Ono Prod: Yoko Ono and Phil Spector
side one
    MEDLEY—3:37
        *NO, NO, NO—*Yoko Ono*—3:37*
        *A LITTLE STORY—*Sean Ono Lennon*—0:42*
side two
    *DOG TOWN—*Yoko Ono*—3:37*
    *I DON'T KNOW WHY—*Yoko Ono*—3:59*
    *SHE GETS DOWN ON HER KNEES—*Yoko Ono*—4:03*

SEP 30, 1981 (US) Geffen GEF 49849
    by Yoko Ono Prod: Yoko Ono and Phil Spector
*A: GOODBYE SADNESS—*Yoko Ono*—3:48*
*B: I DON'T KNOW WHY—*Yoko Ono*—4:19*

NOV 8, 1982 (US) Polydor PD 2224
DEC 3, 1982 (UK) Polydor POSP 541
   by Yoko Ono Prod: Yoko Ono
A: My Man—Yoko Ono—*3:56*
B: Let The Tears Dry—Yoko Ono—*3:26*

NOV 29, 1982 (US) Polydor PD-1-6364 (LP)
DEC 10, 1982 (UK) Polydor POLD 5073 (LP)
   by Yoko Ono
IT'S ALRIGHT Prod: Yoko Ono
side one
My Man—Yoko Ono—*3:56*
Never Say Goodbye—Yoko Ono—*4:25*
Spec Of Dust—Yoko Ono—*3:31*
Loneliness—Yoko Ono—*3:47*
Tomorrow May Never Come—Yoko Ono—*2:26*
side two
It's Alright—Yoko Ono—*4:23*
Wake Up—Yoko Ono—*3:47*
Let The Tears Dry—Yoko Ono—*3:24*
Dream Love—Yoko Ono—*4:53*
I See Rainbows—Yoko Ono—*3:15*

FEB 7, 1983 (US) Polydor 810 556-7
   by Yoko Ono Prod: Yoko Ono
A: NEVER SAY GOODBYE—Yoko Ono—*3:24*
B: LONELINESS—Yoko Ono—*3:21*

FEB 28, 1983 (US) Polydor 810 575-1 (12-inch)
   by Yoko Ono Prod: Yoko Ono
A: NEVER SAY GOODBYE (long version)—Yoko Ono—*4:27*
B: LONELINESS (long version)—Yoko Ono—*4:20*

As part of Yoko Ono's new-found acceptability among listeners and collectors, interest in her previous releases picked up as well. See pages 146--150 for a quick overview of Yoko Ono's solo efforts in the U.S. and the U.K. before 1980. For a more detailed discussion of the material, consult *The Beatles Again* and *All Together Now*.

During that time, there were also three special releases issued in Japan only. Two were commercial singles, one was a promotional album.

APR 1973 (JAPAN) Apple 10344
   by Yoko Ono Plastic Ono Band with Elephant's Memory Prod: Yoko Ono
*A: Josei Joi Banzai—Yoko Ono—*2:51*
*B: Josei Joi Banzai (Part 2)—Yoko Ono—*5:11*

Promotional Album (JAPAN) Apple PRP-8026 (1973)
WELCOME (THE MANY SIDES OF YOKO ONO)
side one
†GROWING PAIN–Yoko Ono–*3:50*
APPROXIMATELY INFINITE UNIVERSE–Yoko Ono–*3:19*
I WANT MY LOVE TO REST TONIGHT–Yoko Ono–*5:11*
NOW OR NEVER–Yoko Ono–*4:57*
SHIRANAKATTA (I DIDN'T KNOW)–Yoko Ono–*3:13*
†RUN, RUN, RUN–Yoko Ono–*5:07*
LOOKING OVER FROM MY HOTEL WINDOW–Yoko Ono–*3:13*
†MEN, MEN, MEN–Yoko Ono–*4:01*
side two
%JOSEI JOI BANZAI–Yoko Ono–*2:51*
$DON'T WORRY KYOKO–Yoko Ono–*4:52*
WOMAN POWER–Yoko Ono–*4:50*
MOVE ON FAST–Yoko Ono–*3:40*
†COFFIN CAR–Yoko Ono–*3:29*
YANG YANG–Yoko Ono–*3:52*
WHAT A MESS–Yoko Ono–*2:41*
†STRAIGHT TALK–Yoko Ono–*3:18*
　　　All tracks taken from the album **Approximately Infinite Universe** except †
from the album **Feeling The Space**, % the A side of the *Josei Joi Banzai* single,
and $ the B side of the *Cold Turkey* single.

FALL 1974 (JAPAN) Odeon EOR-10628
　　　by Yoko Ono and Plastic Ono Super Band　Prod: Yoko Ono and David
　　　　　Spinozza
*A: Yume O Motou (Let's Have A Dream)–Yoko Ono–*3:50*
*B: It Happened–Yoko Ono–*3:51*

　　　Some people unfamiliar with Yoko Ono's solo career mistakenly
assumed that all the tracks on the promotional **Welcome** album were
previously unreleased, thus including some otherwise unavailable
John Lennon recording work. Though Lennon was associated as a
co-producer and/or musician for all but five of the cuts on **Welcome**
(*Growing Pain, Run, Run, Run; Josei Joi Banzai; Coffin Car;* and
Straight Talk), all of those songs had been previously released in both
the U.S. and the U.K. Only *Josei Joi Banzai* could possibly be
considered "rare," having been released only in Japan.
　　　Still, at the time, **Welcome** served its purpose, offering Japanese
DJs a handy sampler of Yoko Ono's most recent album work. This
provided a most appropriate "welcome" vehicle for her solo tour of
Japan in the summer of 1974. The picture sleeve to the tie-in tour
single, *Yume O Motou (Let's Have A Dream)*, even featured a photo
of Yoko and her stage band, though both single tracks were recorded
back in the U.S.
　　　Like both sides of *Josei Joi Banzai*, the A-side of *Yume O Motou*

292

did not turn up outside Japan. However, the B-side song, *It Happened*, ended up on the flip side to *Walking On Thin Ice* in 1981. Though sounding like the same take, the 1974 Japanese record label listed Yoko Ono and David Spinozza as producers, while the sleeve notes for the 1981 release identified John and Yoko as the original producers in 1973.

****

Linda McCartney. Paul McCartney brought wife Linda into his musical career in the early 1970s, first as a backing vocalist on **McCartney**, then as a song co-author (beginning with *Another Day*), and finally as a full-fledged member (on keyboards) of Wings. These moves were greeted with considerable skepticism, especially by McCartney's music publisher. After all, Linda had never done any song writing previously, yet she was listed as co-writer and entitled to half the royalties from many new Paul McCartney compositions. (See page 12.)

Though this was eventually ruled quite acceptable in court, Linda did turn out several songs on her own anyway – if only to prove the point. One of these, *Seaside Woman*, was issued in 1977 under the pseudonym Suzy and the Red Stripes (though everyone knew it was Wings featuring Linda McCartney). *Seaside Woman* was also used as the basis for an animated film short directed by Oscar Grillo. This earned first prize as the official British entry for the short film category at the 1980 Cannes Film Festival. Another solo song, *Oriental Nightfish*, turned up only as the soundtrack to another short film and was not released on disc.

Otherwise, Linda McCartney's solo efforts remained unreleased through 1983. At a 1980 promotion for the commercial release of the *Seaside Woman* film in England, Linda told *Melody Maker*'s Colin Irwin that she had enough in the can for a solo album. In 1982 and 1983 she added to this total, spending some time in the studio with producer Tony Visconti on such tracks as *Love's Full Glory*. Mary Hopkin and Lene Lovich stopped by as backing vocalists for the sessions.

An entire album by Linda McCartney, then, would not be out of the question some time in the future.

MAY 31, 1977 (US) Epic 8-50403
AUG 10, 1979 (UK) A&M AMS 7461
    by Suzy and The Red Stripes   Prod: Paul McCartney
*A: Seaside Woman–McCartney–3:36
*B: B-Side To Seaside–McCartney–2:36

Also issued in the U.K. in 1979 as A&M AMSP 7461, a boxed set containing the record pressed on yellow vinyl, ten "seaside" post-cards, and a badge. The disc was reissued in the U.K. July 18, 1980 under the name Linda McCartney (alias Suzy and the Red Stripes) on A&M AMS 7548 and A&M AMSP 7548 (12-inch). All had the same recording.

When Paul McCartney does guest backing vocals for other performers, Linda is sometimes there as well. However, for the 1979 **Thriller** album by Eddie and the Hot Rods (recorded at Abbey Road studios), only Linda made the album credits as a backing vocalist. Though the liner notes did not offer a track-by-track listing of personnel, she most likely appeared on the *Power And The Glory* cut, also issued as a single.

MAR 2, 1979 (UK) Island ILPS 9563 (LP)
    by Eddie and The Hot Rods
        Linda McCartney: Backing Vocal
THRILLER Prod: Peter Ker; assisted by The Hot Rods
side one
Power And The Glory—Graeme Douglas—*4:17*
Echoes—Steve Nicol/Paul Gray—*3:00*
Media Messiahs—Graeme Douglas—*3:05*
Circles—Dave Higgs—*2:53*
He Does It With Mirrors—Graeme Douglas/Dave Higgs—*4:04*
side two
Strangers—Graeme Douglas—*2:43*
Out To Lunch—Dave Higgs—*4:43*
Breathless—Graeme Douglas/Paul Gray—*3:32*
Take It Or Leave It—Graeme Douglas/Barrie Masters—*4:05*
Living Dangerously—Dave Higgs—*3:34*

MAR 2, 1979 (UK) Island WIP 6474
    by Eddie and The Hot Rods Prod: Peter Ker; assisted by The Hot Rods
A: *Power And The Glory*—Graeme Douglas—*4:17*
B: *(highland one hopefuls two)*

****

Scaffold. Scaffold was a music and humor trio from Liverpool formed in 1963 by Mike McCartney (McGear), Roger McGough, and John Gorman. They did excellent live concert work and turned out some high quality discs for Parlophone Records, including two number ones in Britain: *Thank U Very Much* (1967) and *Lily The Pink* (1968). Along the way, they also had to deal with the fact that to many people Scaffold was merely "that group with Paul McCartney's brother in it." To combat this early on, Mike McCartney changed his professional name to McGear, forcing people to spend at least a few minutes with each group member, trying to determine "Which is the one . . . ?"

Still, having such a famous relative did not hurt. Paul occasionally helped on specific tracks and was around visiting and watching on others. In our main discography section, we have included only those songs that Paul actively took part in as a producer, performer, arranger, or writer. Otherwise, even if he attended the sessions, we've treated him as just an interested observer (the case on *Thank U Very Much* and *Lily The Pink*, for instance). Sometimes a few other superstars came along to play as well, with the likes of Jack Bruce and Graham Nash on *Lily The Pink* and John Mayall, Nash, Dave Mason, Mitch Mitchell, and Jimi Hendrix appearing on the **McGough And McGear** album.

Scaffold's heyday was in the late 1960s. By 1971, Gorman, McGough, and McGear needed a break. McGear recorded a solo album (**Woman**) in 1972, collaborating with McGough and other guest artists, including Paul (see page 443). Then all three helped form a larger conglomeration of poetic musical humorists, dubbed Grimms. McGear left that group after two albums and did a bit more solo work, though he and McGough and Gorman continued to record as Scaffold on and off through 1977 (on Island, Warner Bros., and Bronze Records). For complete details of these Scaffold, Grimms, and Mike McGear solo releases from 1966 to 1977, consult *The Beatles Again* (pages 101–113).

Since 1977, Mike McGear, Roger McGough, and John Gorman have taken off on their own individual pursuits. The only Scaffold tracks issued since 1977 have been repackagings of old material, highlighted by a twenty-two cut compilation album in 1982.

OCT 21, 1977 (UK) EMI 2690 (EP)
    by Scaffold   Prod: Norrie Paramor except † Tony Palmer
side one
    LILY THE PINK—Trad. arr. John Gorman/Mike McGear/Roger McGough—*4:15*
    †*THANK U VERY MUCH*—Mike McGear—*2:30*
side two
    DO YOU REMEMBER?—Mike McGear/Roger McGough—*2:48*
    GIN GAN GOOLIE Trad. arr. Mike McGear/Roger McGough—*2:43*

DEC 2, 1977 (UK) EMI NUT 6 (LP)
Reissued October 1980 as Music For Pleasure MFP 50491
    by Various Artists
20 GOLDEN NUMBER ONES
side two
    cut nine: *LILY THE PINK*—Trad. arr. John Gorman/Mike McGear/Roger
    McGough—*4:15*
        by Scaffold   Prod: Norrie Paramor

JAN 13, 1978 (UK) Double-UP DUOS 1262 (LP)
by Various Artists
40 YEARS FROM LAMBETH WALK
LILY THE PINK—Trad. arr. John Gorman/Mike McGear/Roger McGough—
4:15
by Scaffold Prod: Norrie Paramor

JUL 4, 1980 (UK) Music For Pleasure MFP 55024 (2 LPs)
by Various Artists
HITS FROM THE SWINGING SIXTIES
side three
cut one: *THANK U VERY MUCH*—Mike McGear—*2:30*
by Scaffold Prod: Tony Palmer

OCT 18, 1982 (UK) Charly/See For Miles CM 114 (LP)
by Scaffold
THE SCAFFOLD SINGLES A'S AND B'S Prod: Norrie Paramor except †Paul
McCartney; %George Martin; $Tony Palmer; +Norrie Paramor and Tim
Rice; ††John Burgess; %%Simon Napier Bell and Ray Singer; $$Brian
Gasciogne and Howard Blake; ++Mike McGear
side one
%2 DAY'S MONDAY—John Gorman/Mike McGear/Roger McGough—*2:23*
††GOODBAT NIGHTMAN—Mike McGear/Roger McGough—*2:09*
$THANK U VERY MUCH—Mike McGear—*2:30*
DO YOU REMEMBER?—Mike McGear/Roger McGough—*2:48*
1-2-3—Mike McGear—*3:27*
LILY THE PINK—Trad. arr. John Gorman/Mike McGear/Roger McGough—*4:15*
+CHARITY BUBBLES—Mike McGear/Roger McGough—*2:40*
GIN GAN GOOLIE—Trad. arr. Mike McGear/Roger McGough—*2:43*
LIVER BIRDS—John Gorman/Mike McGear/Roger McGough—*2:27*
%%BUSDREAMS—Mike McGear/Roger McGough—*2:02*
†LIVERPOOL LOU—Dominic Behan—*2:58*
side two
%3 BLIND JELLYFISH—John Gorman/Mike McGear/Roger McGough/*1:58*
$IDE B THE FIRST—Mike McGear/Roger McGough—*2:30*
CARRY ON KROW—Trad. arr. John Gorman—*1:53*
TODAY—Mike McGear—*2:40*
BUTTONS OF YOUR MIND—Mike McGear/Roger McGough—*3:24*
+GOOSE—Mike McGear/Roger McGough—*2:34*
$$ALL THE WAY UP—Howard Blake—*3:23*
PLEASE SORRY—Mike McGear—*2:30*
†TEN YEARS AFTER ON STRAWBERRY JAM—McCartney—*2:52*
COMMERCIAL BREAK—Mike McGear/Roger McGough—*3:00*
++DO THE ALBERT—Mike McGear/Roger McGough—*2:59*

While the See For Miles collection was comprehensive, it still
left out a few single tracks that were never put on any Scaffold
album. These included one 1970 Parlophone cut (*If I Could Start
All Over Again*, the flip of *Busdreams*), a track for Warner Bros. not

296

included on the 1975 **Sold Out** album (*The Wind Is Blowing*, the flip of *Mummy Won't Be Home For Christmas*), and the 1976 and 1977 singles on Bronze (*Wouldn't It Be Funny If You Didn't Have A Nose* backed with *Mr. Noselighter* and *How D'You Do* backed with *Paper Underpants*).

One other Parlophone B-side, *Long Strong Black Pudding* (the flip of *Goodbat Nightman* from 1966), was also omitted from the See For Miles collection, though it did appear on the U.S. **Thank U Very Much** album issued in 1968. That album also included a track never issued in Britain, *Knees Up Mother Brown (Knees Down Mother Brown)*.

* * * * * * * * * *

Mike McGear. Between 1977 and 1983, Mike McGear turned out only two records as a solo artist, *All The Whales In The Ocean* and *No Lar Di Dar (Is Lady Di)*.

All The Whales In The Ocean was a folk-ish ballad celebrating "all creatures great and small" against their human hunters. The track was recorded in Liverpool, where McGear shared production chores with another Mersey man, Billy Kinsley. Together they managed to work in a whale's heartbeat, the sounds of the sea, and Mike's children (in the chorus). Though he did not record this strictly as a rallying tune, McGear did join in on some related "Save The Whales" benefit performances in England and Holland. The song was also used as the final number on a thirteen-track compilation album released in Holland to help support the whale compaign.

Brother Paul found the tune particularly captivating. Mike played him a rough mix before Wings set off for Japan in 1980 and — while in jail — McCartney found he could not get the song out of his head. As he later playfully complained to Mike, "I couldn't stop singing the bloody thing in my cell!"

In contrast to *All The Whales In The Ocean*, which was developed and promoted internationally over several months, *No Lar Di Dar (Is Lady Di)* the following year was a flash inspiration tie-in to the wedding of Lady Diana Spencer and Prince Charles. The song marked the first collaboration between McGear and Roger McGough in four years. Unfortunately for them, the release came out practically on the wedding day and could not ride all the hoopla preceding the event. By the time the record hit the shops, the joke was old news. As a result, it was never necessary to test McGear's conviction behind the promise on the sleeve: "Limited to 5 million copies worldwide."

The *No Lar Di Dar* single also caught Mike in the midst of his metamorphosis from McGear back to McCartney, with the label

297

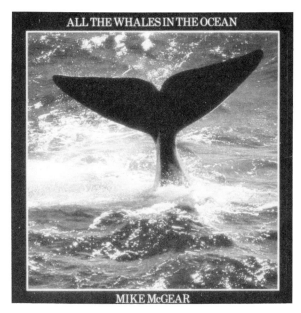

All The Whales In The Ocean   Carrere CAR 144 (45)

No Lar Di Dar (Is Lady Di) Conn Records CONN 29781 (45)

credits including both names. By the end of the year, when his auto-biography/family album came out (*The Macs*, called *Thank U Very Much* in England), he was once again Mike McCartney.

MAY 30, 1980 (UK) Carrere CAR 144
    by Mike McGear   Prod: Mike McGear and Billy Kinsley
A: All The Whales In The Ocean–Mike McGear–*4:07*
B: I Juz Want What You Got–Money–Mike McGear–*3:32*

OCT 27, 1980 (HOLLAND) Philips 6448 097 (LP)
    by Various Artists
WERELD NATUURFONDS GALA/Voor De Walvis
side two
    cut six: *ALL THE WHALES IN THE OCEAN*–Mike McGear–*4:15*
    by Mike McGear   Prod: Mike McGear and Billy Kinsley

JUL 27, 1981 (UK) Conn Records CONN 29781
    by Mike McGear (McCartney) and The Monarchists   Prod: Billy Kinsley
    and Mike McGear
A: No Lar Di Dar (Is Lady Di)–Mike McGear/Roger McGough–*2:40*
B: God Bless The Gracious Queen–Mike McGear–*2:52*

Besides these new tracks, Mike still has five other single sides that have never been placed on any album. These include one 1972 Island track (*Kill*, the flip of *Woman*), two from Warner Bros. (*Sweet Baby*, the flip of *Leave It* in 1974, and *Dance The Do*, the flip of *Norton* in 1975), and two from EMI (*Doing Nothing All Day* and *A To Z* in 1976).

In addition, there are even a few unreleased tracks such as *Thank God For Rock, Thank God For Roll* from the *All The Whales In The Ocean* sessions. Mike also made a demo tape of potential new single material for EMI in April 1977, recorded in the basement studio at Apple with Paul, Denny Laine, Zoot Money, and Vivian Stanshall helping out. EMI executives turned it down. Among other things, they didn't like the drumming. (Sorry, Paul.)

****

Roger McGough and **John Gorman**. John Gorman and Roger Mc-Gough also put out a number of records apart from Mike and Scaffold. The two stuck with Grimms for another album and a few singles in the mid-1970s, then went their separate ways.

Roger McGough recorded only one solo album, an expanded version of his *Summer With Monika* piece previously presented on the 1967 **McGough And McGear** album. Eleven years later and at twice its original length, this poetry and music composition (describing the development and dissolution of a love affair) still remained quite effective, though far too somber to sell well. **Summer With Monika** also came out as a book of poetry and drawings.

John Gorman's first solo releases were done under pseudonyms. As P.C. Plod he put out the single *W.P.C. Hodges* back in 1972, later rerecording it for inclusion on the 1973 Scaffold album, **Fresh Liver**. In 1976 he collaborated with former Grimms associate John Megginson and drummer John Halsey for a novelty Christmas single, rerecording a 1974 Scaffold B-side tune as the Woolpit Carollers.

In 1977 Gorman at last released a pair of discs under his own name, the raucous **Go Man Gorman** album, with *Whole World In His Band* as the accompanying single. Unlike Roger McGough, Gorman filled his solo album with silly songs, funny noises, and nonsense poetry.

Gorman's most successful recordings came a year later, though, in conjunction with the popular British Saturday morning television series, *Tiswas*. There he was one of the quintet hosting the program, appearing along with Sally James, Chris Tarrant, Bob Carolgees, and Lenny Henry. Though presented as a children's show, the series attracted adults as both viewers and guests, including many popular entertainment stars such as Paul McCartney and Wings. They were all eager to participate in some mock interviews and silly slapstick, culminating in a drenching with water (or custard or whatever) to the tune of John Gorman's *Bucket Of Water Song*. In fact, the drenching segment proved so popular that Gorman, James, Tarrant and Carolgees adopted the moniker of the Four Bucketeers and released a pair of singles and an album. They even went on a promotional concert tour in 1980, dousing in person throughout the English countryside.

DEC 8, 1972 (UK) Island WIP 6151
    by P.C. Plod (John Gorman)
A: W.P.C. Hodges—John Gorman
B: B Side Yourself With Plod—John Gorman

JUL 11, 1975 (UK) DJM DJS 393
    by Grimms Prod: Grimms
  A: *Backbreaker*—John Gorman/Roger McGough/Neil Innes/Andy Roberts/
      Dave Richards/John Megginson—*2:39*
B: The Masked Poet—John Gorman/Neil Innes—*2:27*

DEC 5, 1975 (UK) BBC (BEEB) BELP 006 (LP)
by Various Artists
THE CAMERA AND THE SONG
BACKBREAKER—John Gorman/Roger McGough/Neil Innes/Andy
Roberts/Dave Richards/John Megginson—*2:39*
by Grimms Prod: Grimms

MAY 7, 1976 (UK) DJM DJLPS 470 (LP)
by Grimms
SLEEPERS Prod: Peter Jenner and Grimms
side one
The Worst Is Yet To Come—Roger McGough/Neil Innes/Andy Roberts—*2:50*
Blackest Of Blues—Roger McGough/Andy Roberts—*2:55*
Where Am I Now—Roger McGough/Andy Roberts—*2:24*
House Of The Rising Sun—Roger McGough/Neil Innes—*3:50*
Sing Me That Song—Dave Richards—*3:18*
Wiggle Waggle—John Gorman/Roger McGough/Neil Innes/Andy Roberts/Dave
Richards/John Megginson/Timmy Donnell—*0:49*
BACKBREAKER—John Gorman/Roger McGough/Neil Innes/Andy Roberts/
Dave Richards/John Megginson—*2:34*
side two
The Womble Bashers Of Walthamstow—Roger McGough/Neil Innes—*2:56*
Randy Raquel—Neil Innes—*2:38*
Goose—Roger McGough/Andy Roberts—*1:50*
Street—John Gorman/Dave Richards—*1:15*
Slaves Of Freedom—Neil Innes—*3:37*
Bluebird Morning—Andy Roberts—*2:44*
Plenty Of Time—Neil Innes—*4:20*

JUN 11, 1976 (UK) DJM DJS 679
by Grimms Prod: Peter Jenner and Grimms
side one
THE WOMBLE BASHERS OF WALTHAMSTOW—Roger McGough/Neil Innes—
2:56
side two
THE WORST IS YET TO COME—Roger McGough/Neil Innes/Andy Roberts—
2:50
WIGGLE WAGGLE—John Gorman/Roger McGough/Neil Innes/Andy Roberts/
Dave Richards/John Megginson/Timmy Donnell—*0:49*

DEC 3, 1976 (UK) Warner Bros. K 16867
by Woolpit Carollers (A side); John Halsey & Friend (B side)
Prod: John Megginson
*A: The Wind Is Blowing—John Gorman—*2:55*
*B: Without Santa—John Gorman/John Halsey/John Megginson—*3:15*

302

MAY 27, 1977 (UK) DJM DJF 20495 (LP)
    by John Gorman
GO MAN GORMAN   Prod: Peter Jenner
side one
Hello! Hello! Hello!—John Gorman—*1:15*
Poem For Vegetarians—John Gorman—*0:11*
My Lady Of The Waters—John Gorman—*1:35*
Poem Chestnuts—John Gorman—*0:07*
Sticky Fingers (A Protest Song)—John Gorman—*2:13*
Talkin' Boo Hoo's—John Gorman—*2:58*
Poem Marvelous—John Gorman—*0:15*
Whole World In His Band—Trad. arr. John Gorman—*2:25*
Poem For The Sea—John Gorman—*0:12*
Happy Policeman's House—John Gorman—*2:43*
Po_etry Rok—John Gorman—*2:25*
side two
Young Lad's Lament—John Gorman—*3:00*
Rockinest Momma—John Gorman—*2:05*
Flash The Roadie—John Gorman—*2:20*
Whirligig—John Gorman—*1:14*
Policeman's Lot—John Gorman—*3:01*
Old Lag's Lament—John Gorman—*2:32*
Hi Lary Clarissa Sniffleton—John Gorman—*2:38*
Return Of The Bingo Bros.—John Gorman—*0:30*
Two Sleepy People—John Gorman—*2:05*
End Of The L.P. Rock—John Gorman—*1:50*
Etc.—John Gorman—*1:15*
Poem To Album Buyers—John Gorman—*0:10*

JUL 15, 1977 (UK) DJM DJS 10777
    by John Gorman   Prod: Peter Jenner
A: WHOLE WORLD IN HIS BAND—Trad. arr. John Gorman—*2:25*
B: PO_ETRY ROK—John Gorman—*2:25*

SEP 8, 1978 (UK) Island ILPS 9551 (LP)
    by Roger McGough
SUMMER WITH MONIKA   Prod: John Leckie
side one
Prelude—Roger McGough—*1:04*
Prologue—Roger McGough—*2:13*
Epic Film—Roger McGough—*1:04*
I Have Lately Learned To Swim—Roger McGough—*1:50*
Ten Milk Bottles—Roger McGough—*1:40*
Big Bad Dark—Roger McGough—*3:18*
Enemy—Roger McGough—*2:00*
You Are So Very Beautiful—Roger McGough—*1:40*
Sunday Morning—Roger McGough—*1:51*
The Sky Has Nothing To Say—Roger McGough—*0:35*

side two
Ring—Roger McGough—*0:04*
Tightrope—Roger McGough—*2:29*
Nobody's Fool—Roger McGough—*1:29*
Soup—Roger McGough—*0:45*
Trenchwarfare—Roger McGough—*1:30*
Last Waltz—Roger McGough—*1:48*
Porrage—Roger McGough—*1:47*
Teathings—Roger McGough—*2:00*
Epilogue—Roger McGough—*2:29*

APR 11, 1980 (UK) CBS 8393
    by The Four Bucketeers   Prod: Nicky Graham
 A: The Bucket Of Water Song—John Gorman—*2:41*
*B: Mr. Smello—John Gorman—*3:00*

FEB 13, 1981 (UK) CBS 9514
    by The Four Bucketeers   Prod: Nicky Graham (A side); Neil Innes (B side)
A: *Water Is Wonderful*—John Gorman—*3:00*
B: *Raspberry Rock*—John Gorman—*2:06*

OCT 10, 1981 (UK) CBS BUCK 1 (LP)
    by The Four Bucketeers except †Mathew Butler
TISWAS PRESENTS THE FOUR BUCKETEERS   Prod: Neil Innes except
    %Nicky Graham
side one
 Hello And Welcome And Off To A Clean Start—John Gorman/Chris Tarrant/
    Sally James/Bob Carolgees/Lenny Henry—*1:26*
 We Are The Four Bucketeers—John Gorman—*1:29*
 Contents—John Gorman/Chris Tarrant/Sally James/Bob Carolgees/Lenny
    Henry—*0:40*
 Medley—*3:02*
    The Typewriter—Anderson
    The Dying Fly—John Gorman/Mann
 The Wigan And S.E. Lancs. Hopping Club—John Gorman/Chris Tarrant/Sally
    James/Bob Carolgees/Lenny Henry—*1:00*
 It's Fun To Be A Hopper—John Gorman—*2:10*
 David—John Gorman/Chris Tarrant/Sally James/Bob Carolgees/Lenny Henry—
    0:41
 Wuwal Wetweats—John Gorman—*2:33*
 One Of Sally James' Almost Legendary Pop Interviews—John Gorman/Chris
    Tarrant/Sally James/Bob Carolgees/Lenny Henry—*0:46*
 RASPBERRY ROCK—John Gorman—*2:06*
 Chris Gets Carried Away—John Gorman/Chris Tarrant/Sally James/Bob
    Carolgees/Lenny Henry—*1:20*
 %THE BUCKET OF WATER SONG—John Gorman—*2:55*
 Telly Selly Time—Ollie Halsall/John Halsey—*0:05*

side two
Welcome Back—Ollie Halsall/John Halsey—*0:30*
Contents—John Gorman/Chris Tarrant/Sally James/Bob Carolgees/Lenny
   Henry—*0:32*
Funky Spittin' Punk Dog—Lee Brennan/Bob Carolgees—*2:49*
Medley—*0:37*
   The Typewriter—Anderson
   The Dying Fly—John Gorman/Mann
Gabriel Gastropod—John Gorman/Chris Tarrant/Sally James/Bob Carolgees/
   Lenny Henry—*0:30*
The Village Idiots—John Gorman—*2:02*
News Splash—Ollie Halsall/John Halsey—*0:25*
WATER IS WONDERFUL—John Gorman—*2:42*
Algernon Razamataz—John Gorman/Chris Tarrant/Sally James/Bob Carolgees/
   Lenny Henry—*0:45*
Compost Corner—John Gorman—*1:36*
Excuse Me, Chris—John Gorman/Chris Tarrant/Sally James/Bob Carolgees/
   Lenny Henry—*0:18*
*The Fastest Selling Most Fabulous Record Ever To Be Made In The Entire
   History*—Ollie Halsall/John Halsey—*0:10*
Like To Get To Know Me—Smith/Jelly—*3:34*
†*Bright Eyes*—Mike Batt—*4:01*
We Are The Four Bucketeers (Reprise)—John Gorman—*0:48*
Goodbye—John Gorman/Chris Tarrant/Sally James/Bob Carolgees/Lenny
   Henry—*1:09*

* * * * * * * * * *

Denny Laine. For ten years, Denny Laine played with McCartney both as a member of Wings and in solo efforts. When the Wings tour of Japan was canceled in 1980, Laine used the unexpected free time to pursue several solo projects.

In February, he attended a record conference in Cannes to help push the first record release by his wife Jo Jo, *Dancin' Man* (issued February 15, 1980, as Poplar/Hamner HS 305, backed with *Hulk*). *Melody Maker* reported that his promotional press conference was most unusual — nobody played the record. Not surprisingly, it never took off. Neither did the follow-up issued August 1, *When The Boy's Happy* (Mercury MER 30, backed with *Runaway*).

At the same time, Laine also wrote and recorded a song inspired by the events surrounding McCartney's arrest in Tokyo and the cancellation of the Wings tour of Japan. He released it in May, backed with a song he had recorded back in 1978 with Steve Holly, *Guess I'm Only Fooling*. After Paul returned home, it soon became apparent that all plans for a Wings tour that year were out. Beyond that, McCartney also decided that his next album release would not be a Wings record but a solo effort, recorded the previous year completely on his own.

Eager to get back on the road while Paul was busy promoting **McCartney II**, Laine formed his own temporary touring band consisting of himself, Jo Jo, Steve Holly, and Andy Richards on keyboards (from the Alex Harvey band), Mike Piggott on violin, and Gordon Sellar. In June they went into the studio and recorded new versions of two previous Denny Laine hits, *Go Now* and *Say You Don't Mind*, for issuance as a double-A souvenir single. Later in June the band hit the road for a few months, usually playing on weekends to avoid conflicts with other commitments.

To end the year, Laine issued a new solo album, **Japanese Tears**, which was actually his own version of Cold Cuts, McCartney's long-promised collection of finished but unissued tracks gathered from over the years. In fact, three of the songs on Laine's album were actually Wings tracks: one with the original Wings lineup (*I Would Only Smile* from 1973), one recorded in Nashville and co-written with McCartney (*Send Me The Heart* from 1974), and one left over from the **Back To The Egg** sessions at Lympne Castle (*Weep For Love* from 1979). The rest of the package consisted of: both sides of both singles issued earlier in the year, four other songs recorded in 1978 (*Same Mistakes, Silver, Somebody Ought To Know The Way,* and *Nothing To Go By*), a song done at home in 1979 (*Dangerzone*), and two more tracks done in 1980 (*Clock On The Wall* and *Lovers Light*). **Japanese Tears** emerged as one of Denny Laine's best solo albums ever, but it did not do all that well in England and, oddly, did not come out in the U.S. until 1983.

By then, Laine and McCartney had parted company as Wings dissolved in 1981 following Paul's decision to do solo recording with guest musicians rather than any more group efforts. Later in 1981, Laine recorded a completely new solo album called **Anyone Can Fly**, without any involvement by McCartney. Produced by Norman "Hurricane" Smith, the new collection had the following tentative track lineup ready by late fall:

ANYONE CAN FLY   Prod: Norman "Hurricane" Smith

side one	side two
Running Round In Circles	*Various Shapes And Forms*
Be Together	*I Always Thought*
Who Moved The World?	*Could Not Believe*
Racing Cars	*Anyone Can Fly*

In November, *Who Moved The World?* was issued as a lead single, with Norman Smith mistakenly credited as the producer for the *Weep For Love* B-side as well. The album was slated to follow by the end of the year, but it was first postponed, then rescheduled for release only on the European continent early in 1982. Eventually, the entire project was put on the shelf indefinitely.

MAY 2, 1980 (UK) Scratch HS 401
MAY 5, 1980 (US) Arista AS 0511
   by Denny Laine   Prod: Denny Laine
A: *Japanese Tears*—Denny Laine—*3:26*
B: *Guess I'm Only Foolin'*—Denny Laine—*2:32*

AUG 15, 1980 (UK) Scratch Records HS 408
   by Denny Laine   Prod: Denny Laine
A: *Go Now*—Larry Banks/Milton Bennet—*3:20*
A: *Say You Don't Mind*—Denny Laine—*3:07*

DEC 5, 1980 (UK) Scratch SCR L 5001 (LP)
AUG 8, 1983 (US) Takoma TAK 7103 (LP)
   by Denny Laine . . . and Friends
JAPANESE TEARS   Prod: Denny Laine
side one
JAPANESE TEARS—Denny Laine—*4:42*
Dangerzone—Denny Laine—*3:07*
Clock On The Wall—Denny Laine—*2:17*
Send Me The Heart—McCartney/Denny Laine—*3:38*
GO NOW—Larry Banks/Milton Bennet—*3:20*
Same Mistakes—Denny Laine—*3:41*
Silver—Denny Laine—*3:55*
side two
SAY YOU DON'T MIND—Denny Laine—*3:07*
Somebody Ought To Know The Way—Denny Laine—*3:14*
Lovers Light—Denny Laine—*3:02*
GUESS I'M ONLY FOOLING—Denny Laine—*2:29*
Nothing To Go By—Denny Laine—*3:08*
I Would Only Smile—Denny Laine—*3:20*
Weep For Love—Denny Laine—*4:31*

NOV 9, 1981 (UK) Rock City RC 7001
   by Denny Laine   Prod: Norman "Hurricane" Smith (A side); Denny Laine
      (B side)
*A: *Who Moved The World?*—Denny Laine—*5:03*
 B: *WEEP FOR LOVE*—Denny Laine—*4:31*

****

Laurence Juber. Like Denny Laine, Laurence Juber filled his unexpected free time following the cancellation of the 1980 Wings tour of Japan with solo recording activities. He did about ten instrumental cover versions of songs ranging from *You're No Good* to *Stormy Weather*, eventually releasing five of them in 1982 on his own Breaking Records label. *Maisie*, the only Juber original on the album, was recorded with Wings during the **Back To The Egg** sessions. See Entry 708.

307

Standard Time

Breaking Records BREAK 1 (LP)

DENNY LAINE

...and friends
Howie Casey,
Steve Holly,
Jo Jo Laine,
Paul & Linda McCartney,
Henry McCullouch,
Denny Seiwell

"JAPANESE TEARS"

Japanese Tears   Takoma TAK 7103 (LP)

JUL 9, 1982 (US) Breaking Records BREAK 1 (LP)
   by Laurence Juber
STANDARD TIME   Prod: Laurence Juber and Richard Niles
side one
Four Brothers—Jimmy Giuffre—*3:35*
Dinah—Harry Akst/Sam Lewis/Joe Young—*3:05*
Maisie—Laurence Juber—*3:10*
side two
After You've Gone—Henry Creamer/Turner Layton—*4:25*
Stormy Weather—Harold Arlen—*4:45*
The Christmas Song (Chestnuts Roasting On An Open Fire)—Mel Torme/Robert
   Wells—*2:45*

****

Professor Longhair. While working on material for **Venus And Mars**
back in the mid-1970s, Paul and Linda McCartney spent some time
in New Orleans with legendary blues pianist Henry Roeland (Roy)
Byrd, better known as Professor Longhair. Paul even included a tip-
of-the-hat mention of the Professor in the *Venus And Mars/Rock
Show* opening to both that album and his 1976 U.S. concert tour.
   More importantly, McCartney invited Professor Longhair to per-
form at the party held to celebrate the completion of **Venus And
Mars**. The event was staged and recorded on March 24, 1975, aboard
the luxury ship *Queen Mary*, docked at Long Beach, California.
Three years later, that live performance was issued by EMI on its
Harvest label, coinciding with Professor Longhair's first London con-
cert date on March 26, 1978, at the New Theatre, Drury Lane.
   Linda McCartney provided the front cover photography and
MPL did the packaging and funding for this first-ever live album by
the Professor. Though the EMI release was obviously a one-shot deal,
Professor Longhair continued recording for a variety of labels until
his death on January 30, 1980.

MAR 23, 1978 (UK) Harvest SHSP 4086 (LP)
JUL 24, 1978 (US) Harvest SW 11790 (LP)
   by Professor Longhair
LIVE ON THE QUEEN MARY   Prod: Tom Wilson
side one
Tell Me Pretty Baby—Henry R. Byrd—*3:55*
Mess Around—Ahmet Ertegun—*4:02*
Every Day I Have The Blues—Peter Chatman—*5:42*
Tipitina—Henry R. Byrd—*3:49*

310

side two
I'm Movin' On—Hank Snow—*3:42*
Mardi Gras In New Orleans—Henry R. Byrd—*2:55*
Cry To Me—Bert Russell—*2:43*
Gone So Long—Henry R. Byrd—*4:27*
Stagger Lee—Lloyd Price/Harold Logan—*3:03*

APR 7, 1978 (UK) Harvest HAR 5154
    by Professor Longhair Prod: Tom Wilson
A: *MESS AROUND*—Ahmet Ertegun—*4:02*
B: *TIPITINA*—Henry R. Byrd—*3:49*

****

Zoot Money. George Bruno "Zoot" Money was a veteran of the 1960s British blues scene. His *Big Time Operator* single hit the U.K. top thirty in 1966 under the banner Zoot Money and the Big Roll Band (which included future Police star, Andy Summers). Money also played awhile with Eric Burdon, had a stint with Grimms, and worked with Paul McCartney on such projects as the **McGough And McGear** album. In 1980, MPL backed the solo album debut of Mr. Money, issuing the disc on a small, short-lived London-based label, Magic Moon Records.

    Though Paul McCartney was not involved in the recording sessions, he did work with Money on the album cover design. The record itself contained an odd mixture of original Zoot Money compositions and cover versions, including the old McCartney favorite, *Your Feets Too Big.*

SEP 19, 1980 (UK) Magic Moon Records Mach 3.S
    by Zoot Money Prod: Jim Diamond
A: *Your Feets Too Big*—Ada Benson/Fred Fisher—*3:12*
B: *Ain't Nothin' Shakin' But The Bacon*—George B. Money—*2:55*

SEP 25, 1980 (UK) Magic Moon Records LUNE 1 (LP)
    by Zoot Money
MR. MONEY Prod: Jim Diamond
side one
Your Feets Too Big—Ada Benson/Fred Fisher—*3:40*
The Two Of Us—George B. Money/Colin E. Allen—*3:45*
Ac-cent-tchu-ate The Positive—Johnny Mercer/Harold Arlen—*3:25*
Hello—George B. Money/Colin E. Allen—*2:55*
Riders In The Sky—Stan Jones—*3:40*

side two
Can I Get Closer To You—George B. Money/Colin E. Allen—*3:20*
It's Too Soon To Know—Deborah Chessler—*3:05*
Careless Hands—Bob Hilliard/Carl Sigman—*3:35*
Ain't Nothin' Shakin' But The Bacon—George B. Money—*2:55*
Sentimental Journey—Les Brown/Ben Homer/Bud Green—*4:40*

JUN 5, 1981 (UK) Magic Moon Records Mach 6
   by Zoot Money   Prod: Jim Diamond
A: *THE TWO OF US*—George B. Money/Colin E. Allen—*3:45*
B: *AIN'T NOTHIN' SHAKIN' BUT THE BACON*—George B. Money—*2:55*

****

The Cimarons. In the early 1980s, Paul McCartney sent out word that he was looking for musicians to do instrumental reggae versions of some popular music standards (many from the MPL publishing catalog). The Cimarons responded and won the assignment.

McCartney had a long standing affection for reggae, reaching back to the Beatles days with *Ob-La-Di, Ob-La-Da* and continuing through Linda's *Seaside Woman*, the Jamaican slang of *C Moon*, and the light reggae shuffle of *With A Little Luck*. On the *Give Ireland Back To The Irish* single he had even used the Jamaican technique of placing an instrumental "version" of the A-side on the flip. Thus, Paul's desire to see a reggae album with some of his favorite material was quite understandable.

The Cimarons were perfectly suited to the task, with more than a dozen years of experience. Founded by guitarist Locksley Gichie in 1967, the group had turned out several albums and singles for a variety of labels and worked with such reggae stars as Jimmy Cliff, the Maytals, and Bob Marley. For the MPL project, the Cimarons insisted on (and received) strong artistic control and quickly set about the task of interpreting the wide range of songs selected. These included the international flavor of *Arriverderci Roma, Poor People Of Paris*, and Hungarian Eve Boswell's 1956 British top ten hit, *Pickin' A Chicken* – along with Buddy Holly's most popular song, the first Beatles single, two Four Seasons hits, and several McCartney compositions with Wings, including (appropriately) *With A Little Luck* and *C Moon*.

McCartney was obviously pleased with the resulting **Reggaebility** album and included a shot of the Cimarons at the end of the *Ebony And Ivory* promotional video with Stevie Wonder. MPL continued to back the group, promoting both the *Big Girls Don't Cry* single from the album and, the following year, a brand new release, *Love And Affection*. For both of those singles, there was also an extended 12-inch version issued, including a 12-inch picture disc (Safari SAFELX

49) for *Big Girls Don't Cry*. The B-sides to all three Cimarons singles for MPL were not included on **Reggaebility**.

Unlike the 1977 **Thrillington** instrumental album, McCartney had no involvement with the recording sessions for any of these MPL-sponsored Cimarons tracks. However, Paul did direct the promotional film for *Big Girls Don't Cry*, his first such effort since *Magical Mystery Tour.*

JAN 29, 1982 (UK) I.M.P. IMPS 50
    by The Cimarons Prod: Vic Keary and Sid Bucknor
A: With A Little Luck—McCartney—*4:59*
**B: Peggy Sue*—Jerry Allison/Buddy Holly/Norman Petty—*2:31*

FEB 26, 1982 (UK) Pickwick SHM 3106 (LP)
    by The Cimarons
REGGAEBILITY Prod: Vic Keary and Sid Bucknor
side one
With A Little Luck—McCartney—*4:05*
Poor People Of Paris—Marguerite Monnot—*3:45*
Big Girls Don't Cry—Bob Crewe/Bob Gaudio—*2:58*
Pickin' A Chicken—Roberts/Bernfield/de Mortimer—*4:25*
Mull Of Kintyre—McCartney/Denny Laine—*4:27*
side two
Love Me Do—L/McC—*2:32*
Walk Like A Man—Bob Crewe/Bob Gaudio—*3:30*
C Moon—McCartney—*3:44*
Meet Me On The Corner—Roberts/Hart—*3:59*
That'll Be The Day—Jerry Allison/Buddy Holly/Norman Petty—*3:02*
Arriverderci Roma—Garinei/Giovannini/Renato Ranucci—*3:59*

SEP 3, 1982 (UK) Safari SAFE 49
    by The Cimarons Prod: Vic Keary and Sid Bucknor
A: BIG GIRLS DON'T CRY—Bob Crewe/Bob Gaudio—*3:03*
**B: How Can I Prove Myself To You?*—Sonny Binns (as Francis)—*4:07*

SEP 3, 1982 (UK) Safari SAFELS 49 (12-inch)
    by The Cimarons Prod: Vic Keary and Sid Bucknor
side one
BIG GIRLS DON'T CRY (long version)—Bob Crewe/Bob Gaudio—*5:50*
side two
**How Can I Prove Myself To You?*—Sonny Binns—*4:52*
POOR PEOPLE OF PARIS—Marguerite Monnot—*4:37*

MAR 11, 1983 (UK) Cimarons CIM 001
    by The Cimarons Prod: The Cimarons
**A: Love And Affection*—Sonny Binns—*3:43*
**B: Bombs And Guns*—Winston Reid—*3:58*

MAR 11, 1983 (UK) Cimarons 12 CIM 001 (12-inch)
by The Cimarons   Prod: The Cimarons
*A: Love And Affection (long version)–Sonny Binns–6:35
*B: Bombs And Guns (long version)–Winston Reid–8:41

****

Harry Nilsson. Back in the late 1960s, Harry Nilsson caught the attention of the Beatles with his first album releases for RCA, **Pandemonium Shadow Show** and **Aerial Ballet.** Over the next few years, they became friends, with Ringo and John developing into special "drinking buddies" with him during the 1970s. Ringo, George, and John also played on some of Nilsson's records and he returned the favor on several of their solo releases. For complete details on Harry Nilsson's work with the Beatles through 1977, consult *All Together Now* and *The Beatles Again.*

In 1978, RCA issued a pair of Nilsson compilation albums, one for the U.S. and one for the U.K., containing a few of the George and Ringo related tracks (see Entries 592 and 607). Unlike most greatest hits packages, these offered different song lineups in both countries, with the British package getting the edge for quantity and diversity. Harry Nilsson and RCA split following this release.

In 1980, Nilsson released **Flash Harry** (only in England) on Mercury Records (Entry 647). Once again, Ringo was there to play on a few cuts, including a new collaboration between the two, *How Long Can Disco On.* The most unusual track on the album was *Harry,* not sung by Harry Nilsson but by Eric Idle and Charlie Dore, who sent their tape as a surprise musical greeting. Nilsson was so taken with the tune that he used it as the opening cut.

Derek Taylor, who had written the liner notes for **Aerial Ballet** in 1968, did the same for **Flash Harry,** observing that this was Harry Nilsson's nineteenth album and that he had said he would stop after twenty-one. Whether he intended to do so or not, Nilsson did slow down his record output since then, concentrating instead on scores and soundtracks. (For instance, he did the music for the first Ziggy TV cartoon special in 1983.)

There was one exception. On June 27, 1982, Nilsson wrote and recorded *With A Bullet* for release as a privately pressed single to benefit the National Coalition to Ban Handguns, which he became a national spokesman for in 1981.

314

Flash Harry   **Mercury 6302 022 (LP)**

SPECIAL LIMITED EDITION RECORD FOR BEATLEFEST '82-LOS ANGELES

WITH A BULLET
BY HARRY NILSSON

With a Bullet was written, sung and recorded in one take by Harry Nilsson, who stopped by to say hello, during a Buzzy Linhart recording session, on June 27, 1982. When he found out that 10% of Buzzy's record was going to N.C.B.H., he asked "Mind if I play through?", and, to everyone's amazement, he sat at the piano and recorded what you are about to hear, making it up as he went along. Buzzy Linhart then set about the task of adding the Vibes, good vibes indeed they are!, while Harry added the drums. And then the final touch: Phil with blond hair, Mark Lapidos, Buzzy and Harry, who now call themselves *The Awesome Foursome*, harmonized their tuneful way, to the end, while Chris engineered. And thanks to the magic of Rick Riccio, who the next day added a Bass part from a newly unpacked Cassio and who managed to mix the record in record time. And thanks to a stranger (stranger no more) Terry Harrington, who happened to walk by, liked what he heard and added the sax (in one take). Now the results are in your generous hands.

All net proceeds of this record go to the
National Coalition to Ban Handguns (100 Maryland Ave., Washington, DC 20002)

With A Bullet   **Beatlefest R 42874 (45)**

MAY 8, 1978 (US) RCA AFL 1-2798 (LP)
 by Harry Nilsson
GREATEST HITS Prod: Richard Perry except †Rick Jarrard; %Harry Nilsson
 (House)
side one
 †Everybody's Talkin'—Fred Neil—*2:41*
 †Without Her—Harry Nilsson—*2:18*
 †One—Harry Nilsson—*2:50*
 %I Guess The Lord Must Be In New York City—Harry Nilsson—*2:44*
 %Me And My Arrow—Harry Nilsson—*2:04*
 Coconut—Harry Nilsson—*3:48*
side two
 Without You—Pete Ham/Tom Evans—*3:17*
 Jump Into The Fire—Harry Nilsson—*6:54*
 Spaceman—Harry Nilsson—*3:33*
 Remember (Christmas)—Harry Nilsson—*4:07*
 As Time Goes By—Herman Hupfeld—*3:21*
 %Daybreak—Harry Nilsson—*2:43*

NOV 17, 1978 (UK) RCA PL 42728 (LP)
 by Harry Nilsson
HARRY NILSSON'S GREATEST MUSIC Prod: Richard Perry except †Rick
 Jarrard; %Harry Nilsson (House); $Harry Nilsson (House) and Robin
 Geoffrey Cable
side one
 †Everybody's Talkin'—Fred Neil—*2:41*
 †1941—Harry Nilsson—*2:36*
 %I Guess The Lord Must Be In New York City—Harry Nilsson—*2:44*
 %Me And My Arrow—Harry Nilsson—*2:04*
 Spaceman—Harry Nilsson—*3:33*
 %Kojak Columbo—Harry Nilsson—*3:30*
 $Who Done It?—Harry Nilsson—*5:20*
 Coconut—Harry Nilsson—*3:48*
side two
 Without You—Pete Ham/Tom Evans—*3:17*
 %Love Story—Randy Newman—*3:39*
 Remember (Christmas)—Harry Nilsson—*4:07*
 †Without Her—Harry Nilsson—*2:18*
 Makin' Whoopee!—Gus Kahn/Walter Donaldson—*4:25*
 As Time Goes By—Herman Hupfeld—*3:21*
 You Made Me Love You (I Didn't Want To Do It)—Joe McCarthy/James V.
  Monaco—*2:32*
 $All I Ever Think About Is You—Harry Nilsson—*4:04*

SEP 5, 1980 (UK) Mercury 6302 022 (LP)
    by Harry Nilsson except +Eric Idle and Charlie Dore
FLASH HARRY   Prod: Steve Cropper with Bruce Robb except +Eric Idle,
    Trevor Jones, and Andre Jacquemin
side one
+Harry—Eric Idle—*2:22*
Cheek To Cheek—Lowell George/Van Dyke Parks/Kibbe—*2:30*
Best Move—Harry Nilsson/Van Dyke Parks/Hazlewood—*4:04*
Old Dirt Road—Lennon/Harry Nilsson—*4:26*
I Don't Need You—Christian—*3:49*
side two
Rain—Harry Nilsson—*3:51*
I've Got It!—Harry Nilsson/Perry Botkin, Jr.—*3:42*
It's So Easy—Harry Nilsson/Paul Stallworth—*4:43*
How Long Can Disco On—Starkey/Harry Nilsson—*2:54*
Always Look On The Bright Side Of Life—Eric Idle—*4:12*

SEP 5, 1980 (UK) Mercury MER 40
    by Harry Nilsson   Prod: Steve Cropper with Bruce Robb
A: I Don't Need You—Christian—*3:49*
B: It's So Easy—Harry Nilsson/Paul Stallworth—*4:43*

OCT 17, 1980 (UK) Mercury MER 44
    by Harry Nilsson   Prod: Steve Cropper with Bruce Robb
A: ALWAYS LOOK ON THE BRIGHT SIDE OF LIFE—Eric Idle—*4:12*
B: RAIN—Harry Nilsson—*3:51*

JUL 9, 1982 (US) Beatlefest R 42874/R 32182
    by Harry Nilsson   Prod: Harry Nilsson
*A: With A Bullet—Harry Nilsson—*5:15*
*B: Judy—Harry Nilsson—*3:20*

There were four custom pressings of *With A Bullet*, each carrying
a different catalog number and a different spoken intro to the song.
The R 42874 version was for the 1982 Los Angeles Beatlefest, with
Nilsson mentioning that event in the opening rap. The same was
done for the Beatlefests in Chicago (R 82082) and New York (R
102982) later that year. A generic opening (#9) was used for sales
to the rest of the country. As if to prove that fans were right all
along and that record catalog numbers do have (or *should* have)
some special significant, hidden meaning, Beatlefest promoter Mark
Lapidos chose those record numbers to signify: the day he first met
John Lennon and Harry Nilsson (4-28-74), the date of the 1982
Chicago Beatlefest (8-20-82), the date of the 1982 New York Beatlefest (10-29-82), and John Lennon's "magical" number nine.
    The flipside number (32182) referred to the date that a woman
named Judy donated $500.00 to the National Coalition to Ban

Handguns in exchange for a new song for her written by Harry Nilsson. To encourage additional donations, the address of the N.C.B.H. appeared on the picture sleeve (The National Coalition to Ban Handguns at 100 Maryland Ave., Washington, DC 20002).

****

Roxy Music, Phil Collins, Elton John, Queen, Billy Joel, Pink Floyd, Mike Oldfield, and Paul Simon.
Following the death of John Lennon, there was the expected rash of tribute discs. For previous events like this, such releases usually came from sincere but amateurish unknowns with more heart than talent. In Lennon's case, though, the quality was considerably higher as some of the top names in rock felt the need to say something through their music. Closest to home, of course, were the songs by George Harrison (*All Those Years Ago*) and Paul McCartney (*Here Today*), but the others were drawn from the same spirit.

Roxy Music selected a simple but effective tribute and did a cover version of *Jealous Guy*, a popular track from **Imagine** that Lennon had never released as a single. Even the picture sleeve to the new single was tasteful and understated, with only the group name, song title, and the handwritten tag "a tribute" on the pale-colored front. The disc topped the British charts in early 1981 and the song soon became a standard part of the group's concert repertoire, eventually turning up again in 1983 on the live **High Road** mini-album.

Genesis drummer Phil Collins had already recorded a cover version of *Tomorrow Never Knows* in August 1980 for his then forthcoming solo album, **Face Value**. Before releasing the disc in February 1981, though, he added a short bit of *Over The Rainbow* to the end of *Tomorrow Never Knows* as his personal tribute to Lennon.

Elton John, Queen, Billy Joel, Pink Floyd, Mike Oldfield, and Paul Simon chose to do original numbers. Wisely, their songs dealt with the tragedy chiefly through the mood of the music and analogies in the lyrics, rather than dwelling on the event itself. They were all successful artistically, though none of these scored as well as *Jealous Guy* on the charts outside their respective albums. Only Elton John's single of *Empty Garden (Hey Hey Johnny)* cracked the U.S. top twenty.

318

FEB 6, 1981 (UK) Polydor/E.G. ROXY 2
APR 27, 1981 (US) Atco 7329
    by Roxy Music   Prod: Bryan Ferry and Rhett Davies
*A: Jealous Guy—Lennon—6:10
 B: (to turn you on)

APR 10, 1981 (UK) K-tel NE 1118 (LP)
    by Various Artists
CHARTBLASTERS '81
side one
    cut one: *JEALOUS GUY*—Lennon—*6:10*
        by Roxy Music   Prod: Bryan Ferry and Rhett Davies

MAR 11, 1983 (UK) E.G. EGMLP 1 (LP)
MAR 14, 1983 (US) Warner Bros./E.G. 23808 (LP)
    by Roxy Music, recorded live
THE HIGH ROAD   Prod: Rhett Davies and Roxy Music
side two
    cut two: *Jealous Guy (live)*—Lennon—*6:10*

FEB 6, 1981 (UK) Virgin V 2185 (LP)
FEB 16, 1981 (US) Atlantic SD 16029 (LP)
    by Phil Collins
FACE VALUE   Prod: Phil Collins and Hugh Padgham
side two
    cut six: *Medley: 4:46*
            Tomorrow Never Knows—L/McC—*4:15*
            Over The Rainbow—Harold Arlen/E.Y. Harburg—*0:31*

MAR 8, 1982 (US) Geffen GEF 50049
MAY 28, 1982 (UK) Rocket XPRES 77
    by Elton John   Prod: Chris Thomas
A: *Empty Garden (Hey Hey Johnny)*—Elton John/Bernie Taupin—*3:59*
B: *(take me down to the ocean)*

APR 9, 1982 (UK) Rocket HISPD 127 (LP)
APR 19, 1982 (US) Geffen GHS 2013 (LP)
    by Elton John
JUMP UP!   Prod: Chris Thomas
side two
    cut one: *Empty Garden (Hey Hey Johnny)*—Elton John/Bernie Taupin—
    3:59

MAR 7, 1983 (US) Geffen 0436
> by Elton John   Prod: Chris Thomas

A: EMPTY GARDEN (HEY HEY JOHNNY)—Elton John/Bernie Taupin—*3:59*
A: (blue eyes)

APR 19, 1982 (UK) EMI 5293
APR 19, 1982 (US) Elektra 47452
> by Queen   Prod: Queen and Mack

B: Life Is Real (Song For Lennon)—Freddie Mercury—*3:35*
A: (body language)

MAY 10, 1982 (UK) EMI EMA 797 (LP)
MAY 10, 1982 (US) Elektra E1-60128 (LP)
> by Queen   Prod: Queen/Mack

HOT SPACE
side two
> cut two: *Life Is Real (Song For Lennon)*—Freddie Mercury—*3:35*

SEP 20, 1982 (US) Columbia TC 382000 (LP)
SEP 24, 1982 (UK) CBS 85959 (LP)
> by Billy Joel

THE NYLON CURTAIN   Prod: Phil Ramone
side two
> cut four: *Scandinavian Skies*—Billy Joel—*5:59*

MAR 21, 1983 (UK) Harvest SHPF 1983 (LP)
MAR 21, 1983 (US) Columbia QC 38243 (LP)
> by Pink Floyd

THE FINAL CUT   Prod: Roger Waters, James Guthrie, Michael Kamen
side two
> cut five: *Not Now John*—Roger Waters—*4:43*

MAY 2, 1983 (UK) Harvest HAR 5224
MAY 2, 1983 (US) Columbia 38-03905
> by Pink Floyd   Prod: Roger Waters, James Guthrie, Michael Kamen

A: Not Now John (single version)—Roger Waters—*4:20*
B: (the hero's return pts. 1 & 2)

MAY 9, 1983 (UK) Harvest 12HAR 5224 (12-inch)
> by Pink Floyd   Prod: Roger Waters, James Guthrie, Michael Kamen

side one
Not Now John (single version)—Roger Waters—*4:20*
(the hero's return pts. 1 & 2)
side two
NOT NOW JOHN—Roger Waters—*4:43*

THE BEATLES CONCERTO SINGLE

The Beatles Concerto Single   Parlophone R 6024 (45)

pink
floyd
not
now
john

Not Now John   **Harvest 12HAR 5224 (12-inch)**

MAY 6, 1983 (UK) Virgin VS 586
   by Mike Oldfield Prod: Mike Oldfield and Simon Phillips
A: Moonlight Shadow—Mike Oldfield—*3:37*
B: (rite of man)

MAY 23, 1983 (UK) Virgin V 2262 (LP)
   by Mike Oldfield
CRISES Prod: Mike Oldfield and Simon Phillips
side two
   cut one: *Moonlight Shadow*—Mike Oldfield—*5:18*

NOV 28, 1983 (UK) EMI/Virgin NOW 1 (2 LPs)
   by Various Artists
NOW, THAT'S WHAT I CALL MUSIC
side four
   cut four: *MOONLIGHT SHADOW*—Mike Oldfield—*3:37*
      by Mike Oldfield Prod: Mike Oldfield and Simon Phillips

OCT 31, 1983 (US) Warner Bros. 1-23942 (LP)
NOV 4, 1983 (UK) Warner Bros. 923942-1 (LP)
   by Paul Simon Prod: Paul Simon, Russ Titelman, Roy Halee, and Lenny
      Waronker
HEARTS AND BONES
side two
   cut five: *The Late Great Johnny Ace*—Paul Simon—*4:45*

Paul Simon's *The Late Great Johnny Ace* was first performed at the Simon and Garfunkel reunion concert in New York's Central Park on September 19, 1981. However, the song was not included on the live **Concert In Central Park** double-album released the following February. Oddly, it did turn up on the Home Box Office presentation of the concert as a cable television stereo simulcast special, aired February 21, 1982, the day before the album came out. *The Late Great Johnny Ace* was also kept on the commercial video release of the concert (CBS/Fox 7133 in the U.S. and Warner Home Video 99000 in the U.K.).

****

Royal Liverpool Philharmonic Orchestra. Ever since 1963 when London *Times* critic William Mann first described Beatles music using such phrases as "Aeolian cadence," serious musicians have attempted to adapt songs by the Beatles to classical-style performances. Though there have been a few acceptable collections, all too often the results have sounded more like high-brow muzak than the classics.

323

The 1979 **Beatles Concerto** album turned out better than most, recorded with the Royal Liverpool Philharmonic Orchestra at George Martin's AIR London studios. For side one's formal *Beatles Concerto*, director Ron Goodwin and pianists Peter Rostal and Paul Schaefer took the orchestra through an extended twenty-three minute piece consisting of three distinct movements based on nine different Beatles songs. Rostal described it as "a romantic concerto in the style of Greig or Tchaikovsky." George Martin echoed those sentiments in the liner notes to the album, calling the *Beatles Concerto* "not just another medley of tunes by Lennon, McCartney, or Harrison, but a true composition in classical form." By those standards, they apparently succeeded, though squeezing a single from this "classical composition" did seem a bit odd.

JUN 1, 1979 (UK) Parlophone PAS 10014 (LP)
MAY 7, 1980 (US) Moss Music Group MMG-1121 (LP)
    by The Royal Liverpool Philharmonic Orchestra under the direction of
    Ron Goodwin, featuring pianists Peter Rostal and Paul Schaefer
THE BEATLES CONCERTO Prod: An Air London Production, assisted by
    Brian Culverhouse. Arrangement by †Ron Goodwin, or %John Rutter
side one
The Beatles Concerto—23:37
    1st Movement: Maestoso-Allegro moderato—8:00
        She Loves You—L/McC
        Eleanor Rigby—L/McC
        Yesterday—L/McC
        All My Loving—L/McC
        Hey Jude—L/McC
    2nd Movement: Andante espressivo—7:36
        Here, There And Everywhere—L/McC
        Something—Harrison
    3rd Movement: Presto—7:53
        Can't Buy Me Love—L/McC
        The Long And Winding Road—L/McC
side two
The Beatles Impressions—21:16
    %*The Fool On The Hill*—L/McC—*5:09*
    †*Lucy In The Sky With Diamonds*—L/McC—*2:25*
    †*Michelle*—L/McC—*3:15*
    †*Maxwell's Silver Hammer*—L/McC—*2:37*
    %*Here Comes The Sun*—Harrison—*3:25*
    %*A Hard Day's Night*—L/McC—*4:08*

JUN 1, 1979 (UK) Parlophone R 6024
   by The Royal Liverpool Philharmonic Orchestra under the direction of Ron
      Goodwin, featuring pianists Peter Rostal and Paul Schaefer
   Prod: An Air London Production, assisted by Brian Culverhouse
Excerpts from *The Beatles Concerto*
A: *2nd Movement: Andante espressivo- 3:17*
      Here, There And Everywhere–L/McC
      Something–Harrison
B: *3rd Movement: Presto–3:50*
      Can't Buy Me Love–L/McC
      The Long And Winding Road–L/McC

                    ****

Royal Philharmonic Orchestra. Compared to the **Beatles Concerto**,
the **20th Anniversary Concert** album was much more pop than
classical. This was not really surprising because conductor Louis
Clark and the Royal Philharmonic Orchestra were pop stars themselves with the 1981 top ten single *Hooked On Classics*. Still, the
album functioned quite well as a souvenir to a special event: an
evening of Beatles music performed as a benefit concert to celebrate
the twentieth anniversary of the group's first record release in
England. Paul and Linda McCartney attended the show, which was
held at the Royal Albert Hall on December 13, 1982. The event
raised about £30,000 for the Royal Society for the Protection of
Birds, a prestigious conservation group in England.

   Back behind the Royal Box during intermission, Paul and Linda
chatted with the Queen and Prince Philip, who were also in atten-
dance.

FEB 4, 1983 (UK) Solid Rock Foundation SRFL 1001 (LP)
   by The Royal Philharmonic Orchestra with the Royal Choral Society,
      conducted by Louis Clark, and featuring guest performers †Elena
      Duran, %Joan Collins, $Roy Wood, +Honor Heffernan, ††British
      Caledonian Airway Pipe and Drum Band
THE ROYAL PHILHARMONIC ORCHESTRA PLAYS THE BEATLES –
20TH ANNIVERSARY CONCERT Prod: David Richards
side one: Total time–*21:41*
All You Need Is Love–L/McC–*2:40*
A Hard Day's Night–L/McC–*3:05*
I Want To Hold Your Hand–L/McC–*2:56*
†*Medley: 4:09*
      Here, There And Everywhere–L/McC–*1:50*
      Norwegian Wood–L/McC–*2:19*
The Fool On The Hill–L/McC–*3:33*
(continued)

(continued)
Medley: 4:11
> *Got To Get You Into My Life*—L/McC—*0:43*
> *Eight Days A Week*—L/McC—*0:28*
> *Penny Lane*—L/McC—*0:27*
> *Yellow Submarine*—L/McC—*0:30*
> *Get Back*—L/McC—*0:33*
> *Day Tripper*—L/McC—*0:14*
> *Ticket To Ride*—L/McC—*0:25*
> *Ob-La-Di, Ob-La-Da*—L/McC—*0:51*

side two: Total time—*20:52*
%Imagine—Lennon—*3:10*
Blackbird—L/McC—*3:53*
$††Mull Of Kintyre—McCartney/Denny Laine—*5:03*
+$†Happy Xmas (War Is Over)—Lennon/Yoko Ono—*3:05*
Sgt. Pepper Medley—*3:42*
> *Sgt. Pepper's Lonely Hearts Club Band*—L/McC—*1:15*
> *With A Little Help From My Friends*—L/McC—*1:00*
> *Lucy In The Sky With Diamonds*—L/McC—*0:43*
> *Sgt. Pepper's Lonely Heart's Club Band*—L/McC—*0:44*

****

Beatlemania. Touted as "Not The Beatles, But An Incredible Simulation," the live *Beatlemania* stage show astounded critics with its tremendous success at the box office. After all, the production was simply a glorified concert performance by a Beatles soundalike band, with film clips and slides shown in the background.

Yet in an odd way, *Beatlemania* made sense. When it premiered in 1977, the Beatles themselves had not performed in a live concert setting for more than ten years, so a new generation of fans had never had the chance to see a live show devoted entirely to Beatles music. With four surrogates on stage, they could cheer their favorites at last, even calling out for encores. Maybe it was just a simulation, but it was all they had.

While acceptable as a live theatrical event, *Beatlemania* did not transfer well to other formats. The real Beatles were still alive and well on disc and on film, so their clones were superfluous there. An original cast album for *Beatlemania* flopped in early 1978. Later, so did a film of the stage show. In fact, the film closed so quickly that it did not even last the length of its promo slogan: "That Was The Week *Beatlemania* Was." It wasn't.

FEB 6, 1978 (US) Arista AL 8501 (2 LPs)
    by The Original Broadway Cast, recorded live
BEATLEMANIA   Prod: Sandy Yaguda and Kenny Laguna
side one
I Want To Hold Your Hand–L/McC–*1:28*
She Loves You–L/McC–*2:47*
Help–L/McC–*2:22*
Can't Buy Me Love–L/McC–*2:27*
Day Tripper–L/McC–*3:24*
Yesterday–L/McC–*2:56*
side two
Eleanor Rigby–L/McC–*2:08*
Nowhere Man–L/McC–*2:49*
Strawberry Fields Forever–L/McC–*3:34*
Penny Lane–L/McC–*2:54*
Magical Mystery Tour–L/McC–*1:28*
side three
Lady Madonna–L/McC–*2:48*
The Fool On The Hill–L/McC–*3:32*
Got To Get You Into My Life–L/McC–*2:38*
Michelle–L/McC–*2:48*
Get Back–L/McC–*2:36*
side four
All You Need Is Love–L/McC–*3:40*
Revolution–L/McC–*3:34*
Hey Jude–L/McC–*5:47*
I Am The Walrus–L/McC–*2:49*
The Long And Winding Road–L/McC–*2:40*
Let It Be–L/McC–*4:45*

At the time, some people were convinced that the **Beatlemania** soundtrack album was, without a doubt, the worst collection of Beatles cover versions ever put on vinyl. A few months later, there was another nominee . . . .

****

Sgt. Pepper's Lonely Hearts Club Band. Based on advance orders, the two-record soundtrack to the 1978 *Sgt. Pepper's Lonely Hearts Club Band* film (starring Peter Frampton and the Bee Gees) entered *Billboard*'s album charts at number seven, despite a hefty list price of $15.98. The package remained in the top ten for nine weeks, as the film opened to scathing reviews and dismal attendance. Then the album began to sink as record dealers not only failed to reorder but also began returning large quantities of their stock.

Within a few years, the **Sgt. Pepper** soundtrack album was a common sight in record store cut-out piles, marked down to as low

327

as $1.00. At that price, the album became a worthwhile investment, if only to hear George Burns, Steve Martin, and Alice Cooper ham it up. Besides, the set ran more than an hour and even included a bonus poster. In addition, Aerosmith's *Come Together*, Earth, Wind & Fire's *Got To Get You Into My Life*, and Billy Preston's *Get Back* were actually pretty good cover versions, though all three songs were also released as singles and later included on individual albums by the artists.

The rest of **Sgt. Pepper** focused on the Bee Gees and Peter Frampton, who turned in serviceable renditions of the material. Their songs were generally panned by people who didn't like them anyway and enjoyed by fans who did.

JUL 2, 1978 (US) Columbia 3-10796
SEP 22, 1978 (UK) CBS 6553
    by Earth, Wind & Fire Prod: Maurice White
A: Got To Get You Into My Life–L/McC–*4:10*
B: (i'll write a song for you)

JUL 17, 1978 (US) RSO RS 24100 (2 LPs)
JUL 21, 1978 (UK) A&M AMLZ 66600 (2 LPs)
    by Various Artists (see individual cuts)
SGT. PEPPER'S LONELY HEARTS CLUB BAND (Original Soundtrack Album)
    Prod: George Martin except †Maurice White; %George Martin and Jack
        Douglas
side one
Opening Medley: 4:42
    Sgt. Pepper's Lonely Hearts Club Band–L/McC–*1:55*
        by The Bee Gees, Paul Nicholas
    With A Little Help From My Friends–L/McC–*2:47*
        by Peter Frampton, The Bee Gees
Here Comes The Sun--Harrison–*3:05*
    by Sandy Farina
Getting Better–L/McC–*2:46*
    by Peter Frampton, The Bee Gees
Lucy In The Sky With Diamonds–L/McC–*3:41*
    by Dianne Steinberg, Stargard
I Want You (She's So Heavy)–L/McC–*6:31*
    by The Bee Gees, Dianne Steinberg, Paul Nicholas, Donald Pleasence,
        Stargard
side two
Good Morning, Good Morning–L/McC–*1:58*
    by Paul Nicholas, Peter Frampton, The Bee Gees
She's Leaving Home–L/McC–*2:40*
    by The Bee Gees, Jay MacIntosh, John Wheeler
You Never Give Me Your Money–L/McC–*3:07*
    by Paul Nicholas, Dianne Steinberg
(continued)

(continued)
Oh! Darling–L/McC–*3:29*
    by Robin Gibb
Maxwell's Silver Hammer–L/McC–*4:00*
    by Steve Martin
Medley: 5:11
    Polythene Pam–L/McC–*0:40*
        by The Bee Gees
    She Came In Through The Bathroom Window–L/McC–*1:43*
        by Peter Frampton, The Bee Gees
    Nowhere Man–L/McC–*1:24*
        by The Bee Gees
    Sgt. Pepper's Lonely Hearts Club Band–L/McC–*1:24*
        by Peter Frampton, The Bee Gees
side three
†*Got To Get You Into My Life*–L/McC–*3:36*
    by Earth, Wind & Fire
Strawberry Fields Forever–L/McC–*3:31*
    by Sandy Farina
When I'm Sixty-Four–L/McC–*2:40*
    by Frankie Howard, Sandy Farina
Mean Mr. Mustard–L/McC–*2:39*
    by Frankie Howard
Fixing A Hole–L/McC–*2:25*
    by George Burns
Because–L/McC–*2:45*
    by Alice Cooper, The Bee Gees
Medley: 3:24
    Golden Slumbers–L/McC–*1:34*
        by Peter Frampton
    Carry That Weight–L/McC–*1:50*
        by The Bee Gees
side four
%*Come Together*–L/McC–*3:46*
    by Aerosmith
Being For The Benefit Of Mr. Kite–L/McC–*3:12*
    by Maurice Gibb, Peter Frampton, George Burns, The Bee Gees
The Long And Winding Road–L/McC–*3:40*
    by Peter Frampton
A Day In The Life–L/McC–*5:11*
    by Barry Gibb, The Bee Gees
Get Back–L/McC–*2:56*
    by Billy Preston
Sgt. Pepper's Lonely Hearts Club Band–L/McC–*2:13*
    by The Entire Cast

AUG 12, 1978 (US) RSO RS 907
    by Robin Gibb (A side) and The Bee Gees, Jay MacIntosh, John Wheeler
    (B side) Prod: George Martin
A: OH! DARLING–L/McC–*3:29*
B: SHE'S LEAVING HOME–L/McC–*2:40*

AUG 12, 1978 (US) Columbia 3-10802
AUG 25, 1978 (UK) CBS 6584
by Aerosmith Prod: George Martin and Jack Douglas
A: *COME TOGETHER*–L/McC–*3:45*
B: *(kings and queens)*

AUG 28, 1978 (US) A&M 20715
by Billy Preston Prod: George Martin
A: *GET BACK*– L/McC–*2:56*
B: *(space race)*

****

Stars On 45. Over the years, many artists have done medleys of Beatles songs. Harry Nilsson released one of the best on his 1967 **Pandemonium Shadow Show** album. He used *You Can't Do That* as the main theme, then weaved in and out of it with musical riffs, lyric lines, and peculiar sounds from many other Beatles tunes.

Other artists have taken the concept to the extreme and attempted to squeeze in as many Beatles songs as possible. Generally this meant including just the title or one familiar riff. Barclay James Harvest tried that with *Titles* in 1975, to little success. In 1977, Cafe Creme combined 29 songs into a "nonstop Beatles disco single" that was issued in Holland as *Unlimited Citations* (EMI 5C 006-99597). Robert Stigwood's RSO Records picked up the U.S. rights to Cafe Creme's record and reworked it for release in July 1978. Rechristened *Discomania*, the new recording worked in more than 70 tunes for the album version (RSO RS 1-3035) and 13 for the A-side of the single (RSO 899). Despite increased sales of Beatles music at the time due to the publicity surrounding the *Sgt. Pepper* film, no one seemed particularly interested in another soundalike band. Cafe Creme's *Discomania* bubbled under the Hot 100, then disappeared.

The Beatles medley put together in late 1980 by Dutch producer Jaap Eggermont and some session musicians might have suffered the same fate. However, in the early spring of 1981 it took off worldwide, riding the intense international interest in the Beatles rekindled by the death of John Lennon. Eventually, Stars On 45 (called "Star Sound" in England) reached the top of the charts, hitting number 1 in the U.S. and number 2 in the U.K. By the fall, there was even a Stars On 45 musical slotted to begin October 28 at New York's Palladium Theater. The stage show eventually evolved into a successful oldies revue dubbed *Dream Street*, which ran in Las Vegas (of course) in 1982.

In Britain, the chart success of Star Sound touched off a rush of medley records, with another (non-Beatles) release from the group again hitting the U.K. top five. In the U.S., though, the follow-up Beatles medley single from Stars On 45 flopped. A similar second Beatles medley turned up as the B-side to yet another Star Sound single in Britain in 1982. Both British *Beatles Medley* singles were also issued as 12-inch discs (CBS A13 1102 and CBS A13 2296).

APR 1, 1981 (US) Radio Records RR 3810
APR 17, 1981 (UK) CBS A1102
    by Stars On 45 Prod: Jaap Eggermont
A: Beatles Medley—4:03
        Venus Intro—Robby Van Leeuwen—*0:08*
        Sugar Sugar—Jeff Barry/Andy Kim—*0:36*
        I Saw Her Standing There (count)—L/McC—*0:03*
        No Reply—L/McC—*0:16*
        I'll Be Back—L/McC—*0:26*
        Drive My Car—L/McC—*0:30*
        Do You Want To Know A Secret—L/McC—*0:28*
        We Can Work It Out—L/McC—*0:16*
        I Should Have Known Better—L/McC—*0:20*
        Nowhere Man—L/McC—*0:08*
        You're Going To Lose That Girl—L/McC—*0:13*
        Stars On 45—Jaap Eggermont/M. Duiser—*0:39*
B: (stars on 45)

APR 20, 1981 (US) Radio Records RR 16044 (LP)
APR 24, 1981 (UK) CBS 86132 (LP)
    by Stars On 45 (in UK: Star Sound)
STARS ON LONG PLAY (in UK: **STARS ON 45**) Prod: Jaap Eggermont
side one
Beatles Medley: 15:35
    Stars On 45—Jaap Eggermont/M. Duiser—*1:00*
    No Reply—L/McC—*0:17*
    I'll Be Back—L/McC—*0:26*
    Drive My Car—L/McC—*0:30*
    Do You Want To Know A Secret—L/McC—*0:28*
    We Can Work It Out—L/McC—*0:16*
    I Should Have Known Better—L/McC—*0:19*
    Nowhere Man—L/McC—*0:08*
    You're Going To Lose That Girl—L/McC—*0:14*
    Ticket To Ride—L/McC—*0:33*
    The Word—L/McC—*0:24*
    Eleanor Rigby—L/McC—*0:15*
    Every Little Thing—L/McC—*0:39*
    And Your Bird Can Sing—L/McC—*0:47*
    Get Back—L/McC—*0:32*
    Eight Days A Week—L/McC—*0:31*
    It Won't Be Long—L/McC—*0:13*
(continued)

(continued)
Day Tripper—L/McC—*0:45*
Wait—L/McC—*0:34*
Stars On 45—Jaap Eggermont/M. Duiser—*0:21*
Good Day Sunshine—L/McC—*0:12*
My Sweet Lord—Harrison—*0:32*
Here Comes The Sun—Harrison—*0:28*
While My Guitar Gently Weeps—Harrison—*0:31*
Taxman—Harrison—*0:26*
A Hard Day's Night—L/McC—*0:23*
Things We Said Today—L/McC—*0:35*
If I Fell—L/McC—*0:30*
You Can't Do That—L/McC—*0:27*
Please Please Me—L/McC—*0:38*
From Me To You—L/McC—*0:15 [in UK]*
I Want To Hold Your Hand—L/McC—*0:38*
Stars On 45—Jaap Eggermont/M. Duiser—*1:04*
side two
(No Beatles songs covered)

JUN 29, 1981 (US) Radio Records RR 3830
    by Stars On 45 Prod: Jaap Eggermont
A: *Beatles Medley II*—*5:08*
        Stars On 45—Jaap Eggermont/M. Duiser—*0:22*
        Good Day Sunshine—L/McC—*0:11*
        My Sweet Lord—Harrison—*0:31*
        Here Comes The Sun—Harrison—*0:29*
        While My Guitar Gently Weeps—Harrison—*0:31*
        Taxman—Harrison—*0:26*
        A Hard Day's Night—L/McC—*0:23*
        Please Please Me—L/McC—*0:39*
        From Me To You—L/McC—*0:15*
        I Want To Hold Your Hand—L/McC—*0:38*
        Stars On 45—Jaap Eggermont/M. Duiser—*0:43*
B: *(stars on 45 II)*

APR 17, 1982 (UK) CBS A2296
    by Star Sound Prod: Jaap Eggermont
B: *Beatles Medley*—*5:25*
        My Sweet Lord—Harrison—*0:31*
        Here Comes The Sun—Harrison—*0:29*
        While My Guitar Gently Weeps—Harrison—*0:32*
        Taxman—Harrison—*0:25*
        A Hard Day's Night—L/McC—*0:24*
        Things We Said Today—L/McC—*0:35*
        If I Fell—L/McC—*0:30*
        You Can't Do That—L/McC—*0:27*
        Please Please Me—L/McC—*0:40*
        From Me To You—L/McC—*0:15*
        I Want To Hold Your Hand—L/McC—*0:36*
A: *(the greatest rock'n'roll band in the world)*

The extended Beatles medley on side one of the album contained the Beatles material used on both Stars On 45 singles. The other side contained cover versions of songs originally done by artists other than the Beatles, including Shocking Blue's *Venus* and the Archies' *Sugar Sugar* (which were both used on the first *Beatles Medley* single).

Perhaps the most unusual aspect of the Stars On 45 hit single was the fact that, despite the inclusion of riffs from ten Beatles songs, more than one-third of the time was devoted to non-Beatles material. Some radio stations cut out most of this when they aired the medley, going straight to the Beatles songs and fading out early at the end. Still, royalties were split among the publishing companies for all the songs on the discs, including Dayglow Music, which handled *Venus* as well as Jaap Eggermont's *Stars On 45* signature tune.

* * * * * * * * * *

Beatlesongs. In 1982 Rhino Records, an eclectic Los Angeles based label, released a compilation album of novelty songs about the Beatles, drawing from the hundreds issued since 1963.

Eight of the twelve tracks were from 1964 and featured Stateside responses to the initial success of the Beatles in the U.S.

The Invasion was a "break-in" record which mixed humorous narration with bits of other records to tell the story of the arrival of the four "mops."

We Love You Beatles (an adaptation of the *Bye Bye Birdie* tune *We Love You Conrad*) was a teenage girl's unqualified anthem of surrender. The song cracked the U.S. top forty (reaching 39 on *Billboard*'s charts) and was used to open the group's 1964 television special, "Around the Beatles."

My Boyfriend Got A Beatle Haircut also made the charts (peaking at 83) with the lament of a teenage girl mourning the loss of her boyfriend. When he got a Beatle haircut, the other girls began chasing him. Her solution? She got a Beatle haircut, too.

Letter From Elaina featured *American Top 40* disc jockey Casey Kasem (back when he worked for local station KRLA in California) reading a letter from a girl who actually got to see, talk to, and hug George Harrison for a few seconds. An instrumental version of *And I Love Her* provided background accompaniment.

Beatlemania was simply an instrumental by composer Jack Nitzsche, who built his tune around the music to *Please Please Me, From Me To You, I Want To Hold Your Hand*, and his own composition, *Needles And Pins* (written with Sonny Bono).

Pop Hates The Beatles, sung by Allan Sherman to the tune of

Beatlesongs   **Rhino Records RNLP 803 (LP)**

Beatlesongs   **Rhino Records RNLP 803 (LP)**

Pop Goes The Weasel, told the story from the perspective of a harried father with a teenage daughter. His conclusion: dump the Beatles in Boston Harbor, but only *after* they'd been to a barber.

Letter To The Beatles, by the Four Preps, was sung from the point of view of a puzzled boyfriend who could not understand why his girlfriend kept on writing to the Beatles. All she ever received in return was a sales pitch for autographed photos, a fan club membership, and a lock of hair — from a St. Bernard. This record also hit the charts, reaching number 85.

The Beetle was written by Gary Usher and Roger Christian, who also produced the 1964 **Beatles' Story** documentary album for Capitol. Their song was meant to be a fad dance number, but never caught on. Silly lyrics. A good beat. You *can* dance to it.

These eight songs pretty well covered the best of the initial "Beatlemania" novelties. The only two major omissions from the era were *Ringo I Love You* by Bonnie Jo Mason (Cher), a 1964 release produced by Phil Spector, and *All I Want For Christmas Is A Beatle*, a 1963 British hit by Dora Bryan.

Of the remaining songs, *L.S. Bumblebee* (from 1967) was the most unusual because, technically, it had absolutely nothing to do with the Beatles. The song had been hatched by humorists Peter Cook and Dudley Moore back in late 1966 as a satire on the developing psychedelic scene, epitomized at the time by the Beach Boys' *Good Vibrations*. Cook and Moore released their *L.S. Bumblebee* in January 1967 (only in England) and, sometime later, tapes of the song turned up in the U.S. along with the tale that it was an unreleased Beatles track. That story ran virtually unquestioned until 1975 when we checked with Cook and Moore as part of the research for *All Together Now*. For any remaining doubters, the backcover of **Beatlesongs** featured a letter from Dudley Moore, once again confirming the non-involvement of the Beatles.

Rounding out the selections on the album were: *I'm The Meany*, an ode to *Yellow Submarine*'s cartoon villain by Frank Zappa "discovery" Wild Man Fisher, *Hold My Hand* from the Rutles (see page 337), and *Beatle Rap*, a series of amateur Beatles impressions put to a "rap record" beat.

The original front cover to **Beatlesongs** consisted of a cartoon caricature of more than a dozen Beatles fans, but this was quickly changed when some buyers pointed out that one of the characters looked like Mark Chapman. Whether that was intended or not, an innocuous picture of Beatles memorabilia (taken from the back cover) was moved in as a substitute cover for subsequent editions.

335

MAR 1, 1982 (US) Rhino Records RNLP 803 (LP)
by Various Artists (see individual cuts)
BEATLESONGS (A Collection Of Beatles Novelties Volume 1)
side one
The Invasion—Bill Buchanan/Howie Greenfield—*2:53*
by Buchanan and Greenfield
Hold My Hand—Neil Innes—*2:31*
by The Rutles
We Love You Beatles—Lee Adams/Charles Strouse—*2:18*
by The Carefrees
My Boyfriend Got A Beatle Haircut—Jack Wolf/Rose Mehlman/Maurice "Bugs"
Bower—*2:12*
by Donna Lynn
Letter From Elaina—Casey Kasem—*3:16*
by Casey Kasem
Beatlemania—*2:10*
by Jack Nitzsche
side two
Beatle Rap—*3:55*
by The Quorymen
The L.S. Bumble Bee—Peter Cook/Dudley Moore—*2:42*
by Peter Cook and Dudley Moore
I'm The Meany—Wild Man Fischer—*1:20*
by Wild Man Fischer
Pop Hates The Beatles (to the tune *Pop Goes The Weasel*)—*3:04*
by Allan Sherman
Letter To The Beatles—Bruce Belland/Ivan Ulz—*2:48*
by The Four Preps
The Beetle—Gary Usher/Roger Christian—*1:54*
by Gary Usher

****

Peter Sellers. Before George Martin had ever heard of the Beatles,
he worked with Peter Sellers, one of their heroes. (They had grown
up listening to Sellers, Spike Milligan, and Harry Secombe trash the
BBC airwaves on *The Goon Show*.) Appropriately, Martin also produced Peter Sellers' recordings of several Beatles songs: *She Loves
You, A Hard Day's Night*, and *Help*. Though all of them were done
at the same recording sessions in 1965, only *A Hard Day's Night*
and *Help* were released at the time. As a single, they reached the
British top twenty.

The Peter Sellers renditions of *She Loves You* went unreleased
until after his death in the summer of 1980. In January 1981, EMI
issued a single featuring two different interpretations of the song,
one with Sellers using his Dr. Strangelove German accent, the other
with his Phil McCafferty Irish accent. Two years later, EMI released

The Songs of Sellers, an album that included *A Hard Day's Night, Help*, the Dr. Strangelove *She Loves You*, and yet another (previously unreleased) version of *She Loves You* — this one with Sellers doing a William Mate cockney accent.

DEC 10, 1965 (UK) Parlophone R 5393
JAN 31, 1966 (US) Capitol 5580
    by Peter Sellers   Prod: George Martin
A: A Hard Day's Night–L/McC–*1:46*
B: Help–L/McC–*2:22*

JAN 30, 1981 (UK) Parlophone R 6043
    by Peter Sellers   Prod: George Martin
 A: She Loves You–L/McC–*2:16*
  (inspired by Dr. Strangelove)
*B: She Loves You–L/McC–*1:36*
  (inspired by Phil McCafferty, The Irish Dentist)

OCT 31, 1983 (UK) Music For Pleasure MFP 4156401 (LP)
    by Peter Sellers
THE SONGS OF SELLERS Prod: George Martin
side one
    cut two: *A HARD DAY'S NIGHT*–L/McC–*1:46*
    cut four: *SHE LOVES YOU*–L/McC–*2:06*
      (inspired by Dr. Strangelove)
    cut five: *She Loves You*–L/McC–*1:35*
      (inspired by William Mate)
side two
    cut four: *HELP*–L/McC–*2:22*

****

The Rutles. The Rutles were the ultimate Beatles parody. Dubbed the Prefab Four, Dirk, Kevin, Stig, and Nasty first appeared in 1976 on the Eric Idle and Neil Innes British TV series, *Rutland Weekend Television*. They made their U.S. television debut on October 2, 1976, when Idle hosted NBC's *Saturday Night Live* and brought along a film clip of the group performing *I Must Be In Love*. For his return engagement on the show the following April, Idle presented Nasty himself (Innes), who performed *Cheese And Onions* live at the piano. Then Idle and Innes collaborated with *Saturday Night Live* producer Lorne Michaels and resident filmmaker Gary Weis on a full blown Rutles documentary special, *All You Need Is Cash*. That film formally introduced the Rutles lineup to the public, with Eric Idle as Dirk McQuickly (Paul), Neil Innes as Ron Nasty (John), Rikki Fataar as Stig O'Hara (George), and John Halsey as Barry Wom (Ringo). Kevin, like Pete Best, was left on the cutting room floor.

337

Promotion for the special began in early 1978, with a "media invasion" by the Prefab Four. First came an album, complete with a full-color picture booklet based on the documentary. A barrage of newspaper stories followed, with the Rutles winning feature spreads in such publications as the Washington *Post*. The ninety-minute film special hit the NBC airwaves at last on March 22, 1978. It bombed. *All You Need Is Cash* came in as one of the lowest rated television specials that entire season. Obviously, the general public was not ready for the Rutles.

But those that did tune in saw a brilliantly crafted parody that displayed an uncanny knack for coming so close to the original events that sometimes it was nearly impossible to tell reality from parody. In fact, the more a viewer knew about the Beatles and their history, the funnier the show seemed. Particular scenes were dead ringers for familiar documentary clips, down to the quality of the film stock and the angle of the camera shots.

For the story of Rutles Corps. (Apple), George Harrison even made a cameo appearance as an investigative reporter. Later, in his *I Me Mine* book, Harrison urged people interested in the story of the Beatles to see the Rutles film. It was all there, he asserted. And so it was.

All You Need Is Cash aired in Britain March 27 and again July 29. There, enthusiastic Rutles fans boosted the album to number twelve on the charts and the *I Must Be In Love* single into the top forty, peaking at 39. Back in the U.S.,the single never cracked the Hot 100 and the album only reached 63.

The final Rutles record, *Ging Gang Goolie*, was released only in England as a "solo" disc by Dirk and Stig, following the "official break up" of the group. Fans of the Rutles had to wait until 1983 for the next release — video tape and disc versions of the original television special.

FEB 27, 1978 (US) Warner Bros. HS 3151 (LP)
MAR 24, 1978 (UK) Warner Bros. K 56459 (LP)
    by The Rutles
THE RUTLES Prod: Neil Innes
side one
Hold My Hand—Neil Innes—*2:31*
Number One—Neil Innes—*2:50*
With A Girl Like You—Neil Innes—*1:50*
I Must Be In Love—Neil Innes—*2:04*
Ouch!—Neil Innes—*1:49*
Living In Hope—Neil Innes—*2:37*
Love Life—Neil Innes—*2:50*
Nevertheless—Neil Innes—*1:29*

side two
Good Times Roll—Neil Innes—*3:03*
Doubleback Alley—Neil Innes—*2:54*
Cheese And Onions—Neil Innes—*2:37*
Another Day—Neil Innes—*2:09*
Piggy In The Middle—Neil Innes—*4:07*
Let's Be Natural—Neil Innes—*3:23*

MAR 10, 1978 (UK) Warner Bros. K 17125
    by The Rutles Prod: Neil Innes
side one
I Must Be In Love—Neil Innes—*2:04*
side two
Cheese And Onions—Neil Innes—*2:54*
With A Girl Like You—Neil Innes—*1:50*

APR 3, 1978 (US) Warner Bros. WBS 8560
    by The Rutles Prod: Neil Innes
A: I MUST BE IN LOVE—Neil Innes—*2:04*
B: DOUBLEBACK ALLEY—Neil Innes—*2:54*

MAY 26, 1978 (UK) Warner Bros. K 17180
    by The Rutles Prod: Neil Innes
A: LET'S BE NATURAL—Neil Innes—*3:23*
B: PIGGY IN THE MIDDLE—Neil Innes—*4:07*

Promotional 12-inch (US) Warner Bros. PRO E-723 (1978)
    by The Rutles Prod: Neil Innes
side one
I MUST BE IN LOVE—Neil Innes—*2:04*
DOUBLEBACK ALLEY—Neil Innes—*2:54*
WITH A GIRL LIKE YOU—Neil Innes—*1:50*
side two
ANOTHER DAY—Neil Innes—*2:09*
LET'S BE NATURAL—Neil Innes—*3:23*

AUG 18, 1978 (UK) EMI 2852
    by Dirk and Stig Prod: Ricky Fataar and Eric Idle
*A: Ging Gang Goolie—Trad. arr. Eric Idle/Ricky Fataar—*3:11*
*B: Mister Sheene—Eric Idle—*2:25*

ALL YOU NEED IS CASH (Original Television Broadcast: 1978)
Video Issued 1983: As *The Rutles* Pacific Arts PAVR 540 (US) and as
The Complete Rutles Palace Video PVC 2065 (UK)

Get Up And Go	We Were Made For Each Other
Medley:	(Between Us)
Number One	Living In Hope
Love Life	Ouch!
Piggy In The Middle	It's Looking Good
I Must Be In Love	Another Day
Let's Be Natural	Good Times Roll
Goose Step Mama	Love Life
Number One	Nevertheless
We Were Made For Each Other	Piggy In The Middle
(Between Us)	Cheese And Onions
With A Girl Like You	Let's Be Natural
Hold My Hand	You Need Feet
I Must Be In Love	Get Up And Go
	Doubleback Alley

The 1978 **Rutles** album came with the front cover sticker: "Free Record With This 20-Page Book." This was taken literally by the Canadian government, which decided not to apply its record tax rate to the package and treated it instead as a book (with a bonus record).

In the U.S., the album was nominated for a Grammy Award as the best comedy album of the year, but lost out to Steve Martin's **A Wild And Crazy Guy**.

The British single of *I Must Be In Love* came in a picture sleeve. *I Must Be In Love* also appeared on the **Beatlesongs** compilation (see page 335). The U.S. promotional 12-inch disc was issued on yellow vinyl with a banana label logo, while the British Dirk and Stig single was pressed on khaki-colored vinyl and packaged in a cartoon picture sleeve.

There were five songs in the Rutles TV special that did not appear on any of the record releases: *Get Up And Go, Goose Step Mama, We Were Made For Each Other (Between Us), It's Looking Good*, and *You Need Feet*. Generally, the recordings of the other songs in the special were different from those used on the album.

The British *Complete Rutles* was initially packaged as a parody of the design used on the 1982 *Compleat Beatles* video release, then revised. There were also a few minor changes on the video itself, including the addition of about a minute of material.

The Rutles film and album booklet included interviews with Paul Simon and Mick Jagger (playing themselves), who put the entire Rutles phenomenon into "proper historical perspective." Simon explained what effect the Prefab Four had on his work (none), while Jagger expressed his feelings about when the Rutles should get back together (never).

No wonder Harrison loved the Rutles.

Ging Gang Goolie · · · · · · · · · · · · · · · · · · · EMI 2852 (45)

Mister Sheene · EMI 2852 (45)

JOHNNY AND THE MOONDOGS
Silver Days

Johnny And The Moondogs: Silver Days/Air Time
Warwick M 16051/Subway Records MX 4729 (bootleg LP)

ALL SALES FINAL:
BOOTLEGS

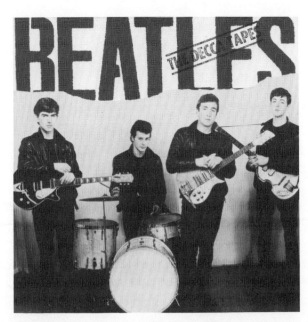

The Decca Tapes   Circuit Records LK 4438-1 (bootleg LP)

The Beatles Broadcasts   Circuit Records LK 4450
(bootleg LP)

Bootlegs
Worth Buying?

There are some dedicated Beatles completists who will purchase virtually any bootleg disc featuring the group. To them, every such recording is simply *assumed* to be worth buying, if only to keep their collections "complete."

Generally, we have left the sorting out of details regarding such packages to people far more dedicated to the task than we are. Charles Reinhart's book *You Can't Do That (Beatles Bootlegs And Novelty Records)* describes more than *one thousand* such releases and is an excellent starting point for bootleg[1] exploration.

We have always approached the topic of bootlegs from the opposite direction, assuming that there are virtually *no* bootlegs worth buying. The reason is simple. Since the late 1960s, bootleggers have foisted upon the Beatles-buying public low-quality, overpriced, blatantly deceptive record releases. "Rare studio-quality tracks" have turned out to be neither rare nor studio-quality (and sometimes not even by the Beatles). New album packages recycled the same old *Let It Be* film outtakes or "mike-in-the-crowd" live recordings in shoddy white cardboard jackets with minimal cover art and information. As such, most bootleg packages were essentially worthless.

Yet through all of this, ever-patient Beatles fans picked through the releases, hoping that *this* time something good would turn up. In the late 1970s, their patience was rewarded as previously unreleased, high-quality studio recordings "hit the streets."

Perhaps buoyed by the increased quality of the tracks, enterprising

----

[1]A quick review of terms: A *bootleg* is any unauthorized disc or tape consisting of previously unreleased studio sessions, live performances, or radio and TV broadcasts. A *counterfeit* is an unauthorized exact copy of an already released legitimate package. A *pirate* is a specially created unauthorized package containing previously released material, but in a new form. Ironically, most fans that collect bootlegs would probably support a crackdown on counterfeits and pirates. Nonetheless, to the record industry all such product has been seen as part of the same problem.

bootleggers also significantly upgraded their packaging. With an eye toward the growing number of collectors willing to pay premium prices for imported singles and albums that featured attractive new photos and picture sleeves, they replaced the nondescript jackets of the past with full color covers and intelligently detailed liner notes. Even the choice of vinyl and pressing plant facilities improved, with some particularly brazen folks not only using the same plants as "real" record companies, but also shipping their product to mainstream record stores. These records projected an air of legitimacy and slipped in comfortably beside regular Beatles product, usually in the "import" section. Knowledgeable fans knew better, but welcomed the opportunity to purchase these discs while waiting for the next official solo release, group repackaging, or always-hoped-for *authorized* studio outtakes.

Unfortunately, it did not take long for bootleggers to realize that they could reissue their familiar old material in slick new packages as well, so once again Beatles fans faced a dizzying assortment of tempting new product. Each promised more top-notch material. Few delivered.

In this section, we've singled out for discussion the few discs that, despite their illegal status, were so good they they *should* have been legitimate. Like a regular Beatles album, they could be played and enjoyed over and over again. In fact, if the material on these had been available through legitimate channels on similar high quality packages, there would have been no need for fans to turn to the bootleg versions at all.

Legitimate record companies, though, have always had to deal with legal complications conveniently skirted by bootleggers (such as who gets paid what for each release). Ironically, such delays have meant that the record packages done without the authorization or approval of the individual Beatles or their record companies have had virtually no competition in the collectors' marketplace. And the truth is that such bootleg product has (and will) always win the support of eager Beatles completists until what they want appears on legitimate releases.

The 1962 Audition
(a.k.a. "The Decca Tapes")

On January 1, 1962, John Lennon, Paul McCartney, George Harrison, and Pete Best formally auditioned at the West Hampstead studios of Decca Records, playing a mixed bag of rock and pop standards plus a few Lennon-McCartney originals. Despite initial positive reaction, Decca's management eventually turned them down. About the only thing the Beatles got out of the session was a copy of the audition tape.

Actually, that tape was a very valuable dividend because it allowed Brian Epstein to approach other record companies with a professional studio recording of the group. He tried virtually every label in London before at last securing a contract with EMI's Parlophone Records. Once the Beatles were signed and on their way, the audition tape was no longer needed and was quickly forgotten.

When Beatles music exploded in 1963 and 1964, companies in both England and the United States quickly released virtually any Beatles-related disc they could think of. Luckier than most, the German-based Polydor label plundered its vaults and came up with some 1961 sessions featuring the Beatles as backing musicians to singer Tony Sheridan, including tracks not issued at the time. As a result, a brand-new release of *Ain't She Sweet* followed the reissued *My Bonnie* onto the charts.

Surprisingly, the Decca audition tapes remained in the company vaults. Apparently Decca felt that the outright rejection of the group certainly left it little claim on the right to release the audition session. For more than ten years, these songs went unheard by the general public. Occasionally a bootleg album would surface touting the Decca audition tracks, but inevitably these turned out to be songs performed on the radio and recorded off the air.

Then, in 1977, a strange new single appeared, on colored vinyl, in a full-color picture sleeve, on the "Deccagone" label. The tracks? *Three Cool Cats* and *Hello Little Girl*. The recording quality? Superb.

The Decca Audition Session

Lineup:

John Lennon: Rhythm Guitar.   Paul McCartney: Bass Guitar.
George Harrison: Lead Guitar.   Pete Best: Drums.

Lead Vocals:

Besame Mucho: Paul   *September In The Rain*: Paul
Crying, Waiting, Hoping: George   *The Sheik Of Araby*: George
Hello Little Girl: John (+ Paul)   *Sure To Fall*: Paul
Like Dreamers Do: Paul   *Take Good Care Of My Baby*: George
Love Of The Loved: Paul   *Three Cool Cats*: George
Memphis, Tennessee: John   *Till There Was You*: Paul
Money: John   *To Know Him Is To Love Him*: John
Searchin': Paul

Session "Producer": Mike Smith

Recording Date: January 1, 1962

Location: West Hampstead studios of Decca Records in London, England.

Note: There were a number of other songs reportedly performed at the Decca audition session, including *Please Mr. Postman, Red Sails In The Sunset*, and *Your Feet's Too Big*. These never turned up on any bootleg release. Perhaps they were held back for subsequent sale. Perhaps they were performed when the tape recorders were not rolling. Or perhaps faulty memories placed them at the audition session when, in reality, they were not performed at all that day. Take your pick.

Quickly the story spread through collectors' circles that some dedicated Beatles fans had somehow acquired a copy of the Decca audition tape, consisting of 15 tracks, and were planning to release them, two at a time, as singles. A collective groan passed through fandom. Why not an album? Seven singles could stretch out over several years!

The reason for the single-by-single strategy was obvious. Each single sold for about $4, so that meant at least $28 for the set. It was unlikely that an album could have been priced that high. More importantly, because bootleggers pirated from each other, an album's worth of material would have had a very short shelf life before being copied and pressed by other people. By parceling out the cuts two at a time, the expected pirating would be postponed sufficiently to recoup the original investment.

Ironically, the single strategy had a curiously exciting side-effect. For the first time in years, Beatles fans had the thrill of awaiting brand-new, previously unheard singles. Through 1977, 1978, and 1979 they willingly paid the $4 for each release, arguing about favorite tracks, picture sleeves, and what should be the next "a" and "b" sides.

As expected, counterfeit copies of the Deccagone singles popped up soon after each release. After the fourth single, an album labeled **The Deccagone Sessions** coupled these eight tracks with some radio broadcast material. Fans quickly recognized the deception and patiently awaited the "official" release of the remaining new singles instead.

In 1979, the seventh single was issued, leaving one track. By then the ultimate strategy had become obvious. The fifteenth track would be the inducement to purchase all 14 once again on an album. Late in the year, **The Decca Tapes** album arrived. First, the package was released as a picture disc (popular at the time). Then, just in time for Christmas, the regular album turned up, complete with all 15 tracks, sharp graphics, detailed liner notes, and a new label identification: Circuit Records.

The Decca Tapes album looked like a legitimate import with appropriate warnings against unauthorized duplication and an address in England for the company. To further support the illusion, the liner notes helpfully explained that, in reality, the album was actually a reissue of a 1962 British album that had originally appeared on Decca Records.

To a knowledgeable Beatles fan, the liner notes were hilarious. In order to explain the album, one thread of Beatles history was deliberately twisted. Instead of rejecting the Beatles after the January 1, 1962 audition, Decca signed them.

Data from the fictional Decca history outlined in the liner notes to THE DECCA TAPES album on Circuit Records

Recording Sessions:

First Recording Session: January 9, 1962.
Besame Mucho; Hello Little Girl; The Sheik Of Araby; September In The Rain; Three Cool Cats.

Second Recording Session: April 4, 1962.
Love Of The Loved; Memphis, Tennessee; Till There Was You.

Third Recording Session: June 5, 1962.
Crying, Waiting, Hoping; Like Dreamers Do; Money; Searchin'; Sure To Fall; To Know Her Is To Love Her.

From January 1, 1962 audition: *Take Good Care Of My Baby.*

Record Releases:

Fictional Singles Data	Actual Decca Releases Assigned Those Numbers
JAN 19, 1962 (UK) Decca F 11339 A: *Three Cool Cats* B: *Hello Little Girl*	MAR 24, 1961 by David Whitfield A: *Climb Ev'ry Mountain* B: *The Sound of Music*
FEB 23, 1962 (UK) Decca F 11364 A: *The Sheik Of Araby* B: *September In The Rain*	JUN 23, 1961 by Robb Storme A: *Near You* B: *Lonely Town*
APR 20, 1962 (UK) Decca F 11405 A: *Memphis, Tennessee* B: *Love Of The Loved*	NOV 17, 1961 by Lionel Bart A: *Give Us A Kiss For Christmas* B: *How Now Brown Cow*
JUN 15, 1962 (UK) Decca F 11487 A: *Searchin'* B: *Like Dreamers Do*	JUL 13, 1962 by Alan Fielding A: *How Many Nights, How Many Days* B: *Building Castles In The Air*
AUG 17, 1962 (UK) Decca F 11533 A: *Sure To Fall* B: *Money*	NOV 2, 1962 by Edumundo Ros & Orchestra A: *Desafinado* B: *One Note Samba*

Contents of Fictional Album:

SEP 27, 1962 (UK) Decca LK 4437 (LP)
THE ORIGINAL BEATLES

side one	side two
Like Dreamers Do	*Hello Little Girl*
Money	*Three Cool Cats*
Till There Was You	*Crying, Waiting, Hoping*
The Sheik Of Araby	*Love Of The Loved*
To Know Him Is To Love Him	*September In The Rain*
Memphis, Tennessee	*Besame Mucho*
Sure To Fall	*Searchin'*

In summary, "The Untold Story of the Decca Tapes" presented the following alternate reality:

Decca signed the Beatles to a five-single contract, primarily as a novelty-type group reflected in the company's choice for the first two single releases: *Three Cool Cats* and *The Sheik of Araby*. When both of those discs flopped, Brian Epstein convinced Decca to promote the Beatles as a solid British band that did serviceable cover versions of rock classics. Chuck Berry's *Memphis, Tennessee* and *Searchin'* from the Coasters followed as singles. Both garnered some positive reviews and moderate sales, convincing both Epstein and the Beatles that Decca was handling them all wrong. They secretly sent out feelers to other companies, jumping to EMI's Parlophone label in the summer of 1962. Miffed at losing a group that apparently had some chance at success, Decca quickly issued the fifth single and then an album in September 1962, just a week before the release of *Love Me Do*. The album contained not only the five singles but also four outtakes. The Beatles and EMI sued Decca and forced the album to be withdrawn before more than a handful of copies were sold. And so it remained until the mid-1970s when EMI agreed to allow Decca to release the 14 tracks as a series of limited edition singles on a special subsidiary label, Deccagone. **The Decca Tapes** album itself was described as an authorized reissue of the original 14-track 1962 album, plus a bonus fifteenth track.

To the uninitiated, the story read as a reasonable account of obscure recording work by the Beatles some 17 years before. Yet it also served as a clever justification for both the Deccagone singles and the Circuit Records album. Both were presented as merely authorized reissuings of material that had, in fact, already come out in England back in 1962. Each "Decca" single from 1962 was given a catalog number and release date, each song was placed at a particular recording session for Decca, and each event was worked into the known history of the Beatles. As a final dig, Circuit Records added an extra flourish at the end of the liner notes with the caption: " 'The Untold Story of the Decca Tapes' is a work of historical fiction." (Translation: Everything you've just read is a lie.)

In a way, the packaging of **The Decca Tapes** was the ultimate fan fantasy, not only creating new singles and a new album, but also concocting a new history for the Beatles as well. Yet it also balanced this enthusiasm with an uncanny business sense. Any Beatles fan collecting the Decca sessions eventually paid approximately $40 for all the singles and the album. Despite that, even fans that complained about the cost generally agreed that, with the high quality of the recordings and the first class packaging, the Decca sessions had been "done right" by people who truly cared about the music. They were consistently cited by fans as the way "new" Beatles product should

Background information for the songs
performed on the Decca Tapes

Besame Mucho (Consuelo Velazquez–Selig Shaftel)
Originally performed in 1943 by Jimmy Dorsey and Orchestra
Released in 1960 by The Coasters on Atco 6163

Crying, Waiting, Hoping (Buddy Holly)
Originally released in 1959 by Buddy Holly on Coral 62134

Hello Little Girl (John Lennon–Paul McCartney)
Given to The Fourmost
First released in 1963 on Parlophone R 5056 (England)

Like Dreamers Do (John Lennon–Paul McCartney)
Given to The Applejacks
First released in 1964 on Decca F 11916 (England)

Love Of The Loved (John Lennon–Paul McCartney)
Given to Cilla Black
First released in 1963 on Parlophone R 5065 (England)

Memphis, Tennessee (Chuck Berry)
Originally released in 1959 by Chuck Berry on Chess 1729

Money (That's What I Want) (Berry Gordy–Janie Bradford)
Originally released in 1959 by Barret Strong on Anna 1111

Searchin' (Jerry Leiber–Mike Stoller)
Originally released in 1957 by The Coasters on Atco 6087

September In The Rain (Al Dubin–Harry Warren)
Originally from the 1935 film *Stars Over Broadway*
Released in 1961 by Dinah Washington on Mercury 71876

The Sheik Of Araby (Harry B. Smith–Ted Snyder–Frances Wheeler)
Originally from the 1940 film *Tin Pan Alley*
Released in 1961 by Fats Domino on Imperial album HAP–2312 (**A Lot Of Dominoes**)

Sure To Fall (In Love With You) (Carl Perkins–William E. Cantrell–Quinton Claunch)
Originally released in 1956 by Carl Perkins on Sun 235

Take Good Care Of My Baby (Gerry Goffin–Carole King)
Originally released in 1961 by Bobby Vee on Liberty 55354

Three Cool Cats (Jerry Leiber–Mike Stoller)
Originally released in 1959 by The Coasters on Atco 6132

Till There Was You (Meredith Willson)
Originally from the 1957 play *The Music Man*
Original cast album released in 1958 on Capitol WAO 990

To Know Him Is To Love Him (Phil Spector)
Originally released in 1958 by The Teddy Bears on Dore 503

be handled – in contrast to such repackagings as **Rock'n'Roll Music**.

To be fair to Capitol and EMI, however, the unidentified people behind the release of these sessions had several tremendous advantages in planning their records. For one thing, they could ignore time-consuming legal maneuvering necessary to obtain clearances and approvals not only from the former Beatles but also from any other record company that might feel it had a claim to the tapes. More importantly, both the singles and the album were targeted to a relatively small audience. Thus, they could succeed with pressings in the thousands rather than in the hundreds of thousands or even a million. As part of the EMI stable, of course, an authorized album would probably have been expected to deliver top ten gold sales – even in competition with popular contemporary product. And *seven* singles would have been out of the question.

So some daring entrepreneurs took a chance and succeeded in bringing these audition sessions to thousands of Beatles fans throughout the world. Once introduced into the world of bootlegs, the tracks were guaranteed a long distribution life as others repackaged and repressed them for subsequent resale.

But that's not quite the end of the story.

By keeping a relatively low profile, the people behind the Deccagone singles and the Circuit Records album neatly avoided ever facing the question of who actually owned the tapes and, more importantly, who had the right to release them. A wise move because the answer was not immediately obvious.

When the tapes were recorded at Decca on January 1, 1962, the Beatles had been under Brian Epstein's wing for barely two months. Previously they had, on their own, signed a limited recording contract with Polydor in Germany when they served as backing vocalists to Tony Sheridan. (Thus their tout back in Liverpool as "Polydor recording artists.") Polydor producer Bert Kaempfert even expressed interest in recording the Beatles alone during one of their visits to Germany in 1962. Conceivably, then, it could be argued that on January 1 the Beatles had some commitment to German Polydor.

Though Decca passed on signing the group it had, of course, provided the facilities for the audition session. A dub of the master tape was given to Brian Epstein almost as a matter of professional courtesy, no doubt with the understanding that he would use it just as he did, for subsequent auditions. While Decca might not ever have been able to claim the sole right to release the material, the company could certainly cite ownership of the original master tape itself and request *some* compensation if it was ever officially released.

Even a claim by EMI would not be crystal clear because the company did not sign the Beatles until well into 1962. Would even worldwide rights to the Beatles extend back to include material recorded *before* the group was under contract? After all, Polydor was able to release the 1961 Tony Sheridan sessions with the Beatles (even the outtakes) and, in 1977, Double H Licensing successfully argued its right to release the live Star Club sessions even though they took place months *after* the Beatles signed to EMI.

Almost from the beginning, then, the Decca sessions floated in an undefined limbo. Following the successful bootleg releases of the Deccagone singles and the Circuit Records album, it was only a matter of time before others entered the fray.

In 1981, a company called United Distributors Lyrics, Ltd. (UDL) tried a somewhat more open sales pitch. UDL packaged ten of the Decca tracks as a $10 mail-order-only item, **Dawn Of The Silver Beatles**, with ads running initially in national publications such as *Rolling Stone* and later locally in such places as Chicago's free weekly newspaper, *The Reader*. After receiving the album, curious collectors discovered that the remaining five tracks were available as well. The catch? The other album, **Lightning Strikes Twice**, cost $12.95 yet contained only one side of Beatles material. (The other side featured five "rare" Elvis Presley tracks.) Though there were never any reports of legal action taken against UDL, by the end of 1981 the company had stopped answering its mail.

In 1982, a consortium of investors decided to release ten of the Decca tracks in an open and deliberate promotional effort to launch a new record label, Backstage Records. Their hook? Former Beatles drummer Pete Best. Their package? A three-record album set called **Like Dreamers Do**.

How could ten tracks be stretched over three records? They couldn't. Instead, one disc (a picture disc) contained an interview with Pete Best plus a few excerpts from some Beatles press conferences. A second picture disc contained the ten tracks. Because sound quality on picture discs was generally not very good, the ten songs appeared again on a higher quality white vinyl disc. The price tag for the entire set? $25-$30.

Taking a cue from the fictional **Decca Tapes** liner notes, Backstage Records also circulated its own "history" of the tapes,[1] claiming that British Decca had sold the rights to a company called Autumn Records in the mid-1960s. Supposedly Autumn Records sat on the package until 1978 when it sold the set to First American Records of Nevada. That company, in turn, merely peddled the material to United Monetary Services of New York, which leased it to the investors who formed Backstage Records. (Why all of these previous "owners" since 1962 had failed to release the songs themselves was never explained.)

---

[1] Recounted in the May 29, 1982, issue of *Billboard* magazine.

In any case, Backstage Records claimed that it had legitimately leased the rights to release the tracks. Playing on the public's curiosity at the reappearance of Pete Best, the company pushed its three-record set behind the former Beatles drummer. Ostensibly Best was touring as part of the resumption of his musical career, but inevitably his sessions on the talk show circuit and in print turned into questions about why he had been dropped by the Beatles. Nonetheless, he generated copy in such publications as *Billboard, Rolling Stone*, and *Oui*. And, inevitably, plugs for the **Like Dreamers Do** album followed as well.[1] The package popped up in real, mainstream record stores — only it did not sell very well. By 1982, most collectors had already acquired the tracks and felt no inclination to spend another $30 for the same material.[2] Members of the general public also balked at the cost of songs they had never heard of. Late in 1982, the package was redone as a two-record set.

Like Dreamers Do marked the fourth major packaging of the audition material since 1977. It was becoming increasingly obvious that no one was certain who could or could not issue the tapes. So in mid-1982 an already established record company entered the market, Audio Fidelity Enterprises.

Audio Fidelity had been around since the 1950s. The company had been one of the pioneers of stereo records and, more recently, had purchased the licensing rights to the 1962 Star Club tapes. Studio audition work from 1962 made sense as a companion release. Unlike all the previous packagers, however, Audio Fidelity decided to target its release of the material to the general record buying public with "popularly priced" sets.

The company took twelve of the fifteen tracks (all the cover versions) and placed them on one album, **The Complete Silver Beatles**,[3] with a list price of $7.98. This was an outright steal compared to the list prices for the packages from Backstage ($20–$30 for ten songs), UDL ($10 for ten songs, $22.95 for fifteen), and Deccagone ($4 for two songs). Only the Circuit Records album ($10 for all fifteen songs) offered a comparable value.

Still, Audio Fidelity came up with its own innovation to squeeze

---

[1]*Oui* went one step further, offering a free promotional single of *Like Dreamers Do/Love Of The Loved* in exchange for a magazine coupon and fifty cents postage. We're still waiting for our copies to arrive.

[2]Collectors were particularly upset that **Like Dreamers Do** was an expensive three-record set that still left out five songs. Had it been done initially as a two-record package it probably would have met much less resistance.

[3]Like UDL's **Dawn Of The Silver Beatles**, Audio Fidelity insisted on using the "Silver Beatles" moniker even though the group had dropped that name well before the Decca audition session.

some extra profit from the tracks: two budget albums for the American market. Labeled **The Silver Beatles Vol. 1** and **The Silver Beatles Vol. 2**, these seven-track packages split the twelve selections from the **Complete** album, with two of the songs appearing on both to fill out the sets. At a list price of $3.98 for seven songs, these budget records practically guaranteed that even the most casual Beatles fan would be able to sample the once inaccessible audition tracks.

But was any of it legal?

Throughout the checkered release history of these tapes since 1977, EMI and Capitol remained strangely silent. No doubt at first this was because both the Deccagone and Circuit packagers had kept a relatively low profile. By 1982, though, both Backstage and Audio Fidelity were confident enough to assert that their releases were legitimate. Both explained that they had paid for the rights and were also paying any necessary royalties. Barring any legal action from EMI and Capitol, it seemed left up to the record industry itself to declare a winner in the "whose right is it, anyway?" contest.

Though *Billboard* magazine had dutifully reported the details of the Backstage release, it stopped short of confirming the company's scenario. In fact, *Billboard* pointed out that no one could find any reference to the Autumn Records mentioned in the Backstage story. More importantly, *Billboard* did not review the Backstage album or even list it in the magazine's weekly "new releases" index. The magazine did not come out and say the release was illegal; but it also did not say it was legal.

It fell to Britain's music industry equivalent to *Billboard, Music Week*, to make the call. In the September 18, 1982 issue of *Music Week*, the Audio Fidelity release was announced with an article headlined: "The Beatles Audition Tapes — Legal At Last." The next week, *Music Week* reviewed the Audio Fidelity album, even predicting a possible top fifty placement on the British charts. When a single of *Searchin'* was issued the following month, that too was treated as a normal, legitimate release.

We're inclined to go along with that judgment — with certain reservations — particularly in light of Audio Fidelity's long history of record releases and leasing agreements stretching back some thirty years. Nonetheless, a case could be made for the Backstage discs being just as legitimate . . . in fact, UDL, Circuit, and Deccagone could make some of the same claims too. After all, just because Audio Fidelity and Backstage paid *somebody* for the rights to the tapes does not mean they paid the legally correct somebody (if there is such a person). No doubt, UDL, Circuit, and Deccagone paid for their tapes as well.

Still, of all the companies to tackle the project, Audio Fidelity was the only one with established service to mainstream record stores. It was not set up solely for the release of this Beatles material. Those simple facts set it apart from all the other packagers.

Even after the Audio Fidelity releases, though, there remained unanswered questions. Pursuing these, Atlanta *Constitution* writer Bill King managed to shake loose some official comments on the whole matter in early 1983. An executive from EMI said his company made no claim to any audition tapes the Beatles recorded before signing their EMI contract. Decca's representative confirmed that Decca did not claim the right to issue the Beatles 1962 audition tracks.[1] And a spokesman for the Beatles' interests claimed that the Beatles themselves were the owners of any audition tapes and that *none* of the releases were legitimate.

Maybe so. Nonetheless, the repackagings by specialty labels continued even after the Audio Fidelity releases, usually under the Silver Beatles banner. Independent entrepreneurs issued the material on yet another picture disc (AR 30-003), as a Japanese audiophile monophonic pressing (Trio AW 25020), as a flexi-disc insert (of *Three Cool Cats* and *Till There Was You*) to *The Complete Beatles U.S. Record Price Guide* book, and in combination with some of the Star Club tracks (Historic Records HIS 11182 in Holland). The Japanese package had the words to all the songs on the back cover, along with an incorrect recording date (the fall of 1962), and an absurd production credit: "Album produced by Pete Best."

Late in 1983, there was even a package that did *not* use the term Silver Beatles! Instead, the British-based Breakaway Records called its collection **The Audition Tapes** (Breakaway BWY 72). Though a relatively new company, Breakaway was similar to Audio Fidelity in that it was not set up just to do the Beatles audition package. Instead, it also had releases by other artists, such as Little Richard and George Benson, as well as albums of the live Star Club material. *Beatles Book* writer Mark Lewisohn did the liner notes for each of the Beatles packages.

Meanwhile, Audio Fidelity came up with an odd combination package (**20 Greatest Hits**) featuring the audition sessions and some Tony Sheridan tracks. The company then ended the year by scheduling for release in early January 1984 a three-record boxed set combining its audition tracks album with its two-disc Star Club set (all to be issued as **The Beatles Historic Sessions** PHX 31).

----

[1]One point that did seem to bother Decca, though, was the identification of the material as "the Decca tapes" because this seemed to imply that the company somehow sanctioned the various packages. Nonetheless, that shorthand label (coined back in the 1960s) stuck and was used by most fans in talking about the tracks.

Ultimately, of course, the entire matter of ownership of the 1962 audition tapes and the right to release them may well have to be settled someday in court. (Where else?) Such action may at last identify the official, authorized custodian of these tracks. Only by then it will probably be too late to make much of a difference — the target audience for the material will already have acquired it (probably several times over). So even if every release since 1977 is eventually and officially declared illegal, it would not necessarily result in a windfall for the winner. The only certain effect would be that thousands of records sitting on home and record store shelves would instantly become textbook examples of "bootlegs worth buying."

Major Packagings of "The Decca Tapes"

APR 1977 (US) Deccagone PRO 1100
A: *Three Cool Cats*
B: *Hello Little Girl*

AUG 1977 (US) Deccagone PRO 1101
A: *The Sheik Of Araby*
B: *September In The Rain*

NOV 1977 (US) Deccagone PRO 1102
A: *Memphis, Tennessee*
B: *Love Of The Loved*

NOV 1977 (US) Deccagone PRO 1103
A: *Searchin'*
B: *Like Dreamers Do*

FEB 1978 (US) Deccagone PRO 1104
A: *Sure To Fall*
B: *Money*

OCT 1978 (US) Deccagone PRO 1105
A: *Crying, Waiting, Hoping*
B: *Till There Was You*

FEB 1979 (US) Deccagone PRO 1106
A: *To Know Him Is To Love Him*
B: *Besame Mucho*

DEC 1979 (US) Circuit Records LK 4438-1 (LP)
THE DECCA TAPES

side one	side two
Like Dreamers Do	*Hello Little Girl*
Money	*Three Cool Cats*
Till There Was You	*Crying, Waiting, Hoping*
The Sheik Of Araby	*Love Of The Loved*
To Know Him Is To Love Him	*September In The Rain*
Take Good Care Of My Baby	*Besame Mucho*
Memphis, Tennessee	*Searchin'*
Sure To Fall	

Picture Disc version of **The Decca Tapes** released November 1979 as
Circuit Records LK 4438, with same contents.

APR 1981 (US Mail Order) PAC Records UDL 2333 (LP)
DAWN OF THE SILVER BEATLES

side one	side two
Love Of The Loved	*Like Dreamers Do*
Money	*Crying, Waiting, Hoping*
Sure To Fall	*Searchin'*
Take Good Care Of My Baby	*Till There Was You*
Three Cool Cats	*Memphis, Tennessee*

MAY 1981 (US Mail Order) PAC Records UDL 2382 (LP)
LIGHTNING STRIKES TWICE
side one (Elvis Presley)   side two (The Beatles)
(good rockin' tonight)   *The Sheik Of Araby*
(baby, let's play house)   *To Know Him Is To Love Him*
(blue moon of kentucky)   *Hello Little Girl*
(i got a woman)   *September In The Rain*
(that's all right mama)   *Besame Mucho*

MAY 1982 (US) Backstage Records BSR 1111 (3 LPs)
LIKE DREAMERS DO
record one/record two (same contents; one a picture disc)
side one   side two
Like Dreamers Do   *Love Of The Loved*
Money   *Memphis, Tennessee*
Take Good Care Of My Baby   *Crying, Waiting, Hoping*
Three Cool Cats   *Till There Was You*
Sure To Fall   *Searchin'*
record three
side one   side two
(an interview with pete best)   *Beatles Press Conferences 1964 and 1965*
LIKE DREAMERS DO was released in October 1982 as a two-record set (Backstage Records
    BSR 2-201), dropping the picture disc containing the songs. In that package, the inter-
    views appeared on record one and the songs on record two.

SEP 1982 (UK) Audio Fidelity AFELP 1047 (LP)
OCT 1982 (US) Audio Rarities AR 2452 (LP)
THE COMPLETE SILVER BEATLES
side one   side two
Three Cool Cats   *To Know Him Is To Love Him*
Crying, Waiting, Hoping   *Take Good Care Of My Baby*
Besame Mucho   *Memphis, Tennessee*
Searchin'   *Sure To Fall*
The Sheik of Araby   *Till There Was You*
Money   *September In The Rain*

OCT 1982 (US) Phoenix PHX 352 (LP)
THE SILVER BEATLES VOLUME 1
side one   side two
Three Cool Cats   *Till There Was You*
Memphis, Tennessee   *Searchin'*
Besame Mucho   *Sure To Fall*
The Sheik Of Araby

OCT 1982 (US) Phoenix PHX 353 (LP)
THE SILVER BEATLES VOLUME 2
side one   side two
Searchin'   *To Know Him Is To Love Him*
Take Good Care Of My Baby   *Three Cool Cats*
Money   *September In The Rain*
                                            Crying, Waiting, Hoping

OCT 1982 (US) Backstage Records BSR-1112
Promotional giveaway from *Oui* magazine

side one
Like Dreamers Do
Love Of The Loved

side two
Like Dreamers Do
Love Of The Loved

OCT 1982 (UK) Audiofidelity AFS1

side one
Searchin'

side two
Money
Till There Was You

NOV 1982 (US) Audio-Rarities AR 30-003 (picture disc LP)
SILVER BEATLES

side one
Besame Mucho
Searchin'
Three Cool Cats
Crying, Waiting, Hoping
September In The Rain

side two
Sure To Fall
To Know Her Is To Love Her
Take Good Care Of My Baby
Memphis, Tennessee
The Sheik Of Araby

NOV 1982 (JAPAN) Trio Records AW 25020 (M) (LP)
SILVER BEATLES

side one
Three Cool Cats
Crying, Waiting, Hoping
September In The Rain
Besame Mucho
Searchin'
The Sheik Of Araby

side two
To Know Her Is To Love Her
Take Good Care Of My Baby
Memphis, Tennessee
Sure To Fall
Money
Till There Was You

FEB 1983 (HOLLAND) Historic Records HIS 11182 (LP)
SILVER BEATLES   (*denotes live Star Club tracks)

side one
Three Cool Cats
Crying, Waiting, Hoping
September In The Rain
Besame Mucho
Searchin'
*Be-Bop-A-Lula

side two
The Sheik Of Araby
To Know Him Is To Love Him
Take Good Care Of My Baby
Memphis, Tennessee
Sure To Fall
*Sweet Little Sixteen

Note: This album package listed several songs in the wrong order, failed to print one title (*Be-Bop-A-Lula*), and mistakenly listed another (*Hallelujah, I Love Her So*). When European fans pointed out the errors, the company promised to correct them on future pressings.

In the late fall of 1983, Historic Records issued a three-record boxed set, combining the **Silver Beatles** with two other discs previously issued in Holland by the company (**The Beatles Live**, Historic Records HIS 10982, a double album containing twenty-six of the live Star Club tracks). The labels on the **Silver Beatles** disc in the new boxed set carried a new track lineup, which was the same as the one used on the Trio Records disc issued in Japan in November 1982. Though that might have been the intended arrangement, the disc itself remained unchanged, rendering the contents information more confusing than ever. In addition, the songs listed on the back cover of the boxed set were in yet *another* running order. This new three-record set had no overall catalog number, no photos or drawings of the group, and only an obvious barebones title: **The Beatles**.

SEP 1983 (UK) Phoenix P20-623 (LP)
20 GREATEST HITS (*denotes Tony Sheridan tracks)

side one
Cry For A Shadow
(let's dance)
If You Love Me, Baby
(what'd i say)
Sweet Georgia Brown
(ruby baby)
(ya ya)
Why
To Know Him Is To Love Him

side two
Three Cool Cats
Crying, Waiting, Hoping
Besame Mucho
Searchin'
The Sheik Of Araby
Money
Take Good Care Of My Baby
Memphis, Tennessee
Sure To Fall
Till There Was You
September In The Rain

DEC 1983 (UK) Breakaway BWY 72 (LP)
THE AUDITION TAPES

side one
Three Cool Cats
Crying, Waiting, Hoping
Besame Mucho
Searchin'
The Sheik Of Araby
Money

side two
To Know Her Is To Love Her
Take Good Care Of My Baby
Memphis, Tennessee
Sure To Fall
Till There Was You
September In The Rain

362

The BBC
Broadcasts

In 1980, *The Beatles Book* reprint series published Mark Lewisohn's extensive documentation of all the appearances by the Beatles on British radio. It was the most important piece of Beatles-related research conducted over the past five years.[1]

Prior to Lewisohn's article, most Beatles fans and researchers (ourselves included) had only a limited knowledge of the group's whirlwind schedule of appearances on the BBC. Lewisohn not only documented every song performed on the air, he also listed songs that were recorded and never aired. In doing so he essentially identified the source of virtually every alleged "studio outtake" from 1962 to 1965: the BBC.

Because the BBC usually taped the songs for their pop music programs at a separate session from the actual broadcast date (sometimes days earlier, sometimes months), the tracks resembled tight studio recordings much more than impromptu "live" sessions. Back then, any alert British fan could have an instant "studio outtake" just by rolling a tape recorder during the actual broadcasts. This was apparently the source of some songs that later appeared in the early 1970s on bootleg albums, many of which were mistakenly identified as containing studio tracks. The best collection at that time included fourteen songs (though of poor sound quality) and was alternately titled **As Sweet As You Are** or **Yellow Matter Custard.**

These over-the-air recordings that were captured back then, however, were only the tip of a treasure trove. As a matter of course the BBC kept on file for years the original master recordings for many of these sessions. Others were unofficially preserved by various sources with access to tapes or copies of them.[2] Occasionally a few

---

[1] "A Complete Catalogue of the Beatles' U.K. Radio Broadcasts" (Parts one and two) by Mark Lewisohn appeared in issues 47 and 48 of *The Beatles Book* (reprint series). These are available for purchase as back issues. See page 455 for details.

[2] For example, if a program aired on the BBC's foreign service, copies would be shipped to other countries for broadcast.

tracks were even aired again, usually in some special holiday broadcast or retrospective.

In 1982, the BBC decided to use the tracks as the basis for a twentieth anniversary celebration of the first radio appearance by the Beatles (March 8, 1962). The result was a two-hour radio special dubbed "The Beatles at the Beeb," which featured concise narration by Andy Peebles, some interviews with BBC personnel at the time, and a generous selection of music drawn from the more than ninety titles performed by the group on the BBC between 1962 and 1965.[1]

"The Beatles at the Beeb" aired in England on Sunday, March 7, 1982, and as an expanded three-hour radio special syndicated in the United States the last weekend in May. Though a few "over-the-air" dubs were included (because some tracks had been discarded or lost over the years), the program generally featured top-of-the-line recordings. Most of this material had not been heard in England since the initial broadcasts. It had never played on American radio, so American fans were given a special treat: forty-eight[2] new recordings by the Beatles, including twenty-six songs that had never been released through EMI. Presumably, thousands of tape recorders captured the entire program for personal replay.

One reason for issuing a virtual worldwide blank check to dub some of the best material from the BBC archives was the fact that, at the time, there was considerable doubt that the tracks would ever be put on record. While the BBC had free use of the songs "in house" (on the air), the company apparently had not been granted the right to release them on disc. (The BBC had its own record label on which it usually issued spoken word and comedy broadcasts — most notably *The Goon Show* — so such an exclusion at the time was understandable.)

There was another reason for the relative unconcern over bootlegging: it was already too late. Some of this high-quality material had already appeared in bootleg form nearly two years before the radio special.

If bootleg packaging notes are to be believed (usually they are not), the same people responsible for the top-notch **Decca Tapes** album decided to use BBC material for the 1980 follow-up releases. This took two forms: a four-song EP and an eighteen-track album.

The EP (**Four By The Beatles**) featured four songs plus some entertaining transition chatter between Rodney Burke and the

---

[1] The BBC also issued a tie-in book, *The Beatles At The Beeb*, by Kevin Howlett, writer and co-producer of the special.

[2] Total includes the opening theme songs to the *From Us To You* and *Pop Go The Beatles* programs.

Beatles, all drawn from a July 1963 broadcast of *Pop Go The Beatles*. The album (**The Beatles Broadcasts**) pulled selections from a number of different radio spots, wisely dispensing with the talk and featuring an uninterrupted run-through of both old and new music. Nine tracks were new studio versions of songs otherwise recorded and released by EMI. Nine[1] other tracks, however, were never officially released. (Of these, only two were titles already used on Circuit's **Decca Tapes** album, though even these were obviously different recordings.)

Both the EP and the album were superbly packaged. In particular, the album featured full color photos against a tasteful dark green backdrop, including an embossed front cover shot. If ever an album looked legitimate, this was it. Apparently the folks behind the release shared this view because the label copy was the height of audacity. It was designed to be easily mistaken for an official authorized BBC product. Around the "BBC Transcription Service" logo, the text read: "Copyright Record Made In England By The British Broadcasting Corporation. Reproduction Restricted to Broadcasting Stations Authorised By The BBC Only."

Even though **The Beatles Broadcasts** had the usual limited pressing of a bootleg project, copies still turned up throughout the United States in both specialty shops and mainstream record stores. Eventually, the album even popped up on NBC's *Today* show as part of a 1982 story on the BBC's "Beatles at the Beeb" radio special. By then, of course, the tracks on **Broadcasts** has been snatched and repackaged onto other bootleg albums.

In 1981, ten more BBC tracks plus seven tracks from a Swedish broadcast appearance formed a new album: **Johnny And The Moondogs: Silver Days/Air Time**. Though the songs were still first-rate recordings, the album packaging marked a dramatic retreat from the brazen attempts at pseudo-authenticity on both **Broadcasts** and **The Decca Tapes**. Though there was an early 1960s photo of the group (with Pete Best), the word "Beatles" was nowhere to be seen, either on the album cover or the record label. In fact, it looked as if the **Johnny And The Moondogs: Silver Days** jacket had been intended for some other project, then quickly drafted for service as the vehicle for more radio material. The actual contents of the album appeared on two stickers slapped onto the shrink wrap. The front read: "Air Time: Featuring 17 Unreleased Classic Tracks From Master Tapes." The back label listed the song titles and recording dates. Most of the

----

[1]Total includes the opening theme song to the *Pop Go The Beatles* program. See pages 375--380 for detailed cross-referencing of songs done for the BBC but never recorded and released on any studio disc.

songs were merely broadcast versions of officially released tracks, but four were otherwise unreleased songs.

The 1982 **Beautiful Dreamer** album marked a guarded return to more elaborate packaging. The front cover featured a full color photo of the group, while the back cover included tongue-in-cheek liner notes focusing on British history as much as on the Beatles. (Perhaps as a deliberate dig at the sometimes stuffy reputation of the BBC, especially since the notes were credited to Sir Richard Dimplebey, a none-too-subtle twist on a real-life BBC newsman, Richard Dimbleby, who died in 1965.)

Unfortunately, the tracks on **Beautiful Dreamer** were nowhere near the sound quality of **Broadcasts** or **Air Time**, leading to the suspicion that the package was rushed out to snare unwary buyers before "The Beatles at the Beeb" aired in the United States. Even so, for completists with a tolerant ear (or a home equalizer unit to clean up the sound), **Beautiful Dreamer** was an essential purchase because it included seven otherwise unavailable songs that did *not* appear in the BBC special. (Eight other non-EMI tracks, plus three familiar Beatles tunes, rounded out the package.)

Since the time "Beatles at the Beeb" aired in the United States, tracks from that program have joined the catalog of bootlegged material packaged time and time again, usually as filler for one or two new songs touted on a new set. However, home copies of the radio special rendered purchase of such records unnecessary.

It is unlikely that *all* of the nearly 300 BBC radio tracks will ever be aired or officially issued on disc. For one thing, some are lost forever. Beyond that, some songs in the repertoire (such as *She Loves You*) were performed a dozen times or more. Surely even the most fanatic fan would not care about every take!

Yet, through the bootleg albums (dating back to **As Sweet As You Are**) and the BBC radio special, millions have shared an important slice of Beatles history. These radio sessions offered a high-quality sampler of the type of music the Beatles performed in their heyday on stage in the small club scene in Germany and in England. Even a plundering of the EMI vaults may never uncover such a concentration of the group at its fresh 1962–1963 performing best.

A Guide to

The Beatles
At The BBC

The Beatles cut nearly 300 tracks for the BBC from 1962 to 1965. These indexes provide a guide to:

● performances included on particular programs;

● all the versions of the 94 different songs done;

● background on songs not written by the Beatles;

● the major bootleg packagings of the BBC tracks; and

● the titles included on "The Beatles at the Beeb."

The song and program indexes have also been designed to be used as indexes to Mark Lewisohn's two-part *Beatles Book* article, "A Complete Catalogue of the Beatles' U.K. Radio Broadcasts." That article covered the BBC material broadcast-by-broadcast in chronological order, including such information as the actual transmission times of the programs, lead vocalists on various songs, and anecdotes about the shows and sessions. We have keyed the numbers in our indexes to coincide with the numbers assigned to each broadcast described in the article.

Note: The first two programs had Pete Best on drums.

Program Key for The Beatles on British Radio:
Alphabetical by Show

The Beat Show 25

The Beatles (Invite You To Take A Ticket To Ride) 52

Easy Beat 12, 21, 27, 40

From Us To You 43, 45, 47, 49

Here We Go 1, 2, 3, 5, 9

The Ken Dodd Show 41

On The Scene 11

Parade Of The Pops 8

Pop Go The Beatles 18, 19, 20, 23, 26, 28, 29, 30, 31, 32, 34, 35, 36, 37, 38

Saturday Club 6, 10, 16, 24, 33, 39, 42, 44, 46, 51

Side By Side 14, 15, 22

Steppin' Out 17

Swinging Sound '63 13

The Talent Spot 4, 7

Teenager's Turn 1

Ticket To Ride 52

Top Gear 48, 50

Program Key for The Beatles on British Radio: Chronological by Show

1) *Teenager's Turn (Here We Go)* aired March 8, 1962
2) *Here We Go* aired June 15, 1962
3) *Here We Go* aired October 26, 1962
4) *The Talent Spot* aired December 4, 1962
5) *Here We Go* aired January 25, 1963
6) *Saturday Club* aired January 26, 1963
7) *The Talent Spot* aired January 29, 1963
8) *Parade Of The Pops* aired February 20, 1963
9) *Here We Go* aired March 12, 1963
10) *Saturday Club* aired March 16, 1963
11) *On The Scene* aired March 28, 1963
12) *Easy Beat* aired April 7, 1963
13) *Swinging Sound '63* aired April 18, 1963
14) *Side By Side* aired April 22, 1963
15) *Side By Side* aired May 13, 1963
16) *Saturday Club* aired May 25, 1963
17) *Steppin' Out* aired June 3, 1963
18) *Pop Go The Beatles* aired June 4, 1963
19) *Pop Go The Beatles* aired June 11, 1963
20) *Pop Go The Beatles* aired June 18, 1963
21) *Easy Beat* aired June 23, 1963
22) *Side By Side* aired June 24, 1963
23) *Pop Go The Beatles* aired June 25, 1963
24) *Saturday Club* aired June 29, 1963
25) *The Beat Show* aired July 4, 1963
26) *Pop Go The Beatles* aired July 16, 1963
27) *Easy Beat* aired July 21, 1963
28) *Pop Go The Beatles* aired July 23, 1963
29) *Pop Go The Beatles* aired July 30, 1963
30) *Pop Go The Beatles* aired August 6, 1963
31) *Pop Go The Beatles* aired August 13, 1963
32) *Pop Go The Beatles* aired August 20, 1963
33) *Saturday Club* aired August 24, 1963
34) *Pop Go The Beatles* aired August 27, 1963
35) *Pop Go The Beatles* aired September 3, 1963
36) *Pop Go The Beatles* aired September 10, 1963
37) *Pop Go The Beatles* aired September 17, 1963
38) *Pop Go The Beatles* aired September 24, 1963
39) *Saturday Club (Fifth Birthday Edition)* aired October 5, 1963
40) *Easy Beat* aired October 20, 1963
41) *The Ken Dodd Show* aired November 3, 1963
42) *Saturday Club* aired December 21, 1963
43) *From Us To You* aired December 26, 1963
44) *Saturday Club* aired February 15, 1964
45) *From Us To You* aired March 30, 1964
46) *Saturday Club* aired April 4, 1964
47) *From Us To You* aired May 18, 1964
48) *Top Gear* aired July 16, 1964
49) *From Us To You* aired August 3, 1964
50) *Top Gear* aired November 26, 1964
51) *Saturday Club* aired December 26, 1964
52) *The Beatles (Invite You To Take A Ticket To Ride)* aired June 7, 1965

Program Key for The Beatles on British Radio:
Chronological by Show

1) *Teenager's Turn (Here We Go)*
   Aired March 8, 1962
   *Dream Baby (How Long Must
   I Dream?)*
   Memphis, Tennessee
   Please Mr. Postman

2) *Here We Go*
   Aired June 15, 1962
   Ask Me Why
   Besame Mucho
   A Picture Of You

3) *Here We Go*
   Aired October 26, 1962
   Love Me Do
   A Taste Of Honey
   P.S. I Love You

4) *The Talent Spot*
   Aired December 4, 1962
   Love Me Do
   P.S. I Love You
   Twist And Shout

5) *Here We Go*
   Aired January 25, 1963
   Chains
   Please Please Me
   Ask Me Why

6) *Saturday Club*
   Aired January 26, 1963
   Some Other Guy
   Love Me Do
   Please Please Me
   Keep Your Hands Off My Baby
   Beautiful Dreamer

7) *The Talent Spot*
   Aired January 29, 1963
   Please Please Me
   Ask Me Why
   Some Other Guy

8) *Parade Of The Pops*
   Aired February 20, 1963
   Love Me Do
   Please Please Me

9) *Here We Go*
   Aired March 12, 1963
   Misery
   Do You Want To Know A Secret
   Please Please Me

10) *Saturday Club*
    Aired March 16, 1963
    I Saw Her Standing There
    Misery
    Too Much Monkey Business
    I'm Talking About You
    Please Please Me
    The Hippy Hippy Shake

11) *On The Scene*
    Aired March 28, 1963
    Misery
    Do You Want To Know A Secret
    Please Please Me

12) *Easy Beat*
    Aired April 7, 1963
    Please Please Me
    Misery
    From Me To You

13) *Swinging Sound '63*
    Aired April 18, 1963
    Twist And Shout
    From Me To You

14) *Side By Side*
    Aired April 22, 1963
    Side By Side
    I Saw Her Standing There
    Do You Want To Know A Secret
    Baby It's You
    Please Please Me
    From Me To You
    Misery

15) *Side By Side*
    Aired May 13, 1963
    Side By Side
    From Me To You
    Long Tall Sally
    A Taste Of Honey
    Chains
    Thank You Girl
    Boys

16) *Saturday Club*
    Aired May 25, 1963
    I Saw Her Standing There
    Do You Want To Know A Secret
    Boys
    Long Tall Sally
    From Me To You
    Money (That's What I Want)

17) *Steppin' Out*
    Aired June 3, 1963
      Please Please Me
      I Saw Her Standing There
      Roll Over Beethoven
      Thank You Girl
      From Me To You

18) *Pop Go The Beatles*
    Aired June 4, 1963
      Pop Go The Beatles
      From Me To You
      Everybody's Trying To Be My Baby
      Do You Want To Know A Secret
      You Really Got A Hold On Me
      Misery
      The Hippy Hippy Shake
      Pop Go The Beatles

19) *Pop Go The Beatles*
    Aired June 11, 1963
      Pop Go The Beatles
      Too Much Monkey Business
      I Got To Find My Baby
      Youngblood
      Baby It's You
      Till There Was You
      Love Me Do
      Pop Go The Beatles

20) *Pop Go The Beatles*
    Aired June 18, 1963
      Pop Go The Beatles
      A Shot Of Rhythm And Blues
      Memphis, Tennessee
      A Taste Of Honey
      Sure To Fall (In Love With You)
      Money (That's What I Want)
      From Me To You
      Pop Go The Beatles

21) *Easy Beat*
    Aired June 23, 1963
      Some Other Guy
      A Taste Of Honey
      Thank You Girl
      From Me To You

22) *Side By Side*
    Aired June 24, 1963
      Side By Side
      Too Much Monkey Business
      Love Me Do
      Boys
      I'll Be On My Way
      From Me To You

23) *Pop Go The Beatles*
    Aired June 25, 1963
      Pop Go The Beatles
      Anna (Go To Him)
      I Saw Her Standing There
      Boys
      Chains
      P.S. I Love You
      Twist And Shout
      Pop Go The Beatles

24) *Saturday Club*
    Aired June 29, 1963
      I Got To Find My Baby
      Memphis, Tennessee
      Money (That's What I Want)
      Till There Was You
      From Me To You
      Roll Over Beethoven

25) *The Beat Show*
    Aired July 4, 1963
      From Me To You
      A Taste Of Honey
      Twist And Shout

26) *Pop Go The Beatles*
    Aired July 16, 1963
      Pop Go The Beatles
      That's All Right (Mama)
      There's A Place
      Carol
      Soldier Of Love (Lay Down Your Arms)
      Lend Me Your Comb
      Clarabella
      Pop Go The Beatles

27) *Easy Beat*
    Aired July 21, 1963
      I Saw Her Standing There
      A Shot Of Rhythm And Blues
      There's A Place
      Twist And Shout

28) *Pop Go The Beatles*
    Aired July 23, 1963
      Pop Go The Beatles
      Sweet Little Sixteen
      A Taste Of Honey
      Nothin' Shakin' (But The Leaves On The Trees)
      Love Me Do
      Lonesome Tears In My Eyes
      So How Come (No One Loves Me)
      Pop Go The Beatles

29) *Pop Go The Beatles*
   Aired July 30, 1963
   Pop Go The Beatles
   Memphis, Tennessee
   Do You Want To Know A Secret
   Till There Was You
   Matchbox
   Please Mr. Postman
   The Hippy Hippy Shake
   Pop Go The Beatles

30) *Pop Go The Beatles*
   Aired August 6, 1963
   Pop Go The Beatles
   I'm Gonna Sit Right Down And Cry
   (Over You)
   Crying, Waiting, Hoping
   Kansas City/Hey Hey Hey Hey
   To Know Her Is To Love Her
   The Honeymoon Song
   Twist And Shout
   Pop Go The Beatles

31) *Pop Go The Beatles*
   Aired August 13, 1963
   Pop Go The Beatles
   Long Tall Sally
   Please Please Me
   She Loves You
   You Really Got A Hold On Me
   I'll Get You
   I Got A Woman
   Pop Go The Beatles

32) *Pop Go The Beatles*
   Aired August 20, 1963
   Pop Go The Beatles
   She Loves You
   Words Of Love
   Glad All Over
   I Just Don't Understand
   (There's A) Devil In Her Heart
   Slow Down
   Pop Go The Beatles

33) *Saturday Club*
   Aired August 24, 1963
   Long Tall Sally
   She Loves You
   Glad All Over
   Twist And Shout
   You Really Got A Hold On Me
   I'll Get You

34) *Pop Go The Beatles*
   Aired August 27, 1963
   Pop Go The Beatles
   Ooh! My Soul
   Don't Ever Change
   Twist And Shout
   She Loves You
   Anna (Go To Him)
   A Shot Of Rhythm And Blues
   Pop Go The Beatles

35) *Pop Go The Beatles*
   Aired September 3, 1963
   Pop Go The Beatles
   From Me To You
   I'll Get You
   Money (That's What I Want)
   There's A Place
   Honey Don't
   Roll Over Beethoven
   Pop Go The Beatles

36) *Pop Go The Beatles*
   Aired September 10, 1963
   Pop Go The Beatles
   Too Much Monkey Business
   Till There Was You
   Love Me Do
   She Loves You
   I'll Get You
   The Hippy Hippy Shake
   Pop Go The Beatles

37) *Pop Go The Beatles*
   Aired September 17, 1963
   Pop Go The Beatles
   Chains
   You Really Got A Hold On Me
   Misery
   Lucille
   From Me To You
   Boys
   Pop Go The Beatles

38) *Pop Go The Beatles*
   Aired September 24, 1963
   Pop Go The Beatles
   She Loves You
   Ask Me Why
   (There's A) Devil In Her Heart
   I Saw Her Standing There
   Sure To Fall (In Love With You)
   Twist And Shout
   Pop Go The Beatles

39) *Saturday Club (Fifth Birthday Edition)*
Aired October 5, 1963
  I Saw Her Standing There
  Memphis, Tennessee
  Happy Birthday
  I'll Get You
  She Loves You
  Lucille

40) *Easy Beat*
Aired October 20, 1963
  I Saw Her Standing There
  Love Me Do
  Please Please Me
  From Me To You
  She Loves You

41) *The Ken Dodd Show*
Aired November 3, 1963
  She Loves You

42) *Saturday Club*
Aired December 21, 1963
  All My Loving
  This Boy
  I Want To Hold Your Hand
  Till There Was You
  Roll Over Beethoven
  She Loves You

43) *From Us To You*
Aired December 26, 1963
  From Us To You
  She Loves You
  All My Loving
  Roll Over Beethoven
  Till There Was You
  Boys
  Money (That's What I Want)
  I Saw Her Standing There
  I Want To Hold Your Hand
  From Us To You

44) *Saturday Club*
Aired February 15, 1964
  All My Loving
  Money (That's What I Want)
  The Hippy Hippy Shake
  I Want To Hold Your Hand
  Roll Over Beethoven
  Johnny B. Goode
  I Wanna Be Your Man

45) *From Us To You*
Aired March 30, 1964
  From Us To You
  You Can't Do That
  Roll Over Beethoven
  Till There Was You
  I Wanna Be Your Man
  Please Mr. Postman
  All My Loving
  This Boy
  Can't Buy Me Love
  From Us To You

46) *Saturday Club*
Aired April 4, 1964
  Everybody's Trying To Be My Baby
  I Call Your Name
  I Got A Woman
  You Can't Do That
  Can't Buy Me Love
  Sure To Fall (In Love With You)
  Long Tall Sally

47) *From Us To You*
Aired May 18, 1964
  From Us To You
  I Saw Her Standing There
  Kansas City/Hey Hey Hey Hey
  I Forget To Remember To Forget
  You Can't Do That
  Sure To Fall (In Love With You)
  Can't Buy Me Love
  Matchbox
  Honey Don't
  From Us To You

48) *Top Gear*
Aired July 16, 1964
  Long Tall Sally
  Things We Said Today
  A Hard Day's Night
  And I Love Her
  I Should Have Known Better
  If I Fell
  You Can't Do That

49) *From Us To You*
Aired August 3, 1964
  From Us To You
  Long Tall Sally
  If I Fell
  I'm Happy Just To Dance With You
  Things We Said Today
  I Should Have Known Better
  Boys
  A Hard Day's Night
  From Us To You

373

50) *Top Gear*
 Aired November 26, 1964
   I'm A Loser
   Honey Don't
   She's A Woman
   Everybody's Trying To Be My
     Baby
   I'll Follow The Sun
   I Feel Fine

51) *Saturday Club*
 Aired December 26, 1964
   Rock And Roll Music
   I'm A Loser
   Everybody's Trying To Be My
     Baby
   I Feel Fine
   Kansas City/Hey Hey Hey Hey
   She's A Woman

52) *The Beatles (Invite You To Take A*
   Ticket To Ride)
 Aired June 7, 1965
   Ticket To Ride
   Everybody's Trying To Be My
     Baby
   I'm A Loser
   The Night Before
   Honey Don't
   Dizzy Miss Lizzy
   She's A Woman
   Ticket To Ride

Program Key for The Beatles on British Radio:
Alphabetical Song List
(* indicates a live performance; NA indicates a track recorded but Not Aired)

Title	Recording Date	Aired
All My Loving #1	December 17, 1963	42
All My Loving #2	December 18, 1963	43
All My Loving #3	January 7, 1964	44
All My Loving #4	February 28, 1964	45
And I Love Her	July 14, 1964	48
Anna (Go To Him) #1	June 17, 1963	23
Anna (Go To Him) #2	August 1, 1963	34
Ask Me Why #1	June 11, 1962	2
Ask My Why #2	January 16, 1963	5
Ask Me Why #3	January 22, 1963	7
Ask Me Why #4	July 2, 1963	NA(26)
Ask Me Why #5	September 3, 1963	38
Baby It's You #1	April 1, 1963	14
Baby It's You #2	June 1, 1963	19
Baby It's You #3	August 1, 1963	NA(35)
Besame Mucho	June 11, 1962	2
Beautiful Dreamer	January 22, 1963	6
Boys #1	April 1, 1963	15
Boys #2	April 4, 1963	22
Boys #3	May 21, 1963	16
Boys #4	June 17, 1963	23
Boys #5	September 3, 1963	37
Boys #6	December 18, 1963	43
Boys #7	July 17, 1964	49
Can't Buy Me Love #1	February 28, 1964	45
Can't Buy Me Love #2	March 31, 1964	46
Can't Buy Me Love #3	May 1, 1964	47
Carol	July 2, 1963	26
Chains #1	January 16, 1963	5
Chains #2	April 1, 1963	15
Chains #3	June 17, 1963	23
Chains #4	September 3, 1963	37
Clarabella	July 2, 1963	26
Crying, Waiting, Hoping	July 16, 1963	30
(There's A) Devil In Her Heart #1	July 16, 1963	32
(There's A) Devil In Her Heart #2	September 3, 1963	38
Dizzy Miss Lizzy	May 26, 1965	52
Do You Want To Know A Secret #1	March 6, 1963	9
Do You Want To Know A Secret #2	March 21, 1963	11
Do You Want To Know A Secret #3	April 1, 1963	14
Do You Want To Know A Secret #4	May 21, 1963	16
Do You Want To Know A Secret #5	May 24, 1963	18
Do You Want To Know A Secret #6	July 10, 1963	29
Don't Ever Change	August 1, 1963	34
Dream Baby (How Long Must I Dream?)	March 7, 1962	1
Everybody's Trying To Be My Baby #1	May 24, 1963	18
Everybody's Trying To Be My Baby #2	March 31, 1964	46
Everybody's Trying To Be My Baby #3	November 17, 1964	50
Everybody's Trying To Be My Baby #4	November 25, 1964	51
Everybody's Trying To Be My Baby #5	May 26, 1965	52
From Me To You #1	April 1, 1963	14
From Me To You #2	April 1, 1963	15

Title	Recording Date	Aired
From Me To You #3	April 3, 1963	12
From Me To You #4	April 4, 1963	22
From Me To You #5	*April 18, 1963	13
From Me To You #6	May 21, 1963	16
From Me To You #7	May 21, 1963	17
From Me To You #8	May 24, 1963	18
From Me To You #9	June 1, 1963	20
From Me To You #10	June 19, 1963	21
From Me To You #11	June 24, 1963	24
From Me To You #12	July 3, 1963	25
From Me To You #13	August 1, 1963	35
From Me To You #14	September 3, 1963	37
From Me To You #15	October 16, 1963	40
From Us To You	December 18, 1963	43,45,47,49
Glad All Over #1	July 16, 1963	32
Glad All Over #2	July 30, 1963	33
Happy Birthday	September 7, 1963	39
A Hard Day's Night #1	July 14, 1964	48
A Hard Day's Night #2	July 17, 1964	49
The Hippy Hippy Shake #1	*March 16, 1963	10
The Hippy Hippy Shake #2	May 24, 1963	18
The Hippy Hippy Shake #3	July 10, 1963	29
The Hippy Hippy Shake #4	September 3, 1963	36
The Hippy Hippy Shake #5	January 7, 1964	44
Honey Don't #1	August 1, 1963	35
Honey Don't #2	May 1, 1964	47
Honey Don't #3	November 17, 1964	50
Honey Don't #4	May 26, 1965	52
The Honeymoon Song	July 16, 1963	30
I Call Your Name	March 31, 1964	46
I Feel Fine #1	November 17, 1964	50
I Feel Fine #2	November 25, 1964	51
I Forgot To Remember To Forget	May 1, 1964	47
I Got A Woman #1	July 16, 1963	31
I Got A Woman #2	March 31, 1964	46
I Got To Find My Baby #1	June 1, 1963	19
I Got To Find My Baby #2	June 24, 1963	24
I Just Don't Understand	July 16, 1963	32
I Saw Her Standing There #1	March 6, 1963	NA(9)
I Saw Her Standing There #2	*March 16, 1963	10
I Saw Her Standing There #3	April 1, 1963	14
I Saw Her Standing There #4	May 21, 1963	16
I Saw Her Standing There #5	May 21, 1963	17
I Saw Her Standing There #6	June 17, 1963	23
I Saw Her Standing There #7	July 17, 1963	27
I Saw Her Standing There #8	September 3, 1963	38
I Saw Her Standing There #9	September 7, 1963	39
I Saw Her Standing There #10	October 16, 1963	40
I Saw Her Standing There #11	December 18, 1963	43
I Saw Her Standing There #12	May 1, 1964	47
I Should Have Known Better #1	July 14, 1964	48
I Should Have Known Better #2	July 17, 1964	49
I Wanna Be Your Man #1	January 7, 1964	44
I Wanna Be Your Man #2	February 28, 1964	45
I Want To Hold Your Hand #1	December 17, 1963	42
I Want To Hold Your Hand #2	December 18, 1963	43
I Want To Hold Your Hand #3	January 7, 1964	44

Title	Recording Date	Aired
If I Fell #1	July 14, 1964	48
If I Fell #2	July 17, 1964	49
I'll Be On My Way	April 4, 1963	22
I'll Follow The Sun	November 17, 1964	50
I'll Get You #1	July 16, 1963	31
I'll Get You #2	July 30, 1963	33
I'll Get You #3	August 1, 1963	35
I'll Get You #4	September 3, 1963	36
I'll Get You #5	September 7, 1963	39
I'm A Loser #1	November 17, 1964	50
I'm A Loser #2	November 25, 1964	51
I'm A Loser #3	May 26, 1965	52
I'm Gonna Sit Right Down And Cry (Over You)	July 16, 1963	30
I'm Happy Just To Dance With You	July 17, 1964	49
I'm Talking About You	*March 16, 1963	10
Johnny B. Goode	January 7, 1964	44
Medley:		
Kansas City/Hey Hey Hey Hey #1	July 16, 1963	30
Kansas City/Hey Hey Hey Hey #2	May 1, 1964	47
Kansas City/Hey Hey Hey Hey #3	November 25, 1964	51
Keep Your Hands Off My Baby	January 22, 1963	6
Lend Me Your Comb	July 2, 1963	26
Lonesome Tears In My Eyes	July 10, 1963	28
Long Tall Sally #1	April 1, 1963	15
Long Tall Sally #2	May 21, 1963	16
Long Tall Sally #3	July 16, 1963	31
Long Tall Sally #4	July 30, 1963	33
Long Tall Sally #5	March 31, 1964	46
Long Tall Sally #6	July 14, 1964	48
Long Tall Sally #7	July 17, 1964	49
Love Me Do #1	October 25, 1962	3
Love Me Do #2	November 27, 1962	4
Love Me Do #3	January 22, 1963	6
Love Me Do #4	*February 20, 1963	8
Love Me Do #5	April 4, 1963	22
Love Me Do #6	June 1, 1963	19
Love Me Do #7	July 10, 1963	28
Love Me Do #8	September 3, 1963	36
Love Me Do #9	October 16, 1963	40
Lucille #1	August 1, 1963	NA(35)
Lucille #2	September 3, 1963	37
Lucille #3	September 7, 1963	39
Matchbox #1	July 10, 1963	29
Matchbox #2	May 1, 1964	47
Memphis, Tennessee #1	March 7, 1962	1
Memphis, Tennessee #2	June 1, 1963	20
Memphis, Tennessee #3	June 24, 1963	24
Memphis, Tennessee #4	July 10, 1963	29
Memphis, Tennessee #5	September 7, 1963	39
Misery #1	March 6, 1963	9
Misery #2	*March 16, 1963	10
Misery #3	March 21, 1963	11
Misery #4	April 1, 1963	14
Misery #5	April 3, 1963	12
Misery #6	May 24, 1963	18
Misery #7	September 3, 1963	37

Title	Recording Date	Aired
Money (That's What I Want) #1	May 21, 1963	16
Money (That's What I Want) #2	June 1, 1963	20
Money (That's What I Want) #3	June 24, 1963	24
Money (That's What I Want) #4	August 1, 1963	35
Money (That's What I Want) #5	December 18, 1963	43
Money (That's What I Want) #6	January 7, 1964	44
The Night Before	May 26, 1965	52
Nothin' Shakin' (But The Leaves On The Trees)	July 10, 1963	28
Ooh! My Soul	August 1, 1963	34
A Picture Of You	June 11, 1962	2
Please Mr. Postman #1	March 7, 1962	1
Please Mr. Postman #2	July 10, 1963	29
Please Mr. Postman #3	February 28, 1964	45
Please Please Me #1	January 16, 1963	5
Please Please Me #2	January 22, 1963	6
Please Please Me #3	January 22, 1963	7
Please Please Me #4	*February 20, 1963	8
Please Please Me #5	March 6, 1963	9
Please Please Me #6	*March 16, 1963	10
Please Please Me #7	March 21, 1963	11
Please Please Me #8	April 1, 1963	14
Please Please Me #9	April 3, 1963	12
Please Please Me #10	May 21, 1963	17
Please Please Me #11	July 16, 1963	31
Please Please Me #12	October 16, 1963	40
Pop Go The Beatles	May 24, 1963	18,19,20,23, 26,28,29,30, 31,32,34,35, 36,37,38
P.S. I Love You #1	October 25, 1962	3
P.S. I Love You #2	November 27, 1962	4
P.S. I Love You #3	June 17, 1963	23
Rock And Roll Music	November 25, 1964	51
Roll Over Beethoven #1	May 21, 1963	17
Roll Over Beethoven #2	June 24, 1963	24
Roll Over Beethoven #3	August 1, 1963	35
Roll Over Beethoven #4	December 17, 1963	42
Roll Over Beethoven #5	December 18, 1963	43
Roll Over Beethoven #6	January 7, 1964	44
Roll Over Beethoven #7	February 28, 1964	45
She Loves You #1	July 16, 1963	31
She Loves You #2	July 16, 1963	32
She Loves You #3	July 30, 1963	33
She Loves You #4	August 1, 1963	34
She Loves You #5	August 1, 1963	NA(35)
She Loves You #6	September 3, 1963	36
She Loves You #7	September 3, 1963	38
She Loves You #8	September 7, 1963	39
She Loves You #9	October 9, 1963	41
She Loves You #10	October 16, 1963	40
She Loves You #11	December 17, 1963	42
She Loves You #12	December 18, 1963	43
She's A Woman #1	November 17, 1964	50
She's A Woman #2	November 25, 1964	51
She's A Woman #3	May 26, 1965	52
Sheila	October 25, 1962	NA(3)

Title	Recording Date	Aired
A Shot Of Rhythm And Blues #1	June 1, 1963	20
A Shot Of Rhythm And Blues #2	July 17, 1963	27
A Shot Of Rhythm And Blues #3	August 1, 1963	34
Side By Side #1	April 1, 1963	14,15
Side By Side #2	April 4, 1963	22
Slow Down	July 16, 1963	32
So How Come (No One Loves Me)	July 10, 1963	28
Soldier Of Love (Lay Down Your Arms)	July 2, 1963	26
Some Other Guy #1	January 22, 1963	6
Some Other Guy #2	January 22, 1963	7
Some Other Guy #3	June 19, 1963	21
Sure To Fall (In Love With You) #1	June 1, 1963	20
Sure To Fall (In Love With You) #2	September 3, 1963	38
Sure To Fall (In Love With You) #3	March 31, 1964	46
Sure To Fall (In Love With You) #4	May 1, 1964	47
Sweet Little Sixteen #1	July 2, 1963	NA(26)
Sweet Little Sixteen #2	July 10, 1963	28
A Taste Of Honey #1	October 25, 1962	3
A Taste Of Honey #2	April 1, 1963	15
A Taste Of Honey #3	June 1, 1963	20
A Taste Of Honey #4	June 17, 1963	NA(23)
A Taste Of Honey #5	June 19, 1963	21
A Taste Of Honey #6	July 3, 1963	25
A Taste Of Honey #7	July 10, 1963	28
A Taste Of Honey #8	September 3, 1963	NA(37)
Thank You Girl #1	April 1, 1963	15
Thank You Girl #2	May 21, 1963	17
Thank You Girl #3	June 19, 1963	21
That's All Right (Mama)	July 2, 1963	26
There's A Place #1	July 2, 1963	26
There's A Place #2	July 17, 1963	27
There's A Place #3	August 1, 1963	35
Things We Said Today #1	July 14, 1964	48
Things We Said Today #2	July 17, 1964	49
This Boy #1	December 17, 1963	42
This Boy #2	February 28, 1964	45
Three Cool Cats #1	January 16, 1963	NA(5)
Three Cool Cats #2	July 2, 1963	NA(26)
Ticket To Ride #1	May 26, 1965	52
Ticket To Ride #2	May 26, 1965	52
Till There Was You #1	June 1, 1963	19
Till There Was You #2	June 24, 1963	24
Till There Was You #3	July 10, 1963	29
Till There Was You #4	September 3, 1963	36
Till There Was You #5	December 17, 1963	42
Till There Was You #6	December 18, 1963	43
Till There Was You #7	February 28, 1964	45
To Know Her Is To Love Her	July 16, 1963	30
Too Much Monkey Business #1	*March 16, 1963	10
Too Much Monkey Business #2	April 4, 1963	22
Too Much Monkey Business #3	June 1, 1963	19
Too Much Monkey Business #4	September 3, 1963	36
Twist And Shout #1	November 27, 1962	4
Twist And Shout #2	*April 18, 1963	13
Twist And Shout #3	May 21, 1963	NA(17)
Twist And Shout #4	June 17, 1963	23

Title	Recording Date	Aired
Twist And Shout #5	July 3, 1963	25
Twist And Shout #6	July 16, 1963	30
Twist And Shout #7	July 17, 1963	27
Twist And Shout #8	July 30, 1963	33
Twist And Shout #9	August 1, 1963	34
Twist And Shout #10	September 3, 1963	38
Words Of Love	July 16, 1963	32
You Can't Do That #1	February 28, 1964	45
You Can't Do That #2	March 31, 1964	46
You Can't Do That #3	May 1, 1964	47
You Can't Do That #4	July 14, 1964	48
You Really Got A Hold On Me #1	May 24, 1963	18
You Really Got A Hold On Me #2	July 16, 1963	31
You Really Got A Hold On Me #3	July 30, 1963	33
You Really Got A Hold On Me #4	September 3, 1963	37
Youngblood	June 1, 1963	19

Background information for the otherwise unreleased songs performed by The Beatles on British Radio

Though the Beatles cut nearly 300 tracks for the BBC, there were only ninety-four different songs involved (including the opening themes for three of the radio programs they appeared on). Forty-two of these titles were not recorded and issued at the time on their regular Parlophone releases, though only two (*I'll Be On My Way* and *From Us To You*) were original group compositions. All of the others were cover versions of songs written by other artists. These titles are listed below along with background information on the original performances.

Songs preceded by an asterisk (*) were included in "The Beatles at the Beeb" radio special. A [Note] or numbers in brackets [B1,B2,B3,B4,B5] indicate an appearance on one or more of the bootleg records detailed in "Major Packagings of the Beatles on British Radio," which follows this listing.

[B5]   *Beautiful Dreamer* (Stephen Foster)
Originally a poem in 1864 by Stephen Foster
Released in 1954 by Slim Whitman on Imperial 8257

           Besame Mucho (Consuelo Velazquez-Selig Shaftel)
Originally performed in 1943 by Jimmy Dorsey and Orchestra
Released in 1960 by The Coasters on Atco 6163

[B2, B3]   *Carol* (Chuck Berry)
Originally released in 1958 by Chuck Berry on Chess 1700

[B2, B3]   *Clarabella* (Frank J. Pingatore)
Originally released in 1956 by The Jodimars on Capitol 3588

[B1, B4]   *Crying, Waiting, Hoping* (Buddy Holly)
Originally released in 1959 by Buddy Holly on Coral 62134

[B1]   *Don't Ever Change* (Gerry Goffin–Carole King)
Originally released in 1962 by The Crickets on Liberty 55441

           Dream Baby (How Long Must I Dream?) (Cindy Walker)
Originally released in 1962 by Roy Orbison on Monument 456

           From Us To You (John Lennon--Paul McCartney)
Opening and Closing Theme Music for the *From Us To You* radio program
Based on *From Me To You*

[B1, B5]   *Glad All Over* (Aaron Schroeder–Sid Tepper–Roy Bennett)
Originally released in 1957 by Carl Perkins on Sun 287

           Happy Birthday (Traditional arr. John Lennon)
Sung on the fifth anniversary of the *Saturday Club* radio program

[B3]   *The Hippy Hippy Shake* (Chan Romero)
Originally released in 1959 by Chan Romero on Del-Fi 4110

[B1, B5]   *The Honeymoon Song* (Mikis Theodorakis–William Sansom)
Originally from the 1959 film *Honeymoon*
Released in 1959 by Manuel and The Music of the Mountains on Capitol 4306

[Note]   *I Forgot To Remember To Forget* (Stanley Kesler–Charles Feathers)
Originally released in 1955 by Elvis Presley on Sun 223

[B1, B3]   *I Got A Woman (Ray Charles)
            Originally released in 1954 by Ray Charles on Atlantic 1050

[B5]   *I Got To Find My Baby (Chuck Berry)
            Originally released in 1960 by Chuck Berry on Chess 1763

[B1]   *I Just Don't Understand (Marijohn Wilkin–Kent Westberry)
            Originally released in 1961 by Ann-Margret on RCA 7894

           *I'll Be On My Way (John Lennon–Paul McCartney)
            Previously given to Billy J. Kramer with The Dakotas
            First released in 1963 on Parlophone R 5023 (England)

[B1, B5]   I'm Gonna Sit Right Down And Cry (Over You) (Joe Thomas–Howard Biggs)
            Originally released in 1954 by Roy Hamilton on Epic 9015
            Released in 1956 by Elvis Presley on RCA 6638

[B5]   I'm Talking About You (Chuck Berry)
            Originally released in 1961 by Chuck Berry on Chess 1779

[B5]   *Johnny B. Goode (Chuck Berry)
            Originally released in 1961 by Chuck Berry on Chess 1691

[B5]   Keep Your Hands Off My Baby (Gerry Goffin--Carole King)
            Originally released in 1962 by Little Eva on Dimension 1003

[B2, B3]   *Lend Me Your Comb (Kay Twomey–Fred Wise–Ben Weisman)
            Originally released in 1957 by Carl Perkins on Sun 287

[B1, B4]   *Lonesome Tears In My Eyes (Johnny Burnette–Dorsey Burnette–Paul Burlison–
            Al Mortimer)
            Originally released in 1956 by The Johnny Burnette Trio on Coral album
            CRL 57080 (Johnny Burnette And The Rock'n'Roll Trio)

           Lucille (Richard Penniman--Albert Collins)
            Originally released in 1957 by Little Richard on Specialty 598

[B3]   *Memphis, Tennessee (Chuck Berry)
            Originally released in 1959 by Chuck Berry on Chess 1729

[B1, B4]   *Nothin' Shakin' (But The Leaves On The Trees) (Cirino Colacrai–Eddie Fon-
            taine–Dianne Lampert–Jack Cleveland)
            Originally released in 1958 by Eddie Fontaine on Sunbeam 105

[B5]   Ooh! My Soul (Richard Penniman)
            Originally released in 1958 by Little Richard on Specialty 633

[Note]   A Picture Of You (Johnny Beveridge–Peter Oakman)
            Originally released in 1962 by Joe Brown on London 10517

[B3]   *Pop Go The Beatles (Traditional arr. Patrick)
            Theme Music for the Pop Go The Beatles radio program
            Based on the traditional nursery rhyme Pop Goes The Weasel

           Sheila (Tommy Roe)
            Originally released in 1962 by Tommy Roe on ABC 10329

[B1]   *A Shot Of Rhythm And Blues (Terry Thompson)
            Originally released by Arthur Alexander in 1961 on Dot 16309

382

Side By Side (Harry Woods)
Theme Music for the *Side By Side* radio program
Based on *Side By Side*, originally released in 1927 by the Paul Whiteman
Orchestra on Victor VI 20627

[B1, B4] *So How Come (No One Loves Me)* (Felice Bryant–Boudaloux Bryant)
Originally released in 1960 by The Omegas on Decca 31094
Released in 1960 by The Everly Brothers on Warner Brothers album WB 1395
(**A Date With The Everly Brothers**)

[B2, B3] *Soldier of Love (Lay Down Your Arms)* (Buzz Cason–Tony Moon)
Originally released in 1962 by Arthur Alexander on Dot 16357

[B5] *Some Other Guy* (Jerry Leiber--Mike Stoller–Richard Barrett)
Originally released in 1962 by Richie Barrett on Atlantic 2142

[B1, B3] *Sure To Fall (In Love With You)* (Carl Perkins–William E. Cantrell–Quinton
Claunch)
Originally released in 1956 by Carl Perkins on Sun 235

[B5] *Sweet Little Sixteen* (Chuck Berry)
Originally released in 1958 by Chuck Berry on Chess 1683

[B5] *That's All Right (Mama)* (Arthur Crudup)
Originally released in 1946 by Arthur Crudup on Victor VI 2205
Released in 1954 by Elvis Presley on Sun 209

Three Cool Cats (Jerry Leiber--Mike Stoller)
Originally released in 1959 by The Coasters on Atco 6132

[B1, B5] *To Know Him Is To Love Him* (Phil Spector)
Originally released in 1958 by The Teddy Bears on Dore 503

[B5] *Too Much Monkey Business* (Chuck Berry)
Originally released in 1956 by Chuck Berry on Chess 1635

[B5] *Youngblood* (Jerry Leiber--Mike Stoller--Doc Pomus)
Originally released in 1957 by The Coasters on Atco 6087

Major Packagings of The Beatles on British Radio

B1.   EARLY 1970s (US) Various Labels
      AS SWEET AS YOU ARE (also: YELLOW MATTER CUSTARD)

side one

I Got A Woman
Glad All Over
I Just Don't Understand
Slow Down
Don't Ever Change
A Shot Of Rhythm And Blues
Sure To Fall

side two

Nothin' Shakin' (But The Leaves On
* The Trees)*
Lonesome Tears In My Eyes
So How Come (No One Loves Me)
I'm Gonna Sit Right Down And Cry
* (Over You)*
Crying, Waiting, Hoping
To Know Her Is To Love Her
The Honeymoon Song

B2.   MAY 1980 (US) BBC Transcription Service ST-8663 (EP)
      FOUR BY THE BEATLES/POP GO THE BEATLES

side one

Carol
Soldier Of Love (Lay Down Your Arms)

side two

Lend Me Your Comb
Clarabella

B3.   AUG 1980 (US) Circuit Records/BBC Transcription Service LK 4450 (LP)
      THE BEATLES BROADCASTS

side one

Pop Go The Beatles
Long Tall Sally
Carol
Soldier Of Love (Lay Down Your Arms)
Lend Me Your Comb
Clarabella
Memphis, Tennessee
I Got A Woman
Sure To Fall
Do You Want To Know A Secret

side two

The Hippy Hippy Shake
Till There Was You
Matchbox
I'm A Loser
She's A Woman
I Feel Fine
Everybody's Trying To Be My Baby
I'll Follow The Sun

B4.   DEC 1981 (US) Warwick M 16051/Subway Records MX 4729 (LP)
      JOHNNY AND THE MOONDOGS: SILVER DAYS/AIR TIME

side one *Swedish Broadcast

*I Saw Her Standing There
*From Me To You
*Money
*Roll Over Beethoven
*You Really Got A Hold On Me
*She Loves You
*Twist And Shout
Nothin' Shakin' (But The Leaves On The
* Trees)*
Lonesome Tears In My Eyes
So How Come (No One Loves Me)

side two

Please Mr. Postman
Crying, Waiting, Hoping
Ticket To Ride
Rock And Roll Music
medley:
* Kansas City/Hey Hey Hey Hey*
This Boy
Can't Buy Me Love

384

B5.   MAR 1982 (US) NEM 61842/Dream Records DH-9561 (LP)
      BEAUTIFUL DREAMER/CLASSIC RADIO BROADCASTS (*See Notes)

side one	side two
*Some Other Guy	That's All Right (Mama)
I'm Talking About You	I'm Gonna Sit Right Down And Cry
*Youngblood	(Over You)
*Too Much Monkey Business	To Know Her Is To Love Her
*I Got To Find My Baby	Sweet Little Sixteen
Johnny B. Goode	*Ooh! My Soul
*Keep Your Hands Off My Baby	There's A Place
*Beautiful Dreamer	I'll Get You
Glad All Over	Words Of Love
	The Honeymoon Song

[Notes]   *I Forgot To Remember To Forget* turned up as one of the songs on the mixed bag bootleg **Youngblood** (Audifon BVP 005).

   A Picture Of You surfaced on the two-disc **Wonderful Picture Of You** (Circle Records SKI 5430), along with more than a dozen *Let It Be* tracks and eleven other BBC songs including *Dream Baby, Happy Birthday Saturday Club,* and six cuts used on **Beautiful Dreamer** (*indicated above).

Titles included in "The Beatles at the Beeb" as broadcast in the United States on Memorial Day weekend (May 29-31), 1982

**added to the 1983 U.S. Memorial Day rebroadcast

Note: Each of the three parts began with bits from the opening theme songs to the *Pop Go The Beatles* and *From Us To You* radio programs.

Part One	Part Two	Part Three
The Hippy Hippy Shake	Matchbox	**Long Tall Sally
Memphis, Tennessee	Sure To Fall	*Rock And Roll Music
**Dream Baby	Lonesome Tears In My Eyes	And I Love Her
Please Mr. Postman	*Sweet Little Sixteen	A Hard Day's Night
*Some Other Guy	*Nothin' Shakin' (But The	Things We Said Today
Too Much Monkey Business	Leaves On The Trees)	*I'll Follow The Sun
Do You Want To Know A	*I Just Don't Understand	I'm A Loser
Secret?	*So How Come (No One	She's A Woman
I'll Be On My Way	Loves Me)	I Feel Fine
Crying, Waiting, Hoping	I Got A Woman	*Johnny B. Goode
Pop Go The Beatles (open)	*I Got To Find My Baby	Medley:
To Know Her Is To Love	The Honeymoon Song	Kansas City
Her	From Us To You (open)	Hey Hey Hey Hey
Don't Ever Change	All My Loving	Everybody's Trying To
*That's All Right (Mama)	Roll Over Beethoven	Be My Baby
Carol	Till There Was You	*Honey Don't
Soldier Of Love (Lay	I Wanna Be Your Man	Dizzy Miss Lizzy
Down Your Arms)	Can't Buy Me Love	Ticket To Ride
Lend Me Your Comb	From Us To You (close)	
Clarabella	**Happy Birthday Saturday	
A Shot Of Rhythm And	Club	
Blues	This Boy	

*Indicates a song not included in the original March 7, 1982, British version of "The Beatles at the Beeb," but added to the expanded three-part program syndicated in America.

When the BBC presented a revised version of the special in England on December 27, 1982, it changed the lineup to include four songs from the American package (*I Got To Find My Baby, Nothin' Shakin', So How Come*, and *Some Other Guy*), plus two other tracks (*Dream Baby* and *Happy Birthday Saturday Club*). These last two were added to the revised American version for 1983, along with *Long Tall Sally*, which had previously been the only song aired on the British version but not on the American. (All three indicated by **.) As of January 1984, there were still six songs not offered on the British version: *That's All Right (Mama), Sweet Little Sixteen, I Just Don't Understand, I'll Follow The Sun, Johnny B. Goode*, and *Honey Don't*.

The syndicated program in the U.S. was shipped to stations on three twelve-inch discs. Counterfeit copies with the revised 1983 song lineup appeared later that year.

What
To Look For
And Where To Find It

Packagings of the 1962 audition tapes and the BBC broadcast tracks are the only bootleg records that can be recommended without hesitation. Significantly, the songs on these are also the ones that have been absorbed into the world of legitimate release — both on disc and through the "Beatles at the Beeb" radio special. Thus, by 1983, there was virtually no reason to bother with the bootleg versions, except to collect the particularly attractive Circuit Records packagings of the tracks on **The Decca Tapes** and **The Beatles Broadcasts** or the Deccagone picture sleeves.

Beyond those records, there are a handful of bootleg releases that contain just a few worthwhile tracks along with marginal-quality filler. Such records should be approached *with reservations*. They are not "so good that they should have been legitimate," but they look slick, occasionally turn up in mainstream record stores, and might prove a tempting purchase at about $10 a disc. Should you succumb, here is what you'll get.

By The Beatles
THE BEATLES (THE BLACK ALBUM) TWK 0169-AIYHO-10 (3 LPs)
Side one: *Tennessee; House Of The Rising Sun; Commonwealth; White Power; Winston, Richard And John; Hi-Ho Silver; For You Blue; Let It Be.*
Side two: *Get Back; Don't Let Me Down; Two Of Us On Our Way Home; Don't Let Me Down; Suzy Parker; I've Got A Feeling; No Pakistanis.*
Side three: *Let It Be; Be-Bop-A-Lula; She Came In Through The Bathroom Window; Hi-Heel Sneakers; I Me Mine; I've Got A Feeling; One After 909.*
Side four: *She Came In Through The Bathroom Window; Penina; Shakin' In The Sixties; Good Rockin' Tonight; Across The Universe; Two Of Us; I Threw It All Away; Momma You've Been On My Mind; Domino.*
Side five: *Early In The Morning; Hi-Ho Silver; Stand By Me; Hare Krishna; Two Of Us; Don't Let Me Down; I've Got A Feeling; One After 909.*
Side six: *Too Bad About Sorrows; She Said She Said; Mean Mr. Mustard; All Things Must Pass; A Fool Like Me; You Win Again; She Came In Through The Bathroom Window; Watching Rainbows; Instrumental.*

Designed to resemble the White Album (including a poster) but done in solid black. The three discs contain material from the 1969 *Let It Be* filming sessions that did not turn up in either the movie or the companion album. There are impromptu jams on golden-oldie rock songs, developing versions of tracks from both **Abbey Road** and **Let It Be**, and odd-ball snippets of dialogue. This provides a nice sampler of outtakes from the most frequently bootlegged period in the Beatles career. Note: Some of the titles listed describe dialogue, not songs. Many of the tracks appeared in the early 1970s on a pair of packages called **Sweet Apple Trax**.

RESERVATIONS: The songs are rough and incomplete. It's like taking the rehearsal and dialogue sections from the *Let It Be* film without any of the finished performances (such as the rooftop concert sequence). If you did not like the film, you will not like this album.

Beautiful Dreamer   NEM 61842/Dream DH-9561
(bootleg LP)

A Guitar's All Right John Audiron R 6015 (bootleg 10-inch)
But You'll Never Earn
Your Living By It

By The Beatles
BEAUTIFUL DREAMER NEM 61842/Dream DH-9561
Side one: *Some Other Guy; I'm Talking About You; Youngblood; Too Much Monkey Business; I Got To Find My Baby; Johnny B. Goode; Keep Your Hands Off My Baby; Beautiful Dreamer; Glad All Over.*
Side two: *That's All Right (Mama); I'm Gonna Sit Right Down And Cry (Over You); To Know Her Is To Love Her; Sweet Little Sixteen; Ooh! My Soul; There's A Place; I'll Get You; Words Of Love; The Honeymoon Song.*

A good selection of obscure BBC radio titles in an attractive package. Unfortunately the sound quality is only fair, with the vocals buried in the mix. However, if your stereo system includes a graphic equalizer, it is a simple matter to boost the vocals, leading to the frustrating question: Why didn't the people responsible for this package do the same in the first place?
RESERVATIONS: Not for casual listeners. Strong sound support system needed.

By John Lennon
A GUITAR'S ALL RIGHT JOHN BUT YOU'LL NEVER EARN YOUR LIVING BY IT Audiron R-6015
Side one: *Whatever Gets You Thru The Night; Lucy In The Sky With Diamonds; I Saw Her Standing There.*
Side two: *Slippin' and Slidin'; Stand By Me; Oh My Love; Lady Marmalade; Working Class Hero; Day Tripper.*

A ten-inch disc issued in 1977. Side one features all three songs performed live by John Lennon at Elton John's concert in Madison Square Garden on November 25, 1974. Oddly, this mike-in-the-audience recording (mixing the music with the excited buzz of the crowd) actually captured the moment more effectively than the somewhat sterile legitimate release issued after Lennon's death. Side two contains the audio portion of two 1975 promotional film performances, a radio broadcast cut that alleges a team-up of Lennon and Jimi Hendrix, and snatches of song fragments such as forty-seven seconds of *Lady Marmalade* mumbled during an interview. Clearly the quest for Lennon material had reached desperate straits during his house-husband period.
RESERVATIONS: Side two is essentially a throw-away.

By John Lennon
JE SUIS LE PLUS MIEUX (THE LAST REUNION) Jazz Series SD-6757
Side one: *Boogaloo At Thirty-Two (Version One)*
Side two: *Boogaloo At Thirty-Two (Version Two)*

A twelve-inch single featuring John Lennon at the piano during the 1973 **Ringo** album sessions singing his composition *I'm The Greatest*. Afterward, Ringo Starr took over the lead vocal for the version that eventually led off his album. This was the one and only musical reunion of John, George, and Ringo — accompanied by friends Klaus Voormann and Billy Preston. The *Je Suis* bootleg package features a superb quality recording, full color photos (Lennon on the front, Aunt Mimi's house on the back), and detailed handwritten liner notes. However, in an almost humorous attempt to be discreet, the bootleggers did not print anybody's real name on the jacket (including Lennon's) or even list the actual name of the song (though the title *Je Suis Le Plus Mieux* was close to the truth, roughly translating to *I'm The Greatest* in French).

RESERVATIONS: Though this is a high-quality recording in an attractive jacket, the fact remains that $10 for two versions of the same three-minute song is rather expensive.

By John Lennon
THE TOY BOY Bag Records 5069
Side one: *As Time Goes By; I Saw Her Standing There; Whatever Gets You Thru The Night; Move Over Ms. L.; Angel Baby; I Found Out; Happy Xmas (War Is Over); Nutopian International Anthem (Long Version); Give Peace A Chance.*
Side two: *I'm The Greatest; Be My Baby; Yer Blues; Do The Oz; What A Shame Mary Jane Had A Pain At The Party; As Time Goes By 2; Starting Over (Postscript); Good Night.*

Essentially John Lennon's "Greatest Bootleg Hits," this includes about anything worthwhile that's ever turned up on a bootleg disc devoted to Lennon. There is a version of *I'm The Greatest* from **Je Suis Le Plus Mieux**, two tracks left off the **Rock 'n' Roll** oldies album, a song from the Rolling Stones' *Rock And Roll Circus* film, brief snatches of *As Time Goes By* from a radio interview, and the infamous *What's The News Maryjane* (called *What A Shame Mary Jane Had A Pain At The Party*), which almost turned up as the B-side to a Plastic Ono Band single in 1969. Instead of the live concert appearance with Elton John there are two tracks identified as studio demos of the songs they sang. Perhaps. Sounds more like a rehearsal session for the concert at Madison Square Garden. The album is

391

rounded out by some relatively obscure Lennon-related tracks pirated from legitimately issued discs. Note: This album came in two forms. The first featured a white cover with gold lettering and a booklet insert (adding several dollars to the price); the second had a blue cover with a color photo, though no booklet.

RESERVATIONS: Though side one is fairly strong (it should be: three tracks are from commercial singles), side two caters to more esoteric Lennon tastes, wrapping up with three song fragments and nearly seven minutes of *What A Shame Mary Jane Had A Pain At The Party*. Frankly, there was a very good reason the track never turned up as a single in *that* form.

By Ringo Starr
OGNIR RRATS' GREATEST HITS Wibble Records 91825
Side one: *Down And Out; Coochy-Coochy; Six O'Clock; Blindman; Band Of Steel; Just A Dream.*
Side two: *I Love My Suit; Press Conference/I'm The Greatest; Act Naturally; You're Sixteen; With A Little Help From My Friends; Heart On My Sleeve; Hard Times; A Man Like Me; Yellow Submarine; Simple Life.*

Essentially Ognir's (Ringo's) "Greatest Bootleg Hits," drawing from his 1978 TV special that featured three songs done in a live performance sequence as well as new renditions of old favorites (including a duet with Carrie Fisher on *You're Sixteen*). Rounding out the package are a half-dozen obscure commercial oddities (such as *Band Of Steel*, a Ringo Starr original composition sung by Guthrie Thomas) and the audio tracks to a pair of clothing commercials for Japanese television.

RESERVATIONS: The live songs lose a bit without the context of the special. Otherwise the package is not bad, helped chiefly by the fact that all of the material was taken from fully produced sources: a TV special, TV commercials, and commercially released records.

By George Harrison
BY GEORGE! Handmade Records NSU-001
Side one: *Miss O'Dell; Deep Blue; I Don't Care Anymore; Dark Horse; Here Comes The Sun; Homeward Bound; Awaiting On You All; The Pirate Song; Far East Man; I Still Don't Care Anymore; Think For Yourself.*
Side two: *Flying Hour; Lay His Head; Sat Singing; Tears Of The World; Dream Away.*

Essentially George Harrison's "Greatest Bootleg Hits." Side two is the real draw because it includes Harrison's closing song to the hit film *Time Bandits* plus the four songs from **Somewhere In England** that were replaced by more upbeat tunes before release in 1981. Unfortunately the tracks were obviously not taken from the original master tapes. In fact, the song from *Time Bandits* sounds as if it was recorded from a seat in the audience at a theater. Side one includes snatches of alternate recordings of Harrison solo tunes (from radio interviews and the studio), assorted obscure B-sides from commercial singles, and several songs performed on television in America (two from *Saturday Night Live*) and Britain (*The Pirate Song* from Eric Idle's *Rutland Weekend Television*).

RESERVATIONS: Side one varies widely in quality and consistency. Side two's main draw, the four **Somewhere In England** tracks, also turned up in their original context on a full-fledged counterfeit of the original album package with much better quality.

By George Harrison
SOMEWHERE IN ENGLAND Dark Horse DHK 3492
Side one: *Hong Kong Blues; Writing's On The Wall; Flying Hour; Lay His Head; Unconsciousness Rules.*.
Side two: *Sat Singing; Life Itself; Tears Of The World; Baltimore Oriole; Save the World*.

A counterfeit copy of the aborted 1980 version of George Harrison's **Somewhere In England** album, faithfully duplicating the original's greyish front cover featuring a closeup of Harrison's head with a map of England superimposed on his hair. The package also came with a full-color Dark Horse label and an alternate track arrangement, including the four songs dropped from the 1981 set: *Flying Hour, Lay His Head, Sat Singing*, and *Tears Of The World*. Each of these was written by Harrison except *Flying Hour*, which was a Harrison/Ralphs composition.

The album flows rather well and the sound quality is surprisingly good, though it is easy to see why the record was ultimately rejected in this form: the tone is extremely lowkey. Ironically, had **Somewhere In England** come out as originally intended, it would no doubt have been quickly forgotten. Instead, it became the first genuine "alternative version" of a Beatles record since the **Get Back** album.

RESERVATIONS: There are only four songs on this record that were not carried over to the 1981 commercial release.

Je Suis Le Plus Mieux   Jazz Series SD 6757 (bootleg 12-inch)
(The Last Reunion)

Somewhere In England   **Dark Horse DHK 3492**
                                             (counterfeit LP)

By Paul McCartney
ODD SOX RC-78894 (2 LPs)
Side one: *Girls' School; Daytime Nightime Suffering; Coming Up (Live At Glasgow); The Mess; Oh Woman, Oh Why; Goodnight Tonight (Short Version).*
Side two: *Give Ireland Back To The Irish; Mary Had A Little Lamb; Little Woman Love; C Moon; I Lie Around; Walking In The Park With Eloise; Bridge On The River Suite.*
Side three: *Lunch Box/Odd Sox; Country Dreamer; Sally G; Seaside Woman; B-Side To Seaside; Wonderful Christmastime; Rudolph The Red-Nosed Reggae (Reindeer); Give Ireland Back To The Irish (Instrumental Version).*
Side four: *Check My Machine; Secret Friend; Zoo Gang; Goodnight Tonight (Long Version).*

Not exactly Paul McCartney's "Greatest Bootleg Hits" because *all* of these tracks were previously released commercially. Instead this is the definitive pirate album, gathering all of McCartney's singles-sides that were never included on an album through 1980. This easily filled the four sides, underscoring the fact that there is quite a stockpile of such material begging for a legitimate compilation release. The sound quality is excellent, of course, even as a second generation copy of commercial releases.

RESERVATIONS: Though technically some of the tracks such as *Secret Friend* were virtually impossible to find in America, this is exactly the type of "greatest hits" piracy package that has driven the recording industry bonkers.

By Paul McCartney
SUITABLE FOR FRAMING MPL JPM 40-IF
Side one: *I'll Give You A Ring; Rainclouds; Maise; I Would Only Smile; Take It Away; Send Me The Heart; Ebony And Ivory (solo version).*
Side two: *Waterspout; Hi, Hi, Hi; Waterfalls; Arrow Through Me; Winter Rose; Love Awake; Weep For Love; Complain To The Queen.*

A hybrid pirate-bootleg follow-up to **Odd Sox**, containing eight obscure commercial releases as well as a handful of outtakes, alternate recordings, and broadcast tracks. The previously released cuts come from the B-sides to singles from **Tug Of War** and Wings tracks included on solo records by Laurence Juber and Denny Laine. These flow nicely together on side one, leaving the flip for the less consistent bootleg material. This includes three alternate takes from **Back To The Egg** (the extended version of *Love Awake* is quite effective), a track from the unreleased 1980 version of **Cold Cuts** (*Waterspout*), and an impromptu radio jam (*Complain To The Queen*).

RESERVATIONS: The deceptively detailed track information

on the back cover is often misleading. For instance, songs from the Denny Laine and Laurence Juber solo discs are identified as out-takes. More importantly, the sound quality on a few of the bootleg cuts (most notably *Waterfalls*) is below the consistency of the pirated material.

By The Beatles/Paul McCartney
NO. 3 ABBEY ROAD NW 8 AR-8-69 ($10 or less)
Side one: *Golden Slumbers; Carry That Weight; Her Majesty; You Never Give Me Your Money; Octopus's Garden; Maxwell's Silver Hammer; Oh! Darling; Something.*
Side two: *How Do You Do; Blackbird; The Unicorn; Lalena; Heather; Mr. Wind; The Walrus And The Carpenter; Land Of Gisch.*

Though touted as a Beatles bootleg, the real draw is side two which features a fifteen-minute studio warm-up between Paul Mc-Cartney and Donovan Leitch from the White Album era. Playing their acoustic guitars, the two exchanged songs-in-the-works with Paul offering *Blackbird* and *Heather* (for Linda's daughter) and Donovan selecting numbers from what eventually became **H.M.S. Donovan** (a British children's album). A thoroughly delightful, relaxed performance. Side one, in the meantime, features average quality alternate takes of songs from **Abbey Road**.
RESERVATIONS: Side one is of only marginal interest.

****

Inevitable question: Where can I buy bootleg records?
Honest answer: We don't know. Really.
Why?
With the exception of the handful of records previously noted, we simply do not find *any* bootlegs "worth buying." So we've never gone bootleg shopping. And the ones we do like have been so effectively packaged that we've seen them in mainstream record stores.
Still, we can offer some suggestions, warnings, and a bit of history.
Despite their illegal status, bootleg records were relatively easy to find in the late 1960s and early 1970s, especially at open-air flea markets, swap meets, and shops that catered to the "counter-culture." This reached a peak of sorts in the mid-1970s when there was so much bootleg product that there were even "cut-out" sales, with albums going for as low as $2.99 each. The packages put out during this time generally featured plain white jackets with a cheap insert sleeve identifying the contents. They looked bogus even to a casual buyer.

Probably the best sets to come out of that era were **Sweet Apple Trax** (the *Let It Be* sessions), **As Sweet As You Are** (British radio appearances), and **Wings From The Wings** (three records covering Paul McCartney's 1976 tour of America). That last package was issued several months before the legitimate **Wings Over America** release and no doubt contributed to a step-up in legal action against bootleggers. For the next few years, bootlegs became increasingly difficult to find. Few mainstream stores touched them and they only turned up in secondhand shops and at swap meets.

In the meantime, American interest in foreign pressings of records surged. As a result, there were more and more unfamiliar packages on store shelves featuring legitimate Beatles product in unusual picture sleeves from various countries. Canny bootleggers found this the perfect opportunity to slide back into action. In the next great rush of bootleg product – led by the high-quality Decca audition tapes and the BBC radio broadcasts in 1979 and 1980 – the albums were designed to look like foreign pressings. With this air of legitimacy, they once again slipped into some mainstream record stores, usually ending up in the "import" bin. For the next few years, bootlegs were relatively easy to find.

However, in 1982 this began to change. For one thing, record industry campaigns and legal actions against all unauthorized product stepped up, motivated chiefly by sagging sales and the proliferation of pirates and counterfeits. And in this latest campaign, there are new federal laws backing the proceedings.

Previously, people that produced and sold bootleg product faced relatively minor fines. Even if they were caught, it was no big deal. Now it is. So there is every reason to believe that – unlike the mid-1970s – bootlegging will not "bounce back" to the same scale of just a few years ago. It won't be worth the risk. There will be better ways to earn a quick buck.

Yet this is not really such a great loss. Most of the Beatles material from 1962–1969 that was really worth issuing has come out: early auditions, radio performances, film outtakes, and a few live concerts. That only leaves the studio outtakes in the EMI vaults (see page 405, "Outtakes We'd Like To See Out"). Rest assured those *will* eventually come out officially. That has happened with other major rock artists (including Elvis Presley and Buddy Holly) and there is no reason to believe the situation with the Beatles will be any different.

In the meantime, if you insist on searching for bootleg product:

*Decide on the price you are willing to pay for particular items and be ready to pay it as soon as you see them – whether at a mainstream record store, a second-hand shop, a swap meet, a fan convention, or anywhere else. You do not have the luxury of comparison shopping. If you decide the price is too high, you really don't want the records.

*In most cases you really *don't* want the records. Trust our ears.

*Be careful if you purchase by mail. Even if the seller is 100% honest, unexpected legal action can deplete the warehouse (garage) stockpile before your order can be filled (but just after your check has cleared).

*Do not walk into a store or up to a dealer at a swap meet and say, "Got any bootlegs?" They'll think you're an undercover agent.

*If you *are* an undercover agent, get a new line. Anybody dumb enough to say "Yes" has already been caught.

*Remember, most bootleg records are of interest only to the most dedicated Beatles completists. Perhaps the best indication of the general reliability of bootleg product is the warning sticker most stores attach to the discs:

"No Returns – All Sales Final."

YOU
CAN'T SAY
WE NEVER
TOLD YOU

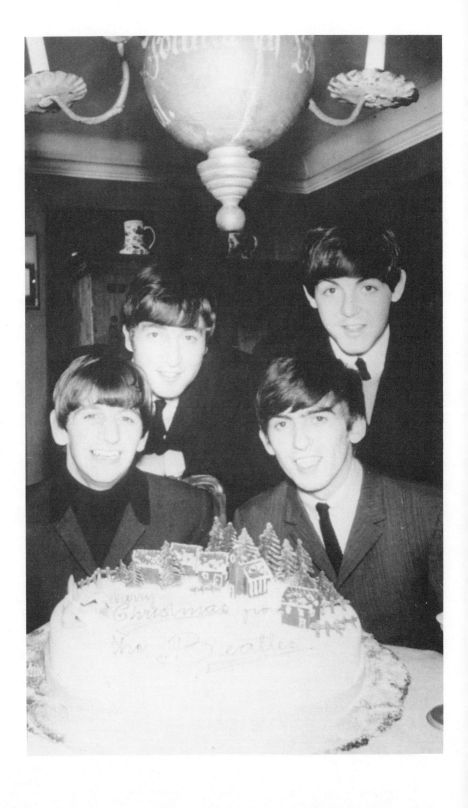

You Can't Say

We Never Told You

In mid 1980, *Beatles Book* writer Mark Lewisohn in England came across the sheet music for a song called *You Can't Say I Never Told You*. The folio came complete with a picture of the Beatles on the cover, publishing credit to Northern Songs, a 1965 copyright, and the line "words and music by John Lennon and Paul McCartney." A scan of the lyrics quickly revealed that they were obviously written for another performer because they were from a woman's point of view. However, there was *no* reference to the identity of the singer.

Was this just a misprint or was it a previously undiscovered Lennon and McCartney tune that had been "given away" in the mid-1960s? If the latter, who recorded it? And how had it escaped detection for fifteen years?

Eventually these questions ended up with us. After some Stateside digging, we unearthed a bit of the release history for the song. *You Can't Say I Never Told You* had never been issued in the U.S. but had been released in England during the fall of 1965 as a single on CBS Records (CBS 201792) with *And Now I Don't Want You* on the flip side. The artist? Suzy Cope.

We had never heard of Suzy Cope. Neither, apparently, had Mark Lewisohn. But, armed with this new information, he once again took up the search, now certain that the sheet music was definitely for a song that had actually come out back then. Meanwhile, hoping to find someone who might have a copy of the single, we reported this "research work in progress" in the April 1981 issue of *Beatlefan* magazine (in an article dubbed "Mystery of the Missing Beatles Song"). Soon thereafter, Mark Lewisohn found a copy of the record in England and the solution to the mystery.

Yes, Suzy Cope had indeed sung *You Can't Say I Never Told You*, just as it appeared on the sheet music. No, John Lennon and Paul McCartney did not write the song and, in fact, had absolutely nothing to do with the record, the published lyrics and music, or

401

Suzy Cope. The Beatles photo and the Lennon/McCartney writing credits had been a misprint back in 1965 after all.

Was this a letdown?

Not really. We had always known that might prove to be the case. In fact, we were pleased to see that a potential bogus Beatles connection had been quashed before it could catch on and assume a life of its own.

Besides, we did get one thing out of it all — a great title for this section of the book.

Outtakes
We'd Like To See Out

From July 18 to September 11, 1983, more than 20,000 visitors to EMI's Abbey Road studios were treated to a special pop culture event: a ninety-minute film, video, and slide documentary show built around the music of the Beatles. This special program, "The Beatles at Abbey Road," was presented three times daily in studio number two, where, from 1962 to 1969, the Beatles had recorded most of their music.

The studio was free for such an event because EMI had to close it anyway for a few months as part of a major equipment refurbishing job. This presented a once-in-a-lifetime opportunity to use the studio as a stage for a unique retrospective, celebrating EMI's most famous recording artists. "The Beatles at Abbey Road" received international press coverage and attracted visitors from all over the world. They came away suitably impressed.

To set the proper mood in the studio, there was a display of musical instruments (including a drum set and piano), professional tape recorders, microphones, loudspeakers, and old photos. One wall chart listed the titles of all the songs recorded by the Beatles, at Abbey Road. About 100 chairs were set up, facing two large video screens. After a brief welcoming speech, the room darkened and the program began.

The show, narrated by London disc jockey Roger Scott, opened with some background history on the Abbey Road studios, including an excerpt from the first recording ever made there back on November 12, 1931 (Sir Edward Elgar conducting the London Symphony Orchestra). Moving up thirty years, there was a film of Helen Shapiro performing her number one British hit, *Walkin' Back To Happiness*. Then came the voices of the Beatles taken from the 1964 Christmas message to their fans, sending greetings from studio number two. With the opening notes of *Love Me Do*, the program was truly on its way. Over the next ninety minutes, there were two dozen Beatles numbers presented (in whole or part).

"The Beatles at Abbey Road" was divided into two forty-five

"The Beatles at Abbey Road"

Conceived by Ken Townsend and John Barrett

Written and Narrated by Roger Scott

Daily Performances at 10:30 a.m., 3:30 p.m., and 7:30 p.m.
from July 18 to September 11, 1983

Admission: £4.50 ($7.00)

PART ONE.
Orchestra warm-up
Pomp And Circumstance March No. 2 excerpt (1931)
Sir Edward Elgar conducting the London Symphony Orchestra
Walkin' Back To Happiness (1961)
Helen Shapiro
Another Beatles Christmas Record excerpt (1964)
Love Me Do (1962)
How Do You Do It (1962)
I Saw Her Standing There (1963)
(take 1, handclaps to take 12, finished version)
Twist And Shout (1963)
One After 909 (1963)
Don't Bother Me (1963)
(false start, take 11, take 12)
A Hard Day's Night (1964)
(false start, take 2, take 3)
Leave My Kitten Alone (1964)
I'm A Loser (1964)
She's A Woman (1964)
(take 1)
Ticket To Ride (1965)
Help (1965)
(minus vocals and lead guitar)

PART TWO.
Norwegian Wood (This Bird Has Flown) (1965)
(take 1)
I'm Looking Through You (1965)
(handclaps take 1)
Paperback Writer (1966)
Rain (1966)
Penny Lane (1966)
Strawberry Fields Forever (1966)
(take 1, take 7, take 26)
A Day In The Life (1967)
Hello Goodbye (1967)
Lady Madonna (1968)
Hey Jude (1968)
(early version)
While My Guitar Gently Weeps (1968)
(take 1)
Because (1969)
(minus instruments)
No. 9 Dream (1974)
(John Lennon solo recorded at New York's Hit Factory)

minute segments. The first section set most of the music to film and photo montages. Part two drew on the special promotional films that the Beatles had done at the time to accompany their songs. The result was a generally well balanced, entertaining program that took the audience from the simple energy of *Love Me Do* to the rich textured harmonies of *Because*.

Of course, for many Beatles fans just *visiting* Abbey Road would have been exciting enough. To sit there and hear some of their favorite Beatles songs played over the studio's superb sound system, accompanied by a slick visual show, was sheer magic. But, there was more. As often as possible, the program offered excerpts from unreleased, alternate versions of familiar songs. In two cases, this involved selections from songs that had never been officially issued by the group: *How Do You Do It* and *Leave My Kitten Alone*.

In many instances, the outtakes were used to demonstrate the development of the music. For example, there were excerpts from three takes of *I Saw Her Standing There*, several false starts on *A Hard Day's Night*, take one of *She's A Woman* (which sounded a bit like *Dr. Robert* at that stage), *Help* without vocals or lead guitar, a clapping track for *I'm Looking Through You*, versions one, seven, and twenty-six of *Strawberry Fields Forever* (providing an aural explanation of how the finished single combined different takes), and *Because* without instrumental backing. Most impressive of all was the initial acoustic version of *While My Guitar Gently Weeps*, with George Harrison in perfect voice through the entire take. This included an extra verse not used on the commercially released version which was take forty-four.

Such specific references to song takes, recording dates, and musical personnel was sometimes accompanied by flashes of the session sheets themselves on the video screens.[1] This underscored one of the most important facts about the research that made "The Beatles at Abbey Road" possible: EMI at last had an organized, detailed guide to the storehouse of tapes from the Beatles recording sessions. For the first time, then, it was possible to learn once and for all whether or not there were any Beatles outtakes that might someday be released.

"The Beatles at Abbey Road" dealt with that question directly. According to the program, there were only four previously unreleased,

----

[1] These detailed the four songs done at Pete Best's one-and-only EMI recording session with the Beatles: *Besame Mucho, Love Me Do, P.S. I Love You*, and *Ask Me Why*. None of these takes were ever used on any of the Beatles releases.

Abbey Road On Record

In addition to "The Beatles at Abbey Road," material by the group also turned up on some special promotional packages tied in with the studio.

One was a limited edition promo album (500 copies) issued only in England by EMI as part of the 1982 promotion for Brian Southall's book *Abbey Road* — subtitled "The story of the world's most famous recording studios." (Paul McCartney did the Foreword and George Martin did the Preface.) A sampler album of the music from Abbey Road was a natural tie-in, so copies of **The Abbey Road Collection** (EMI PSLP 366) went out to interviewers and reviewers at radio stations, newspapers, and magazines throughout England. There were twenty-four cuts on the disc including, naturally, a Beatles track, *She Loves You* (once the best selling single ever in Britain until it was passed by Paul McCartney's *Mull Of Kintyre* — also on the record). There were also a number of other cuts with a Beatles connection (all listed below). For this album, George Harrison's *My Sweet Lord* was trimmed to a running time of 3:51.

THE ABBEY ROAD COLLECTION (1982 UK PROMO)
side one
cut nine: *Lily The Pink* by Scaffold
cut eleven: *My Sweet Lord* by George Harrison
side two
cut five: *She Loves You* by The Beatles
cut six: *Bad To Me* by Billy J. Kramer and The Dakotas
cut seven: *A World Without Love* by Peter and Gordon
cut twelve: *Mull Of Kintyre* by Wings

In the U.S., Abbey Road engineer-turned-producer-turned performer, Alan Parsons, put out a special two-record DJ package in 1979 featuring material he had worked on over the years. This **Radio Guide To The Alan Parsons Project** (Arista SP-68) included three songs by the Beatles and three songs by Paul McCartney. Oddly, the back cover incorrectly listed *The End* instead of *Get Back* in the contents lineup. That was corrected three years later when the set was reissued as a *three* disc package called **The Complete Audio Guide To The Alan Parsons Project** (Arista SP-140). The side and track placements for the Beatles and McCartney songs remained the same as on the 1979 edition.

RADIO GUIDE TO THE ALAN PARSONS PROJECT (1979 US PROMO)
Reissued in 1982 with an additional record as
THE COMPLETE AUDIO GUIDE TO THE ALAN PARSONS PROJECT
(1982 US PROMO)
side one
cut two: *A Day In The Life* by The Beatles
cut three: *Get Back* by The Beatles
cut four: *Maxwell's Silver Hammer* by The Beatles
cut five: *Maybe I'm Amazed* by Paul McCartney
cut six: *I Am Your Singer* by Wings
cut seven: *Hi Hi Hi* by Wings

otherwise unavailable songs by the Beatles that remained in the vaults:

How Do You Do It (John and Paul vocal)
Leave My Kitten Alone (John vocal)
That Means A Lot (Paul vocal)
If You've Got Troubles (Ringo vocal)

How Do You Do It (written by Mitch Murray) had been recorded by the Beatles in 1962 at the behest of George Martin as a possible second single. Instead, the group insisted on its own composition, *Please Please Me*, and Gerry and the Pacemakers got *How Do You Do It* instead. They took it to number one in Britain.

Leave My Kitten Alone was a cover version of a 1959 rhythm and blues hit by Little Willie John. The song was done by the Beatles in 1964 but did not make it onto **Beatles For Sale**, which already had a half-dozen cover versions of other songs.

That Means A Lot was an original Lennon-McCartney tune recorded in 1965 but never used. Instead, the song was given to P.J. Proby, who took it to number thirty on the British charts.

Finally, *If You've Got Troubles* was a Ringo novelty vocal left over from the 1965 **Rubber Soul** sessions.

And that, according to "The Beatles at Abbey Road," was it.

On the surface, such a claim seemed incredible. For years, ardent fans had heard that there were hundreds of hours of tape in storage at Abbey Road. How could these yield only four finished songs?

In part, the answer was that some long-held assumptions about the Beatles recorded output had not been correct.[1] For instance, many fans assumed that for every Lennon and McCartney tune given to another artist, there was a finished Beatles version to serve as a demo. This was not the case. John or Paul might do a guide recording, but that was likely to be a simple piano or guitar piece rather than a full-fledged studio production.

Another assumption was that the Beatles recorded dozens of cover versions of rock and pop standards in between sessions for their own songs. As the *Let It Be* movie clearly showed, the group did indeed use old songs to warm-up in the studio, but these were hardly finished, releaseable versions.

----

[1] By 1982, the legends regarding Beatles outtakes had reached such proportions that writer J.P. Russell unflinchingly listed 215 titles "assumed to have been recorded by the Beatles but not released" in his book *The Beatles On Record*. Though acknowledging the existence of all 215 was "doubtful," the underlying implication was that the correct total was much nearer several hundred rather than only four. See the "Margin Of Error" section (page 446) for a further discussion of this myth, including (gasp) our own role in it. Also consult the July 1982 issue of *Record Collector* (#35) for an excellent debunking article, "The Beatles' Unreleased Recordings."

Then there were the *Let It Be* film sessions themselves. For almost an entire month in 1969, the Beatles performed before the cameras with nearly one-hundred hours of rehearsals, jams and developing songs. Since the early 1970s, this material had served as the basis for dozens of bootleg packages, so fans assumed that EMI might one day release several similar legitimate albums on its own. Unfortunately, stripped of their aura as "purloined treasures," most of these meandering and unfinished tracks were not particularly impressive. The Beatles themselves barely salvaged one album from the sessions back in 1970, so EMI could hardly be expected to find more than a handful of additional useable cuts. As a final strike against the material, it was not even done at Abbey Road, so the recordings were not left on file at the studio. (In fact, some of them were no doubt completely lost long ago to sticky-fingered bootleggers.)

Finally, and most important, many people simply failed to understand the reality of day-to-day studio production. They assumed that, for instance, a half-hour's worth of leftover material translated into several brand-new, completely finished numbers. In truth, what it usually meant was a dozen or so takes of the same song, with outtake material adding up very quickly. One fourteen-song British album could result in seven hours of unused recordings, assuming only a dozen takes of each track (and there were cases when this number approached one hundred). Thus, the material on even several hundred hours of tape could be easily accounted for. It simply represented take after take leading to the finished versions of commercially released Beatles songs.

Ardent fans, of course, might argue that such alternate takes would be worth releasing. However, from a business point of view that might not be true. Rough working versions of Beatles tracks might be fascinating to historians and collectors, but not to the general public. And, ultimately, that is to whom EMI must cater; not to thousands of dedicated collectors, but to millions of mainstream record buyers. These are the people who did *not* send the live Hamburg tapes or the 1962 audition tracks to the top of the charts. Would they really have any interest in "take sixteen" of *I Saw Her Standing There*?

Perhaps they would, in the proper setting. If such alternate versions were carefully selected to emphasize dramatically different interpretations of familiar songs, they could help fill out a package built around *How Do You Do It, Leave My Kitten Alone, That Means A Lot*, and *If You've Got Troubles*. For instance, the acoustic version of *While My Guitar Gently Weeps*, the rocking 1963 recording of *One After 909* (also used in "The Beatles at Abbey Road"), the full length version of the *Christmas Time Is Here Again* signature tune from the 1967 Christmas record, and the alternate take of *It's All Too Much* used in the *Yellow Submarine* film would be excellent candidates for inclusion.

The package could also extend into Beatles versions of a few solo songs, such as the group's 1968 rendition of George Harrison's *Not Guilty* or (if they could be retrieved from the *Let It Be* film sessions) group recordings of Paul McCartney's *Teddy Boy*, John Lennon's *Give Me Some Truth*, or George Harrison's *All Things Must Pass*. Squeezing *Let It Be* further would turn up *Suzy Parker*, the original presentation of *Get Back*, and a handful of nearly finished rock oldies. All of these could bring the lineup of a well-balanced outtakes album to about twelve to sixteen cuts.

And that's just about where we'd end it. Why bother with any more? That would take care of any truly saleable unreleased material, especially when coupled with an authorized album issuing of the BBC broadcast tracks and a clearly sanctioned package of the 1962 audition sessions (both showcasing the group's otherwise unreleased cover versions).

Of course, should an outtakes package do extremely well, EMI might be tempted to take another look at its stockpile of tapes. A follow-up collection of more marginal material might result (every take of *Maxwell's Silver Hammer*?). Perhaps the company might even convince Paul McCartney to allow the issuance of two songs from a 1958 demo disc made by John, Paul, and George.[1] With the outtakes sales gate open, there might be no stopping it.

After all, the catalogs of other departed acts such as Buddy Holly, Jimi Hendrix, and Elvis Presley were eventually expanded to include new overdubs on half-finished demos, remixes of previously released tracks, alternate takes of established hits, and various concert and film outtakes. On one 1983 Elvis Presley album, the original vocal tracks to some of Presley's most popular songs were even given *newly-recorded* instrumental backing to "punch them up." For Buddy Holly and Jimi Hendrix, the number of posthumous packages eventually exceeded what they put out when they were still alive.

For the Beatles, though, we sincerely hope that it all ends with the release of just the best of the outtakes. The world does not really need a Beatles equivalent to that overblown eight-record **Elvis Aron Presley** boxed set of sometimes inaudible "rarities" (originally foisted on the public in 1980 at $50+ and currently sitting in your local cut-out bin for $24.95). Just a *few* good quality

----

[1]Paul McCartney won possession of that disc through a 1982 court order. The two songs on it were a group original called *In Spite Of All The Danger* and a cover version of Buddy Holly's *That'll Be The Day*. Another demo disc, cut in Germany in 1960, reportedly had John, Paul, George, and Ringo involved on cover versions of *Fever* (by Little Willie John), *September Song* (by Kurt Weill and Maxwell Anderson), and *Summertime* (by George Gershwin and DuBose Heyward). There are no known copies of that German disc still in existence.

outtake tracks would be a big enough treat for Beatles fans.

And their release is inevitable. Apparently EMI does not even need the permission of the former Beatles to issue the material (though the company has consulted them anyway). So, though it may not be much consolation *now* to impatient fans, rest assured that anything worth releasing (and then some) will no doubt come out, eventually. Just remember, once that's gone from the vaults, we will have truly come to the end of the Beatles.

****

Afterward – Paul, John, George, and Ringo

As solo artists, each of the former Beatles also accumulated outtakes. Of the four, Paul McCartney has ended up with the most extensive back catalog of unreleased material, reflecting his consistent release schedule since 1970. In fact, McCartney had put out so much material by 1983 that it would take a two-record set just to cover the commercially released single tracks that never appeared on an album.

Since the mid-1970s, McCartney has tossed around a proposal to put some of his finished but unreleased songs onto a special collection dubbed "Cold Cuts." The closest this ever came to being ready for release was in late 1980 when McCartney had a track lineup selected and was working on a few last overdubs. He put this aside, though, in the aftermath of John Lennon's death.

Obviously, then, there is definitely one album's worth of high-quality, unreleased McCartney material ready to go. There could probably be another full album (or two), drawing on three sources: live concerts with Wings, studio recordings, and improptu jam sessions from film and studio work.

From 1972 to 1979, Wings concert performances inevitably included material that was not out on record at the time, showcasing both cover versions and original compositions. Later, commercially released live recordings of *The Mess, Soily*, and *Coming Up* taken from such shows illustrated the high quality and high energy of this work. Further digging through Wings shows, especially those done in 1972 to 1975 and in 1979, would certainly turn up other strong tracks, including: *1882, Best Friend, Tragedy, Blue Moon Of Kentucky, Twenty-Flight Rock, Say You Don't Mind* (Denny Laine) and *Henry's Blues* (Henry McCullough).

Because McCartney set up Wings to function as a group on record as well as on the road, some of the studio tracks occasionally featured vocals and even compositions by the other members. Obviously, these were the first to be put aside when *the* Wing, McCartney, had more than enough material to fill an album. (A few of these did turn up later on solo releases by Denny Laine and Laurence Juber — see Entries 662 and 708).

Having a functioning group ready in the studio was also helpful to McCartney's own compositions. Even a "quick trial demo" or an alternate interpretation of a song with Wings would have a more complete and finished sound than, say, the same thing done completely alone. Such songs, as well as any leftover album tracks, would be candidates for Cold Cuts release. These might include: *Boil Crisis, All Stand Together, Mama's Little Girl, Waterspout, My Carnival, Cage, Hey Diddle, Wide Prairie Maid, Oriental Nightfish, Tragedy, Did We Meet Somewhere Before*, and *Same Time, Next Year*, as well as a number of tracks for the Rupert Bear project (done during the **Back To The Egg** sessions).

Paul McCartney's solo recordings (completely alone or working with guest musicians) also produced some leftovers. For instance, reaching back to the late 1960s, there were demo versions of *Goodbye* and *Come And Get It*, as well as otherwise unreleased songs such as *Heather* (see page 396). Moving up a dozen years to some finished recordings, several tracks were dropped from **McCartney II** as it was compressed into a single disc from a proposed double album. Later, during the recording for **Tug Of War** and **Pipes Of Peace**, a few cuts that did not quite work on the sets were put aside, such as a medley built around *Sweetest Little Show*.

There were also many impromptu studio jams, especially at Montserrat, inevitably leading back to favorites from the past such as the Carl Perkins classics *Honey Don't, Boppin' The Blues*, and *Lend Me Your Comb*, Eddie Cochran's *Cut Across Shorty*, and even *When The Saints Go Marching In* and *Red Sails In The Sunset*. That same spirit often surfaced during "studio concert jams" that helped fill the inevitable breaks during such film projects as the 1975 *One Hand Clapping* documentary or the feature length *Give My Regards To Broad Street*. McCartney's performance during the making of the *Take It Away* promotional film was probably the most appreciated of this type. It was done on June 23, 1982, before an audience of British fan club members invited to serve as extras on the set (playing an audience). They were treated to such songs as Buddy Holly's *Bo Diddley* and *Peggy Sue*, Eddie Cochran's *Twenty Flight Rock*, Little Richard's *Lucille* and *Send Me Some Lovin'*, Chuck Berry's *Reelin' And Rockin'*, and even *The Theme From Hill Street Blues*.

Of course, though exciting to watch and (no doubt) to play, all of these jam sessions were not in the same polished and finished category as the other outtakes. Nonetheless, they helped build McCartney's large stockpile of alternate material — adding to the inevitable leftovers that reflected not only his prolific output but also Paul's meticulous approach to studio work: mixing, remixing, and fine-tuning a project for as long as a year or two.

411

Milk And Honey   **Polydor 817 160-1 Y-1 (LP)**

John Lennon, in contrast, made his solo records in concentrated spurts, taking weeks and months rather than months and years. As a result, he usually did not have very much left over. Even most of his live concert appearances eventually turned up on disc. There were only two cases in which Lennon left behind a quantity of outtakes: the 1974 rock oldies sessions with Phil Spector, and the 1980 comeback with Yoko Ono. In the case of the oldies, Lennon rejected about five tracks when assembling the **Rock'n'Roll** album in 1975 because he thought they sounded terrible — so much so that he went back into the studio and recorded some new ones. Release of this material would be a fascinating career footnote, though otherwise nothing special.

The songs left from **Double Fantasy** were working versions set aside for the follow-up **Milk And Honey** album. In 1983, Yoko Ono at last assembled them for release the following year, digging even further to come up with a pair of vocals the two had made only on cassette (*Let Me Count The Ways/Grow Old With Me*). At the same time, she also retrieved an alternate version of her own *Every Man Has A Woman Who Loves Him* from **Double Fantasy** (with a lead vocal by John) for use on a compilation album of songs written by Yoko Ono but recorded by other artists. That number, plus the back-and-forth Lennon/Ono song exchange on the **Milk And Honey** package, essentially took care of the unreleased tracks from 1980, as follows:

On **Milk And Honey**: *I'm Stepping Out* (John), *Sleepless Night* (Yoko), *I Don't Wanna Face It* (John), *Don't Be Scared* (Yoko), *Nobody Told Me* (John), *O'Sanity* (Yoko), *Borrowed Time* (John), *Your Hands* (Yoko), *(Forgive Me) My Little Flower Princess* (John), *Let Me Count The Ways* (Yoko), *Grow Old With Me* (John), *You're The One* (Yoko in 1983).

There were a few other odd Lennon recordings, beginning with *What's The News Maryjane*, done back in 1968 by John, Yoko, and George Harrison and originally slated for **The Beatles** double album. Among the live recordings that did not appear on disc, there were a few rock oldies such as *Hound Dog* and *Memphis, Tennessee*, but not any otherwise unavailable Lennon originals. There was also a Lennon rehearsal version of *I'm The Greatest* (see page 391) and, no doubt, demo versions of a few other songs given to other artists such as *Rock And Roll People* (for Johnny Winter), *God Save Us* (for the Elastic Oz Band) and *Mucho Mungo* (for Harry Nilsson).

In the book *Loving John*, May Pang described two Lennon demo sessions for Ringo, one involving *Goodnight Vienna* and the other the oldie *Only You* that Ringo put on the same album. That book also presented the details behind two unreleased songs from a pair of exceptional studio sessions: a Lennon produced cover version of *Too*

Many Cooks sung by Mick Jagger, and a 1974 late night superstar recording of the oldie *The Midnight Special*, with a musical line-up of John Lennon, Paul McCartney, Stevie Wonder, Linda McCartney, Jesse Ed Davis, Danny Kortchmar, Harry Nilsson, and May Pang (on tambourine).

Still, it seems clear that, unlike Paul McCartney, Lennon left virtually no finished, original studio solo work behind for future release. At best, then, we could see one catch-all disc, using the **Rock'n'Roll** outtakes as the anchor.

George Harrison and Ringo Starr have also not been as prolific as Paul McCartney, though through 1983 they did both have a few leftovers. When Harrison's original version of **Somewhere In England** was rejected in 1980, that put four finished songs on the shelf: *Flying Hour, Lay His Head, Sat Singing*, and *Tears Of The World*. He also never released *The Pirate Song*, an original composition with Eric Idle that he performed on Idle's *Rutland Weekend Television* series in Britain back in 1975.

Ringo had extra tracks from the sessions for his first two solo albums: *Autumn Leaves* and *I'll Be Looking At The Moon* from **Sentimental Journey** and an extended *Nashville Jam* from **Beaucoups Of Blues**. Then he had some compositions left from the 1976 **Roto-gravure** era: *All Right, It's Hard To Be Lovers*, and *Party*. A few years later, he also discarded four tracks produced by Russ Ballard in 1978, the year **Bad Boy** was released. He also had a live version of *Act Naturally* performed for the concert segment of his 1978 *Ringo* special, but not used. Finally, Ringo even dropped the initial title cut (*Can't Fight Lightning*) to his 1981 **Stop And Smell The Roses** disc, along with *Life Begins At Forty*, a Lennon original that probably seemed inappropriate to use after his death.

Otherwise, George and Ringo have generally used most of the finished material they've recorded. Taken together, though, there might be enough between them for one solid combined outtakes package.

Of course, by 1983, some of the original *commercial* solo releases had become hard-to-find collector's items in their own right. Outtakes aside, someone in search of a complete collection of recordings from John, Paul, George, and Ringo would have quite a task anyway. But, that's another topic for another time.

Audiophiles

During the first wave of Beatlemania in the 1960s, newly purchased singles and albums often ended up being played on low-quality "hi-fi" sets with limited reproduction range and sensitivity. As systems grew more sophisticated, American fans began to notice that Beatles albums imported from England performed far better than their domestic counterparts. The sound seemed clearer, there were more cuts, and sometimes even more elaborate artwork. By the late 1960s, a British Beatles collection had become the standard collecting status symbol among American fans.

By the mid-1970s, the horizons of collecting had expanded into other parts of the world, especially into Japan. There, record companies not only used extremely high quality vinyl but also added lyric sheets and even gatefold covers to packages that lacked both in their British or American releases. A number of fans eagerly snapped up imported copies of these records as the new "preferred" pressings, despite the relatively high prices (sometimes twice the cost of a Capitol album).

During the late 1970s, a domestic specialty label, Mobile Fidelity Sound Lab, added still another plateau to the quest for state-of-the-art sound by including the Beatles in its "Original Master Recordings" series. These records were touted as a first generation transfer from the original stereo master tapes onto a special vinyl compound disc designed to present clean, clear sound that eliminated as much surface noise and tape hiss as possible. To protect the discs themselves from damage, each one was packaged in heavy cardboard with a special anti-static rice paper inner sleeve.

Abbey Road, Magical Mystery Tour, and **The Beatles** (The White Album) each received this treatment. In 1982, Mobile Fidelity put together its equivalent to the boxed **Beatles Collection** from EMI by gathering thirteen Beatles album packages into an Original Masters set dubbed **The Collection**. The list price? $350.00.

At the same time, the company also selected **Sgt. Pepper** for its limited edition *"beyond* the state-of-the-art" UHQR series. A super high quality pressing of **Sgt. Pepper** was packaged in a thick library-type blue presentation box with a double layer of impact-protective foam, a rice paper inner sleeve, and a cardboard jacket. The price? About $50.

After years of seeing inflated prices attached to records due to such spurious features as a "rare" label design or a simple misprint, it was refreshing to find the emphasis shift to the quality of the package and the reproduction of the music. These were records meant to be played and enjoyed over and over again by discriminating audiophiles.

Still, before someone takes the inevitable next step and launches a super-superior-ultra-fine-highest-quality series, we'd like to deal with an obvious question: Are these for everybody?

Even the companies putting together audiophile packages would immediately answer "No." After all, Mobile Fidelity pressed only about 25,000 copies of **The Collection** for distribution worldwide. Obviously, this was not meant to replace every copy of the millions of standard Beatles albums already sold.

The key to deciding whether or not to purchase audiophile pressings is simple: How closely, carefully, and often do you listen to your Beatles records — and on what sort of equipment?

If you have a basic compact stereo unit (nothing flashy, just dependable) there is no point in acquiring records that may run more than your system itself cost! Any domestic releases will do just fine.

If you have a good quality component system, it would probably be worthwhile to pick up the British albums — not only because of the pressings but also because those packages are how the songs were originally released.

If you have a state-of-the-art system, you've probably purchased all of the audiophile pressings already.

If you're still uncertain, the best strategy is to do a side-by-side comparison on a Beatles album you are particularly familiar with, listening to both the standard pressing and an audiophile version. Let your ears decide.

Listener's Reference Guide

Japanese records:

There is a Japanese equivalent to virtually every British and American Beatles package, even **The Beatles Story** documentary set. We've found the 66000 series used in the boxed **Beatles Collection** to be the best of the Japanese pressings.

Mobile Fidelity Original Master Recordings:

Abbey Road (1-023)
Magical Mystery Tour (1-047)
   Cassette Tape (C-047)
The Beatles (The White Album) (2-072)

The Beatles: The Collection (Boxed Set)
1. **Please Please Me** (1-101)
2. **With The Beatles** (1-102)
3. **A Hard Day's Night** (1-103)
4. **Beatles For Sale** (1-104)
5. **Help!** (1-105)
6. **Rubber Soul** (1-106)
7. **Revolver** (1-107)
8. **Sgt. Pepper** (1-100)
9. **The Beatles** (2-072) (A/B)
10. **The Beatles** (2-072) (C/D)
11. **Yellow Submarine** (1-108)
12. **Abbey Road** (1-023)
13. **Let It Be** (1-109)
14. **Magical Mystery Tour** (1-047)

The sleeve for each disc in **The Collection** boxed set featured a photo of the original EMI master tape box. Some of the individual discs from the boxed set not previously issued were slated for separate release, but not in the special sleeves.

Like the original EMI **Beatles Collection** package, Mobile Fidelity's **The Collection** was not a complete set of all the songs released by the Beatles. (Many were not included on the original British albums.) Mobile Fidelity's set omitted the following twenty-five songs: *Bad Boy, The Ballad Of John And Yoko, Day Tripper, Don't Let Me Down, From Me To You, Hey Jude, I Call Your Name, I Feel Fine, I Want To Hold Your Hand, I'll Get You, I'm Down, The Inner Light, Lady Madonna, Matchbox, Old Brown Shoe, Paperback Writer, Rain, She Loves You, She's A Woman, Slow Down, Thank You Girl, This Boy, We Can Work It Out, Yes It Is, You Know My Name (Look Up The Number),* plus the German language versions of *I Want To Hold Your Hand* and *She Loves You,* the alternate version of *Across The Universe,* and the single versions of *Get Back, Let It Be,* and *Revolution.*

There was also an album size hardcover photo book included in the package. This contained pictures of the original covers for each of the albums.

Mobile Fidelity UHQR Recordings:

Sgt. Pepper's Lonely Hearts Club Band 1--100

Columbia Records Half-Speed Mastered Series:

Band On The Run (Paul McCartney and Wings) Columbia HC-46482

Nautilus Super Disc:

Double Fantasy (John Lennon and Yoko Ono) Nautilus/Geffen NR-47

Notes:
Though the Japanese often add material such as lyric sheets to their album packages, this is not the case with every audiophile set. The initial Mobile Fidelity release of **Magical Mystery Tour**, for instance, did not include the twenty-four page program booklet (despite a store price of more than $15). So even after purchasing an audiophile pressing of an album, you might still need to pick up a regular copy of the package in order to get any special inserts such as posters or lyric sheets.

Sometimes flaws slip by in even the best packages. For instance, the Mobile Fidelity "original stereo master recording" of **Magical Mystery Tour** was first issued with several tracks in *mono*. This occurred because the master tape used by Mobile Fidelity apparently did not contain stereo versions of the singles on side two. Eventually the company dug out some master tapes from EMI in Germany that had the songs in stereo and used that version for a special cassette package in 1982.

If you are looking primarily for variations in mixing and a more lively sound to your discs, sample some of the monophonic issuings as well as the audiophile sets. It may turn out that what you really want in available on the less expensive mono packages.

You may discover that the most impressive aspect of an audiophile pressing is not what you hear but what you don't hear. After all, every pressing contains the same basic information. However, sometimes on a standard pressing the tape hiss, pops, clicks, and other surface noise make it a bit hard to hear every sound. Oddly, this had led to one unusual criticism of the ever-improving audiophile packages (especially on some of the compact digital laser discs): they sometimes expose studio noise and recording flaws not previously apparent. Still, that might be an acceptable trade-off if we can tell at last, once and for all, whether it's "I buried Paul," "cranberry sauce," or "I'm very bored."

Digital Notes

Will digital "laser discs" replace even the best vinyl pressings? Perhaps. After all, the sound quality of a digital recording played over a digital system is quite impressive. Beyond that, the compact digital discs themselves resist scratching, warping, and (if you believe some promotions) even a heavy footstomp. They can be played thousands of times without suffering any loss in quality.

However, there is one flaw.

Presently, material that was not originally recorded and mixed using the digital process has to be adapted for the new system. It's almost as if we were back in the days of monophonic to stereophonic to duophonic to quadrophonic. Sometimes the changeover is not all that impressive.

None of the records turned out by the Beatles as a group were done using the digital process. The same holds true of most of the solo efforts before 1980. So shop carefully as any and all of these records are issued in this new form, as they inevitably will be. If you like what you hear, by all means buy it. But if not, trust your ears and take a pass.

Of course, if you think the digital process is awful and has no chance of catching on, as a collector you should therefore pick up *all* of the digital releases that you can. After all, how many copies of the quadrophonic **Imagine** album or the **Band On The Run** quad tape have you seen lately?

Compact Digital Discs:

Band On The Run by Paul McCartney
(US) Columbia CK 36482
Tug Of War by Paul McCartney
(Japan) EMI/Odeon/Toshiba CP 35-3001
(US) Columbia CK 37462
Pipes Of Peace by Paul McCartney
(US) Columbia CK 39194
(UK) Parlophone CDP 7460182
Abbey Road by The Beatles
(Japan) EMI/Odeon/Toshiba CP 35-3016

Final Note:

If you have the money, the interest, and the high quality sound system at your disposal, by all means purchase the various audiophile packages. But don't lose sight of the fact that eventually you will reach a point at which you have to admit that there is just not any more to be squeezed out of the recordings. You have heard all there is to hear. This is especially true of some of those early discs such as *Love Me Do*, which were very simple songs that were more-than-adequately captured on their original British pressings. After all, those basic Beatles tracks first made their mark without any super-enhancement or audiophile clean-up. They became worldwide smashes by reaching millions of people over crackling car radios and worn-out phonograph needles. That magic is still there on every available package.

Monophonics

The Beatles released both stereophonic and monophonic versions of all their albums in Britain through 1969's **Yellow Submarine** soundtrack. Unlike American packages of mono to stereo (or stereo to mono) which often just "rechanneled" the existing tracks into the other format, British Beatles albums were separately mixed for both mono and stereo. As a result, occasional quirks turned up, most noticeably on the monophonic packages for **The Beatles** (The White Album) and **Sgt. Pepper**. Beyond that, there was a different feel to some tracks, especially on the early albums, which seemed a bit louder and livelier carrying the same musical information through both channels.

Though the monophonic albums were allegedly available ever since their original issuings, during the 1970s they were all but impossible to find. As a result, monophonic packages of **The Beatles** and **Sgt. Pepper** became highly sought items among collectors. Capitol Records even included selections from the monophonic version of **The Beatles** on its 1980 **Rarities** album.

In 1981, EMI officially rereleased ten Beatles albums in monophonic form and, the following year, gathered the discs together into a monophonic equivalent to the original boxed **Beatles Collection**, dubbed **The Beatles Mono Collection**. This was a limited edition package (only 1,000 of the black boxes were offered) designed to appeal to collectors eager to purchase the entire set.

Are the monophonics worth a separate purchase? Though there are indeed minor mixing differences scattered throughout the mono and stereo editions, they would hardly justify purchasing complete sets of both. Yet, for Beatles fans tempted by the exotic high quality Japanese or audiophile pressings of the albums, the monophonics make just as much sense to own — perhaps even more. After all, the monophonic releases originally came out right alongside the stereophonic copies and, to many first generation British fans, were actually their personal preference.

421

A sampling of mono releases is probably the best route to take today, purchasing one or two of the early albums (especially effective in mono) plus **Sgt. Pepper** and **The Beatles** (collector favorites). You might even want to cover two collecting worlds at once by including some Japanese pressings in the sampling of monophonics. (In 1982 Japan issued its own equivalents to the British monophonic discs, using colored vinyl and including lyric sheets.)

Title	British Number (Parlophone/Apple†)	Japanese Number (Odeon/EMI/Toshiba/ Apple†)
*Please Please Me	PMC 1202	EAS-70130
*With The Beatles	PMC 1206	EAS-70131
*A Hard Day's Night	PMC 1230	EAS-70132
*Beatles For Sale	PMC 1240	EAS-70133
*Help!	PMC 1255	EAS-70134
*Rubber Soul	PMC 1267	EAS-70135
*Revolver	PMC 7009	EAS-70136
A Collection Of Beatles Oldies	PMC 7016	———————
*Sgt. Pepper	PMC 7029	EAS-70137
*The Beatles (The White Album)	PMC 7067/8†	EAS-67157/58†
*Yellow Submarine	PMC 7070†	EAS-70138†
Rarities (see notes)	PCM 1001	----------------

*Indicates a title reissued in 1981 and subsequently included in the British boxed set below:

The Beatles Mono Collection   Parlophone BM 1

Notes:

Twelve of the seventeen cuts on **Rarities** were in mono.

All of the original British EPs and every original British single track (except *Get Back, Don't Let Me Down, Something, Come Together*, and *Let It Be*) were issued in monophonic. See Entries 693 and 734 for lists of the British EPs and singles.

In Japan there were also three special monophonic compilation albums issued in addition to the ten packages listed above. The contents of these were as follows:

MEET THE BEATLES (Japan) Apple EAS-70100 (LP)

side one

I Want To Hold Your Hand
She Loves You
From Me To You
Twist And Shout
Love Me Do
Baby It's You
Don't Bother Me

side two

Please Please Me
I Saw Her Standing There
P.S. I Love You
Little Child
All My Loving
Hold Me Tight
Please Mr. Postman

THE BEATLES' SECOND ALBUM (No. 2) (Japan) Apple EAS-70101 (LP)

side one

Can't Buy Me Love
Do You Want To Know A Secret
Thank You Girl
A Taste Of Honey
It Won't Be Long
I Wanna Be Your Man
There's A Place

side two

Roll Over Beethoven
Misery
Boys
Devil In Her Heart
Not A Second Time
Money (That's What I Want)
Till There Was You

BEATLES No. 5 (Japan) Apple EAS-70102 (LP)

side one

Long Tall Sally
Sie Liebt Dich
Anna (Go To Him)
Matchbox
You Really Got A Hold On Me
She's A Woman
Ask Me Why

side two

I Feel Fine
Komm, Gib Mir Deine Hand
Chains
Slow Down
All I've Got To Do
I Call Your Name
This Boy

Sgt. Pepper's Lonely
Hearts Club Band

Capitol SEAX 11840
(picture disc LP)

McCartney — A Sample From
"Tug Of War" — April 1982

Columbia AS 1444
(12-inch promo)

Stamp Collecting

Some records are purchased to be seen, not heard. These include such items as discs pressed on brightly colored vinyl, picture discs, cassette singles, and exotic foreign releases. In most cases, the sound quality of the music is absolutely irrelevant because the records will never be played. Rather, they will be accumulated for their visual appeal, much like a collection of stamps.

Though such an approach to record collecting has obvious limitations (it virtually ignores the whole point of records, the music), a handful of these releases can serve as amusing conversation pieces.

****

Picture Discs and Colored Vinyl

Picture discs and records pressed on colored vinyl have been around for decades, especially on packages aimed at young children. During the 1970s, small independent record companies as well as bootleg manufacturers embraced both techniques as ways to make their product stand out as more desirable, especially to collectors. Major record companies followed, first with promotional items aimed at record stores and radio stations. For instance, Ringo Starr's *Heart On My Sleeve* turned up on a various artists picture disc sampler album issued to radio stations in 1978 (see page 32). Then came material touted directly to the general public.

This reached a peak in the late summer of 1978 when Capitol released the first authorized Beatles picture disc, **Sgt. Pepper's Lonely Hearts Club Band,** to tie in with the publicity surrounding the Bee Gees/Peter Frampton *Sgt. Pepper* film. The company announced a pressing of 150,000 records to be allocated throughout the country. In New York City, these were in such demand that copies could be sold *above* the $15.98 list price. A sign at a King Karol record store there read: "Originally issued at $15.98 list. Our price $24.95. While they last." Reportedly, more than one hundred copies were sold at that price.

Along with the **Sgt. Pepper** picture disc, Capitol also released colored vinyl editions of three sets that had long before been given "color nicknames" by fans, who referred to them by the album jacket colors: the "white" album for **The Beatles**, the "red" album for **The Beatles 1962--1966**, and the "blue" album for **The Beatles 1967--1970**. These were pressed on white, red, and blue vinyl respectively. As with the **Sgt. Pepper** picture disc, there were about 150,000 copies made and they each carried a list price of $15.98. Boosted by these new packages and the *Sgt. Pepper* film publicity, all four albums returned to *Billboard*'s charts, with **The Beatles** and **The Beatles 1967--1970** cracking the Hot 100 and **Sgt. Pepper** reaching the top twenty.

The British **Sgt. Pepper** picture disc featured a different cover photo cropping from the U.S. version, but EMI ran into some pressing delays so this one did not come out until January 1979. By then, interest in the novelty was already waning, especially in the U.S. There, Capitol's follow-up **Abbey Road** and **Band On The Run** picture discs failed to do as well as **Sgt. Pepper**. The company did not issue any other Beatles-related picture discs.

There were several reasons for this quick fade in popularity. As with any fad, there had been too many such items dumped at one time on the market. It seemed as if *everybody* had a picture disc out or in the works: Peter Frampton, Linda Ronstadt, Barry Manilow, . . . even Groucho Marx! Beyond that, record buyers had quickly discovered that the warning printed on the **Sgt. Pepper** package was quite accurate: "Sound quality may not be comparable to conventional edition." Records with low quality sound and twice the list price of a standard pressing soon lost their appeal to the general public. Picture discs returned to the realm of special promotion aimed at radio stations and ardent collectors, with far more limited pressings.

In 1982, EMI included carefully limited quantities of picture disc singles as part of its twentieth anniversary celebration of the Beatles. As a special promotion, the company began to formally reissue each single as near to the anniversary of the original release date as possible, beginning with *Love Me Do*. Each one was offered in either a standard black vinyl pressing with a new picture sleeve or as a picture disc incorporating the new sleeve picture. *Love Me Do* made the British top five, but subsequent rereleases did not do as well. By the end of 1983 it was obvious that the picture disc/rerelease promotion would not make it through all twenty-two original British singles (up to *Let It Be*).

Colored vinyl was never as big a deal as picture discs, so it did not have a dramatic fade. Instead, record companies continued to use the technique occasionally for commercial releases and, more frequently, on special promotions. In 1982 Capitol issued some gold vinyl copies of **Reel Music** for radio station giveaways, and then extended the promotion to the retail level with red, blue, and white flexi-disc "soundsheets" to tie-in with the "red," "blue," and "white" albums. These were used as record store giveaways, offering two songs from the appropriate color album on the disc and a complete list of available Capitol Beatles albums on the cardboard backing sheet.

Later in 1982, Columbia Records sent out a twelve-inch white vinyl promotional disc, **McCartney — A Sample From "Tug Of War"** April, **1982**, containing *Ebony And Ivory* b/w *Ballroom Dancing* and *The Pound Is Sinking*. Serving as a sneak preview teaser to the **Tug Of War** album (which soon followed), the package was particularly effective in using the black and white motif. The label had a black background with white lettering (to contrast with the white vinyl) and the front cover featured a striking black and white photo of McCartney dressed as he was for the *Ebony And Ivory* promotional film with Stevie Wonder.

COMMERCIALLY RELEASED PICTURE DISCS BY THE BEATLES

Sgt. Pepper's Lonely Hearts Club Band
(US)   Capitol SEAX 11840 (August 21, 1978)
(UK)   Parlophone PHO 7027 (January 15, 1979)

Abbey Road
(US)   Capitol SEAX 11900 (December 1, 1978)

Band On The Run by Paul McCartney and Wings
(US)   Capitol SEAX 11901 (December 1, 1978)

Faster/Your Love Is Forever by George Harrison
(UK)   Dark Horse K 17423P (July 13, 1979) (Entry 627)

Love Me Do/P.S. I Love You
(UK)   Parlophone RP 4949 (October 4, 1982)

Please Please Me/Ask Me Why
(UK)   Parlophone RP 4983 (January 10, 1983)

From Me To You/Thank You Girl
(UK)   Parlophone RP 5015 (April 11, 1983)

Love Me Do   Parlophone RP 4949
(picture disc 45)

Please Please Me   Parlophone RP 4983
(picture disc 45)

From Me To You   Parlophone RP 5015
(picture disc 45)

She Loves You   Parlophone RP 5055
(picture disc 45)

She Loves You/I'll Get You
(UK)   Parlophone RP 5055 (August 22, 1983)

I Want To Hold Your Hand/This Boy
(UK)   Parlophone RP 5084 (November 14, 1983)

First Movement by The Beatles Featuring Tony Sheridan
(UK)   Audiofidelity PXS 339P (October 10, 1983)

COMMERCIALLY RELEASED COLORED VINYL DISCS BY THE BEATLES

Happy Christmas/Listen The Snow Is Falling by John Lennon and Yoko Ono
      (Green)
(US)   Apple 1842 (December 1, 1971) (Entry 303)
(UK)   Apple R 5970 (November 24, 1972) (Entry 303)

The Beatles (White)
(US)   Capitol SEBX 11841 (August 21, 1978)
(UK)   Apple PCS 7067/8 (September 29, 1978)

The Beatles 1962--1966 (Red)
(US)   Capitol SEBX 11842 (August 21, 1978)
(UK)   Apple PCSPR 717 (September 29, 1978)

The Beatles 1967--1970 (Blue)
(US)   Capitol SEBX 11843 (August 21, 1978)
(UK)   Apple PCSPB 718 (September 29, 1978)

Seaside Woman/B-Side To Seaside by Suzy and the Red Stripes (Yellow)
(UK)   A&M AMSP 7461 (August 10, 1979) (Entry 627a) (See page 293)

Eva-Tone Soundsheet 420826-CS (April 1982) (Red)
      Two songs from **The Beatles 1962--1966** on side one
      All My Loving and *You've Got To Hide Your Love Away*

Eva-Tone Soundsheet 420827-CS (April 1982) (Blue)
      Two songs from **The Beatles 1967--1970** on side one
      Magical Mystery Tour and *Here Comes The Sun*

Eva-Tone Soundsheet 420828-CS (April 1982) (White)
      Two songs from **The Beatles** on side one
      Rocky Raccoon and *Why Don't We Do It In The Road?*

During the colored vinyl rush of 1978 and 1979 in the U.S., special pressings from other countries often turned up in the import bins, with the Canadian **Love Songs** (gold vinyl) and **Sgt. Pepper** (marble vinyl) the most common. There were also British export versions of **Magical Mystery Tour** (gold vinyl), **Abbey Road** (green vinyl) and **Let It Be** (white vinyl), as well as a gold vinyl version of the German **Beatles Greatest**.

For true completists, there were also Beatles-related discs such as Michael Jackson's **Thriller** picture disc and *The Girl Is Mine* (available on red vinyl and as a picture disc). Others included **Along The Red Ledge** by Daryl Hall and John Oates (on red vinyl), **Stage** by David Bowie (on yellow vinyl), and (our favorite) *Ging Gang Goolie* by Dirk and Stig (on khaki vinyl).

****

Cassette Singles

Ever since cassettes were introduced to the mass market, record companies have attempted to package a cassette equivalent to a single, but with little success. Listeners simply did not want to bother with such short length tapes. In 1981, several record companies in Britain tried again, skirting the time problem by promoting cassette singles as special collector's items, like colored vinyl and picture discs, meant to be looked at, not played.

There were four Beatles-related singles issued in this form.

Woman/Beautiful Boys by John Lennon and Yoko Ono
(UK)   Geffen K 79195M (January 16, 1981)

Walking On Thin Ice/It Happened/Hard Times Are Over by Yoko Ono
(UK)   Geffen K 79202M (February 20, 1981)

Watching The Wheels/I'm Your Angel by John Lennon and Yoko Ono
(UK)   Geffen K 79207M (March 27, 1981)

All Those Years Ago/Writing's On The Wall by George Harrison
(UK)   Dark Horse K 17807M (May 15, 1981)

This gimmick packaging faded soon thereafter.

A far more popular cassette innovation was the twofer/double series, which offered two albums worth of material on one tape. George Harrison's **Thirty Three & 1/3** and **George Harrison** albums were released in this form in July 1981 (Warner Bros. Dark Horse K 466101). Elton John offered an even better deal in May 1981,

430

combining his two live albums (**Here And There** and **17/11/70**) onto one cassette, with an added bonus: the three songs performed live in 1974 with John Lennon. Thus, *Whatever Gets You Thru The Night, Lucy In The Sky With Diamonds*, and *I Saw Her Standing There* turned up on this cassette package (DJM TWO 419) even though they had not been included on the original **Here And There** album from that 1974 tour.

****

Russian and Polish Pressings

Few items can match the packaging obscurity of Beatles music as officially released in Poland and Russia.

Back in the mid-1970s, the U.S.S.R. put out a half dozen seven-inch EPs, each containing three or four songs by either the Beatles or Paul McCartney. None of the sleeves for these had any photos of the group. Instead, the records came in Melodiya's standard generic sleeves that could be used with any disc. A later issuing of the **Band On The Run** album improved the situation a bit (Paul, Linda, and Denny Laine appeared on the cover), though, oddly, the title cut was replaced with *Silly Love Songs*.

Poland, on the other hand, specialized in "postcard" records, with vinyl pressed onto rectangular pieces of cardboard. As with the Russian discs, there were no photos of the actual performers on these packages. Instead, there were pictures of Polish tourist sights such as castles or the countryside. Songs released in 1981 in this format included three Lennon solo recordings from **Double Fantasy** and one track by Paul McCartney.

RUSSIAN MELODIYA RELEASES

C62-05613/05614 by The Beatles

side one	side two
Golden Slumbers	*Here Comes The Sun*
Carry That Weight	*Sun King*

M62-35691/35692 by The Beatles

side one	side two
Can't Buy Me Love	*Lady Madonna*
Maxwell's Silver Hammer	*I Should Have Known Better*

M62-35903/35904 by The Beatles

side one	side two
When I'm Sixty-Four	*With A Little Help From My Friends*
Lovely Rita	*Penny Lane*

431

M62-36701/36702 by Paul and Linda McCartney

side one
Heart Of The Country
Ram On

side two
Dear Boy
Eat At Home

M62-36715/36716 by The Beatles

side one
Across The Universe
I Me Mine

side two
Let It Be

M62-38133/38134 by The Beatles

side one
Octopus's Garden
Something

side two
Come Together

Band On The Run by Paul McCartney and Wings
(LP)   Melodiya ROCT 5289-73

POLISH POSTCARD RELEASES 1981

Tonpress R-1054
Coming Up by Paul McCartney

Tonpress R-1124
(Just Like) Starting Over by John Lennon

Tonpress R-1151
Woman by John Lennon

Tonpress R-1158
Watching The Wheels by John Lennon

The sound quality on both the Russian discs and the Polish postcards was awful. In fact, this seems an appropriate spot to wrap up the discussion of stamp-like collectibles. After all, where can you go after records that feature a dull label design, low-quality pressings, and no Beatles-related artwork? What possible value could they have?

Well . . . a 1982 survey of the "top 1000 rare records" published in the British *Record Collector* fan magazine placed a premium on something even worse: Beatles tracks released in India as scratchy ten-inch 78 rpm records. These were valued at £110 ($170) each — ten times the price of a pristine audiophile pressing of **Abbey Road**.

This really is an area of collecting best appreciated by philatelists.

New Numbers

In the numbered chronological discography (Entries 1--767) appearing in *All Together Now, The Beatles Again*, and this volume, we have listed the catalog numbers assigned to each record at the time of its initial release. Some of these numbers have been changed over the years, usually as part of a general reorganization by the respective record companies or a switch in record labels. Because the music on the records themselves remained unchanged, we have always considered such revised number assignments to be similar to a label or design variation. Therefore, none of these discs with new catalog numbers have been treated as separate entries in the discography.

Nonetheless, there have been enough changes that we felt they should be noted somewhere — if only to make special ordering from your local record store less difficult. We have divided these lists of American and British discs into three sections: records by the Beatles, solo releases, and Beatles-related discs. They are listed in chronological order (first for America, then for Britain) and all are keyed by the entry numbers in the main discography sections of *All Together Now, The Beatles Again*, and *The End of the Beatles*.

The revised catalog numbers are those in effect as of 1984. We have *not* included any other numbers assigned in the years between the initial release and these listings.

By The Beatles

U.S. Albums and Singles

All the U.S. Beatles singles and albums and all the solo releases once issued on Apple have been reissued with a standard Capitol Records label. In the process, any special one-time custom label designs were dropped (for example, the "star" label for the **Ringo** album and associated singles). Generally, posters, booklets, and other special inserts have also been eliminated.

Nonetheless, most of these records retained the same catalog number and prefix from the original release. This listing only includes packages given completely new numbers in the process.

U.S. Albums

(Entry)	New Number	(Previous Number)	Title
(75)	Capitol SW 11921	(United Artists UAS 6366)	**A Hard Day's Night**
(248)	Capitol SW 11922	(Apple/UA AR 34001)	**Let It Be**

Note: The **Rock'n'Roll Music** two-record set (Entry 515, Capitol SKBO 11537) was replaced by two individual packages that coupled the sides in a different way from the original release. These have been treated as new discs. See Entries 653 and 654.

U.S. Singles

(Entry)	New Capitol Number	(Previous Capitol /Apple Number)	Title
(33)	6278	(5112)	*I Want To Hold Your Hand/I Saw Her Standing There*
(50)	6279	(5150)	*Can't Buy Me Love/You Can't Do That*
(80)	6281	(5222)	*A Hard Day's Night/I Should Have Known Better*
(82)	6282	(5234)	*I'll Cry Instead/I'm Happy Just To Dance With You*
(83)	6283	(5235)	*And I Love Her/If I Fell*
(93)	6284	(5255)	*Matchbox/Slow Down*
(107)	6286	(5327)	*I Feel Fine/She's A Woman*

U.S. Singles continued . . .

(Entry)	New Capitol Number	(Previous Capitol /Apple Number)	Title
(114)	6287	(5371)	*Eight Days A Week/I Don't Want To Spoil The Party*
(117)	6288	(5407)	*Ticket To Ride/Yes It Is*
(121)	6290	(5476)	*Help/I'm Down*
(126)	6291	(5498)	*Yesterday/Act Naturally*
(135)	6293	(5555)	*We Can Work It Out/Day Tripper*
(142)	6294	(5587)	*Nowhere Man/What Goes On*
(145)	6296	(5651)	*Paperback Writer/Rain*
(151)	6297	(5715)	*Eleanor Rigby/Yellow Submarine*
(165)	6299	(5810)	*Penny Lane/Strawberry Fields Forever*
(169)	6300	(5964)	*All You Need Is Love/Baby You're A Rich Man*

By The Beatles

U.K. Albums

In the U.K. nearly all of the Beatles singles and albums still in print have retained their original catalog number and label design. Only records shifted to a budget label have received new numbers.

U.K. Albums

(Entry)	New Number	(Previous Number)	Title
(74)	Contour CN 2007	(Polydor 236 201)	The Beatles Featuring Tony Sheridan (was The Beatles First)
(160)	Fame FA 4130811	(Parlophone PCS 7016)	A Collection Of Beatles Oldies
(713)	Breakaway BWY 72	(Audiofidelity AFELP 1047)	The Audition Tapes (was The Complete Silver Beatles)

Note: As in the U.S., the **Rock'n'Roll Music** two-record set (Entry 515, Parlophone PCSP 719) was replaced by two individual packages that coupled the sides in a different way from the original release. These have been treated as new discs. See Entries 653 and 654.

Solo Releases

U.S. Albums and Singles

By John Lennon

(Entry)	New Capitol Number	(Previous Capitol /Apple Number)	Title
(230)	ST 12239	(SW 3362)	**Live Peace In Toronto**
(367)	SN 16068	(SW 3414)	**Mind Games**
(432)	SN 16069	(SK 3419)	**Rock'n'Roll**

By Paul McCartney (Albums and Single)

(Entry)	New Columbia/ *United Artists Number	(Previous Capitol /Apple, *United Artists, †Columbia Number)	Title
(246)	PC 36478	(STAO 3363)	**McCartney**
(282)	JC 36479	(SMAS 3375)	**Ram**
(305)	PC 36480	(SW 3386)	**Wild Life**
(349)	PC 36481	(SMAL 3409)	**Red Rose Speedway**
(354)	*LMAS 100	*(LA 100-G)	**Live And Let Die**
(372)	JC 36482	(SO 3415)	**Band On The Run**
(447)	PC 36801	(SMAS 11419)	**Venus And Mars**
(508)	PC 37409	(SW 11525)	**Wings At The Speed Of Sound**
(509)	18-02171	(4256)	*Silly Love Songs/Cook Of The House*
(633)	38-04127	†(1-11162)	*Wonderful Christmastime/Rudolph The Red-Nosed Reggae*

By George Harrison

(Entry)	New Capitol Number	(Previous Capitol /Apple Number)	Title
(352)	SN 16216	(SMAS 3410)	**Living In The Material World**
(422)	SN 16055	(SMAS 3418)	**Dark Horse**
(455)	SN 16217	(SW 3420)	**Extra Texture**

By Ringo Starr

(Entry)	New Capitol Number	(Previous Capitol /Apple Number)	Title
(245)	SN 16218	(SW 3365)	**Sentimental Journey**
(257)	SN 16235	(SMAS 3368)	**Beaucoups Of Blues**
(366)	SN 16114	(SWAL 3413)	**Ringo**
(415)	SN 16219	(SW 3417)	**Goodnight Vienna**
(466)	SN 16236	(SW 3422)	**Blast From Your Past**

Solo Releases

U.K. Albums

Among the solo releases from EMI in Britain, only a handful still carry the Apple label. Otherwise, most have shifted to a standard Parlophone label with the catalog numbers remaining the same. As with the group efforts, only records moved to a budget label have received new numbers.

A special note regarding Paul McCartney's releases: Unless there is a custom-design label for a particular package, McCartney's British records generally carry the Parlophone label. Technically, though, it might be more accurate to describe them as EMI/MPL releases that happen to use the Parlophone label.

By John Lennon

(Entry)	New Music For Pleasure Number	(Previous Apple/ Parlophone Number)	Title
(367)	MFP 50509	(PCS 7165)	**Mind Games**
(432)	MFP 50522	(PCS 7169)	**Rock'n'Roll**

By Paul McCartney

(Entry)	New Fame Budget Number	(Previous Apple/ Parlophone Number)	Title
(246)	FA 413100-1	(PCS 7102)	**McCartney**
(305)	FA 413101-1	(PCS 7142)	**Wild Life**

By George Harrison

(Entry)	New Music For Pleasure Number	(Previous Apple/ Parlophone Number)	Title
(422)	MFP 50510	(PAS 10008)	**Dark Horse**
(533)	MFP 50523	(PAS 10011)	**The Best Of George Harrison**

By Ringo Starr

(Entry)	New Music For Pleasure Number	(Previous Apple/ Parlophone Number)	Title
(366)	MFP 50508	(PCTC 252)	**Ringo**
(466)	MFP 50524	(PCS 7170)	**Blast From Your Past**

Beatles-Related Discs

U.S. Albums and Singles

(Entry)	New Numbers	(Previous Numbers)	Title (Artist)
(54)	Imperial 047	(Imperial 66027)	*Bad To Me/(little children)* (Billy J. Kramer)
(170b)	Capitol N 16158	(Brother ST 9001)	**Smiley Smile** (Beach Boys)
(193a)	Epic 15-2296	(Epic 5010434)	*Atlantis/(to susan on the west coast waiting)* (Donovan)
(193b)	Epic PE 26439	(Epic BXN 26439)	**Greatest Hits** (Donovan)
(194)	RSO 1-3013	(Atco SD 7001)	**Goodbye** (Cream)
(212)	Capitol SN 16078	(Capitol SKAO 184)	**Brave New World** (Steve Miller)
(244)	MCA 682	(Shelter SHE 1001)	**Leon Russell** (Leon Russell)
(264)	Columbia F3M 38858	(Columbia M3X 30353)	**The Way It Was–The Sixties** (was **I Can Hear It Now**) (Walter Cronkite)
(301)	Pickwick SPC 3733	(A&M SP 3507)	**I Wrote A Simple Song** (Billy Preston)
(324)	A&M 3133	(A&M SP 4348)	**Wind Of Change** (P. Frampton)
(327)	RCA AYL 1-3812	(RCA LSP 4714)	**Son Of Schmilsson** (Harry Nilsson)
(356)	Warner Bros. BSK 3252	(Ode SP 77019)	**Los Cochinos** (Cheech & Chong)
(364)	Columbia PC 31721	(Columbia KC 31721)	**It's Like You Never Left** (Dave Mason)
(368)	Columbia C 32729	(Columbia KC 32729)	**On The Road To Freedom** (Alvin Lee & Mylon LeFevre)
(383)	UA/EMI LWB 321	(United Artists LA 321-H2)	**History Of The Bonzos** (Bonzo Dog Band)
(439)	RCA AQL 1-0998	(RCA APL 1-0998)	**Young Americans** (David Bowie)
(467)	Elektra 6E 109	(Elektra 7E 1048)	**Best Of** (Carly Simon)
(468)	Epic-Ode PE 34959	(Ode SP 77033)	**New York Connection** (Tom Scott)
(512)	RCA AQL 1-1732	(RCA APL 1-1732)	**Changesonebowie** (David Bowie)
(526)	MCA 37118	(Shelter SRL 52007)	**Best Of** (Leon Russell)
(556)	MCA 37031	(MCA 2271)	**One Of The Boys** (R. Daltrey)
(564a)	Capitol SN 16084	(Capitol Starline ST 2549)	**Best Of** (Peter & Gordon)
(565)	Capitol N 16077	(EMI M 11690)	**Hits Of Mersey Era 1** (Various)
(571)	MCA 5225	(MCA 3027)	**Greatest Hits II** (Elton John)
(600)	RCA AYL 1-4231	(RCA AFL 1-2804)	**Along The Red Ledge** (Daryl Hall and John Oates)

Beatles-Related Discs

U.K. Albums and Singles

(Entry) New Numbers   (Previous Numbers) Title (Artist)

(Entry)	New Numbers	(Previous Numbers)	Title (Artist)
(194)	RSO 2394 178	(Polydor 583 053)	**Goodbye** (Cream)
(215)	RSO 2394 131	(Polydor 583 060)	**Best Of** (Cream)
(244)	Island ISA 5005	(A&M AMLS 982)	**Leon Russell** (Leon Russell)
(245a)	Atlantic K 30030	(Atlantic 2400 013)	**On Tour** (Delaney & Bonnie)
(263)	Atlantic K 40341	(Atlantic 2401 004)	**Stephen Stills** (Stephen Stills)
(299)	ABC-USA AB 730	(Probe SPB 1041)	**In London** (B.B. King)
(319)	RSO 2671 107	(Polydor 2659 012)	**History Of** (Eric Clapton)
(324)	A&M AMLH 68099	(A&M AMLS 98099)	**Wind Of Change** (Peter Frampton)
(339)	Polydor 2657 014	(Ode 99001)	**Tommy** (London Symphony Orchestra & Guests)
(356)	Warner Bros. BSK 3252	(ODE 77019)	**Los Cochinos** (Cheech & Chong)
(358)	RSO SPELP 23	(Polydor 2394 116)	**Eric Clapton's Rainbow Concert** (Eric Clapton)
(439)	RCA LP 3009	(RCA RS 1006)	**Young Americans** (David Bowie)
(449)	RCA BOW 507	(RCA 2579)	*Fame/(right)* (David Bowie)
(547)	Fame FA 3030	(Capitol EST 24058)	**Best Of** (Steve Miller)
(562)	See For Miles CM 106	(EMI NUT 8)	**World Without Love** (was **Best Of**) (Peter & Gordon)
(563)	See For Miles CM 107	(EMI NUT 9)	**Listen** (was **Best Of**) (Billy J. Kramer)
(580)	Music For Pleasure MFP 50491	(EMI NUT 6)	**20 Golden Number Ones** (Various)
(598)	See For Miles CM 108	(EMI NUT 14)	**Got To Get You Into My Life** (was **Best Of**) (Cliff Bennett & the Rebel Rousers)
(634)	Polydor SPELP 30	(Polydor POLD 5029)	**Freeze Frame** (Kevin Godley & Lol Creme)
(662)	Breakaway BLY 110	(Scratch SCR 1 5001)	**In Flight** (was **Japanese Tears**) (Denny Laine)
(736)	Music For Pleasure MFP 41-5653-1	(Parlophone EMTV 38)	**Very Best Of** (Cilla Black)

Note: The 1971 **Radha Krsna Temple** album (Entry 283) was re-issued in 1977 on the Spiritual Sky label as **Goddess Of Fortune**. However, this was an unauthorized private pressing.

Margin Of Error

When told that the premise behind the main discography section in *All Together Now, The Beatles Again*, and *The End Of The Beatles* was to chronicle every appearance on disc by John Lennon, Paul McCartney, George Harrison, and Ringo Starr, Harry Nilsson chuckled and said, "You'll never do it. There are too many nobody knows about."

He's right.

Realizing that, we've always recognized that "sins of omission" are inevitable. Unfortunately, so are a few outright errors. This section deals with instances of both.

* * * * * * * * * *

Paul McCartney and Donovan

Back in 1966, when *Mellow Yellow* was near the top of the U.S. charts, a story made the Stateside rounds that Paul McCartney was on the disc, whispering "quite rightly." Even a casual listen proved that to be false because Donovan himself was quite clearly doing that voice. Unfortunately that dismissal stuck with us so strongly nine years later that in our research we completely by-passed a Donovan interview in *New Musical Express* in which he confirmed McCartney's presence *elsewhere* on the track. About two-thirds of the way through the song, Paul (who had dropped by the studio) unexpectedly sang out (in a nasal voice), "Mel-low Yel-low."

This very popular song appeared on singles issued in both Britain and America, on **Mellow Yellow** and **Donovan's Greatest Hits** albums in the U.S., and no doubt on a dozen other discs we haven't tracked down yet.

Paul McCartney and Mike (McGear) McCartney

In our main discography, we have included the instances in which Paul McCartney took an active part in his brother Michael's recording sessions (on his own or with Scaffold), acting as a producer,

443

performer, arranger, or writer. Two more cases have recently come to light: Paul's guitar work on the 1969 Scaffold single *Charity Bubbles* b/w *Goose* and his co-authorship with Mike and Roger McGough on the song *Bored As Butterscotch* on Mike's 1972 **Woman** album. (For the latter, Paul used the pseudonym "Friend.") See pages 294 and 297, as well as page 101 in *The Beatles Again*, for further discussions of Mike's career and his brother's occasional involvement in it.

Paul McCartney and the Beach Boys

Ace Beach Boys researcher Brad Elliott presented us with a six-page report outlining his views on the extent of Paul McCartney's involvement with the song *Vegetables*. Considering Brad's impressive Beach Boys credentials[1] and dedication to accuracy and detail, we have little trouble accepting his scenario: Paul McCartney was one of several people in the studio making munching sounds for the song, and that particular effects track probably survived to the final mix. That's it. McCartney did not sing on, nor co-produce, the track.

Thanks, Brad. For your next assignment, please convince Capitol and/or the Beach Boys to retrieve and release the legendary **Smile** album . . . .

Paul McCartney and Percy "Thrills" Thrillington

In *The Beatles Again* we cited a press release/news item that assured the public that Percy "Thrills" Thrillington was "for real." Well, he wasn't. We've since confirmed that there was no such person. Thus, the **Thrillington** album, which contained instrumental versions of songs from Paul McCartney's **Ram** album, was actually done under McCartney's direction. That, of course, made him the producer and places both the album and a British single of *Uncle Albert/Admiral Halsey* into the main chronological discography.

Apparently the "Thrillington" promotion was quite a put-on in Britain, so we don't feel too bad about this. After all, at the time EMI even sent out gifts and placed romantic personal ads – signed by Percy Thrillington.

Paul McCartney, Alma Cogan, and The Escorts

Back in *All Together Now* we identified Paul McCartney as the tambourine player on an obscure Alma Cogan single, *I Knew Right Away* (Entry 102). Since then we've dug up an original copy of the disc and discovered that there was no tambourine on the cut! Further checking revealed that McCartney had nothing to do with that single,

----

[1] Brad Elliott wrote *Surf's Up*, a superb Beach Boys discography, and also supervised work on Capitol's 1983 **Beach Boys Rarities** album (even slipping in a previously unreleased Beach Boys cover version of *With A Little Help From My Friends*).

though we have been unable to determine whether he might have appeared on a different track instead.

In *All Together Now* we also identified Paul as the tambourine player and producer on a 1966 British single by the Escorts, *From Head To Toe* b/w *Night Time* (Entry 158). The tambourine involvement on the A-side is undisputed. However, when contacted recently by British writer/researcher Spencer Leigh, the former members of the Escorts insisted that Paul did not produce the single, though they honestly did not remember who did. In any case, this limits McCartney's involvement to just the A-side, *From Head To Toe*.[1]

John Lennon and Yoko Ono and the Aspen Flexi-Disc
In 1969, a John Lennon and Yoko Ono flex-disc was included in the Spring/Summer issue (number seven) of a limited edition art magazine called *Aspen* (known as "the magazine in a box"). The magazine had an unusual format: it came in a box, with each section (including the box itself) considered to be a separate work of art. For issue seven (dubbed "The British Box"), the John and Yoko flexi-disc was section eleven, while a sheet of paper containing the words to the songs was section nine. Two tracks on the disc credited to Yoko Ono and John Lennon (*No Bed For Beatle John* and *Radio Play*) appeared on **Life With The Lions** (Entry 203), which was also issued that spring. However, one five-minute segment credited just to Yoko Ono (*Song For John*) did not turn up anywhere else. That was recorded at the same time as *No Bed For Beatle John* and *Radio Play* (November 1968), as John camped by Yoko's hospital bedside.

Aspen Flexi Disc (Issue 7, Section 11)
    Manufactured by Eva-Tone EV-330707
    by Yoko Ono and John Lennon except † by Yoko Ono
side one
†*Song For John*—Yoko Ono—*4:55*
    Part 1. *Let's Go On Flying—1:08*
    Part 2. *Snow Is Falling All The Time—1:30*
    Part 3. *Mum's Only Looking For Her Hand In The Snow—2:17*
No Bed For Beatle John—Lennon/Yoko Ono—*4:45*
side two
Radio Play—Lennon—*8:10*

----

[1]And, as if to prove that it's never too late to make another mistake, we missed citing in the main discography section of this volume a reissue of *From Head to Toe* on a 1982 Escorts retrospective album, **From The Blue Angel**. See page 449.

The *All Together Now* entry for **Life With the Lions** mistakenly included *Song For John* in the song listing. It did not appear on that album.

Another section (number eight) of that same issue of *Aspen* consisted of an otherwise unavailable John Lennon book, *The Lennon Diary 1969*. This was a small datebook for the year 1969, with a week's worth of blank spaces on each two-page spread. Before the year began, Lennon filled in the entire book with variations on the same dull routine virtually every day: Get Up, Go To Work, Come Home, Watch TV, Go To Bed, Have Sex. He signed and dated the book Wednesday November 29, 1968, also including one telephone number (9.9.9), two "dates to remember" (his birthday on October 9 and Yoko's birthday on February 18), and an important reminder: get a new diary for the next year.

George Harrison and Bobby Whitlock

After Derek and the Dominos split, guitarist Bobby Whitlock began a solo recording career. Guest appearances by other rock superstars such as fellow Domino Eric Clapton and friend George Harrison were almost inevitable. *One Day At A Time* author Anthony Fawcett, who was around when the Whitlock album **Raw Velvet** was done, confirmed that Harrison did appear on that disc.

Ringo Starr and Rory Storm

The liner notes to a 1983 compilation album, **Liverpool 1963-1968** (Entry 743) revealed that Ringo Starr appeared as a guest backing vocalist on a 1964 single release by his former group, Rory Storm and the Hurricanes. See page 242 for further details.

Ringo Starr Titles and the Mouth Sax Solo

First, a few title changes. The Randy Newman song appearing on the **Ringo** album is really called *Have You Seen My Baby*, not *Hold On*. (A label error, but one we should have caught.) On Ringo's **Beaucoups Of Blues**, the title *Woman Of The Night* has been officially changed to *Women Of The Night*. (We have no idea why.) Finally, on **Goodnight Vienna**, the *No No Song* is now listed as a medley of Hoyt Axton's *No No Song* and a 1954 South African tune called *Skokiaan*.[1] (If they say so!)

In another area, it seems that the credits on the **Ringo** album were precisely correct for *You're Sixteen*, identifying Paul McCartney's contribution as a "mouth sax solo." We assumed that was just a clever way of saying he played a kazoo. Apparently, so did most

---

[1]Named after a South African Zulu drink. The song was written by Tom Glazer and August Msarurgwa and first introduced in South Africa by the Bulawayo Sweet Rhythms Band on Gallotone Records.

other people. But, in a post-album interview, McCartney explained that, yes, he'd really "played" the solo through his mouth and nose.

Unconfirmed Reports and Mythical Outtakes

We know of about a dozen other instances in which one or more of the Beatles might have appeared as guest performers on records by other artists. However, we have not listed them because we have been unable to confirm the rumored involvement (nor, for that matter, entirely discount it). We will have to keep these cases "open" until we can double check the stories once and for all.

This careful policy has meant that occasionally we have missed a few likely connections that later turned out to be genuine (such as McCartney's involvement with *Bored As Butterscotch*). However, it has also meant that we've had very few errors in the continuing chronological discography begun in *All Together Now*.

Unfortunately, when we first researched *All Together Now* back in 1975, we did not have that same luxury of cross reference checking regarding potential studio outtakes. Instead, we extracted as much as we could from the British music press, various books, magazines, and personal interviews. In retrospect, we should have put stronger qualifiers on our presentation in the "Bootleg" section of *All Together Now*, stressing the unconfirmed nature of some titles.

Since then, we have learned far more about the status of various Beatles outtakes and we have attempted to incorporate that information throughout this book, especially in the "All Sales Final" and "Outtakes We'd Like To See Out" sections. Unfortunately, some of the titles we cited in *All Together Now* have taken on a life of their own as other writers have extracted them from our text and incorporated them into ever larger lists of "outtakes *definitely* finished and in the vault ready for release." T'ain't so. We hope that the detailed discussions of the BBC sessions, the 1962 audition tracks, and other confirmed outtakes in this volume will go a long way in deflating those mythical numbers.

Writing Wrap-Up

We welcome corrections, critical comments, and even compliments. A stamped self-addressed envelope usually makes us feel an obligation to respond rather quickly, especially to very specific and direct questions. Send all correspondence to:

Pierian Press
Box 1808
Ann Arbor, Michigan 48106

Margin of Error Discography Inserts

Entry numbers for the following discs key their placement into the main chronological discography sections in *All Together Now, The Beatles Again,* and *The End Of The Beatles.*

105a. NOV 13, 1964 (UK) Parlophone R 5197
by Rory Storm and the Hurricanes Prod: Brian Epstein
A: *America*—Leonard Bernstein/Stephen Sondheim—*2:29*
    Ringo: Backing Vocal
B: *(since you broke my heart)*

157a. OCT 24, 1966 (US) Epic 5-10098
by Donovan Prod: Mickie Most
A: *Mellow Yellow*—Donovan Leitch—*3:42*
    Paul: Backing Vocal
B: *(sunny south kensington)*

163a. JAN 13, 1967 (UK) Pye 7N-17267
by Donovan Prod: Mickie Most
A: *MELLOW YELLOW*—Donovan Leitch—*3:42*
    Paul: Backing Vocal
B: *(preachin' love)*

164a. JAN 30, 1967 (US) Epic BN 26239 (LP)
by Donovan
MELLOW YELLOW Prod: Mickie Most
side one
    cut one: *MELLOW YELLOW*—Donovan Leitch—*3:42*
    Paul: Backing Vocal

193b. JAN 27, 1969 (US) Epic BXN 26439 (LP)
by Donovan
DONOVAN'S GREATEST HITS Prod: Mickie Most
side two
    cut one: *MELLOW YELLOW*—Donovan Leitch—*3:42*
    Paul: Backing Vocal

213a. JUN 27, 1969 (UK) Parlophone R 5784
AUG 18, 1969 (US) Bell 821
by Scaffold Prod: Norrie Paramor and Tim Rice
    Paul: Guitar
A: *Charity Bubbles*—Mike McGear/Roger McGough—*2:34*
B: *Goose*—Mike McGear/Roger McGough—*2:34*

320a. APR 21, 1972 (UK) Island ILPS 9191 (LP)
by Mike McGear
WOMAN   Prod: Mike McGear
side two
> cut four: *Bored As Butterscotch*—Mike McGear/Roger McGough/
> Paul McCartney (as "Friend")—*2:49*

552a. APR 22, 1977 (UK) EMI 2594
by Percy "Thrills" Thrillington (Paul)   Prod: Paul McCartney (as
Percy "Thrills" Thrillington)
A: *Uncle Albert/Admiral Halsey*—Paul and Linda McCartney—*4:57*
B: *Eat At Home*—Paul and Linda McCartney—*3:30*

552b. APR 29, 1977 (UK) EMI EMC 3175 (LP)
MAY 17, 1977 (US) Capitol ST 11642 (LP)
by Percy "Thrills" Thrillington (Paul)
THRILLINGTON   Prod: Paul McCartney (as Percy "Thrills"
Thrillington)
side one
> *Too Many People*—Paul McCartney—*4:30*
> *3 Legs*—Paul McCartney—*3:42*
> *Ram On*—Paul McCartney—*2:49*
> *Dear Boy*—Paul and Linda McCartney—*2:47*
> *Uncle Albert/Admiral Halsey*—Paul and Linda McCartney—*4:57*
> *Smile Away*—Paul McCartney—*4:39*
side two
> *Heart Of The Country*—Paul and Linda McCartney—*2:25*
> *Monkberry Moon Delight*—Paul and Linda McCartney—*4:32*
> *Eat At Home*—Paul and Linda McCartney—*3:30*
> *Long Haired Lady*—Paul and Linda McCartney—*5:44*
> *Back Seat Of My Car*—Paul McCartney—*4:54*

717a. OCT 15, 1982 (UK) Edsel Records FORD 1 (LP)
by The Escorts
FROM THE BLUE ANGEL
side two
> cut five: *From Head To Toe*—William Robinson—*2:31*
> Paul: Tambourine

McGraw-Hill Paperbacks
$8.95
THE
BEATLES
FOREVER
400 ILLUSTRATIONS
HOW THEY CHANGED OUR CULTURE
THE LARGEST COLLECTION OF BEATLE MEMORABILIA EVER GATHERED
RECORD COVERS NEVER APPEARING IN A BOOK BEFORE (INCLUDING THE BANNED "BUTCHER" SLEEVE IN FULL COLOR)
NICHOLAS SCHAFFNER

For
Further
Reading

The music of John Lennon, Paul McCartney, George Harrison, and Ringo Starr speaks for itself. Yet, it has also served as the catalyst for hundreds of books, covering such topics as "who slept with whom" and "who played what when," with so many in print that a definitive list would be a book in itself.

Not surprisingly, Pierian Press put one together for publication in 1984 (though not written by us), *Here, There And Everywhere: The First International Beatles Bibliography, 1962–1982* (edited by Carol Terry), using a computerized database of about 8,000 citations to books, articles, reviews, and other published texts. As a spinoff from the preparations for this bibliography, Pierian's managing editor Tom Schultheiss wrote a detailed guide to building a Beatles library for the February 1981 issue of *Wilson Library Bulletin*. That article was reprinted (with minor revisions) in the June/July 1981 issue of *Beatlefan* (Volume 3, Number 4), along with an expanded bibliography combining listings from the Schultheiss article, Nicholas Schaffner's bibliography in *The Beatles Forever*, and the reference collection at the *Beatlefan* office. Either version of the article should do until Pierian's *Here, There And Everywhere* reaches your home bookshelf or library reference desk.

Obviously, we've read, used, or at least seen many of these Beatles titles, sometimes extracting obscure bits of information from even the worst of them. For this section, we've selected ten of our favorite Beatles books for a few brief comments. This list is completely subjective and should in no way be mistaken for a definitive guide to building a Beatles library (though it won't serve badly as a starting point). Of course, it goes without saying that we really like *All Together Now, The Beatles Again?*, and *The End Of The Beatles?*, though for obvious reasons they have been excluded from this listing.

1) *The Beatles Forever* by Nicholas Schaffner is truly the "ultimate Beatles history," even though it was done by someone far from their inner circle. Well researched and illustrated, this has rightly become one of the most popular and respected Beatles-books. An excellent companion is Schaffner's *British Invasion*, which integrates the Beatles into the larger story of the British musical scene.

2) *Mersey Beat: The Beginnings Of The Beatles* (compiled and edited by Bill Harry) is like coming across a scrapbook of articles collected by a British Beatles fan from back in the early 1960s. Bill Harry served as editor of the *Mersey Beat* music paper back then and for this book chose with care the ads, articles, and news items to be reprinted, including the famous "Beatles Top Poll" front page headline from 1962.

3) *The Playboy Interviews With John Lennon And Yoko Ono* (conducted by David Sheff and edited by G. Barry Golson) captures John and Yoko in their best public state of mind ever: at peace, articulate, and eager to share their new work. This also contains Lennon's song-by-song commentary on most of his own solo releases and Beatles tracks.

4) *The Writings Of John Lennon* (published in 1981 by Simon and Schuster) is one of the best combined packagings of *In His Own Write* and *A Spaniard In The Works*. Unlike the cheaper paperback version out around the same time, this hardcover retained the proportions and layout style of the original editions. Should you want a detailed analysis of the material to compare with your own reactions, try *The Literary Lennon* by Dr. James Sauceda.

5) *I Me Mine* by George Harrison is strictly for ardent collectors and rare book buffs in its original $300+ 1980 leather-bound edition from Genesis Publications. The more popularly priced hardcover reprint, however, serves as a pleasant and accessible visit with Harrison and friend Derek Taylor (who wrote the linking text), including comments on most of George's compositions. The two reversed roles for Taylor's own limited edition book for Genesis, with Harrison doing editing and commentary on *Fifty Years Adrift In An Open-Necked Shirt.*

6) *With The Beatles: The Historic Photographs Of Dezo Hoffmann* is a fine collection of photos from the beginning days of Beatlemania in Britain. Robert Freeman's *Yesterday — The Beatles 1963–1965* makes an excellent companion.

7) *John Lennon: In My Life* is an "I-remember-John Lennon-from-back-then" book by someone who really was there, child-hood chum Pete Shotton. Written in collaboration with Nicholas Schaffner, the book affectionately traces Shotton's continuing friendship with Lennon right through to the end in 1980. For those interested in more controversial reading, Peter Brown's *The Love You Make* and May Pang's *Loving John* offer far more scandalous revelations. The most important aspect of these (and any other[1]) books of personal reminiscences is to recognize that they represent one person's point of view rather than an objective, balanced history. Before starting any of these, it is essential to read some basic biography material such as the Hunter Davies *Beatles Authorized Biography* or *The Beatles Forever*. Some specialized background history can also help, such as *The Beatles At The Beeb* by Kevin Howlett, *Abbey Road* by Brian Southall, or even *Making Music (The Guide To Writing, Performing, And Recording)* edited by George Martin.

8) *The Beatles: An Illustrated Record* by Roy Carr and Tony Tyler is still one of the best packagings of basic Beatles history and discographic information into a glossy full color format. Among other "competing" discographies we like *The Beatles On Record* by Mark Wallgren for its generally dependable information and easy to follow format, and *The Complete Beatles U.S. Record Price Guide* by Perry Cox and Joe Lindsay for detailing all sorts of label variations we've never cared about. Now we have someplace to steer people with such questions.

9) *The Beatles In Richard Lester's "A Hard Day's Night": A Complete Pictorial Record Of The Movie.* The title just about says it all — the best Beatles film, shot by shot, with dialogue and

---

[1] Such as Richard DiLello's *The Longest Cocktail Party*, Brian Epstein's *A Cellarful of Noise*, Cynthia Lennon's *A Twist Of Lennon*, Derek Taylor's *As Time Goes By*, Allan Williams' *The Man Who Gave The Beatles Away*, George Martin's *All You Need Is Ears*, Mike McCartney's *The Macs*, and even John Lennon's *Lennon Remembers*.

stage directions (including sequences that were cut), plus a few essays and reviews to explain to the unbaptized what it all meant.

10) *A Day In The Life: The Beatles Day-By-Day* by Tom Schultheiss. The first Pierian Press catalog to include a display ad for *All Together Now* placed it beside more typical fare from the company at the time (*Articles On The Middle East 1947-- 1971*). By 1980, the emphasis had shifted and Pierian's managing editor Tom Schultheiss put together his own Beatles book (because he couldn't talk us into doing it!). This turned out to be a surprisingly useful day-by-day guide to Beatles activities and events through 1970. Now, the company has more than a dozen Beatles and other rock-related books out, with more on the way. We never dreamed it would go this far. Honest.

454

Keeping Current

Despite the fact that the last new Beatles studio album came out in 1970, there is still a surprising amount of news relating to John Lennon, Paul McCartney, George Harrison, and Ringo Starr even today. Publications such as *Rolling Stone, The Record, Billboard*, and *Music Week* in Britain carry many of the music items, while specific celebrity-oriented stories usually turn up in magazines such as *People* or in the entertainment sections of local newspapers.

Interested fans can keep up with it all (and then some) through these and several special Beatles-oriented magazines, newsletters, and conventions.

Magazines and Newsletters

The Beatles Book (Monthly in the U.K.)

This revival of *The Beatles Book* from the 1960s started in 1976, packaging a glossy paper reprint edition of the original magazine (first published in Britain from 1963 to 1969) with a wraparound eight pages of new material. This went on at the rate of one a month through the initial seventy-seven issue run. Since October 1982 (when the reprints ran out) the entire magazine has featured all new articles and layouts, with an excellent selection of photos (many previously unpublished) and full color front and back covers. The monthly news column by Mark Lewisohn is an excellent way to stay on top of special new releases of every type (records, films, books). Though writing from a British point of view, the magazine still manages to keep an eye on important Stateside events as well. We highly recommend a subscription and, in fact, suggest picking up all the available back issues as well.

The Beatles Book	Annual subscription rate to the
Beat Publications Ltd.	U.S. (sent airmail):
45 St. Mary's Road	$33.00
Ealing, London	
W5 5RQ, England	

Beatlefan (Bi-monthly in the U.S.)

Atlanta *Constitution* writer Bill King started *Beatlefan* in 1978, bringing to it his years of newspaper experience. Since then, the magazine has flourished as a no-nonsense "Beatles publication of record," which presents detailed reports on virtually any activity relating to John, Paul, George, and Ringo. If you missed it in your local paper, you'll probably find it here. There are also feature articles, reviews, and interviews (see page 461), as well as regular columns on new books, promotional films, and bootleg records — plus one of the toughest annual trivia contests we've ever seen.

Selected back issues are available, along with special reprint editions combining material on specific subjects (such as Badfinger) that was originally spread over several issues.

Beatlefan
The Goody Press
P.O. Box 33515
Decatur, Georgia 30033

Annual subscription rate in the U.S.:
$8.00

Club Sandwich (Paul McCartney's official fan club newsletter, published several times each year in the U.K.)

For more than ten years, Paul McCartney has maintained his official British-based fan club organization. Currently the newsletter is done in an oversize format (12 by 18 inches, sometimes larger) and printed on glossy paper in color. There are photos, articles, a fan letter column, a fan art gallery, and a brief news column. Issues tied in with a new McCartney release offer behind the scenes tidbits, sometimes even going over new album material track by track. Club members are also given the opportunity to purchase authorized merchandise such as t-shirts and photos. Over the years, British club members have been tapped to participate in a handful of special events, such as the filming of the *Take It Away* promotional film.

This is a must for McCartney fans.

Club Sandwich
P.O. Box 4UP
London W1, 4UP
England

Annual members dues for the U.S.:
$10.00

Beatles Unlimited (Bi-monthly in Holland)

The Beatles, as seen from the European continent. This offset magazine has been around since 1975 and, over the past eight years, has caught a number of events and promotional appearances that would never have been covered by the Beatles fan magazines in either Britain or America. Artillio Bergholtz of the Beatles Information Center in Sweden does a detailed regular column on new record releases in the U.S., the U.K., and other selected countries. There is also an international news column, reviews, interviews, and retrospective articles.

Beatles Unlimited also published three special editions: *Starr Unlimited* (an all-Ringo issue), *The Beatles Concert-ed Efforts* (concert appearances), and *Lots Of Liverpool* (seven trips through the Merseyside area).

Beatles Unlimited
P.O. Box 602
3430 AP Nieuwegein
The Netherlands

Annual subscription rate to the U.S. (sent airmail):
$13.00

****

The Write Thing (Quarterly in the U.S.)

Barbara Fenick, who put together a price guide to Beatles collectibles in 1982 (*Collecting The Beatles*), has been publishing her *Write Thing* newsletter since 1974. Each issue includes the latest news and reviews, as well as sections devoted to personal anecdotes and observations from fans. Naturally, there are detailed features on collecting, along with an extensive selection of photos offered for sale each issue.

The Write Thing
P.O. Box 18807
Minneapolis, MN 55418

Annual subscription rate in the U.S.:
$8.00

****

Strawberry Fields Forever (Bi-monthly in the U.S.)

Though sometimes *Strawberry Fields Forever*'s bi-monthly schedule seems more a goal than a reality (there was a two-year hiatus between issues in 1981 and 1983), it's hard to get too upset. Obviously publisher Joe Pope is still doing his magazine for the fun of it as an enthusiastic fan. For instance, *Strawberry Fields Forever* not only had the lowest advertised price we ever saw for both *I Me Mine* in 1977 and the Mobile Fidelity **Collection** in 1983, there were even provisions made in both cases for installment payments! Of course, when the issues do arrive, there is selected news, reviews, and interviews. A few issues have been sent out as special flexi-discs.

Strawberry Fields Forever   Subscription rate in the U.S.:
310 Franklin St., No. 117 $10.00 for six issues
Boston, Massachusetts 02110

****

Beatles Now (Bi-monthly in the U.K.)

Begun in 1981, this relatively new British Beatles magazine is printed on glossy paper and includes (of course) the latest news and reviews plus detailed background features and photos. Though British based, the magazine also displays an international flavor – for instance, the fifth issue had an interview with a Beatles DJ from Israel.

Beatles Now   Annual subscription rate to the
73 Kirchener Road   U.S.
Walthamstow, London $12.00 (sea mail)
E17 4LJ, England   Inquire about air mail rates.

****

Goldmine (Twice monthly in the U.S.)
Record Collector (Monthly in the U.K.)

In 1979 *The Beatles Book* launched a glossy paper spinoff publication, *Record Collector*, devoted to the general subject of rock record collecting (with a British slant). Naturally, the articles and sales lists frequently focus on Beatles-related items. Stateside, the long-running monthly *Goldmine* magazine offers similar mixed bag coverage of rock, with frequent Beatles-related articles.

Both magazines contain hundreds of classified ads offering thousands of records for sale each month.

Goldmine   *Record Collector*
700 E. State St.   45 St. Mary's Road
Iola, Wisconsin 54990   Ealing, London
                                 W5 5RQ, England

****

If that is still not enough for you, we suggest consulting the ads in any of the above publications for other fan club organizations. There are dozens worldwide, including some Beatles-related spinoffs. For instance, the Mike McCartney (McGear) Fan Club puts out a bi-monthly newsletter following the activities of Paul's younger brother. That, and a few others, are listed below:

The Mike (McGear) McCartney
  Fan Club
Barbara Paulson
P.O. Box 164
Genoa, Illinois 60135

With A Little Help From My
  Friends
10290 Pleasant Lake No. F21
Cleveland, Ohio 44130

The Beatles Information Center
Artillio Bergholtz
Box 7481
S-10392 Stockholm
Sweden

The Harrison Alliance
Patti Murawski, Editor
67 Cypress St.
Bristol, Connecticut 06010

Club Des 4 De Liverpool
(written in French)
43, bis Boulevard Henri IV
75004 Paris, France

The Beatles Information Center
Rainer Moers
Crackerbox Palace
Im Weidenbruch 4
D-5000 Koln 80
West Germany

The Beatles Information Center organizations in Sweden and West Germany are two different set-ups. Both gladly accept English-language correspondence.

Finally, for those that cannot wait for a bi-monthly or even a monthly news magazine, New York rock writer Lou O'Neill, Jr. includes a good deal of Beatles news in his bi-weekly "Rock Wire Report" (annual U.S. subscriptions available for $16.50 from P.O. Box 56, Rego Park, New York 11374).

****

Conventions

Conventions of Beatles fans are held regularly throughout the world. These provide the perfect opportunity to meet other fans and swap stories, to watch film and TV clips, to buy records and memorabilia, to dance to Beatles soundalike bands, and to meet a celebrity or two. For dates and locations consult the news columns and ads appearing in various Beatles magazines and newsletters, especially in *The Write Thing, Beatlefan, Beatles Now*, and *Beatles Unlimited*.

The two most widely known conventions are the Beatlefests in the U.S. and the Mersey Beatle Extravaganza in the U.K.

Beatlefest
Mark and Carol Lapidos stage annual Beatlefest shows in New York, Chicago, and Los Angeles, with other cities such as Houston added as the schedule permits. Over the years, the Beatlefest guest

list has been quite impressive, including such speakers as Mike Mc-Cartney, Clive Epstein, Mal Evans, Laurence Juber, Steve Holly, and Victor Spinetti. Harry Nilsson has also appeared, selling kisses and a record (see page 317) to raise money for the National Coalition to Ban Handguns. There have been more than thirty Beatlefests since 1974, so the program operation is smooth and professional. In 1980, Mark and Carol Lapidos instituted an appropriate spinoff from the Beatlefests, Caromar Records, their own independent record company.

Beatlefest National Headquarters
P.O. Box 436
Westwood, New Jersey 07675
(201) 666-5450

Mersey Beatle Extravaganza (MBE)

For Britain, what could be more appropriate than a Beatles convention held in Liverpool? Instituted in 1981 by Liz and Jim Hughes, operators of Cavern Mecca (Liverpool's top Beatles information center and store), the Mersey Beatle Extravaganza has quickly become a special international event. Guests have included Billy J. Kramer, Derek Taylor, Cavern Club owner/founder Ray McFall, and Cavern Club emcee Bob Wooler. With a bar set up right at the center of the activities, the atmosphere is very casual, encouraging informal chats and friendly mixing. For Stateside fans, the MBE is a perfect excuse to journey to Liverpool. And to top it off, Liz and Jim Hughes can steer you to some excellent guides that can give you a delightful tour of all the sites you've wanted to visit – from the gates at Strawberry Field to the pub from the cover of **Sentimental Journey** to the bus shelter and roundabout at Penny Lane.

There is also a Cavern Mecca club, which sends out about four newsletters each year. An information packet is available for two international reply coupons (sold at the post office) sent to the MBE/Cavern Mecca headquarters.

Cavern Mecca
9 Cavern Walks
Mathew Street
Liverpool L2 6RE
Merseyside, England

****

The Sotheby's Rock And Roll Auction

For the well-heeled fan (or ambitious investor), Sotheby Parke Bernet & Co. offers an annual opportunity to spend thousands of dollars on Beatles-related items ranging from original manuscripts of song lyrics to souvenir lunch boxes and toy guitars. Strictly speaking, the auction is not devoted exclusively to the Beatles but actually encompasses a variety of rock artists including the Rolling Stones, Buddy Holly, Elvis Presley, Marc Bolan, and even Barry Manilow. However, since 1981, the Beatles-related items have brought the event an international audience and publicity, with spirited bidding by participants from all over the world. Admission is open to anyone with a catalog for the auction, which costs about $8.00.[1] You do not have to bid on any item, though if you do you'll be expected to arrange payment on the spot.

If you want to get a close look at some of the articles being sold, the best time to visit Sotheby's is actually a day or two prior to the auction. There is no admission charge and most of the items are on display and available for personal inspection. Beginning in 1983, Sotheby's arranged to have its rock-related auction held within a week of the Merseyside Beatles Extravaganza.

Sotheby Parke Bernet & Co.
34-35 New Bond Street
London W1A 2AA
England

There are other offices throughout the world which can supply information on upcoming auctions, including the procedure for putting an item up for bid.

****

Perhaps the most fascinating aspect of all these resources is that they have behind them people who are not only willing to dig for detailed information but who are also capable of presenting it in entertaining and informative packages. As a result, fans have been able to follow the public and artistic activities of Lennon, McCartney, Harrison, and Starr with far more background details than would ever be carried in regular mainstream newspapers, magazines, or radio and television features. For instance, as part of an interview that appeared in the February 1983 issue of *Beatlefan*, Carl Perkins had the opportunity to explain a minor recording oddity: his laughter at the end of *Get It*, his duet track with Paul McCartney on **Tug Of War**. He turned the point into a delightful personal anecdote:

> . . . One night [in Montserrat] we set out in some little rubber rafts to a big boat [owned by] a billionaire, a real good friend of George Martin's. Anyway, they had a meal,

---

[1]Consult pages 245-267 of Barbara Fenick's *Collecting The Beatles* for reprinted excerpts from the 1981 rock auction catalog offerings.

I'm tellin' you! 'Course, they were puttin' on the big dog for Paul. It's a big converted English battleship. So anyway, I'm sitting between Paul and Linda and they had china and all these forks and things you don't use. I said, "Man, there's more silverware around my plate than I got at home. How many damn forks can you use?" I got him tickled. Then I said, "I tell you one thing, this is shittin' in high cotton for a country boy."

Paul says, "What's that mean?" I said, "See, I was raised where they had out-houses and if the cotton came up to the back door and you had a good crop, you didn't even have to go to the out-house, you could just squat in the field and they couldn't see you from the road." And he fell on the floor.

The next day [when Perkins and McCartney were recording *Get It*] with the tapes rolling, [McCartney] asked, "Hey Carl, what's that quaint old saying you were telling me last night? Something about *sitting* in high cotton?"

I said, "You almost right." . . . and he said, "Well, have I misquoted you or something?" I said, "Yeah, you got one word wrong." He said, "Cotton, right?" and I just cracked up and he left the damn laughing on it![1]

It's hard to imagine that detailed story running intact anywhere but in a specialty magazine such as *Beatlefan*. In fact, we would not expect a general entertainment reporter to necessarily even make the Carl Perkins/Paul McCartney connection, much less ask about an obscure moment during the recording sessions.

Once again, then, we heartily recommend that you sample at least one or two of the resources we've outlined above. If nothing else, you'll probably enjoy the point of view: people writing about the people and music they really care about.

So, don't say we never told you.

****

---

[1]Copyright 1983 by The Goody Press. Reprinted with permission from *Beatlefan* magazine Volume 5, Number 2 (February/March 1983) pages 16--17.

INDEXES
AND
INSTRUCTIONS

Indexes And Instructions

This index section consists of fifteen separate indexes.

The first thirteen indexes are keyed to the ENTRY NUMBERS used in the main chronological discography sections of *All Together Now*, *The Beatles Again*, and *The End Of The Beatles*. (Please see pages 469-472 for a brief "Nuts & Bolts" explanation of the chronological discography system.)

Indexes two through thirteen are cumulative, covering Entry Numbers in all three volumes, while the first index cites only initial Entry Numbers in *The End Of The Beatles*.

The two remaining indexes are keyed to PAGE NUMBERS in *The End Of The Beatles*.

****

SIMPLE RULE OF THUMB

When in doubt as to where to begin the search for an item, use the General Title Index (Index 14, beginning on page 525) and the General Name Index (Index 15, beginning on page 543). They will guide you by page number to essentially any spot in this volume.

****

For those interested in extracting more complicated details, what follows is:

a list of the fifteen indexes in this section;

a summary of other title listings in this book; and

a brief explanation of the assumptions behind the style of the chronological discography entries ("Nuts & Bolts")

A LIST OF THE INDEXES APPEARING IN THIS SECTION OF
THE END OF THE BEATLES

****

OTHER HELPFUL LISTS INCLUDED IN
THE END OF THE BEATLES

There are also a number of other listings throughout *The End Of The Beatles*. These isolate particular areas of information in the context of various discussions. They can be used in conjunction with the indexes in this section.

A. All the songs recorded and released by the Beatles for EMI between 1962 and 1970. Alphabetical. Pages 112, 114, 116. Use with indexes 2 and 14.
B. All the songs recorded at the Beatles' 1961 sessions in Germany backing singer Tony Sheridan and released by various labels beginning in 1961. Alphabetical. Page 194. Use with indexes 2 and 14.
C. All the songs recorded live at the Star Club in Germany in 1962 and released by various labels beginning in 1977. Alphabetical, with lead vocalists. Page 152. Use with indexes 2 and 14.
D. All the songs recorded at the Beatles' 1962 audition sessions and released by various labels beginning in 1977. Alphabetical, with lead vocalists. Page 348. Use with indexes 2 and 14.
    In addition, on page 352 there is an alphabetical listing of the original versions of the songs from these sessions not written by the Beatles.
E. All the songs recorded by the Beatles for broadcast by the BBC between 1962 and 1965. Alphabetical, cross-referenced to individual programs. Pages 375-380.
    In addition, on pages 381-383 there is an alphabetical listing of the original versions of the songs from these sessions not written by the Beatles.
F. The contents of **The Beatles Collection** (Albums). All Beatles albums of new material issued by EMI in Britain from 1963 to 1970, plus a bonus disc from 1978. Includes complete track listings for each disc. Pages 39, 41, 43, 45, 47, 49, 51. Use with indexes 2, 12, and 14.
G. The contents of **The Beatles EP Collection** (EPs). All the Beatles EPs issued by EMI in Britain from 1962 to 1983. Includes complete track listings for each disc. Also includes an alphabetical listing of all the songs in the set. Pages 165-171. Use with indexes 2, 12, and 14.
H. The contents of **The Beatles Singles Collection** (Singles). All Beatles singles issued by EMI in Britain from 1962 to 1983. Includes complete track listings for each disc. Also includes initial recording dates for each song. Pages 217-222. Use with indexes 2, 12, and 14.
I. The contents of **The John Lennon Collection** (Albums). All Lennon solo albums issued by EMI in Britain from 1969 to 1975. Includes complete track listings for each disc. Also includes (in slightly less detail) all John Lennon and Yoko Ono album collaborations and all Yoko Ono solo albums through 1974. Pages 144-151. Use with indexes 3, 8, 12, and 14.
J. Commercial and promotional-only spoken word packages released between 1963 and 1983, featuring the Beatles as a group or individually. Alphabetical. Pages 282-283. Use with indexes 2 and 14.
K. Beatles singles and albums issued in Britain between 1964 and 1970 for the export market. Chronological. Page 72. Use with indexes 2, 12, and 14.
L. Illustrations included in *The End Of The Beatles*. Alphabetical by LPs, EPs, singles, 12-inches, and miscellaneous others. Pages xi-xiv. Use with index 14.

****

467

Nuts and Bolts

The chronological disc history begun in *All Together Now* and continued in *The Beatles Again* and *The End Of The Beatles* presents the detailed particulars concerning hundreds of records (albums, singles, 12-inch singles, and EPs). Using the samples below as reference, the following line-by-line guide should clearly explain what information is covered.

599. AUG 7, 1978 (US) Capitol 4612
SEP 22, 1978 (UK) Parlophone R 6022
by The Beatles   Prod: George Martin
A: MEDLEY—4:45
SGT. PEPPER'S LONELY HEARTS CLUB BAND—1:59
WITH A LITTLE HELP FROM MY FRIENDS—2:46
B: A DAY IN THE LIFE—5:03

601. AUG 21, 1978 (US) RCA AFL 1-2804 (LP)
SEP 29, 1978 (UK) RCA PL 1-2804 (LP)
by Daryl Hall and John Oates
ALONG THE RED LEDGE   Prod: David Foster
side one
cut three: *The Last Time—*Daryl Hall*—2:47*
George: Guitar

607. NOV 17, 1978   RCA PL 42728 (LP)
by Harry Nilsson   Prod: Harry Nilsson
Ringo: Drums
HARRY NILSSON'S GREATEST MUSIC
side one
cut five: *SPACEMAN—*Harry Nilsson*—3:33*
cut six: *KOJAK COLUMBO—*Harry Nilsson*—3:30*

707. JUL 5, 1982 (UK) Parlophone 12R 6056 (12 inch)
JUL 26, 1982 (US) Columbia 44-03019 (12 inch)
by Paul McCartney   Prod: George Martin
side one
TAKE IT AWAY—McCartney—*3:59*
side two
**I'll Give You A Ring*—McCartney—*3:05*
DRESS ME UP AS A ROBBER—McCartney—*2:40*

757. NOV 25, 1983 (UK) Old Gold OG 9367
by Billy J. Kramer with The Dakotas   Prod: George Martin
A: DO YOU WANT TO KNOW A SECRET—L/McC—*1:59*
B: (trains and boats and planes)

first line
A number beginning an entry is its chronological reference number.

After the number, the release date appears, followed by the country of release, then the record label and the record number. If the disc is a seven-inch extended play record (EP), a twelve-inch single (12-inch), or an album (LP), those identifications follow the record number. The record is otherwise understood to be a seven-inch 45 rpm single.

All releases in both Great Britain (UK) and the United States (US) are listed.

When both countries release exactly the same disc with exactly the same cuts in exactly the same order, the release dates are stacked one over the other. If there are any differences in the discs, the releases are listed as separate entries.

The release dates generally reflect when a record was available to the general public rather than the "official" release date. Still, given varying distribution patterns throughout both countries, there is an error margin of plus or minus about a week on any given release date.

Records issued in other countries are listed only if they affected the British or American markets in an important way, or if the material on them was released only in those foreign markets.

on the next line
The name of the performer is listed.

on the next lines
The name of the album or EP is listed, followed by the contents. Or the two sides of the single are listed.

Notes:
1. Writing credits, titles, and timings listed for each entry reflect,

to the best of our knowledge, what is actually on the record. This is sometimes different from the information listed on the record itself.

2. All songs performed by the Beatles are written by John Lennon and Paul McCartney unless otherwise stated. Therefore, for those Beatles tracks, the Lennnon/McCartney song authorship credit is not listed.

In all other cases, though, the song authorship is spelled out in full, reflecting all available information. The only abbreviations used are the last names for Lennon, McCartney, Harrison, and Starkey, and a special code L/McC. The L/McC code applies to that body of songs credited to the Lennon/McCartney writing team while they were members of the Beatles.

If any of these songs appear in the numbered chronological discography performed by other artists (and without any involvement by John, Paul, George, or Ringo as producers or backing performers), then they have been included because they were specifically given to those artists. (See Sample Entry 757.)

3. Producer (Prod) credits appear after the performer's name if they apply just to the cuts listed from an album or EP, but appear after the album or EP title if they apply to that entire disc. On singles, producer credits always appear after the performer's name.

4. If Lennon, McCartney, Harrison, or Starr are listed as guest musicians immediately after the name of the performer, then that applies to all cuts listed. Otherwise, their presence is noted under each individual cut. NOTE: Backing musician credits appear in the main chronological discography entries only if that is the sole reason for the discs being included in the chronological listing. Otherwise, all such musician credit information should be sought in the Musician Credits index beginning on page 473.

5. A song title appearing in ALL CAPITAL LETTERS is a reissue — that is, a song that has appeared previously on an album or single. The general rules we used to determine a reissue are: Cuts released at about the same time in the US and the UK are not reissues; singles which are released at about the same time as the album they are from are not reissues; however, singles released after the album are reissues.

6. A song in parentheses and in all lower case italics is completely unrelated to our discussions of the disc. That song is listed merely to show what else was on the record. This is usually done only for singles and EPs.

7. An asterisk (*) before a song title on a single indicates that the song appeared only on a single (seven or twelve inch) and was never subsequently issued on an album in either the US or the UK as of January 1984. NOTE: Several songs marked with an asterisk in *All Together Now* and *The Beatles Again* can now be found on al-

471

bums listed in this book. These songs (with their Entry Numbers) include: *Love Me Do* (version one) (**5**), *Tip Of My Tongue* (**17**), *Sie Liebt Dich* (**49**), *One And One Is Two* (**59**), *Like Dreamers Do* (**70**), *From Head To Toe* (**158**), *How I Won The War* (**171**), *Give Peace A Chance* (**214**), *Penina* (**216a**), *You Know My Name (Look Up The Number)* (**241**), *Another Day* (**275**), *Hi Hi Hi* (**340**), *Ten Years After On Strawberry Jam* (**384**), *Junior's Farm* (**411**), and *I Saw Her Standing There* (**436**).

Final Note:

The same style of discography listing is used throughout *The End Of The Beatles*. The chief variations outside the main chronological discography section are: entries are not numbered; many discs do not have direct involvement by Lennon, McCartney, Harrison, or Starr; and symbols such as ALL CAPS or an asterisk apply in a much more limited sense only to the area then under discussion.

Though only numbered chronological discography entries are included in Indexes 1 through 13 (keyed to Entry Numbers), every title and artist is included in the two master indexes to this book, Indexes 14 and 15 (keyed to Page Numbers).

Musician Credits

This section includes in one alphabetical listing the musician credits for all the songs appearing for the first time in the chronological discography between October 21, 1977 and December 31, 1983 (Entries 573 to 767). Reissued material is *not* included. For musician information on previously released tracks appearing in the main discography, consult *The Beatles Again* (covering Entries 501 to 573 released between January 1, 1976 and October 21, 1977) and *All Together Now* (covering everying prior to 1976).

There is a lead vocalist listed for every song in this section. Beyond that, the amount of information varies from track to track. Some are quite detailed. In many cases, though, a basic lineup of players is resonsible for an entire set of sessions and songs on an album or in a live concert performance. Generally in these situations the musician lineup is listed once (under an umbrella heading such as an album title) and individual tracks are cross-referenced back. However, even in these cases, any noteworthy variations applying to specific songs are listed by the individual titles.

This section is not designed to serve as a general index to the main chronological discography — those are the next ten indexes, beginning on page 485. However, for convenient cross referencing, we have included the Entry Number for the first appearance of each song, as well as its category from the following list:

The Beatles (B)	Beatles For Others (BFO)
John Lennon (JL)	Lennon For Others (LFO)
Paul McCartney (PM)	McCartney For Others (MFO)
George Harrision (GH)	Harrison For Others (HFO)
Ringo Starr (RS)	Starr For Others (SFO)

The format used in this index section is as follows:

Song Title (Category) Entry Number
Performer's Name (if *not* the Beatles or John, Paul, George, or Ringo)
Lead Vocalist
Musicians for the song or Cross Reference citation.

After The Ball (PM) 625
Lead Vocal: Paul McCartney
See **Back To The Egg**
Again And Again And Again (PM) 625
Lead Vocal: Denny Laine
See **Back To The Egg**
Alibi (RS) 746
Lead Vocal: Ringo Starr
See **Old Wave**
All Those Years Ago (GH) 671
Lead Vocal: George Harrison
Ringo Starr: Drums
Paul McCartney, Linda McCartney, Denny
Laine: Backing Vocals
See **Somewhere In England**
Always Look On The Bright Side Of Life
(HFO) 631
By Monty Python
Lead Vocal: Eric Idle
George Harrison, Phil MacDonald: Mixing
Arrow Through Me (PM) 625
Lead Vocal: Paul McCartney
See **Back To The Egg**, plus Tony Dorsey,
Steve Howard, Thaddeus Richard,
Howie Casey: Brass Overdub
As Far As We Can Go (RS) 745
Lead Vocal: Ringo Starr
See **Old Wave**, plus Joe Vitale
Attention (RS) 687
Lead Vocal: Ringo Starr
Linda McCartney, Sheila Casey, Lezlee
Livrano Pariser: Backing Vocals
Paul McCartney: Bass, Piano, Percussion
Ringo: Drums
Laurence Juber: Guitars
Howie Casey: Saxes
Audition Session–1962 (by The Beatles)
John Lennon: Vocals, Rhythm Guitar
Paul McCartney: Vocals, Bass Guitar
George Harrison: Vocals, Lead Guitar
Pete Best: Drums
Average Person (PM) 754
Lead Vocal: Paul McCartney
See **Pipes Of Peace**
Baby Don't Run Away (GH) 727
Lead Vocal: George Harrison
George: Synthesizer
George, Billy Preston, Rodina Sloan:
Backing Vocals
Jim Keltner: Drums
Mike Moran: Synthesizer, Keyboard, and
Bass Synthesizer
Ray Cooper: Percussion
Baby's Request (PM) 625
Lead Vocal: Paul McCartney
See **Back To The Egg**
Back Off Boogaloo (version two) (RS) 687
Lead Vocal: Ringo Starr

Ringo and Jim Keltner: Drums
Harry Nilsson, Rick Riccio: Backing
Vocals
Ritchie Zito, Dennis Budimir, Fred
Tacket: Guitars
Jane Getz: Piano
Dennis Belfield: Bass
Jerry Jummonville: Tenor Sax
Bruce Paulson: Trombone
Jim Gordon: Baritone Sax
Lee Thornburg: Trumpet
Van Dyke Parks: Arrangements
Back To The Egg (PM) 625
Paul McCartney: Vocals, Guitar, Bass,
Keyboards, Backing Vocal
Linda McCartney: Keyboards, Backing
Vocal
Denny Laine: Vocal, Guitar, Bass, Key-
boards, Backing Vocal
Laurence Juber: Guitars
Steve Holly: Drums, Percussion
Backwards Traveller (PM) 587
Lead Vocal: Paul McCartney
See **London Town**
Bad Boy (RS) 591
Ringo Starr: Vocals, Drums, with Ringo's
Roadside Attraction (see page 28)
credited only as: Push-a-lone (Lead
Guitar), Git-tar (Rhythm Guitar),
Diesel (Bass), and
Hamisch Bisonette: Synthesizer
Morris Lane: Keyboards, plus
Vini Poncia's Peaking Duck
Orchestra and Chorus
Bad Boy (RS) 591
Lead Vocal: Ringo Starr
See **Bad Boy**
Ballroom Dancing (PM) 704
Lead Vocal: Paul McCartney
Paul: Piano, Drums, Bass, Electric Guitar,
Percussion
Denny Laine: Electric Guitar
Jack Brymer: Clarinet Gliss
Peter Marshall: Narration
Paul, Linda McCartney, Eric Stewart:
Backing Vocals
Baltimore Oriole (GH) 672
Lead Vocal: George Harrison
See **Somewhere In England**
Be My Baby (RS) 746
Lead Vocal: Ringo Starr
See **Old Wave**, plus
Barbara Bach: Handclaps
Be What You See (PM) 704
Paul McCartney: Guitar, Vocoder
Beautiful Boy (Darling Boy) (JL) 656
Lead Vocal: John Lennon
See **Double Fantasy**, plus

Robert Greenidge: Steel Drum
Beautiful Boys (LFO) 656
by Yoko Ono and John Lennon
Lead Vocal: Yoko Ono
See **Double Fantasy**
Besame Mucho (B) 713
Lead Vocal: Paul McCartney
See Audition Session–1962
Blood From A Clone (GH) 672
Lead Vocal: George Harrison
See **Somewhere In England**
Blow Away (GH) 612
Lead Vocal: George Harrison
See **George Harrison**
Boat Ride (RS) 581
Lead Vocal: Ringo Starr
See **Scouse The Mouse**, plus
Pete Zorn: Flute Arrangement
Bogey Music (PM) 642
Lead Vocal: Paul McCartney
See **McCartney II**
The Broadcast (PM) 625
Instrumental backing to *The Sport Of
King* and *The Little Man* read by
Harold Margary
See **Back To The Egg**
Cafe On The Left Bank (PM) 588
Lead Vocal: Paul McCartney
See **London Town**
Check My Machine (PM) 643
Lead Vocal: Paul McCartney
See **McCartney II** sessions
Children Children (PM) 588
Lead Vocal: Denny Laine
See **London Town**
Circles (GH) 727
Lead Vocal: George Harrison
George: Bass, Synthesizer, Guitars
Henry Spinetti: Drums
Billy Preston: Organ, Piano
Ray Cooper: Percussion
Mike Moran: Synthesizer
Jon Lord: Synthesizer
Cleanup Time (JL) 656
Lead Vocal: John Lennon
See **Double Fantasy**
Coming Up (PM) 640
Lead Vocal: Paul McCartney
Linda McCartney: Backing Vocal
See **McCartney II**
Coming Up (Live At Glasgow) (PM) 640
Lead Vocal: Paul McCartney
Paul: Bass
Linda McCartney: Keyboards
Denny Laine: Guitar
Laurence Juber: Guitar
Steve Holly: Drums
Howie Casey: Tenor Sax

Tony Dorsey: Trombone
Steve Howard: Trumpet
Thaddeus Richard: Soprano Sax
Coming Up (Live For Kampuchea) (PM)
670
Lead Vocal: Paul McCartney
See *(Live At Glasgow)* lineup
Crying Waiting Hoping (B) 713
Lead Vocal: George Harrison
See Audition Session–1962
Cuff Link (PM) 587
Instrumental featuring Paul McCartney
on drums
See **London Town**
Dark Sweet Lady (GH) 614
Lead Vocal: George Harrison
See **George Harrison**
Darkroom (PM) 642
Lead Vocal: Paul McCartney
See **McCartney II**
Daytime Nightime Suffering (PM) 616
Lead Vocal: Paul McCartney
Paul: Bass
Linda McCartney: Keyboards
Laurence Juber: Guitar
Denny Laine: Guitar
Steve Holly: Drums
Baby James: Crying
Dead Giveaway (RS) 687
Lead Vocal: Ringo Starr
Ringo: Drums
Ringo, Ron Wood: Backing Vocals
Ron Wood: Guitars, Acoustic Bass, Saxes
Greg Mathieson, Joe Sample: Pianos
Wilton Felder: Electric Bass
Dear Yoko (JL) 656
Lead Vocal: John Lennon
See **Double Fantasy**
Deliver Your Children (PM) 588
Lead Vocal: Denny Laine
See **London Town**
Don't Let It Bring You Down (PM) 588
Lead Vocal: Paul McCartney
See **London Town**
Double Fantasy (JL) 656
John Lennon: Vocals, Guitars
Yoko Ono: Vocals
Earl Slick, Hugh McCracken: Guitars
Tony Levin: Bass Guitar
George Small: Keyboards
Andy Newmark: Drums
Arthur Jenkins, Jr.: Percussion
Ed Walsh: Oberheim
Cas Mijac (Michelle Simpson), Cassandra
Wooten, Cheryl Mason Jacks, Eric
Troyer, Benny Cummings Singers/
Kings Temple Choir: Background
Singers

475

Randy Stein: English Concertina
Howard Johnson, Grant Hungerford, John
Parran, Seldon Powell, George "Young"
Opalisky, Roger Rosenberg, David
Tofani, Ronald Tooley: Horns
Dream Away (GH) 727
Lead Vocal: George Harrison
George: Guitars
George, Billy Preston, Syreeta, and Sarah
Ricor: Backing Vocals
Dave Mattacks: Drums
Alan Jones: Bass
Mike Moran: Piano, Synthesizer
Ray Cooper: Percussion
Dress Me Up As A Robber (PM) 704
Lead Vocal: Paul McCartney
Paul: Guitars, Bass, Backing Vocal
Linda McCartney: Backing Vocal
Dave Mattacks: Drums, Percussion
Denny Laine: Synthesizer, Electric
Guitar
George Martin: Electric Piano
Drumming Is My Madness (RS) 686
Lead Vocal: Ringo Starr
Ringo, Jim Keltner: Drums
Jerry Jummonville: Tenor Sax
Bruce Paulson: Trombone
Jim Gordon: Baritone Sax
Lee Thornburg: Trumpet
Dennis Budimir: Guitar
Ritchie Zito: Guitar
Jane Getz: Piano
Fred Tacket: Guitar
Dennis Belfield: Bass
Rick Riccio: Flute
Van Dyke Parks: Arrangement
Ebony And Ivory (PM) 701
Lead Vocal Duet: Paul McCartney and
Stevie Wonder
Paul: Bass, Guitar, Synthesizers, Vocoder,
Percussion, Piano
Stevie Wonder: Electric Piano, Drums,
Synthesizers, Percussion
Paul & Stevie Wonder: Backing Vocals
Ebony And Ivory (solo version) (PM) 703
Lead Vocal: Paul McCartney
Same as above version, but without the
Stevie Wonder vocal
Ending Jam (SFO) 589
by The Band
Instrumental Jam with Ringo on Drums
See *I Shall Be Released* lineup
Every Man Has A Woman Who Loves Him
(LFO) 656
by Yoko Ono and John Lennon
Lead Vocal: Yoko Ono
See **Double Fantasy**
Every Night (live) (PM) 670

Lead Vocal: Paul McCartney
See Wings Live—1979
Everybody's In A Hurry But Me (RS) 746
Jam with Ringo Starr Vocal Rap
See **Old Wave**, plus additional musicians
listed (usual instruments in parentheses)
John Entwistle (Bass)
Ray Cooper (Percussion)
Waddy Wachtel (Guitar)
Eric Clapton (Guitar)
Russell Kunkel (Drums)
Fame (live) (LFO) 602
by David Bowie
Lead Vocal: David Bowie
John Lennon: Co-Author
Live Concert Lineup:
Carlos Alomar: Rhythm Guitar
Andrian Belew: Lead Guitar
Dennis Davis: Drums, Percussion
Simon House: Electric Violin
Sean Mayes: Piano, String Ensemble
George Murray: Bass Guitar
Roger Powell: Keyboards, Synthesizer
Carlos Alomar, Adrian Belew, Sean
Mayes, George Murray, Roger Powell:
Backing Vocals
Famous Groupies (PM) 588
Lead Vocal: Paul McCartney
See **London Town**
Faster (GH) 614
Lead Vocal: George Harrison
George: Bass
See **George Harrison**
Front Parlour (PM) 642
Instrumental
See **McCartney II**
Frozen Jap (PM) 642
Instrumental
See **McCartney II**
George Harrison (GH) 614
George Harrison: Vocals, Backing Vocals,
Guitars
Andy Newmark: Drums
Willie Weeks: Bass
Neil Larsen: Keyboards, Mini Moog
Ray Cooper: Percussion
Steve Winwood: Polymoog, Harmonium,
Mini Moog, Backing Vocals
Emil Richards: Marimba
Gayle Levant: Harp
Del Newman: String & Horn Arrangements
Get It (PM) 704
Lead Vocal Duet: Paul McCartney and
Carl Perkins
Paul: Acoustic Guitar, Percussion,
Synthesizer, Bass
Carl Perkins: Electric Guitar
Get Well Soon (MFO) 634

by Kevin Godley and Lol Creme
Lead Vocal: Kevin Godley
Paul McCartney, Lol Creme, Kevin God-
ley: Backing Vocals
Lol Creme: Guitars, Keyboards, Har-
monica
Kevin Godley: Percussion, Cowbell
Getting Closer (PM) 624
Lead Vocal: Paul McCartney
See **Back To The Egg**
The Girl Is Mine (MFO) 720
by Michael Jackson
Lead Vocal Duet: Michael Jackson and
Paul McCartney
Dean Parks, Steve Lukather: Guitars
Louis Johnson: Bass
Jeff Porcaro: Drums
David Paich: Piano
Greg Phillinganes: Rhodes
David Foster: Synthesizer
Steve Porcaro: Synthesizer Programming
Girlfriend (PM) 588
Lead Vocals: Paul and Linda McCartney
See **London Town**
Girls' School (PM) 578
Lead Vocal: Paul McCartney
Paul: Bass
Jimmy McCulloch: Guitar
Denny Laine: Guitar
Joe English: Drums
Linda McCartney: Opening Cheer, Key-
boards, Backing Vocal
Give Me Something (LFO) 656
by Yoko Ono and John Lennon
Lead Vocal: Yoko Ono
See **Double Fantasy**
Gone Troppo (GH) 727
Lead Vocal: George Harrison
George: Guitars, Marimba, Jal-Tarang
George, Joe & Vicki Brown: Backing
Vocals
Henry Spinetti: Drums
Herbie Flowers: Bass
Mike Moran: Keyboards
Ray Cooper: Percussion, Marimba, and
Effects
Jim Keltner: Percussion
Goodnight Tonight (PM) 616
Lead Vocal: Paul McCartney
Paul: Guitar, Bongo Drums, Keyboards,
Percussion, Backing Vocals
Linda McCartney: Backing Vocals
Denny Laine: Guitars, Backing Vocals
Laurence Juber: Guitars
Steve Holly: Percussion
Got To Get You Into My Life (live) (PM)
670
Lead Vocal: Paul McCartney

See Wings Live 1979 with Horns
Greece (GH) 723
Instrumental with Vocal Chant by
George Harrison
George: Guitars
Henry Spinetti: Drums
Herbie Flowers: Bass
Billy Preston, Mike Moran: Keyboards,
Synthesizers
Ham'n'Eggs (SFO) 582
by Lonnie Donegan
Lead Vocal: Lonnie Donegan
Ringo Starr: Drums
Lonnie Donegan: 12-String Guitar
Peter Jameson: Acoustic Guitar, Slide
Guitar
Dave Wyntor: Bass
Peter Banks: Guitar
Peter Wingfield: Piano
Leo Sayer: Harp
Hard Times (RS) 591
Lead Vocal: Ringo Starr
See **Bad Boy**
Hard Times Are Over (LFO) 656
by Yoko Ono and John Lennon
Lead Vocal: Yoko Ono
See **Double Fantasy**
Have A Drink On Me (Take A Whiff On Me)
(SFO) 582
by Lonnie Donegan
Lead Vocal: Lonnie Donegan
Southern California Community Choir
(arranged by Rev. James Cleveland):
Backing Vocals
Ringo Starr: Drums
Dave Wyntor: Bass
Peter Jameson: Acoustic Guitar, Slide
Guitar
Albert Lee: Lead Guitar
Lonnie Donegan: Banjo
Peter Wingfield: Piano
Heart Of Mine (SFO) 675
by Bob Dylan
Lead Vocal: Bob Dylan
Ringo Starr: Drums, Tom Tom
Ron Wood: Guitar
Donald "Duck" Dunn: Bass
Wm. "Smitty" Smith: Organ
Heart On My Sleeve (RS) 591
Lead Vocal: Ringo Starr
See **Bad Boy**, plus
James Newton Howard: Strings
Here Comes The Moon (GH) 614
Lead Vocal: George Harrison
See **George Harrison**
Here Today (PM) 704
Lead Vocal: Paul McCartney
Paul: Guitar

477

Jack Rothstein: Violin
Bernard Partridge: Violin
Ian Jewel: Viola
Keith Harvey: Cello
Hey Hey (PM) 754
Instrumental featuring Paul McCartney,
Stanley Clarke, and Steve Gadd
See **Pipes Of Peace**
Hong Kong Blues (GH) 672
Lead Vocal: George Harrison
See **Somewhere In England**
The Honorary Consul (Theme) (MFO) 763
by John Williams
Instrumental
Hopeless (RS) 746
Lead Vocal: Ringo Starr
See **Old Wave**
Hot As Sun (MFO) 689
by Elaine Paige
Lead Vocal: Elaine Paige
Chris Rainbow, Elaine Paige: Backing
Vocals
Morris Pert: Percussion
David Paton, Ian Bairnson: Guitars
Mike Moran: Keyboards
How Long Can Disco On? (SFO) 647
by Harry Nilsson
Lead Vocal: Harry Nilsson
Ringo Starr: Co-Author and Drums
(27 other musicians listed in general
credits for **Flash Harry** album — not
all applicable to this cut)
I Keep Forgettin' (RS) 746
Lead Vocal: Ringo Starr
See **Old Wave**
I Know A Place (RS) 581
Lead Vocal: Ringo Starr
See **Scouse The Mouse**
I Really Love You (GH) 727
Lead and Backing Vocals: George
Harrison, Willie Greene, Bobby King,
and Pico Pena
Henry Spinetti: Drums
Herbie Flowers: Bass
Mike Moran: Keyboards
Ray Cooper: Feet, Fender Rhodes,
Glockenspiel
I Shall Be Released (SFO) 589
by The Band
Lead Vocal Duet: Bob Dylan and Richard
Manuel
Ringo Starr, Levon Helm: Drums
Gareth Hudson: Keyboards
Robbie Robertson, Rick Danko, Paul
Butterfield, Eric Clapton, Neil Young,
Bob Dylan, Ron Wood: Guitars
Neil Young, Joni Mitchell, Ronnie
Hawkins, Dr. John, Neil Diamond, Paul

Butterfield, Bobby Charles, Eric
Clapton, Van Morrison: Backing Vocals
I Would Only Smile (MFO) 662
by Denny Laine
Lead Vocal: Denny Laine
Paul McCartney: Bass
Linda McCartney: Keyboards
Denny Seiwell: Drums
Henry McCulloch: Guitar
Denny Laine: Guitar
If You Believe (GH) 614
Lead Vocal: George Harrison
See **George Harrison**, plus
Gary Wright: Oberheim
I'll Give You A Ring (PM) 706
Lead Vocal: Paul McCartney
Paul, Linda McCartney, Eric Stewart:
Backing Vocals
Tony Coe: Clarinet
Paul: All other instruments
I'm Carrying (PM) 588
Lead Vocal: Paul McCartney
See **London Town**
I'm Going Down (RS) 746
Lead Vocal: Ringo Starr
See **Old Wave**, plus
Barbara Bach: Screaming
I'm Losing You (JL) 656
Lead Vocal: John Lennon
See **Double Fantasy**
I'm Moving On (LFO) 656
by Yoko Ono and John Lennon
Lead Vocal: Yoko Ono
See **Double Fantasy**
I'm Your Angel (LFO) 656
by Yoko Ono and John Lennon
Lead Vocal: Yoko Ono
See **Double Fantasy**, plus
John Lennon: Whistle
Tony Davilio: Horn Arrangement
In My Car (RS) 745
Lead Vocal: Ringo Starr
See **Old Wave**
It Happened (LFO) 666
by Yoko Ono
Lead Vocal: Yoko Ono
John Lennon, Yoko Ono: Spoken Intro
David Spinozza, Hugh McCracken:
Guitars
Gordon Edwards: Bass
Kenny Asher: Keyboard
Rick Marotta: Drums
Arthur Jenkins, Jr.: Percussion
I've Got It! (SFO) 647
by Harry Nilsson
Lead Vocal: Harry Nilsson
Ringo Starr: Drums
See musician note on *How Long Can Disco
On?*

478

I've Had Enough (PM) 588
Lead Vocal: Paul McCartney
See **London Town**
Keep Under Cover (PM) 754
Lead Vocal: Paul McCartney
See **Pipes Of Peace**
Kiss Kiss Kiss (LFO) 652
by Yoko Ono and John Lennon
Lead Vocal: Yoko Ono
See **Double Fantasy**
The Last Time (HFO) 601
by Daryl Hall & John Oates
Lead Vocals: Daryl Hall & John Oates
George Harrison: Acoustic Guitar
The Band for the **Along The Red Ledge**
album:
Kenny Passarelli: Bass
Caleb Quaye: Lead Guitar
Roger Pope: Drums
David Kent: Synthesizer
Charlie DeChant: Saxophone
David Foster: Keyboards
Let It Be (live) (PM) 670
Lead Vocal: Paul McCartney
See Rockestra—Live, with
Paul: Piano
Life Itself (GH) 672
Lead Vocal: George Harrison
See **Somewhere In England**
Lipstick Traces (On A Cigarette) (RS) 590
Lead Vocal: Ringo Starr
See **Bad Boy**
Living In A Pet Shop (RS) 581
Lead Vocal: Ringo Starr
See **Scouse The Mouse**
London Town (PM) 588
Paul McCartney: Vocals, Guitar, Bass,
Keyboards, Drums, Percussion, Violin,
Flageolet, Recorder
Denny Laine: Vocals, Guitar, Bass,
Flageolet, Recorder, Percussion
Jimmy McCulloch: Guitar, Percussion
Joe English: Vocals, Drums, Percussion,
Harmonica
Linda McCartney: Vocals, Keyboards,
Percussion
London Town (PM) 588
Lead Vocal: Paul McCartney
See **London Town**
Love Awake (PM) 625
Lead Vocal: Paul McCartney
See **Back To The Egg**
Love Comes To Everyone (GH) 614
Lead Vocal:George Harrison
See **George Harrison**, plus
Eric Clapton: Guitar Intro
Lucille (live) (PM) 670
Lead Vocal: Paul McCartney

See Rockestra—Live
Lucy In The Sky With Diamonds (live)
(LFO) 668
by The Elton John Band
Lead Vocal: Elton John
John Lennon: Backing Vocal, Guitar
Elton John: Piano
Dee Murray: Bass
Davey Johnstone: Guitar
Nigel Olsson: Drums
Ray Cooper: Percussion
The Muscle Shoals Horns
Lunch Box/Odd Sox (PM) 640
Instrumental by Wings from 1975,
including Paul, Linda McCartney,
Denny Laine, Jimmy McCulloch, and
Geoff Britton
McCartney II (PM) 642
Paul McCartney: All vocals and instru-
ments including Drums, Guitars, Syn-
thesizers, Keyboards
Linda McCartney: Backing Vocals
Maisie (MFO) 708
by Laurence Juber
Instrumental
Paul McCartney: Bass
Laurence Juber: Guitar
Steve Holly: Drums
Denny Laine: Harmonica
The Man (PM) 754
Lead Vocal Duet: Paul McCartney and
Michael Jackson
See **Pipes Of Peace**
A Man Like Me (RS) 591
Lead Vocal: Ringo Starr
See **Bad Boy**, plus
Doug Riley: Strings
Million Miles (PM) 625
Lead Vocal: Paul McCartney
Paul: Concertina Squeeze Box
No one else on the track.
Memphis, Tennessee (B) 713
Lead Vocal: John Lennon
See Audition Session—1962
Mineral Man (HFO) 697
by Gary Brooker
Lead Vocal: Gary Brooker
George Harrison: Guitar
(14 other musicians listed in the general
Lead Me To The Water credits – not
all applicable to this cut)
Money (That's What I Want) (B) 713
Lead Vocal: John Lennon
See Audition Session—1962
Monkey See-Monkey Do (RS) 591
Lead Vocal: Ringo Starr
See **Bad Boy**
Morse Moose And The Grey Goose (PM) 588

Lead Vocal: Paul McCartney
See **London Town**
A Mouse Like Me (RS) 581
Lead Vocal: Ringo Starr
See **Scouse The Mouse**
Mull Of Kintyre (PM) 578
Lead Vocal: Paul McCartney
Paul, Denny Laine: Acoustic Guitars
Paul, Linda McCartney, Denny Laine,
   Joe English: Backing Vocals
Campbeltown Pipe Band
Mystical One (GH) 727
Lead Vocal: George Harrison
George: Guitars, Mandolin, Synthesizer
Henry Spinetti: Drums
Mike Moran: Keyboards
Joe Brown: Mandolin
Ray Cooper: Percussion, Synthesizer
Name And Address (PM) 588
Lead Vocal: Paul McCartney
See **London Town**
Never Say Goodbye (LFO) 733
by Yoko Ono
Lead Vocal: Yoko Ono
John Lennon: Shout
Main Band for the **It's Alright** album:
   Elliot Randall, John Tropea: Guitars
   Neil Jason: Bass Guitar
   Pete Cannarozzi, Paul Griffin: Synthe-
     sizers
   Paul Griffin, Michael Holmes, Paul
     Shaffer: Keyboards
   Yogi Horton, Alan Schwartzberg:
     Drums
   Rubens Bassini, David Friedman,
     Sammy Figeroa, Roger Squitero:
     Percussion
Nobody Knows (PM) 642
Lead Vocal: Paul McCartney
See **McCartney II**
Not Guilty (GH) 614
Lead Vocal: George Harrison
See **George Harrison**
Ode To A Koala Bear (PM) 752
Lead Vocal: Paul McCartney
From **Pipes Of Peace** sessions
Old Dirt Road (LFO) 647
by Harry Nilsson
Lead Vocal: Harry Nilsson
John Lennon: Co-Author
See musician note at *How Long Can
   Disco On?*
Old Siam Sir (PM) 623
Lead Vocal: Paul McCartney
See **Back To The Egg**
Old Time Relovin' (RS) 590
Lead Vocal: Ringo Starr
See **Bad Boy**

Old Wave (RS) 745
Ringo Starr: Vocals, Drums
Joe Walsh: Backing Vocals, Guitars
Mo Foster: Bass
Chris Stainton, Gary Brooker: Keyboards
On The Way (PM) 642
Lead Vocal: Paul McCartney
See **McCartney II**
One Of These Days (PM) 642
Lead Vocal: Paul McCartney
Linda McCartney: Backing Vocal
See **McCartney II**
The Other Me (PM) 754
Lead Vocal: Paul McCartney
Paul alone playing Synthesizer, Piano,
   and Guitar
Picture Show Life (RS) 746
Lead Vocal: Ringo Starr
See **Old Wave**
Pipes Of Peace (PM) 754
Paul McCartney: Vocals, Guitar, Piano,
   Keyboards, Bass, Synthesizer, Acoustic
   Guitar, Electric Guitar
George Martin, Paul: Arrangements
Kenneth Sillitoe: Orchestra Leader
No instruments listed for musicians at
   the sessions. Performers' usual instru-
   ments listed here. Other players listed
   on individual cuts when known.
   Ringo Starr: Drums
   Linda McCartney: Backing Vocals
   Steve Gadd: Drums
   Eric Stewart: Guitar, Backing Vocals
   Stanley Clarke: Bass
   Andy Mackay: Tenor Sax
   Dave Mattacks: Drums
   Denny Laine: Guitar
   Hughie Burns: Guitar
   Geoff Whitehorn: Guitar
   Gavin Wright: Violin
   Gary Herbig: Flute
   Jerry Hey: Horns/Strings
   Gary E. Grant: Horns
   Ernie Watts: Tenor Sax
   Nathan Watts, David Williams, Bill
     Wolfer, Ricky Lawson
Pipes Of Peace (PM) 754
Lead Vocal: Paul McCartney
See **Pipes Of Peace**, plus
   James Kippen: Tabla
   Pestalozzi Children's Choir: Backing
     Vocal
The Pound Is Sinking (PM) 704
Lead Vocal: Paul McCartney
Paul: Acoustic Guitar, Electric Guitar,
   Synthesizer
Stanley Clarke: Bass
Denny Laine: Acoustic Guitar

Paul, Linda McCartney, Eric Stewart: Backing Vocals

Private Property (RS) 687
Lead Vocal: Ringo Starr
Paul McCartney: Bass, Piano
Ringo: Drums
Paul, Linda McCartney, Sheila Casey, Lezlee Livrano Pariser: Backing Vocals
Howie Casey: Saxes
Laurence Juber: Acoustic, Electric Guitars

Rainclouds (PM) 701
Lead Vocal: Paul McCartney

Reception (PM) 625
Instrumental by Wings with overdubs of random radio broadcast sounds and the voice of Dierdre Margary.
See **Back To The Egg**

Rockestra—Studio (PM) 625
Paul McCartney, John Paul Jones, Ronnie Lane, Bruce Thomas: Basses
Paul McCartney, Gary Brooker, John Paul Jones: Pianos
Denny Laine, Laurence Juber, Dave Gilmour, Hank Marvin, Pete Townshend: Guitars
Steve Holly, John Bonham, Kenney Jones: Drums
Linda McCartney, Tony Ashton: Keyboards
Speedy Acquaye, Tony Carr, Ray Cooper, Morris Pert: Percussion
Howie Casey, Tony Dorsey, Steve Howard, Thaddeus Richard: Horns

Rockestra—Live (PM) 670
Paul McCartney, John Paul Jones, Ronnie Lane, Bruce Thomas: Basses
Paul McCartney, Gary Brooker: Pianos
Denny Laine, Laurence Juber, Pete Townshend, Billy Bremner, Dave Edmunds, James Honeyman-Scott, Robert Plant: Guitars
Steve Holly, John Bonham, Kenney Jones: Drums
Linda McCartney, Tony Ashton: Keyboards
Speedy Acquaye, Tony Carr, Morris Pert: Percussion
Howie Casey, Tony Dorsey, Steve Howard, Thaddeus Richard: Horns

Rockestra Theme (PM) 625
Instrumental with Vocal Chant by Paul McCartney.
See Rockestra—Studio

Rockestra Theme (live) (PM) 670
Instrumental with Vocal Chant by Paul McCartney
See Rockestra—Live

Rudolph The Red-Nosed Reggae (Reindeer) (PM) 633
Instrumental by Paul McCartney with guest violin solo (see page 82).

Running Free (RS) 581
Lead Vocal: Ringo Starr
See **Scouse The Mouse**

Save The World (GH) 672
Lead Vocal: George Harrison
See **Somewhere In England**

Say Say Say (PM) 752
Lead Vocal Duet: Paul McCartney and Michael Jackson
See **Pipes Of Peace**, plus
Chris Smith: Harmonica

Say Say Say (instrumental) (PM) 753
Same as above, minus lead vocals.

Scouse The Mouse (RS) 581
Ringo Starr: Vocals
Henry Spinetti: Drums
Gary Taylor: Bass
Tommy Eyre: Piano
Pete Solley: Piano, Organ
Phil Palmer, Ray Russell, Nigel Jenkins: Electric Guitars
Roger Brown, Gary Taylor: Acoustic Guitars
Rod King: Steel Guitar, Dobro
Keith Nelson: Banjo
Graham Preskett: Fiddle, Mandolin
Simon Morton: Percussion
Raph Ravenscroft: Flute
Gary Taylor, Joanna Carlin, Pete Zorn, Paul Da Vinci, Roger Brown: Backing Vocals
Gary Taylor: Voices in Pet Shop
Sylvia King, Joan Baxter: Sopranos

Scouse The Mouse (RS) 581
Lead Vocal: Ringo Starr
See **Scouse The Mouse**

Scouse's Dream (RS) 581
Lead Vocal: Ringo Starr
See **Scouse The Mouse**

Searchin' (B) 713
Lead Vocal: Paul McCartney
See Audition Session—1962

Secret Friend (PM) 648
Lead Vocal: Paul McCartney
See **McCartney II** sessions

Send Me The Heart (MFO) 662
by Denny Laine
Lead Vocal: Denny Laine
Paul McCartney: Backing Vocal, Bass
Denny Laine: Guitar
Buddy Emmens: Steel Guitar

September In The Rain (B) 713
Lead Vocal: Paul McCartney
See Audition Session—1962

481

482

See **Somewhere In England**
That's The Way It Goes (GH) 727
Lead Vocal: George Harrison
George: Guitars, Synthesizer
Willie Greene: Bass Vocal
Henry Spinetti: Drums
Herbie Flowers: Bass
Mike Moran: Keyboard and Synthesizer
Ray Cooper: Percussion
Three Cool Cats (B) 713
Lead Vocal: George Harrison
See Audition Session–1962
Through Our Love (PM) 754
Lead Vocal: Paul McCartney
See **Pipes Of Peace**, plus
George Martin: Bicycle Percussion
(hitting a revolving cycle wheel with
a ratchet)
Till There Was You (B) 713
Lead Vocal: Paul McCartney
See Audition Session–1962
To Know Her Is To Love Her (B) 713
Lead Vocal: John Lennon
See Audition Session–1962
To You (PM) 625
Lead Vocal: Paul McCartney
See **Back To The Egg**, plus
Laurence Juber, Steve Holly: Backing
Vocals
Tomorrow (MFO) 595
by Kate Robbins
Lead Vocal: Kate Robbins
Paul McCartney: Producer
Tonight (RS) 591
Lead Vocal: Ringo Starr
See **Bad Boy**, plus
James Newton Howard: Strings
Tug Of Peace (PM) 754
Lead Vocal: Paul McCartney
See **Pipes Of Peace**, plus
Paul, George Martin: Garden Canes
Tug Of War (PM) 704
Lead Vocal: Paul McCartney
Paul: Acoustic Guitar, Bass, Drums,
Electric Guitar, Synthesizer
Campbell Maloney: Military Snares
Denny Laine: Electric Guitar
Eric Stewart: Electric Guitar
Paul, Linda McCartney, Eric Stewart:
Backing Vocals
Orchestra led by Kenneth Sillito
Unconsciousness Rules (GH) 672
Lead Vocal: George Harrison
See **Somewhere In England**
Unknown Delight (GH) 727
Lead Vocal: George Harrison
George: Guitars, Synthesizer
Jim Keltner: Drums

Willie Weeks: Bass
Neil Larsen: Piano
Gary Brooker: Synthesizer
Ray Cooper: Percussion
Willie Greene, Bobby King, Pico Pena:
Backing Vocals
Wake Up My Love (GH) 723
Lead Vocal: George Harrison
George: Bass, Guitars
Henry Spinetti: Drums
Mike Moran: Keyboards, Synthesizer
Ray Cooper: Percussion
Walk A Thin Line (HFO) 674
by Mick Fleetwood
Lead Vocal: George Hawkins
George Harrison: 12-String Guitar, Slide
Guitar, Backing Vocals
Adjo group, Sara Recor: Backing Vocals
Mick Fleetwood: Drums, Percussion
George Hawkins: Bass, Piano, Guitar
Walking On Thin Ice (LFO) 666
by Yoko Ono
Lead Vocal: Yoko Ono
John Lennon: Lead Guitar, Keyboards
High McCracken, Earl Slick: Rhythm
Guitars
Tony Levin: Bass Guitar
Andy Newmark: Drums
Jack Douglas: Percussion
Wanderlust (PM) 704
Lead Vocal: Paul McCartney
Paul: Piano, Bass, Acoustic Guitars
Adrian Sheppard: Drums, Percussion
Denny Laine: Bass
Philip Jones: Brass Ensemble
Paul, Linda McCartney, Eric Stewart:
Backing Vocals
Watching The Wheels (JL) 656
Lead Vocal: John Lennon
See **Double Fantasy**, plus
Matthew Cunningham: Hammer Dulci-
mer
Waterfalls (PM) 642
Lead Vocal: Paul McCartney
See **McCartney II**
Weep For Love (MFO) 662
by Denny Laine
Lead Vocal: Denny Laine
Denny Laine, Laurence Juber: Guitars
Paul McCartney: Bass
Steve Holly: Drums
Paul, Linda McCartney, Steve Holly:
Backing Vocals
We're Open Tonight (PM) 625
Lead Vocal: Paul McCartney
See **Back To The Egg**
Whatever Gets You Thru The Night (live)
(LFO) 668

483

by The Elton John Band
Lead Vocal: John Lennon
John: Guitar
Elton John: Piano, Backing Vocals
Dee Murray: Bass
Davey Johnstone: Guitar
Nigel Olsson: Drums
Ray Cooper: Percussion
The Muscle Shoals Horns
What's That You're Doing? (PM) 704
Lead Vocal Duet: Paul McCartney and
Stevie Wonder
Paul: Bass, Drums, Electric Guitar
Stevie Wonder: Synthesizer
Andy Mackay: Lyricon
Paul, Linda McCartney, Eric Stewart:
Backing Vocals
Where Did Our Love Go (RS) 591
Lead Vocal: Ringo Starr
See **Bad Boy**, plus
Doug Riley: Strings
Who Needs A Heart (RS) 591
Lead Vocal: Ringo Starr
See **Bad Boy**
Wings Live—1979
Paul McCartney: Vocals, Bass, Piano,
Guitars, Keyboards
Denny Laine: Vocals, Guitar, Bass, Key-
boards
Linda McCartney: Keyboards, Backing
Vocals
Laurence Juber: Guitars, Keyboards
Steve Holly: Drums, Backing Vocals
Horn Section:
Howie Casey: Tenor Sax
Tony Dorsey: Trombone
Steve Howard: Trumpet
Thaddeus Richard: Soprano Sax
Winter Rose (PM) 625
Lead Vocal: Paul McCartney
See **Back To The Egg**, plus
Black Dyke Mills Brass Band: Overdub
With A Little Luck (PM) 587
Lead Vocal: Paul McCartney
See **London Town**

Woman (JL) 656
Lead Vocal: John Lennon
See **Double Fantasy**
Wonderful Christmastime (PM) 633
Lead Vocal: Paul McCartney
Paul: All instruments
Wrack My Brain (RS) 686
Lead Vocal: Ringo Starr
Ringo: Drums
George Harrison: Lead Guitar, Acoustic
Guitar
Herbie Flowers: Bass, Tuba
Al Cooper: Piano, Electric Guitar
Ray Cooper: Piano, Percussion, Synthe-
sizer, Lead Guitar
George, Ray Cooper, Vocoder: Backing
Vocals
Writing's On The Wall (GH) 671
Lead Vocal: George Harrison
See **Somewhere In England**
(Yes) I'm Your Angel
See *I'm Your Angel*
You Belong To Me (RS) 687
Lead Vocal: Ringo Starr
Ringo: Drums
George Harrison: Lead Guitar
Al Cooper: Piano, Synthesizer
Ray Cooper: Piano, Synthesizer,
Tambourine
Your Love Is Forever (GH) 614
Lead Vocal: George Harrison
See **George Harrison**
You've Got A Nice Way (RS) 687
Lead Vocal: Ringo Starr
Ringo: Drums
Stephen Stills: Lead Guitar
Mike Finnigan: Piano, Organ
Mike Stergis: Rhythm Guitar
Joe Lala: Percussion
Harley Thompson: Bass
Stephen Stills, Mike Finnigan, Mike
Stergis: Backing Vocals

Cumulative Indexes

The following ten indexes are keyed to Entry Numbers in the main chronological discography sections of *All Together Now*, *The Beatles Again*, and *The End Of The Beatles*.

INDEX 2.   Songs Recorded and Released By The Beatles.
INDEX 3.   Songs Recorded and Released By John Lennon.
INDEX 4.   Songs Recorded and Released By Paul McCartney.
INDEX 5.   Songs Recorded and Released By George Harrison.
INDEX 6.   Songs Recorded and Released By Ringo Starr.
INDEX 7.   Beatles For Others.
INDEX 8.   Lennon For Others.
INDEX 9.   McCartney For Others.
INDEX 10.   Harrison For Others.
INDEX 11.   Starr For Others.

These indexes reflect the most up-to-date information available. As a result, there are a few additional citations as well as a few omissions from the Entry Numbers listed in *All Together Now* and *The Beatles Again*. The exclusions (listed below) reflect cases in which there is now some doubt as to the involvement of Lennon, McCartney, Harrison, or Starr on the specific cuts.

INDEX 9. (McCartney For Others) excludes *Night Time* by the Escorts and *Lontano Dagli Occhi* by Mary Hopkin.

INDEX 10. (Harrison For Others) excludes *Fascinating Things, I Can't See The Reason, Love To Survive, Stand For Our Rights,* and *Two Faced Man* by Gary Wright. There is no doubt that George Harrison appeared on the Gary Wright album **Footprint** (which contained all those tracks). However, we are not certain that he appeared on every cut. Therefore, we are now treating it like other albums with similar non-specific musician credits. Thus, not every packaging of every track is considered a regular entry.

INDEX 11. (Starr For Others) excludes *Alyce Blue Gown*, *Cloud Man*, *Crying In My Sleep*, *Feet In The Sunshine*, *It's A Sin*, *Just This One Time*, *Lady Fits Her Bluejeans*, *Land's End/Asleep At The Wheel*, and *Ocean In His Eyes* by Jimmy Webb. There is no doubt that Ringo Starr appeared on the Jimmy Webb album **Land's End** (which contained all those tracks). However, we are now treating it like other albums with similar non-specific musician credits. Thus, not every repackaging of every track is considered a regular entry.

By The Beatles

All EMI studio recordings except:

> *Recorded live at the Star Club in Germany in 1962
> **Recorded live at the Hollywood Bowl in 1964 and 1965
> †Beatles Christmas Message
> %1961 studio recording in Germany backing Tony Sheridan
> +1961 studio recording in Germany
> $1962 studio audition

489

490

By John Lennon

All studio recordings with John Lennon lead vocal except

> *Experimental track by John Lennon and Yoko Ono (cuts on **Two Virgins, Life With The Lions, Wedding Album,** and the Zappa disc from **Some Time In New York City**)
> %By the Elastic Oz Band with John Lennon lead vocal (pseudonym for Plastic Ono Band)
> Lead vocals and duets with Yoko Ono from **Some Time In New York City** and **Double Fantasy** are listed here. Yoko Ono lead vocals are listed under Lennon For Others

494

By Paul McCartney

All solo studio recordings except

> *By Wings with lead vocals by Paul McCartney except lead vocals by Denny
> Laine (dl), Jimmy McCulloch (jm), Joe English (je), or Linda McCartney (lm)
> %By Suzy and the Red Stripes, pseudonym for Linda McCartney and Wings with
> Linda McCartney lead vocal
> $By Rockestra
> †By the Country Hams, pseudonym for Paul McCartney, Chet Atkins,
> Floyd Kramer, and Geoff Britton.

By George Harrison

All studio recordings with George Harrison lead vocal except

> *An instrumental track from the **Wonderwall** soundtrack
> %An experimental instrumental from **Electronic Sound**
> **A live recording from **The Concert For Bangla Desh** with George Harrison
> lead vocal
> Songs from **The Concert For Bangla Desh** that did not feature a George Harrison
> lead vocal are listed under Harrison For Others

By Ringo Starr

All studio recordings with Ringo Starr lead vocal

*Indicates a track from **Scouse The Mouse** with Ringo lead vocal
Indicates a live recording from **The Concert For Bangla Desh with Ringo
Starr lead vocal

Beatles
For Others

Lennon
For Others

*Indicates a Yoko Ono lead vocal on **Some Time In New York City** and **Double Fantasy**

$Indicates John Lennon's voice as part of an excerpt from a soundtrack

506

McCartney
For Others

Harrison For Others

*Indicates a live track from **The Concert For Bangla Desh** that did not feature a George Harrison lead vocal

312,323,545
The Holdup – two (by David Bromberg) 373
How Can You Say Goodbye (by Jackie Lomax) 200
How Do You Sleep (by John Lennon)
How The Web Was Woven (by Jackie Lomax) 235,242
I Am Missing You (by Shankar Family) 398,401
I Am Missing You – *Reprise* (by Shankar Family) 401
I Apologize (by Splinter) 572
I Don't Want To Discuss It – live (by Delaney & Bonnie Bramlett) 245a
I Don't Want To Be A Soldier Mama (by John Lennon)
I Don't Want You To Pretend (by Billy Preston) 255
I Fall Inside Your Eyes (by Jackie Lomax) 200,205,207,242,286
I Just Don't Know (by Jackie Lomax) 200,207
I Need Your Love (by Splinter) 572,583
I Wrote A Simple Song (album by Billy Preston) 301
I Wrote A Simple Song (by Billy Preston) 301,308,730
I'd Die Babe (by Badfinger) 306
If I Find The Time (by Rudy Romero) 336a
If You've Got Love (by Dave Mason) 364
I'll Bend For You (by Splinter) 566
I'll Still Love You (by Ringo Starr)
I'm The Greatest (by Ringo Starr)
I'm Your Spiritual Breadman (by Ashton, Gardner & Dyke) 258,277
Instant Karma (by John Lennon)
Is This What You Want (by Jackie Lomax) 200,207
It Doesn't Matter (by Billy Preston) 219
It Don't Come Easy (by Ringo Starr)
*It Don't Come Easy – live (by Ringo Starr)
*It Takes A Lot To Laugh/It Takes A Train To Cry – live (by Bob Dylan) 307
I've Got A Feeling (by Billy Preston) 255
Jacob's Ladder (by Doris Troy) 252,254
Jaya Jagadish Hare (by Shankar Family) 401
Jenny, Jenny – live (by Delaney & Bonnie Bramlett) 245a
Joi Bangla (by Ravi Shankar) 292
*Jumpin' Jack Flash – live (by Leon Russell) 307
*Just Like A Woman – live (by Bob Dylan) 307
Ka Han Gayelava Shyam Salone (by Shankar Family) 401

Kajri (by Ravi Shakar) 503
Kinnara School (by Ravi Shankar) 304
The Last Time (by Daryl Hall & John Oates) 601,603
Leon Russell (album by Leon Russell) 244,748
Let The Music Play (by Billy Preston) 255
Let Us All Get Together Right Now (by Billy Preston) 219
Little Girl (by Billy Preston) 255,267
Little Girl (by Splinter) 572,577
Little Yellow Pills (by Jackie Lomax) 200,207,216
Lonely Man (by Splinter) 457,527 (in Japanese): 527
Long As I Got My Baby (by Billy Preston) 253
Long Tall Sally – live (by Delaney & Bonnie Bramlett) 245a
Love Dance Ecstasy (by Shankar Family) 401
Love Is Not Enough (by Splinter) 572
Lovely Lady (by Rudy Romero) 336a
Lumberjack Song (by Monty Python) 465,530
Lust (by Shankar Family) 398,401
Make Love Not War (by Peter Skellern) 456
Mineral Man (by Gary Brooker) 697
*Mr. Tambourine Man – live (by Bob Dylan) 307
Morning Star (by Billy Preston) 219
Motions Of Love (by Splinter) 572,583
My Sweet Lord (by Billy Preston) 253, 255,267
Naderdani (by Ravi Shankar) 503
Name Of The Game (by Badfinger) 306
Never Tell Your Mother She's Out Of Tune (by Jack Bruce) 220,261,334
New York City (Who Am I) (by Splinter) 572,586
Nothin' Gonna Get You Down (by Rudy Romero) 336a
Oh Bhaugowan (by Ravi Shankar) 292
Oh My Love (by John Lennon)
Only You Know And I Know – live (by Delaney & Bonnie Bramlett) 245a,334a
Overture (by Shankar Family) 401
Peace And Hope (by Shankar Family) 401
Photograph (by Ringo Starr)
The Place I Love (by Splinter) 400
Poor Elijah – live (by Delaney & Bonnie Bramlett) 245a
Prayer To The Spiritual Master (by Radha Krsna Temple) 218
Raga Desh (by Ravi Shakar) 304
Raga Hem Bihag – live (by Ravi Shankar)

510

343

Starr
For Others

*Indicates a live track from **The Concert For Bangla Desh** that did not
feature a Ringo Starr lead vocal
$Indicates Ringo Starr's voice as part of an excerpt from a soundtrack

Album Titles

Albums and EPs are identified as follows:

(B) The Beatles
(B/TS) The Beatles with Tony Sheridan
(BFO) Contains Beatles-for-others material
(JL) John Lennon
(LFO) Contains Lennon-for-others material
(PM) Paul McCartney
(MFO) Contains McCartney-for-others material
(GH) George Harrison
(HFO) Contains Harrison-for-others material
(RS) Ringo Starr
(SFO) Contains Starr-for-others material
*Indicates a Various Artists album containing material from one or more of the above categories.

Best Of Leon (SFO) 526
The Best Of Peter And Gordon (BFO/
  MFO) 148
The Best Of Peter And Gordon (BFO/
  MFO) 562
Best Of Rod Stewart (MFO) 510
Best Of Stephen Stills (SFO) 539
Best Of Steve Miller 1968--1973 (MFO)
  547
*The Big Hits From England And The
  USA (B/BFO) 94
Blast From Your Past (RS) 466
Bobby Keys (HFO/SFO) 326
Brave New World (MFO) 212
*British Gold (B/BFO) 606
*British Rock Classics (B/TS) 611
Brother (HFO/SFO) 331
Changesonebowie (LFO) 512
*Chartbusters Vol. 4 (B) 61
A Collection Of Beatles Oldies (B) 160
Coming Out (SFO) 521
The Complete Silver Beatles (B) 713
*The Concert For Bangla Desh (H/HFO)
  307
*Concerts For The People Of Kampuchea
  (PM) 670
Crosswords (HFO) 520
Dark Horse (GH) 422
David Bromberg (HFO) 312
*Deep Ear (MFO) 417a
Delaney And Bonnie On Tour (HFO)
  245a
*Do It Now (B) 273
Donovan's Greatest Hits (MFO) 193b
Doris Troy (HFO/SFO) 254
Double Fantasy (JL) 656
Duit On Mon Dei (SFO) 442
The Early Beatles (B) 115
*The Early Years (B/TS) 285
Early Years (1) (B) 677
Early Years (2) (B) 678
Elaine Paige (MFO) 689
Electronic Sound (GH) 204
Elephant's Memory (LFO) 330
Elton John's Greatest Hits Volume II
  (LFO) 571
Encouraging Words (HFO) 255
*England's Greatest Hits (HFO/LFO/MFO)
  170a
Eric Clapton's Rainbow Concert (HFO)
  358
Extra Texture (GH) 455
The Family Way (MFO) 163
Feeling The Space (LFO) 365
First And Fourmost (BFO) 696
*First Movement (B/TS) 702
*First Vibration (B) 206
Flash Harry (SFO/LFO) 647
Fly (LFO) 296

Footprint (HFO) 300
*The Force (MFO) 431
Freeze Frame (MFO) 634
Friends/Smiley Smile (MFO) 412a
From The Blue Angel (MFO) 717a
From Then To You (B) 270
George Harrison (GH) 614
Get Stoned (BFO/LFO/MFO) 576
Gone Troppo (GH) 727
Good News (SFO) 554
Goodbye (HFO) 194
Goodnight Vienna (RS) 415
Got To Get You Into Our Life (MFO)
  164
Greatest Hit (HFO) 685
Greatest Hits (HFO/SFO) 592
*The Guinness Album: Hits Of The 70's
  (GH) 664
The Hamburg Tapes Volume One (B) 765
The Hamburg Tapes Volume Two (B) 766
The Hamburg Tapes Volume Three (B)
  767
A Hard Day's Night (B) 75,77,605
*Hard Goods (MFO) 382a
Hard Times (HFO) 456
Harder To Live (HFO) 457
Harry Nilsson's Greatest Music (SFO) 607
Hear The Beatles Tell All (B) 637
Heart Play – unfinished dialogue (JL)
  760
Heavy Cream (HFO) 333
Help (B) 122,123,605
Hey Jude (also called The Beatles Again)
  (B) 239,620a
The Historic First Live Recordings (B)
  641
Historic Sessions (B) 681
*History Of British Rock (BFO/HFO/LFO/
  MFO) 378
*History Of British Rock Vol. 2 (B/BFO/
  MFO) 419
*History Of British Rock Vol. 3 (B/TS/
  BFO/HFO/MFO) 461
*History Of Eric Clapton (HFO) 319
*History Of Rock--Volume 16 (HFO) 749
The History Of The Bonzos (MFO) 383
*History Of The Mersey Era--Vol. 1 (BFO)
  537
*History Of The Mersey Era Volume 1
  (BFO) 565
*Hit '69 (HFO) 228
*Hits From The Swinging Sixties (BFO/
  MFO) 644
Holly Days (MFO) 555
*Hot Platter Cordon Bleu (HFO) 577
Hot Rods (MFO) 649
*I Can Hear It Now--The Sixties (B) 264
I Don't Want To See You Again (BFO)
  109

Ram (PM) 282
Rare Beatles (B) 694
Rarities (B) 605,605a,605b,639
Ravi Shankar's Music Festival From India
    (HFO) 503
*Ready, Steady, Go (BFO) 39
Red Rose Speedway (PM) 349
Reel Music (B) 700
*Remember . . . A Collection Of Pop
    Memories (BFO/LFO) 740
Revolver (B) 150,154,605
Ringo (RS) 366
Ringo The 4th (RS) 570
Ringo's Rotogravure (RS) 524
*Rock On Through The 60s (MFO) 638
Rock 'n' Roll (JL) 432,673
Rock 'n' Roll Music (B) 515
Rock 'n' Roll Music--Volume One (B)
    653
Rock 'n' Roll Music--Volume Two (B)
    654
Rolled Gold--The Very Best Of The
    Rolling Stones (BFO/LFO/MFO)
    463
The Rolling Stones Greatest Hits (LFO/
    MFO) 561
Rubber Soul (B) 136,137,605
*The Savage Young Beatles (B/TS) 709
Save The Last Dance For Me (LFO/SFO)
    626
*Savile's Time Travels (20 Golden Hits Of
    1963) (B/BFO) 688
*Savile's Time Travels (20 Golden Hits Of
    1964) (B/BFO) 744
The Scaffold Singles A's & B's (MFO)
    719
*Scouse The Mouse (RS) 581
Sentimental Journey (RS) 245
Sgt. Pepper's Lonely Hearts Club Band
    (B) 168,605
Shankar Family & Friends (HFO/SFO)
    401
Shaved Fish (JL) 458,673
Ship Imagination (SFO) 364a
Shot Of Love (SFO) 680
The Silver Beatles--Vol. 1 (B) 714
The Silver Beatles--Vol. 2 (B) 715
*Sixties Lost And Found Volume 2 (BFO)
    762
Smiler (MFO) 405
Smiley Smile (MFO) 170b,412a
Sold Out (MFO) 428
Solid Rock (BFO) 650
Some Time In New York City (JL) 325,
    673
Something New (B) 84
Somewhere (BFO) 548
Somewhere In England (GH) 672

*Son Of Dracula (SFO/HFO) 381
Son Of Schmilsson (HFO/SFO) 327
Songs For A Tailor (HFO) 220
*The Songs Lennon And McCartney Gave
    Away (BFO/MFO/RS) 618
Songs, Pictures & Stories Of The Fabulous
    Beatles (B) 99
Spark In The Dark (SFO) 569
Stage (LFO) 602
Standard Time (MFO) 708
*Stardust (BFO) 412
*The Stars Sing Lennon And McCartney
    (BFO) 276a
Sta*rtling Music (SFO) 433
Step Inside Love (BFO) 362a
Stephen Stills (SFO) 263
Stills (SFO) 449a
Stop And Smell The Roses (RS) 687
Story Of The Stones (BFO/LFO/MFO)
    731
Straight Up (HFO) 306
Strange Brew--The Very Best Of Cream
    (HFO) 742
*The Summit (PM) 636
Sunshine Dream (MFO) 705
*Supergroups Vol. 2 (HFO) 261
Tadpoles (MFO) 217
That Was Only Yesterday (HFO) 507
That's The Way God Planned It (HFO)
    219
Thirty Three & 1/3 (GH) 535
*This Is Where It Started (B/TS) 155
Those Were The Days (MFO/BFO) 332
Thriller (MFO) 734
Thrillington (MFO) 552b
Through The Past, Darkly (Big Hits Vol.
    2) (LFO/MFO) 221
The Tin Man Was A Dreamer (HFO) 348
To The World (HFO) 336a
*Tommy (SFO) 339
*Tribute To Michael Holiday (BFO) 85
Troublemaker (SFO) 635
Tug Of War (PM) 704
*20 Golden Number Ones (BFO) 580
20 Great Hits (B) 751
20 Greatest Hits (B) 716,717
20 Greatest Hits (B/TS) 750
*20 Monster Hits (MFO) 327a
*20 One Hit Wonders (MFO) 718
Twist And Shout (B) 32
Two Man Band (HFO) 572
2 Originals Of Steve Stills (SFO) 462
Two Sides Of The Moon (SFO) 441
Two Virgins (also called Unfinished Music
    No. 1) (JL) 189
Ululu (HFO) 317
Unfinished Music No. 2 (also called Life
    With The Lions) (JL) 203
Unfinished Music No. 1 (also called Two

518

EP Titles

Albums and EPs are identified as follows:

(B) The Beatles
(B/TS) The Beatles with Tony Sheridan
(BFO) Contains Beatles-for-others material
(JL) John Lennon
(LFO) Contains Lennon-for-others material
(PM) Paul McCartney
(MFO) Contains McCartney-for-others material
(GH) George Harrison
(HFO) Contains Harrison-for-others material
(RS) Ringo Starr
(SFO) Contains Starr-for-others material
*Indicates a Various Artists disc containing material from one or more of the above categories.

General Indexes

The following two indexes are keyed to Page Numbers in *The End Of The Beatles*.

INDEX 14.   General Title Index.
Includes song, album, film, book, magazine, play, and radio/ television program titles.

INDEX 15.   General Name Index.
Includes individual and group names.

Album and EP titles are in **boldface**. All other titles are in *italics*. When the same title applies to several items (for instance, a song, a book, a television series), each is listed separately, with short parenthetical descriptions to help sort out the distinctions.

Some title citations in the General Title Index are accompanied by a brief artist identification (an abbreviation in parentheses). This is to help avoid confusion when two different songs have the same title, or when a number of different artists have done cover versions of the same Beatles song.

The following is the list of abbreviations used in the Title Index to identify each artist:

Apl – Applejacks
BJK – Billy J. Kramer
BP   – Billy Preston
BTM – *Beatlemania* show
CBen– Cliff Bennett
CBla – Cilla Black
CIM – Cimarons
DL   – Denny Laine
EHR– Eddie & The Hot Rods
EJ   – Elton John

EP   – Elaine Paige
Fm – Fourmost
Gms – Grimms
HN – Harry Nilsson
IM   – Ian McLagen
JN   – Jack Nitzsche
LR   – Leon Russell
MH – Mary Hopkin
MJ   – Michael Jackson
MM – Mike (McGear) McCartney
P&G – Peter & Gordon
PC   – Phil Collins
PJP – P.J. Proby
PS   – Peter Sellers
PT   – Percy Thrillington
Ring – Ringo Starr
RLP – Royal Liverpool
        Philharmonic Orchestra
RPO – Royal Philharmonic
        Orchestra (London)
RS   – Rolling Stones
RTL – Rutles
RxM – Roxy Music
Scf – Scaffold
SPF – *Sgt. Pepper* film
S45 – Stars On 45 (Star Sound)
Tws – *Tiswas* cast
YO   – Yoko Ono
ZM – Zoot Money

General Title Index

526

529

532

534

535

537

539

General Name Index

544

About the Authors

Walter J. Podrazik was born in 1952 and, like millions of other baby boomers, was seated in front of the television set on Sunday night, February 9, 1964. Unlike most of his peers, though, he was watching "The Scarecrow Of Romney Marsh" on *Walt Disney's Wonderful World Of Color* rather than the Beatles on *The Ed Sullivan Show*. Since then, however, Wally has more than made up for that, becoming a recognized Beatles historian.

Besides co-authoring with Harry Castleman two previous books on the group (*All Together Now* and *The Beatles Again*), Wally's Beatles-related projects have included: serving as one of the credited research consultants for the 1980 Beatles **Rarities** album from Capitol Records, writing the liner notes for **The Complete Silver Beatles** album package in 1982, and — as part of the twentieth anniversary celebration in 1984 — acting as one of the key contacts recommended by Capitol's publicity agency for "fact checking" background information on the Fab Four's arrival in America.

Wally has written four other pop culture books with Harry Castleman. In addition, Wally also maintains an interest in animals of every sort, especially buffalo and penguins. He is currently lusting after a trip to the Antarctic.

Harry Castleman was born in Salem, Massachusetts in 1953 and, unlike his co-author Walter J. Podrazik, saw the Beatles' February 9, 1964 appearance on *The Ed Sullivan Show*, having already purchased *I Want To Hold Your Hand* and **Meet The Beatles** on the first day they went on sale at his local record store. Harry and Walter began their Beatles-related partnership in 1971 by collaborating on a radio program about the group, went on to co-produce an 18-hour Beatles radio documentary in 1974, and then co-authored two previous books on the Beatles (*All Together Now* and *The Beatles Again*). Harry and Wally have also been the featured speakers at numerous conventions of Beatles fans.

Harry is a lawyer in Jacksonville, Florida, is married, and still regrets the day he let his mother throw out his baseball card collection.

On Beyond Beatles

In discussing the art of song writing for the 1982 book *Making Music* (edited by George Martin), composer Paul Simon noted that one of the frustrations of popular music was that the average age of the bulk of the purchasing audience stayed about the same (teens) while the artists grew older. Consequently, the two groups had less and less in common as time went on because a thirty-year-old adult was not particularly interested in the pains of being sixteen, and vice versa.

One of the most amazing aspects of the careers of John Lennon, Paul McCartney, George Harrison, and Ringo Starr was their success as top forty artists in *three decades* – the 1960s, 1970s, and 1980s. They scored as the Beatles, then again as new solo artists, and finally as established pop music veterans.

Still, it would be absurd to expect the same pace and success rate for the rest of their performing lives. Though at any time along the way they might still have a big hit – just as artists such as Frank Sinatra, Elvis Presley, or Rick Nelson did after the British invasion of 1964 – strictly speaking, they are no longer even in that game anymore. There is a new generation devoting full time to the task of topping the charts.

Instead, while still making pop music, the former Beatles have shifted from the concerns of sixteen-year-olds to a more adult and family-oriented perspective. Of course, their new projects will never be as popular as their Beatles work. But for those willing to see "beyond the Beatles," they offer special pleasure of a different sort: the opportunity to grow up with the maturing work of artists who have had a special place in the hearts of several generations.

For all of these people, then, there will never really be an "end" to the Beatles.